# Innovating Business Education:

## AI, Skill Development, and Hybrid and Blended Models

Anatoly Zhuplev
https://orcid.org/0009-0008-5124-5063
*Loyola Marymount University, USA*

Bryan Christiansen
https://orcid.org/0000-0001-7282-8497
*Southern New Hampshire University, USA*

IGI Global
Scientific Publishing
Publishing Tomorrow's Research Today

Vice President of Editorial Melissa Wagner
Director of Acquisitions Mikaela Felty
Director of Book Development Jocelynn Hessler
Production Manager Mike Brehm
Cover Design Jose Rosado

Published in the United States of America by
IGI Global Scientific Publishing
701 East Chocolate Avenue
Hershey, PA, 17033, USA
Tel: 717-533-8845 | Fax: 717-533-7115
Website: https://www.igi-global.com E-mail: cust@igi-global.com



Library of Congress Cataloging-in-Publication Data

Names: Zhuplev, Anatoly, 1948- editor | Christiansen, Bryan, 1960- editor
Title: Innovating business education : AI, skill development, and hybrid and blended models / edited by: Anatoly Zhuplev, Bryan Christiansen.
Description: Hershey, PA : IGI Global Scientific Publishing, [2026] | Includes bibliographical references and index. | Summary: "This book discusses the emerging innovations in business education, focusing on AI, skill development, and hybrid and blended models"-- Provided by publisher.
Identifiers: LCCN 2025045804 (print) | LCCN 2025045805 (ebook) | ISBN 9798337375236 hardcover | ISBN 9798337375243 paperback | ISBN 9798337375250 ebook
Subjects: LCSH: Business education--Technological innovations | Artificial intelligence--Business applications | Artificial intelligence--Educational applications
Classification: LCC HF1106 .I56 2026 (print) | LCC HF1106 (ebook) | DDC 650.071--dc23/eng/20260130
LC record available at https://lccn.loc.gov/2025045804
LC ebook record available at https://lccn.loc.gov/2025045805
British Cataloguing in Publication Data
A Cataloguing in Publication record for this book is available from the British Library.

# Table of Contents

# Detailed Table of Contents

to AI adoption in education. The chapter concludes with recommendations for educators and policymakers on leveraging AI to enhance academic outcomes and offers directions for future research.



In the evolving landscape of business education, the line between physical and digital learning is no longer clear-cut. Blended and hybrid learning models have emerged not merely as logistical solutions, but as pedagogical innovations that prioritize adaptability, engagement, and learner autonomy. This chapter explores how these models are reshaping business colleges by bridging traditional classroom rigor with digital flexibility. Drawing on empirical observations, institutional practices, and theoretical insights, it highlights both the possibilities and the pitfalls of integrating online and face-to-face instruction. Rather than championing technology for its own sake, the discussion centers on intentional design—learning environments where method serves purpose. Ultimately, this chapter argues that the real promise of blended and hybrid learning lies not in convenience, but in cultivating more responsive, inclusive, and future-ready educational experiences.



This chapter explores the transformative potential of cooperative learning (CL) in fostering intrinsic motivation (IM) and self-directed learning (SDL) within blended learning (BL) business education environments. Drawing on a design-based, mixed-methods study conducted at a South African TVET college, it presents the Cooperative–Self-Directed–Blended Learning (C–SD–BL) framework. The chapter unpacks theoretical foundations, empirical findings, and practical implications, demonstrating how structured CL strategies in BL contexts enhance learner engagement, autonomy, and competence. Insights are drawn exclusively from the author's doctoral research, presenting a contextually grounded, theoretically rigorous contribution to active learning scholarship in business education.

This chapter examines the use of hybrid learning models as a means of improving the level of student engagement in a business learning context, taking the Indian institutions as an example. With its roots in a mixed-methods design, the study will supplement the quantitative survey design to quantify the characteristics of the sample with the qualitative interview-based design to understand individual personality and challenges faced by them. The pedagogical practices used by the methodology include case methods, simulations, role-plays, active learning strategies, and the usage of hybrid tools. The research demonstrates that the combination of technology and participatory pedagogy ensures a significant margin of emotional, behavioral, and cognitive involvement, which results in enhanced learning, positive knowledge results, and satisfaction, being one of the brightest innovations of higher education.



This chapter explores integrating blended and hybrid learning models in business education to enhance flexibility, accessibility, and engagement. Grounded in constructivist, sociocultural, and cognitive load theories, it presents the FOT Model—Flexible Instructional Design, Outcomes-Focused Pedagogy, and Technology-Enabled Interaction—as a framework for optimal hybrid learning. Drawing on case studies from Harvard Business School, IIM Bangalore, Wharton, IE Business School, and Kristu Jayanti (Deemed to be University), it showcases best practices in aligning pedagogy, technology, and assessment to create scalable, inclusive, and active learning environments. Benefits like personalization, real-world skill development, and scalability are discussed alongside challenges like digital equity, faculty readiness, and instructional quality. The chapter concludes by examining emerging trends—AI, immersive technologies, and predictive analytics—and proposing future research directions to strengthen the sustainability and effectiveness of hybrid learning for industry-ready graduates.

This chapter examines how collaborative learning and peer instruction improve critical business skills in postsecondary education. As business conditions are subject to frequent changes, educational orientation should also change to develop students' abilities for the future. Pedagogies of partnership strengthen communication, leadership, decision-making, and cultural intelligence. This chapter develops a rich framework for integrating these practices with technology use, diversity in groups, and integrating the real world into the classroom setting. This framework offers practical guidance for educators and institutions on developing students' job-ready skills through active learning.



Fostering creative confidence is essential for innovation and enables students to tackle problems with optimism and resilience. Organizations and businesses are increasingly interested in creativity and innovation in the workplace and are concerned that students are not developing that skill set in college. Many students express that they don't feel creative. However, creativity can be rejuvenated. In an era where employers rank creativity among the most critical skills for the future, nurturing creative confidence in students has become a priority. The 21-day creativity challenge is a structured approach that engages students regardless of their starting point. They are introduced to seven design mindsets (adapted from IDEO and Stanford's Hasso Plattner Institute of Design) and select from a menu of activities. This chapter outlines the premise for the activity, detailing the conceptual and theoretical foundations, considerations made during the assignment's creation, and a thematic analysis of reflection papers from 30 students in an entrepreneurship course taken in Spring 2023



This chapter introduces a novel approach to enhancing business simulations by integrating Mixpanel-based behavioral analytics, aiming to improve students' decision-making, teamwork, leadership, and job preparedness. The system captures real-time interaction data, using machine learning to segment behaviors

# Preface

Business education stands at an intersection of rapid technological advancement, evolving learner expectations, and the urgent demand for skills that match the dynamic realities of global industries. The traditional boundaries of instruction are blurring, giving way to learner-centered approaches that reimagine the role of educators, technologies, and institutional structures.

This edited volume, *Innovating Business Education: AI, Skill Development, and Hybrid and Blended Models*, brings together international perspectives and empirical insights on how higher education, particularly in business disciplines, is adapting to this changing landscape. Spanning continents and educational contexts, the chapters explore forward-thinking models, AI integration, blended and hybrid delivery, cooperative and experiential learning, and next-generation skill development strategies.

Our contributors examine these themes through qualitative, quantitative, and mixed-methods research designs, offering readers a comprehensive view of the shifts underway. More than just showcasing emerging practices, this book provides actionable frameworks, evidence-based recommendations, and critical reflections that educators, administrators, and policymakers can apply to their unique institutional environments.

## CHAPTER OVERVIEW

### Chapter 1: Enhancing Academic Innovation Through the Academic CHANGE Model

By Akhilesh Bacchoo, Prashant Mishra, and Adrian Archer

This chapter introduces the Academic CHANGE Model focusing on Curriculum, Human Resources, Assessments and Assimilation, Novelty, Gamification, and Engagement to drive relevance and responsiveness in academic institutions.

The model's components are analyzed through qualitative research, offering a roadmap for institutions seeking systemic academic reform in response to cultural and technological shifts.

## Chapter 2: The Cognitive Intersection of Artificial Intelligence (AI) Usage and Academic Excellence

By Mei Peng Low and Wie Jane Chin

Focusing on six types of AI usage, this chapter assesses how strategic deployment of AI tools influences academic performance. Guided by Self-Determination Theory, the study underscores the necessity for intentional, pedagogically aligned AI integration to boost student outcomes.

## Chapter 3: Blended and Hybrid Learning Approaches: Flexibility and Innovation in Business Colleges

By Mustafa Kayyali

This chapter examines the pedagogical implications of blended and hybrid models in business education, advocating for intentional learning design that balances rigor and flexibility. The discussion centers on student engagement, autonomy, and the evolving role of educators.

## Chapter 4: Fostering Intrinsic Motivation and Self-Directed Learning Through Cooperative Learning in Blended Business Education

By Dorothea Lowes, Christo van der Westhuizen, and Chantelle Bosch

Through a design-based, mixed-methods study, the authors present the Cooperative–Self-Directed–Blended Learning (C–SD–BL) framework, demonstrating how cooperative learning strategies in blended environments can deepen intrinsic motivation and learner autonomy.

## Chapter 5: Engaging Minds with Hybrid Models in Business Education: Insights from India's B-Schools

By Pravin Kumar

Drawing on research across Indian business schools, this chapter illustrates how hybrid learning, coupled with participatory pedagogies like simulations and role-plays, fosters emotional, cognitive, and behavioral engagement among students.

## Chapter 6: Blended and Hybrid Learning Approaches in Business Education: Innovating Flexible and Interactive Pedagogy

By Surjit Singha

Singha introduces the FOT Model (Flexible Instructional Design, Outcomes-Focused Pedagogy, and Technology-Enabled Interaction) as a framework for scalable, inclusive hybrid education. Case studies from top global institutions illustrate effective practice and emerging trends.

## Chapter 7: Collaborative Learning and Peer Instruction: Fostering Critical Business Skills in Modern Education

By Surjit Singha

This chapter continues the conversation on active learning by outlining a framework that integrates collaborative learning, peer instruction, and technology to develop job-ready skills such as leadership, communication, and decision-making.

## Chapter 8: Instilling Creative Confidence through Experiential Challenge: The 21-Day Creativity Challenge

By Stacy Grau

Grau explores the importance of cultivating creative confidence through experiential learning. The 21-day creativity challenge offers a structured, research-backed approach that activates students' innovation potential and problem-solving capabilities.

### Chapter 9: Enhancing Student Skill Development through Behavioral Analytics in Business Simulations

By Hélder Martins

This chapter introduces a Mixpanel-integrated approach to business simulations that uses behavioral analytics and machine learning for real-time, personalized learning feedback. The results indicate measurable improvements in core business skills and student engagement.

### Chapter 10: Skill Development Exercises in International Business Venturing and "Glocal" Socio-Economic Development

By Anatoly Zhuplev

Focusing on global business contexts, this chapter presents skill development exercises that merge international business venturing with socio-economic impact. The five-stage export development model offers practical tools for preparing students for complex, real-world challenges.

### Chapter 11: From Classroom to Community: Optimizing Public Relations Education in Vietnam

By Tuong-Minh Ly-Le and Kim Chi Dang

The final chapter explores how blending outcome-based and experiential education enhances PR training in Vietnam. It highlights the balance of professional and personal competencies, and how experiential learning fosters both practical and societal impact.

These chapters reflect the diversity and dynamism of contemporary business education. Whether through AI, cooperative learning, hybrid models, or analytics, a common thread emerges: educators must be agile, intentional, and student-centered to prepare learners for a complex, fast-moving world.

We hope this book serves as both a guide and an inspiration for those seeking to innovate with purpose in the evolving realm of business education.

**Anatoly Zhuplev**
*Loyola Marymount University, USA*

**Bryan Christiansen**
*Southern New Hampshire University, USA*

# Chapter 1
# Enhancing Academic Innovation Through the Academic CHANGE Model:
## Keeping the Education Industry Relevant Through Change

**Akhilesh D Bacchoo**
https://orcid.org/0009-0007-5985-6144
*Global College, Malta*

**Prashant Kumar Mishra**
https://orcid.org/0009-0003-8774-5864
*Global College, Malta*

**Adrian Xuereb Archer**
https://orcid.org/0000-0002-8932-5973
*Global College, Malta*

## ABSTRACT

*This chapter explores the potential of implementing the new Academic CHANGE model, focusing on Curriculum, Human Resources, Assessments and Assimilation, Novelty, Gamification, and Engagement within an academic setting. Through qualitative analysis, the study aims to uncover how these elements contribute to enhanced educational outcomes and overall institutional effectiveness. The research was performed to analyse the changes which need to be made at different levels of academia to reflect the changes in technology and culture that have happened in*

DOI: 10.4018/979-8-3373-7523-6.ch001

*the last few years which have forced a reform in the way educational institutions operate and dispense education to their respective students. The research is qualitative in nature and incorporates interviews, focus groups, and thematic analysis to comprehensively understand each component's impact.*

## INTRODUCTION

Education has undergone a significant transformation, driven by advancements in technology and evolving societal interests. The digital era has not only introduced new tools for teaching and learning but has also reshaped the ways in which knowledge is accessed, shared, and evaluated (Kryukov & Gorin, 2017). Social media has emerged as a powerful force, influencing perceptions of educational relevance and challenging traditional paradigms. Platforms like Twitter, Instagram, and TikTok have given rise to new forms of communication and knowledge exchange, often bypassing conventional academic structures (Imran et al., 2019). This shift has prompted critiques of educational institutions, with some voices on social media questioning their relevance in preparing students for contemporary challenges (Selwyn, 2016).

In response to these pressures, the pursuit of excellence in education has never been more critical. Educational institutions are continuously tasked with addressing the diverse and dynamic needs of their student populations (Januszyk et al, 2016) while adapting to rapid technological advancements (Halili, 2019) and shifting societal expectations (Cabau, 2014). This dual challenge has highlighted the need for comprehensive, adaptable frameworks that support both academic rigor and innovation.

The Academic CHANGE Model represents such a framework, offering a holistic approach to educational improvement. By focusing on Curriculum, Human Resources, Assessments and Assimilation, Novelty, Gamification, and Engagement, the model seeks to create learning environments that are not only aligned with academic standards but also responsive to the demands of a rapidly changing world. Its emphasis on integrating innovative practices, such as gamification and interdisciplinary approaches, positions the model as a solution for fostering student engagement and preparing learners for the complexities of modern life (Dede, 2009; Fullan, 2011).

This chapter aims to explore the continuous implementation of the Academic CHANGE Model in academia, emphasizing its effectiveness in delivering high-quality education to students. By conducting a qualitative analysis, this study seeks to uncover the challenges and successes experienced by institutions that have adopted the model. The research highlights best practices in implementation, identifies areas for refinement, and examines the model's impact on educational outcomes. Ultimately, the findings of this study are intended to contribute to the ongoing discourse on educational innovation and excellence. By providing evidence-based insights, this research offers valuable guidance for policymakers, educators, and administrators striving to enhance the educational experience and maintain relevance in a rapidly evolving global landscape.

## LITERATURE REVIEW

### Curriculum

The curriculum is the cornerstone of any educational system, serving as the primary vehicle through which knowledge and skills are transmitted. According to Tyler (1949), a well-designed curriculum must align with the educational objectives of an institution, ensuring that the content delivered is relevant, comprehensive, and adaptable to the needs of students. This foundational perspective has been supported and expanded by contemporary scholars, who argue that the curriculum must function as a living framework that reflects the evolving demands of society (Pinar, 2012; Kelly, 2009).

Building on Tyler's framework, Doll (2012) highlights the importance of "curriculum visioning," emphasizing the necessity of incorporating critical thinking, creativity, and adaptability into curricular structures. In the context of global educational reforms, Eisner (2002) stresses that a curriculum should not only disseminate knowledge but also foster aesthetic and emotional development, underscoring the need for a holistic educational approach.

Recent studies have further underlined the importance of a dynamic curriculum that evolves in response to societal changes and technological advancements (Pinar, 2012; Kelly, 2009). This perspective aligns with the principles of 21st-century education, where flexibility and interdisciplinary approaches are critical (Beane, 1997). For instance, Spady (1994) advocates for outcomes-based education, a model that integrates practical skills and real-world problem-solving into the curriculum to enhance student readiness for post-academic challenges.

The Academic CHANGE Model exemplifies this progressive approach, advocating for a curriculum that not only covers traditional academic subjects but also incorporates interdisciplinary and experiential learning opportunities. This model's emphasis on experiential learning resonates with Dewey's (1938) philosophy, which posits that education should be rooted in the experiences of the learner. Furthermore, the inclusion of interdisciplinary elements is supported by contemporary research, which indicates that such approaches foster critical thinking, collaboration, and innovation—skills essential for navigating the complexities of the modern world (Drake & Burns, 2004; Barnett, 2000).

## Human Resources

Human resources, particularly the quality and commitment of educators, play a crucial role in the successful implementation of any educational model (Qawasmeh et al.,2024). Research has consistently demonstrated that teacher effectiveness is one of the most significant factors influencing student achievement (Hattie, 2009). Effective educators not only possess strong content knowledge but also the ability to inspire, engage, and adapt their teaching to diverse learning needs. As Darling-Hammond et al. (2017) argue, professional development and continuous training are essential for educators to stay abreast of the latest pedagogical techniques and technological tools. These developmental opportunities are not merely supplementary but fundamental to maintaining the quality of instruction in a rapidly changing educational landscape.

In addition to pedagogical training, teachers need to cultivate technological literacy, particularly as digital tools and online platforms become integral to education (Koehler & Mishra, 2009). The Technological Pedagogical Content Knowledge (TPACK) framework highlights the importance of integrating technology, pedagogy, and content knowledge to enhance teaching effectiveness. This perspective aligns with the principles of the Academic CHANGE Model, which emphasizes the critical role of equipping teachers with both traditional and digital competencies.

The Academic CHANGE Model underscores the necessity of investing in human resources by providing ongoing professional development, fostering a collaborative culture among educators, and ensuring that teachers are equipped to deliver high-quality, engaging instruction. A collaborative culture, as noted by Fullan (2007), not only supports knowledge sharing and innovation but also strengthens teacher morale and reduces burnout. When educators engage in professional learning communities (PLCs), they have the opportunity to reflect, share best practices, and address common challenges collaboratively, ultimately enhancing their effectiveness in the classroom (DuFour & Eaker, 1998).

Furthermore, the model recognizes the importance of aligning professional development with the broader goals of the institution. Training initiatives should not only focus on immediate skill acquisition but also on fostering a mindset of lifelong learning and adaptability among educators (Guskey, 2002). This strategic investment in human resources ensures that teachers are well-prepared to navigate the complexities of modern education while contributing to the overall success of the academic institution.

While the Academic CHANGE Model provides a holistic structure, its positioning alongside existing models would enhance clarity and scholarly utility. The SAMR model (Puentedura, 2013) focuses on the transformative use of technology in learning design, moving from substitution to redefinition. Although widely adopted, it has been criticised for lacking contextual and pedagogical depth (Hamilton et al., 2016). Similarly, Universal Design for Learning (UDL) offers a neuroscience-informed approach to inclusive curriculum design (Meyer et al., 2014), promoting flexibility and accessibility. The CASEL framework (Collaborative for Academic, Social, and Emotional Learning, 2021) emphasises socio-emotional competencies, an area that intersects with the 'Engagement' pillar of the CHANGE Model. By drawing conceptual links to these models, the CHANGE framework may be better positioned as a system-level integration of inclusive design, digital innovation, and human-centred pedagogies.

## Assessments and Assimilation

Assessment is a critical component of the educational process, providing valuable insights into student learning and informing instructional practices. Traditional assessment methods, such as standardized testing, have been widely criticized for their inability to capture the full range of student abilities and for fostering a narrow focus on rote memorization (Harlen, 2007). Critics argue that these methods often fail to account for critical thinking, creativity, and problem-solving skills, which are increasingly essential in today's complex and dynamic world (Shepard, 2000).

In contrast, contemporary educational models advocate for a more comprehensive and nuanced approach to assessment. The Academic CHANGE Model exemplifies this shift by promoting a more holistic approach that integrates multiple forms of assessment. Formative assessments, for example, are instrumental in providing real-time feedback to students and teachers, fostering a learning-oriented environment that emphasizes progress and mastery over time (Black & Wiliam, 1998). Summative assessments, when thoughtfully designed, can serve as a capstone to measure cumulative learning while still allowing room for critical reflection and deeper understanding.

Additionally, the incorporation of qualitative measures such as portfolios, self-assessments, and peer evaluations aligns with the principles of constructivist learning theories. According to Sadler (1989), self-assessment encourages students to develop metacognitive skills, enabling them to take ownership of their learning journey. Portfolios, in particular, offer a dynamic medium for students to showcase their achievements, creativity, and growth over time, providing a richer and more personalized narrative of their educational experiences (Barrett, 2007).

The Academic CHANGE Model also emphasizes the critical role of data assimilation, ensuring that assessment outcomes are effectively used to inform instructional practices and support student growth. This approach is grounded in the principles of data-driven decision-making, which advocate for the strategic use of assessment data to identify learning gaps, tailor instruction, and enhance student outcomes (Marsh, Pane, & Hamilton, 2006). By integrating assessment seamlessly into the learning process, this model fosters a culture of continuous improvement and student-centered education.

## Novelty

Innovation is a key driver of educational excellence, encouraging institutions to explore new teaching methods, technologies, and curricular designs. The concept of novelty in education encompasses a wide range of practices, from the integration of digital tools to the adoption of project-based learning and flipped classroom models (Bergmann & Sams, 2012). These approaches are grounded in the idea that traditional, lecture-centered methods often fail to meet the diverse learning needs of students, particularly in an era marked by rapid technological and societal change (Prensky, 2010).

The integration of digital tools has been a focal point in educational innovation. Digital platforms, adaptive learning technologies, and virtual reality have been shown to create more personalized and engaging learning environments (Dede, 2009; Zhao et al., 2002). For instance, the use of learning management systems (LMS) enables teachers to deliver content flexibly and interactively, catering to the unique needs of each learner (Filho et al.,2024). Moreover, digital simulations and gamified learning experiences have proven to increase motivation and improve concept retention among students (Gee, 2003).

Project-based learning (PBL) is another innovative approach that emphasizes real-world problem-solving and collaboration (Wijna et al.,2024). PBL encourages students to take an active role in their education by engaging in meaningful, interdisciplinary projects that mimic professional challenges (Thomas, 2000). This method has been linked to higher levels of critical thinking, creativity, and teamwork skills—key competencies for the modern workforce (Barron & Darling-Hammond, 2008). Similarly, flipped classroom models, where students explore instructional content at home and engage in hands-on activities in the classroom, have been shown to improve both academic outcomes and classroom dynamics (Bishop & Verleger, 2013).

The Academic CHANGE Model advocates for a culture of continuous innovation, encouraging educators to experiment with new ideas and adapt their practices to meet the evolving needs of their students. This aligns with Fullan's (2011) concept of "whole system reform," which emphasizes that sustainable educational change requires a systemic commitment to innovation at all levels. Moreover, fostering an innovative mindset among educators involves not only professional development but also creating an institutional culture that values risk-taking, creativity, and adaptability (Hargreaves & Fullan, 2012).

The post-pandemic education landscape has seen an exponential increase in the deployment of artificial intelligence (AI) tools and hybrid learning environments, yet these are only partially addressed within the CHANGE framework. AI-driven platforms now offer adaptive feedback, automated assessment, and data-driven learning personalisation (Luckin et al., 2016; Holmes et al., 2021). However, such technologies also raise ethical concerns around surveillance, data privacy, and equity of access (Selwyn, 2022). Meanwhile, hybrid learning models—blending synchronous and asynchronous, in-person and online formats—are gaining traction for their flexibility but challenge traditional notions of engagement and classroom management (Raes et al., 2020). The CHANGE Model could be augmented by explicitly incorporating strategies for navigating AI ethics, hybrid infrastructure, and the digital divide, thereby reinforcing its relevance in emerging pedagogical contexts.

By embedding innovation into the core of educational practices, institutions can enhance student engagement, motivation, and achievement while preparing learners for an increasingly complex and interconnected world (Adinoyo et al.,2024).

## Gamification

Gamification, the application of game design elements in non-game contexts, has gained traction as an effective strategy for enhancing student engagement and motivation. As defined by Deterding et al. (2011), gamification involves incorporating elements such as points, badges, leaderboards, and challenges into non-gaming environments to encourage specific behaviours. In education, these elements have been shown to foster increased student participation, collaboration, and improved learning outcomes (Hamari et al., 2014; Kapp, 2012).

Gamified learning experiences are particularly effective because they leverage intrinsic and extrinsic motivation. Deci and Ryan's (1985) self-determination theory suggest that gamification supports intrinsic motivation by addressing core psychological needs for autonomy, competence, and relatedness. For example, challenges that are appropriately tailored to a student's skill level can enhance their sense of competence, while collaborative gamified tasks foster social connectedness.

Moreover, gamification can enhance formative assessment by providing real-time feedback, helping students track their progress and identify areas for improvement (Domínguez et al., 2013). The use of leaderboards and point systems, while often associated with extrinsic rewards, can also drive engagement by creating a healthy sense of competition and achievement (Hamari et al., 2014).

The Academic CHANGE Model incorporates gamification as a core component, recognizing its potential to transform traditional educational environments into dynamic, interactive learning spaces. By integrating elements such as points, badges, leaderboards, and challenges, educators can create a more engaging and motivating learning experience for students. For instance, research by Nah et al. (2014) highlights that gamification enhances not only academic engagement but also the development of critical thinking and problem-solving skills when coupled with interactive learning activities.

Furthermore, the adaptability of gamification to various educational contexts is a key strength. It can be applied to diverse disciplines, ranging from STEM fields to humanities, and is equally effective in face-to-face, hybrid, and fully online learning environments (Sailer et al., 2017). By aligning game mechanics with learning objectives, educators can ensure that gamified strategies support meaningful educational outcomes rather than serving as mere entertainment (Kapp, 2012).

The Academic CHANGE Model's emphasis on gamification as a transformative tool aligns with contemporary trends in education that prioritize active, student-centered learning. By fostering a sense of achievement and providing opportunities for creativity and collaboration, gamification not only enhances engagement but also helps students develop the skills and mindset needed for lifelong learning.

While gamification can enhance learner motivation and engagement, the literature cautions against an overreliance on extrinsic rewards and superficial mechanics. Research indicates that points, badges, and leaderboards can be effective short-term motivators, but may fail to foster long-term intrinsic engagement or deep learning unless thoughtfully integrated into pedagogy (Hanus & Fox, 2015). Moreover, gamification risks creating competitive anxiety and exclusionary dynamics, particularly for neurodiverse learners or those from underrepresented backgrounds (Toda et al., 2019). Inclusive gamification strategies should focus on narrative, collaboration, and mastery-based progression rather than high-stakes competition. Additionally, design considerations such as accessibility, low-bandwidth adaptability, and cultural sensitivity are crucial in global or diverse educational settings. The CHANGE Model would benefit from incorporating a more critical stance on gamification, highlighting when and how it should be applied, and embedding it within inclusive, purpose-driven learning experiences.

## Engagement

Student engagement is a critical determinant of academic success, encompassing cognitive, emotional, and behavioral dimensions (Fredricks et al., 2004). Cognitive engagement involves the investment of effort in learning tasks and the use of deep learning strategies, emotional engagement relates to positive and negative reactions to teachers, peers, and the overall learning environment, and behavioral engagement includes participation in academic, social, and extracurricular activities (Fredricks et al., 2016). Engaged students are more likely to attend classes, participate actively in learning activities, and achieve higher academic outcomes (Kuh, 2009). Conversely, disengagement is associated with poor academic performance, higher dropout rates, and diminished lifelong learning skills (Finn & Zimmer, 2012).

The Academic CHANGE Model emphasizes the importance of fostering a supportive and inclusive learning environment that promotes student engagement. Such environments are characterized by meaningful interactions, positive relationships, and opportunities for student voice and agency. Research underscores that students are more likely to engage when they perceive their learning environment as supportive and when their contributions are valued (Zyngier, 2008). This aligns with Deci and Ryan's (1985) self-determination theory, which highlights the importance of autonomy, competence, and relatedness in fostering intrinsic motivation and engagement.

Engaging instructional strategies are central to this effort. Active learning methods, such as collaborative projects, problem-based learning, and discussions, encourage students to take ownership of their learning and connect theoretical knowledge to real-world applications (Prince, 2004). Technology also plays a pivotal role in engagement, offering tools that personalize learning experiences and make them more interactive (Reeve, 2012). For example, digital platforms can provide immediate feedback, allowing students to track their progress and maintain motivation.

Creating a school culture that values student voice and agency is equally important. Students who feel that their opinions are respected and that they have some control over their learning environment are more likely to remain engaged (Cook-Sather, 2006). The Academic CHANGE Model aligns with this approach by advocating for practices that prioritize inclusivity, equity, and responsiveness to student needs.

Furthermore, promoting engagement requires addressing systemic barriers that contribute to disengagement, such as socio-economic challenges, cultural mismatches, and unequal access to resources (Fredricks et al., 2016). Strategies to overcome these barriers include implementing culturally responsive teaching practices and ensuring that all students have access to high-quality learning opportunities (Gay, 2010). By fostering a culture of belonging and inclusivity, educators can create environments where all students are motivated to learn and succeed.

Socio-emotional learning has gained prominence as an essential dimension of student engagement. It involves the development of skills such as self-awareness, emotional regulation, empathy, and responsible decision-making, all of which underpin positive academic and social outcomes (Durlak et al., 2011). Engagement strategies that integrate SEL foster deeper connections between students and their learning environments, enabling not just participation but a sense of belonging and purpose. Programmes that embed SEL into the curriculum have been shown to improve motivation, classroom behaviour, and academic achievement (Taylor et al., 2017). Despite its importance, SEL is often treated as peripheral or remedial rather than integral to academic design. The CHANGE Model would be enhanced by incorporating SEL as a foundational element of its engagement pillar, thereby recognising the whole learner and supporting inclusive and emotionally intelligent learning environments.

Engagement cannot be fully realised without addressing the structural inequities that shape students' educational experiences. Learners from marginalised backgrounds often face systemic barriers such as unequal access to technology, culturally irrelevant curricula, and bias in assessment and instruction (Gorski, 2013). These conditions not only limit participation but also reduce students' sense of agency and belonging within educational settings. To foster equitable engagement, institutions must adopt culturally responsive pedagogies, ensure digital inclusivity, and involve learners in decision-making processes related to their education (Gay, 2010; Paris & Alim, 2017). Within the CHANGE Model, this could be operationalised through co-designed learning experiences, inclusive representation in curriculum content, and adaptive technologies that meet diverse needs. Equity-oriented engagement strategies are not simply ethical imperatives but pedagogical necessities for building resilient and socially just learning communities.

## Implementation of the Academic CHANGE Model and a comparison with Michael Fullan's Model of Educational Change

Implementing the Academic CHANGE Model requires a strategic and collaborative approach, involving all stakeholders in the educational community. The success of any educational innovation hinges on a confluence of factors, including strong leadership, clear communication, and sustained support systems (Fullan, 2007). These elements create the foundation for change and ensure that the model is embedded effectively into the institution's culture and practices.

The academic change model can be considered to pick up from the trail of the Fullan's Model of Educational Change which is considered as a foundational text in the comprehension of change in an educational setting (Fullan, 2016). This particular model shares many similarities with the academic CHANGE model since both of them have a focus on system-wide educational transformation, stakeholder involvement and perpetual change in the academic world.

Fullan's model emphasises on a system-wide reform implying that change needs to happen on various levels such as policy, institutional leadership, faculty and students which again connects to the academic CHANGE model which takes a holistic approach as in integrates **curriculum**, **human resources**, **assessments**, **novelty**, **gamification** and **engagement** as interdependent pillars. Both models of change recognise that isolated changes are not effective without complementary improvements in other areas.

Michael Fullan stresses the importance of collaborative leadership, teacher engagement and student involvement which are consolidated under the two pillars of **Human Resources** and **Engagement** in the academic CHANGE model. Both highlight the human factor in education and confirm that change cannot succeed unless faculty and students actively play an important role in the implementation of change.

Moreover, Fullan's model describes education as a continuous improvement process which requires reflection, adaptation and refinement whereas the academic Change model encourages **Novelty,** in the form of innovation in teaching methods and curriculum design and **Gamification** where technology is used to enhance learning experiences. Despite the terminologies being different, both models emphasise continuous transformation rather than a one-time reform which ensures that institutions remain adaptable to further change.

The main difference stems from the difference in the emphasis on technology. Michael Fullan encourages the use of digital tools but unlike the academic CHANGE model where technology is central to the change process, in Fullan's model of educational change, technology is not a core pillar.

Both models are aligned in their system-wide approach, emphasis on stakeholder involvement, continuous improvement, leadership and assessment-driven change. However, the academic CHANGE model expands more on the components of innovation, gamification and the role of technology which makes it more suited for the modern academic world. Using the model developed by Michael Fullan, there are still some gaps to be filled in modern academia and these gaps can be filled using the academic CHANGE model.

The successful implementation of the CHANGE Model is closely linked to institutional readiness and the strategic vision of leadership. Research has consistently demonstrated that transformative educational change depends on leadership that is collaborative, adaptive, and responsive to context (Fullan, 2016; Harris & Jones, 2018). Leaders must be willing to navigate uncertainty, build coalitions among staff, and model the values of innovation and inclusion. Institutional audits or readiness assessments can help identify gaps in capacity—such as staff digital literacy, policy alignment, or infrastructure availability—that may hinder implementation (OECD, 2020). Moreover, implementation efforts must be aligned with quality assurance frameworks and national accreditation systems to avoid resistance from regulatory bodies. By embedding the CHANGE Model within institutional strategies and performance indicators, educational leaders can foster a culture of sustained innovation rather than short-lived experimentation.

Real-world applications of models such as CHANGE must account for localised constraints and socio-cultural dynamics. For example, a case study by Al-Freih and Alkhalaf (2021) investigating curriculum digitalisation in Saudi Arabian higher education revealed that institutional inertia, limited staff training, and misalignment between national policy and institutional autonomy were key barriers. Similarly, studies in European contexts have highlighted how fragmented funding streams and uneven broadband infrastructure limit the scalability of technology-enhanced learning (Redecker, 2017). To counter these challenges, a phased or modular implementation of the CHANGE Model may be more effective than an institution-wide rollout. Piloting specific pillars—such as Assessment or Engagement—within targeted departments or programmes can yield localised evidence of impact and build momentum for broader adoption. Additionally, involving students, administrative staff, and external partners in the design and evaluation of implementation phases helps ensure that the model remains responsive to diverse stakeholder needs.

## Strong Leadership and Vision

Strong leadership is a cornerstone of successful implementation. Leaders who articulate a clear vision for change, model commitment, and inspire collaboration are better positioned to guide their institutions through the complexities of reform (Leithwood et al., 2004). Transformational leadership has been shown to foster a sense of ownership and motivation among educators, enabling them to embrace and adapt to new models like the Academic CHANGE Model (Bass & Riggio, 2006).

## Collaborative Stakeholder Engagement

Meaningful change requires the active participation of all stakeholders—teachers, administrators, students, parents, and the wider community. Kotter's (1996) model of change management emphasizes the importance of building coalitions and generating buy-in at all levels to ensure the initiative's success. This collaborative approach not only strengthens implementation efforts but also helps to address resistance to change, a common barrier in educational innovation (Evans, 1996).

## Professional Development and Resources

Ongoing professional development is critical for equipping educators with the skills and knowledge necessary to implement the model effectively. Research by Guskey (2002) highlights that professional development must be continuous, practical, and aligned with teachers' daily responsibilities to achieve lasting impact. Additionally, institutions must provide adequate resources—technological tools, instructional materials, and time for collaboration—to support the implementation process (Desimone, 2009).

## Culture of Continuous Improvement

A culture of continuous improvement is essential for sustaining change over time. Such a culture emphasizes reflection, feedback, and adaptability, enabling institutions to refine their practices in response to challenges and evolving needs. Senge's (1990) concept of the learning organization underscores the importance of creating environments where staff and stakeholders continually expand their capacity to achieve desired outcomes.

Therefore, the conceptual framework of the CHANGE model can be illustrated as follows:

## A COMPARISON OF THE ACADEMIC CHANGE MODEL WITH THE TPACK MODEL

Our Academic CHANGE Model shares similarities with the TPACK Framework (Koehler & Mishra, 2009), which emphasizes the integration of technology, pedagogy, and content knowledge. Both models stress the importance of aligning technology with educational practices; however, the Academic CHANGE Model extends beyond TPACK by integrating gamification, engagement, and novelty as core components. Where TPACK focuses on teacher competence in blending technology and content, the Academic CHANGE Model adopts a systemic perspective, encompassing curriculum design, assessments, and student engagement.

The two frameworks are holistic in nature and are somehow interconnected. The TPACK model emphasises on three core areas namely, technology, pedagogy and content which then work together to create an effective teaching environment. The model stresses that knowledge domains cannot function in isolation and should intersect with one another to form a comprehensive approach to education. Similarly, the Academic CHANGE Model is built on six interdependent pillars—Curriculum, Human Resources, Assessments, Novelty, Gamification, and Engagement—which collectively enhance educational quality. The model acknowledges that isolated improvements in one area are ineffective without complementary advancements across the other components.

Technology is one of the three core domains in the TPACK model. It emphasises that teachers must understand how to effectively integrate digital tools into their pedagogy and content delivery, creating technology-enhanced learning environments. Technology integration is central to several pillars of the CHANGE model, particularly in Novelty, Gamification, Assessments, and Engagement. The model promotes using digital platforms, interactive tools, gamification, and real-time assessments to increase student participation and personalise learning experiences.

Both models prioritise technology as a driver of innovation in education, recognising that digital tools can enhance pedagogy, assessment, and engagement when aligned with learning objectives.

*Figure 1. Conceptual Framework of The Academic CHANGE Model*

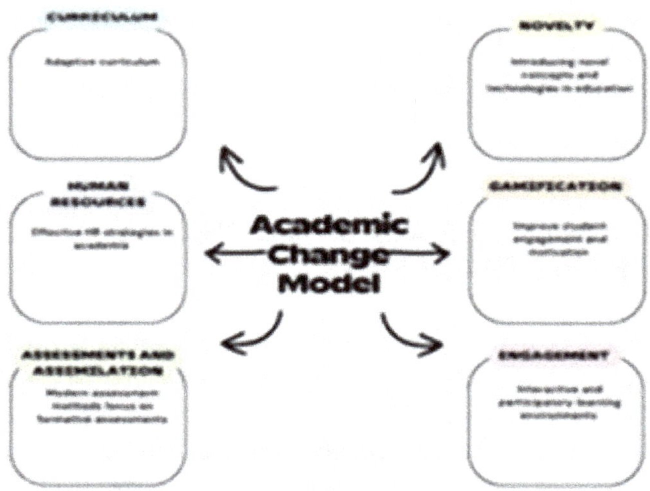


Pedagogy is a core component of TPACK (Niess, 2011), emphasising the importance of active learning strategies, such as project-based learning, inquiry-based methods, and collaborative exercises, which are enhanced through technology. The CHANGE model strongly advocates active and experiential learning, particularly under the pillars of Curriculum, Novelty, and Engagement. Methods such as project-based learning, gamification, and collaborative assignments are highlighted as effective ways to drive student involvement and creativity.

TPACK highlights that educators must develop technological, pedagogical, and content knowledge to integrate digital tools effectively into their teaching. It underscores ongoing professional development to build these competencies. The Human Resources pillar of the CHANGE model similarly stresses the importance of continuous professional development for educators. The model advocates training programs to enhance teachers' digital literacy and pedagogical techniques, ensuring they can implement new technologies and active learning methods effectively. Both models recognise that teacher preparedness and professional development are critical for successful educational reform.

TPACK encourages using technology-enhanced assessment tools (e.g., online quizzes, digital portfolios, and real-time feedback systems) to track student progress and inform teaching adjustments. The Assessments and Assimilation pillar promotes holistic and formative assessments, advocating for real-time feedback systems, digital assessment tools, and data-driven instructional improvements to enhance student outcomes (Shin et al., 2009). Both models emphasise the importance of assessments and data-driven decision-making to ensure that teaching methods are effective and that learning outcomes are continuously improved.

TPACK encourages the use of interactive technologies (e.g., gamification, virtual simulations, and digital collaboration tools) to increase student engagement and participation. Engagement is a core pillar of the CHANGE model, advocating for gamification, digital platforms, and inclusive teaching practices to promote student participation, collaboration, and voice in the learning process. Both models highlight the importance of student engagement and active participation, facilitated through technology and interactive learning environments.

While the TPACK model focuses on teacher competencies (Wang et al., 2018) and the integration of technology with pedagogy and content, the Academic CHANGE model provides a broader institutional framework for improving educational quality (Polly and Brantley-Dias, 2009). However, both models are complementary, as TPACK's focus on teacher preparedness and technology integration aligns with the Human Resources, Novelty, and Assessment pillars of the Academic CHANGE model.

Together, these models highlight that successful educational reform requires both well-equipped educators and systemic institutional change. Implementing both frameworks simultaneously can lead to a more comprehensive, technology-driven, and student-centred approach to academic innovation and excellence.

## Challenges and Recommendations

While the benefits of the Academic CHANGE Model are evident, its implementation is not without challenges. Common obstacles include resistance to change, limited resources, and the need for sustained professional development (Hall & Hord, 2011). Resistance to change is often rooted in fear of the unknown, perceived threats to existing roles, and skepticism about the effectiveness of new practices (Evans, 1996). To overcome this, institutions must take deliberate steps to create an environment that encourages openness to innovation.

## Phased Implementation Approach

A phased approach to implementation is critical for ensuring that stakeholders are adequately prepared and supported. Gradual rollouts allow for pilot testing, the identification of potential challenges, and the opportunity to refine strategies before full-scale adoption. Rogers' (2003) diffusion of innovations theory underscores the importance of engaging early adopters as champions of change who can influence broader acceptance. Pilot programs not only provide proof of concept but also build confidence and momentum among educators and administrators.

## Collaborative Culture and Open Communication

Building a culture of collaboration and open communication is fundamental to mitigating resistance and fostering buy-in. Kotter (1996) identifies establishing a clear vision and maintaining transparent communication as key elements in successful change initiatives. Professional learning communities (PLCs) can serve as valuable platforms for collaboration, enabling educators to share insights, address concerns, and co-develop solutions (DuFour & Eaker, 1998). This collaborative engagement fosters a sense of ownership and shared responsibility for the success of the implementation process.

## Resource Allocation

Institutions must prioritise the allocation of resources to support the implementation of the Academic CHANGE Model. Investments in technology infrastructure, such as interactive tools and learning management systems, are essential for enabling innovative teaching practices. Additionally, sustained professional development programs are necessary to equip educators with the skills and confidence to leverage these resources effectively (Desimone, 2009). Institutions should also provide dedicated time for educators to engage in professional development and collaborative planning, which are often overlooked in resource allocation discussions.

## Evaluation and Feedback Mechanisms

Regular evaluation and feedback mechanisms are indispensable for monitoring progress and making data-informed adjustments to the model (Lindeman and Lipsett, 2016). These mechanisms enable institutions to assess both the implementation process and its impact on educational outcomes. Guskey's (2002) framework for evaluating professional development highlights the importance of measuring outcomes at multiple levels, from participant satisfaction to changes in instructional practice and student achievement. Incorporating both qualitative and quantitative data ensures a comprehensive understanding of successes and areas for improvement (Moore and Kuol, 2005).

## Sustaining the Change

To ensure long-term success, institutions must embed the principles of the Academic CHANGE Model into their organizational culture. This requires continuous reflection, adaptation, and reinforcement of the model's practices. Fullan (2011) emphasizes that systemic change is sustainable only when it becomes part of the institutional fabric, supported by ongoing leadership, collaboration, and resource commitment.

Another crucial aspect that warrants further integration within the CHANGE Model is equity of access to digital tools and learning environments. The COVID-19 crisis exposed—and in many cases deepened—inequities in educational access, particularly among marginalised communities (UNESCO, 2022; Williamson & Hogan, 2020). Students in low-income households often face limited internet access, device shortages, and lower levels of digital literacy, all of which impair their ability to benefit from technology-driven innovation. Moreover, teachers in resource-constrained environments may lack the training or infrastructure to implement novel pedagogies effectively. To support truly inclusive innovation, the CHANGE Model should incorporate design-for-equity principles, recommend tiered resource models, and promote cross-sector collaborations with governments and NGOs.

By addressing these challenges through strategic planning, resource prioritization, and stakeholder engagement, institutions can maximize the benefits of the Academic CHANGE Model and foster meaningful, lasting improvements in educational quality.

# RESEARCH METHODOLOGY

## Research Design

This study employed a qualitative research design to explore the implementation and effectiveness of the Academic CHANGE Model in educational institutions. A thematic analysis approach was adopted to identify recurring themes from semi-structured interviews conducted with various stakeholders, including educators, administrators, and policymakers. This method was chosen for its ability to capture nuanced insights into the lived experiences and perceptions of participants, offering a rich understanding of the challenges and successes associated with the model.

## Participants

The study involved 21 participants selected through purposive sampling. The participants represented diverse educational contexts, including primary, secondary, and higher education institutions. Stakeholders were chosen based on their involvement in the adoption or implementation of innovative educational frameworks, ensuring that the data collected reflected a range of perspectives and experiences. The sample size was determined by the point of saturation, where no new themes or insights were emerging during the analysis.

## Data Collection

Data was collected through semi-structured interviews, each lasting approximately 45–60 minutes. The interview protocol was designed to align with the six components of the Academic CHANGE Model: Curriculum, Human Resources, Assessments and Assimilation, Novelty, Gamification, and Engagement. Open-ended questions encouraged participants to share their experiences, perceptions, and recommendations related to the model's implementation and its impact on educational quality.

Interviews were conducted via video conferencing platforms to accommodate participants from various locations. With participants' consent, all interviews were recorded and transcribed verbatim for analysis.

## Data Analysis

Thematic analysis was conducted following Braun and Clarke's (2006) six-phase framework:

1. **Familiarization with Data**: Transcripts were reviewed multiple times to ensure familiarity with the content.
2. **Generating Initial Codes**: Relevant data segments were coded systematically using QDA Miner software.
3. **Searching for Themes**: Codes were grouped into potential themes that aligned with the Academic CHANGE Model's components.
4. **Reviewing Themes**: Themes were reviewed and refined to ensure they were coherent, distinct, and representative of the data.
5. **Defining and Naming Themes**: Clear definitions and names were assigned to each theme.
6. **Producing the Report**: The findings were synthesized and presented in relation to the study's research questions.

Inter-rater reliability was ensured by having a second researcher independently review the codes and themes, with discrepancies resolved through discussion.

## Ethical Considerations

The study adhered to ethical research standards to protect participant confidentiality and well-being. Ethical approval was obtained from the relevant institutional review board. Participants were provided with detailed information about the study's purpose and procedures and were required to sign informed consent forms. Data was anonymized during transcription and securely stored to ensure confidentiality

## Limitations

While the qualitative approach provided in-depth insights, it is important to acknowledge limitations related to the study's generalizability. The findings are context-specific and may not fully capture the experiences of all educational institutions. Additionally, reliance on self-reported data introduces the potential for bias, as participants' accounts may reflect personal perceptions rather than objective realities.

## Analysis

A thematic analysis was conducted on 21 interviews with stakeholders from various educational institutions to explore their perspectives on factors influencing the quality of education. The interviews reached saturation, and six recurring themes were identified: Curriculum, Human Resources, Assessments and Assimilation, Novelty, Gamification, and Engagement. These themes align closely with the intended conceptual framework of the Academic CHANGE Model, confirming its relevance and validity as a comprehensive approach to enhancing educational quality.

## Curriculum

The theme of Curriculum emerged as the most frequently mentioned aspect. Participants highlighted the need for curricula to be relevant, adaptable, and aligned with both institutional goals and societal demands. Many respondents emphasized the importance of integrating interdisciplinary content and experiential learning opportunities to equip students with critical thinking and problem-solving skills. This validates the Academic CHANGE Model's emphasis on a dynamic curriculum as a cornerstone of quality education.

A recurring concern heard in these discussions focused on the need for ongoing curriculum evolution to keep pace with shifting industry expectations, advances in technology, and wider socio-economic changes. Participants showed their concern that traditional curricular structures, which often prioritize theoretical knowledge over practical application, are at risk of becoming obsolete in rapidly changing professional landscapes. Many stakeholders stressed that higher education institutions should constantly update their curricula to be in line with both academic development and the changing needs of the labour market, otherwise graduates might not have those competencies relevant for contemporary work life.

This will be a much-needed factor of adaptability that will be more and more needed in curriculum development, especially as institutions seek to accommodate diverse needs of students or the integration of emerging academic disciplines. Many of the interviewees commented that rigidity within more conventional curricula challenges interdisciplinary collaboration, lifelong learning, and incorporation of fields like artificial intelligence, sustainability, and digital transformation. Most people felt that allowing the curriculum to be cross-disciplinary in nature and allowing for practical applications would be critical in driving innovation and giving students employable skills.

From these findings, several recommendations emerged on how to apply more dynamic curricular frameworks. The curriculum must be regularly reviewed in order to check its relevance with the industry as well as knowledge areas that are emerging. The institutions should further work towards a modular learning architecture that will be more flexible to let the student be exposed to multiple disciplines, acquiring qualifications via more personalized and adaptable learning paths. It is important to stress that one of the main linking mechanisms between study and application can be through including opportunities for experiential learning, such as work placements, industry partnerships, and project-based assessments. By embedding such strategies, curricula are able to better prepare students for the demands of an increasingly complex and technologically driven society.

## Human Resources

Human Resources was identified as a critical determinant of educational quality, particularly the role of educators in delivering effective instruction and fostering a supportive learning environment. Respondents stressed the importance of professional development, collaboration among teachers, and leadership support in ensuring teaching excellence.

One common thread running through the discussions was the need for continued professional growth as a means of improving teacher effectiveness. The participants reiterated that only with continuous training can teachers be updated on new methodologies, the evolution of technologies, and subject matters related to pedagogy. Without professional development, there is always a chance that pedagogical staff will be unprepared for emerging demands in education, which might result in slippage into poor-quality instruction. Most of the interviewees stressed that institutions really need to invest in some structured development programs, which give academics an opportunity to sharpen their teaching methods, be current with research, and learn new techniques in pedagogy.

Another important aspect was the collaborative culture of the educators themselves. Most of the participants mentioned that an institution that promotes a collaborative atmosphere where knowledge sharing between and amongst the faculties is the most common basis for achieving high institutional success. These were seen to be supported by professional learning communities, mentorship initiatives, and cross-discipline collaboration that create a culture of continuous improvement and shared excellence in pedagogy. Those interviewed felt that when faculty are encouraged to solve problems and support each other, they are much more likely to innovate and adopt best practices that enhance student learning outcomes.

Other factors are resource allocation and provision of incentives to retain the motivation and dedication of educators. Most of the participants were concerned about resources made available to the teaching staff about technological infrastructure, academic materials, and research engagement. On the motivational aspect, it was established that the aspects of career development opportunities, workload pressures, and financial rewards might be detrimental to sustainability in teacher motivation. As such, these issues needed to be addressed to ensure that teachers remained motivated toward the provision of quality education.

Evaluation and Integration: The meeting also discussed the aspect that needed a formalized approach regarding human resources. The participants recommended that there should be mechanisms for assessing the effectiveness of professional development, faculty collaboration efforts, and resource allocation strategies. This, it was felt, would help integrate educator feedback into the policies and decision-making processes of the institution to create an enabling academic environment that is adaptive and responsive. Consequently, with structured methodologies of assessment embedded within the routines of institutions, their support to educators would be continually refined; likewise, HR strategies would surely be better harmonized with overall educational excellence objectives.

The interview analysis will establish that human resources, with the greatest insight into sustained high-quality education, lie at the very heart of professional development opportunities, collaboration cultures, resource availability, and proper structured assessment mechanisms-all these ingredients put together as institutional interventions important for motivating better academic contributions by teachers and sustaining their participation in academic matters.

## Assessments and Assimilation

The theme of Assessments and Assimilation focused on the role of both formative and summative assessments in informing instructional practices and supporting student growth. Interviewees expressed a preference for assessments that go beyond rote memorization to evaluate deeper understanding and skills. Assimilation of assessment data into teaching strategies was also emphasized as a mechanism for continuous improvement.

A dominant theme of the interviews held was the dire need for the assessment that covers critical thinking, problem-solving, and practical competency rather than merely memorization and standardized testing. Most participants complained that conventional modes of assessment very often fail to capture the complete learning of a student, specifically in those subjects which require a great deal of creativity, analytical reasoning, and applied knowledge. Accordingly, formative assessment practices such as coursework, project-based assessment methods, and portfolios of reflective learning were considered superior in monitoring the students' progress and involvement. Again, there is an urgent need to integrate means for continuous feedback so as to enable the student to monitor his or her progress and hence obtain deeper insights into his or her subject area.

Data-driven decision-making within an assessment practice also came up during the discussions between the stakeholders. The participants emphasized that education institutions should effectively use the data from assessment to refine their curriculum, improve teaching methods, and identify areas in which students need extra help. The ability to assimilate the results of assessment into pedagogical strategies makes instruction responsive and student-centered. This approach was seen as being especially important for bridging the gap between theoretical knowledge and practical application. Also, on account of this regular monitoring of student performance, the trends enable the teachers to try out new teaching methods which best suit various learning needs and hence result in increased academic performance.

Fairness and Inclusion in Assessment: The discussions mainly centered around the assessment frameworks providing for differences in learning styles and ability so that the students are assessed based on their strengths and progress. It therefore follows that the multi-method approach, such as oral presentations, case studies, peer assessment, and self-assessment, is thus recommended for reducing assessment bias and building an inclusive academic environment. Those present at the event also spoke of the transparency of grading criteria and clear assessment rubrics as factors that will raise student awareness of expectations and enhance academic integrity.

Moreover, the respondents asserted that this process of assimilation should be continuous from student assessment to the path that leads towards institutional self-evaluation. In this respect, most of the interviewees declared that mechanisms to evaluate whether the educational programs, teaching methodologies, and institutional policies are efficient should be established. This process is in need of continuous interaction with the faculty and students for perceptions regarding teaching effectiveness and curriculum relevance. This is in tune with integrating these insights into institutional decision-making processes that are critical for keeping academic programmes tuned to current educational and professional demands.

Taken together, these insights reinforce a key message in interviews about adopting an enabling approach that makes the process of assessments and assimilation dynamic, information-driven, and inclusive. It calls on the institutions to transcend the fixed, examination-centered evaluation model toward more formative, continuous, and varied methods of assessment that are seen as crucial to promote deeper learning. Results of assessment should also be systematically fed into teaching strategies and institutional planning for continuous improvement. With meaningful evaluation processes and effective strategies for assimilation, academic institutions will be in a better position to ensure quality in the overall education and better equip students to face the complexities of the modern professional world.

## Novelty

Novelty was a recurring theme, reflecting the need for innovation in teaching methods, curricular design, and institutional practices. Many respondents discussed the importance of embracing new ideas and technologies to remain competitive and relevant in the evolving educational landscape.

A recurring theme throughout the presentation was the extent to which novelty serves as a catalyst for creativity and adaptability in education. Participants acknowledged that while traditional teaching methods are highly valued, they often fail to engage students at a deeper level, limiting opportunities for fostering independence and problem-solving skills. Pedagogical innovation was widely recognised as essential for promoting meaningful learning beyond mere rote memorisation. Many interviewees referred to active learning strategies, such as inquiry-based learning, problem-based learning, and interdisciplinary teaching, as effective approaches for developing students' adaptability. By incorporating novelty into curriculum design and instructional methods, educators can better equip students to navigate an increasingly complex and ever-changing world.

Another significant theme that emerged from the discussions was the integration of digital tools and platforms, with technology frequently cited as a key driver of innovation. Many participants observed that advancements in artificial intelligence, virtual learning environments, and interactive digital platforms have transformed traditional learning experiences, making them more personalised, accessible, and engaging. The use of learning management systems, gamification strategies, and real-time assessment technologies was widely regarded as instrumental in enhancing teaching effectiveness and increasing student motivation. Additionally, interviewees noted that technology provides greater flexibility in learning, particularly in the context of blended and online education. While the potential of digital tools was broadly recognised, some participants expressed concerns about overreliance on technology, cautioning that meaningful education is underpinned by critical human interaction.

One of the principal challenges highlighted was the need to strike an effective balance between tradition and innovation. While there was widespread agreement that continuous evolution in educational practices is necessary, many participants also felt strongly that core academic values and rigour must not be compromised. There was a consistent emphasis on the need for institutions to introduce new approaches while preserving the pedagogical integrity that has defined education for generations. The challenge, therefore, lies in ensuring that innovation serves to strengthen and reinforce, rather than disrupt, the fundamental principles of teaching and learning. Many participants advocated for a hybrid approach in which traditional academic foundations—such as critical thinking, analytical reasoning, and ethical discourse—are complemented by modern pedagogical tools and digital resources. By embedding novelty within structured and well-defined educational frameworks, institutions can ensure that innovation enhances, rather than replaces, established best practices.

Overall, the insights gathered from these interviews suggest that a balanced integration of creativity, technological advancements, and academic rigour is essential for the future of education. While innovation is increasingly necessary to enhance student engagement and sustain institutional competitiveness, it must be implemented in a manner that respects the traditional values of education. The extent to which educational institutions can successfully adopt novel learning methodologies while safeguarding core academic objectives will determine their ability to remain forward-thinking and committed to high standards in pedagogical principles.

## Gamification

The theme of Gamification was identified as a transformative approach to engaging students. Respondents noted the effectiveness of game-based elements, such as points, badges, and leaderboards, in increasing motivation and participation.

One of the threads that emerged was the level at which gamification actually inspires active participation and adds to the learning experience. Indeed, a lot of participants shared experiences of how traditional lecture-based methods tend to be ineffective in keeping the attention of students for a longer period, while gamification does. By incorporating points systems, leaderboards, badges, rewards, and challenges, gamification builds up an element of intrinsic motivation-inspiring students toward being more active in the whole learning process. Several interviewees mentioned that pupils remember more successfully when learning takes the form of some characteristic features of playing or competing, because this way a record of their achievements and successes is built up. Moreover, gamification was viewed as being particularly effective for collaborative learning because team-based challenges and problem-solving activities compel peer interaction and cooperative engagement.

Even while participants widely acknowledged the benefits of gamification, they equally placed emphasis that there is a need to make sure gamified elements are meaningfully aligned with learning objectives. Many interviewees warned about the overuse of shallow game mechanics and underlined that gamification should not be used as a form of entertainment per se but rather as a systematic enhancement of pedagogy. Gamification, when used properly, supports the core learning objectives through the introduction of scaffolded challenges that put students' comprehension, application, and solving skills into test. Indeed, several participants indicated that gamification could be very well integrated into project-based learning, case studies, and simulations, since students are at work with applied knowledge. Finally, being able to track performance through interactive dashboards and a feedback mechanism should be noted for its value: students are thereby able to chart their performance to identify areas in which they must improve. On the other hand, however, most were worried that the implementations might be tokenistic, using points and badges as elements of gamification for no apparent educational values. Indeed, participants echoed again that gamification will be effective only when it is designed with pedagogical intent-so that learning would always be the driving force.

On the other hand, accessibility and competition have also raised concerns with gamification, which the participants have expressed quite frequently. A number of interviewees also identified that not all students take to competitive learning; indeed, a student may become defeated with continued lower performances in leaderboards or gamified assessments. Sometimes very high levels of competition have a negative effect: a student may disengage, or anxiety can set in through an inability to compete with very high-achieving peers. To avoid this, most of the participants recommended the inclusion of collaborative gamification features, such as team-based activities and cooperative challenges, rather than competing on individual performance metrics. Another important issue that was raised concerned ensuring equal access to the gamified learning platform. Digital inequity in schools, for instance, means that students have unequal access to technology, internet connectivity, or digital literacy skills, which could lead to differences in engagement and learning outcomes. Institutions should therefore ensure that any game experience is inclusive, adaptable, and accessible to students of all abilities and backgrounds, whether these students have prior technological experiences or not.

Overall, results from interviews with stakeholders show how gamification can potentially change educational experiences if it is implemented with clarity of pedagogical intention, sensitive to student needs. While gamification nurtures creativity and motivation in students, effective integration into the curriculum will have to be one which upholds valuable learning outcomes. It therefore behooves institutions to strike a balance between intrinsic and extrinsic motivators, individual and collaborative elements, and competitive and non-competitive frameworks in creating an enabling learning environment. By tackling issues of accessibility and competition, educational institutions are able to position gamification as a tool that enhances learning, promotes inclusivity, creativity, and long-term academic success.

## Engagement

Engagement emerged as a fundamental theme, encompassing cognitive, emotional, and behavioral dimensions. Participants agreed that fostering student engagement is essential for academic success, and they emphasized the role of active learning strategies, inclusive practices, and student voice in achieving this goal.

One dominant theme in the discussions was indeed the value of active learning methods, in particular project-based learning, for increasing engagement. Several participants noted that the traditional lecture-based method of teaching is heavily dependent on passive content delivery, which can often result in disengagement and low retention of knowledge. On the other hand, active learning methods include activity-oriented teaching, such as problem-solving assignments, case analysis, role plays, and team projects. Many of the educators responding to this survey said that project-based learning offers great efficiency in developing critical thinking, creativity, and problem-solving skills of students in a real-world setting by calling them to apply theoretical knowledge in practical settings. Of these, many identified that active learning instills a sense of ownership and responsibility because students can independently explore topics, collaborate with colleagues, and be engaged in self-directed inquiry. Of these, many have identified that active learning instills ownership and responsibility because students can independently explore topics, collaborate with colleagues, and be engaged in self-directed inquiry.

Another important dimension of engagement that emerged from the interviews was the importance of creating inclusive learning environments that value and include student voices. As participants noted, when students feel that their perspectives, experiences, and contributions are valued, they are more likely to engage actively and meaningfully in their studies. This understanding also emerged strongly through many interviews where the structure of traditional education, perforce, puts students always in a receiving role rather than as contributors and agents of change in knowledge generation. Instead, an inclusive class promotes discursive culture for collaboration, together with sharing choices and responsibilities of decision-making as co-knowledge constructors together with educators. Most of the respondents explained that the student feedback mechanism, such as course evaluations, peer discussions, and advisory panels, is crucial in curriculum design and instructional methods. Other important aspects were using different teaching approaches to meet various learning styles and cultural backgrounds so all students would feel reflected and supported. Inclusion allows institutions to create an atmosphere in which students feel valued, respected, and motivated to take responsibility for their learning process.

Technology was very often mentioned as one of the main enablers of engagement, especially for increasing accessibility and interactivity within education. Indeed, many participants emphasized that with effective use, digital tools can bridge gaps in learning by providing personalized and flexible learning experiences. The interviewees observed that learning management systems, virtual collaboration platforms, and multimedia resources allow students to learn course materials at their own pace, which caters to the demand for individual differences in learning style and preference. Other instructional uses of interactive technologies include gamified learning platforms, virtual simulations, and real-time feedback systems, which have also been found instrumental in increasing participation and motivation. It is further elaborated that many stakeholders highlighted added value for ensuring inclusive education via digital tools: "Digital means alternative ways to access learning for students with disability, language limitations, or socio-economic constraints." One issue was overdependence on technology itself; interviewees pointed out that it is very important that digital engagement not replace, but rather complement, other more traditional forms of interaction. But participants also indicated that technology is best used when it is thoughtfully integrated into pedagogy to balance face-to-face collaboration with digital accessibility and create a rich, interactive learning experience.

Overall, findings from stakeholder interviews underline the interplay between engagement, inclusivity, and technology in constructing an effective learning environment. The integration of active learning, student voice, and agency, together with a thoughtful use of digital tools, creates a far more engaging, accessible, and student-centered experience. By fostering participation, representation, and flexibility in a truly holistic approach, institutions can promote learning environments which enhance academic achievement but at the same time nurture curiosity and creativity for students' lifelong success.

## Validation of the Conceptual Framework

The recurrence of these six themes validates the initial conceptual framework of the Academic CHANGE Model. Each theme was not only prevalent in the interviews but also interconnected, highlighting the multifaceted nature of educational quality.

1. A dynamic **Curriculum** depends on skilled Human **Resources** to implement it effectively.
2. Effective **Assessments** drive curricular improvements and enhance **Engagement**.

3. **Novelty** and **Gamification** act as catalysts for maintaining interest and relevance in education.

The alignment between the themes identified in the interviews and the Academic CHANGE Model demonstrates that these elements collectively influence the quality of education. Furthermore, the analysis underscores the importance of adopting a holistic approach that integrates these components seamlessly.

The thematic analysis of interviews confirms the robustness of the Academic CHANGE Model as a conceptual framework for enhancing educational quality. The findings emphasize the need for institutions to prioritize these six interconnected themes to address the complex and evolving demands of contemporary education. By focusing on curriculum, human resources, assessments, novelty, gamification, and engagement, institutions can create transformative learning environments that meet academic standards and inspire innovation.

## DISCUSSION

Results reinforce the importance of the Academic CHANGE Model as a systematic means of striving for quality enhancement in modern academic institutions. Confirmatory thematic analysis confirms these six components-Curriculum, Human Resources, Assessments and Assimilation, Novelty, Gamification, and Engagement-relevant but also linked together to present a holistic model of institutional development. The results align with existing research on curriculum adaptation, faculty development, student engagement and assessment strategies.

### Comparison with Existing Literature

The importance of curriculum adaptability has been widely acknowledged in recent literature. Research emphasizes that higher education institutions must regularly update curricula to reflect industry trends, digital advancements, and interdisciplinary approaches. The Academic CHANGE Model aligns with this perspective by advocating for a curriculum structure that integrates both traditional and emerging disciplines. However, regulatory rigidity in many institutions limits the rapid evolution of curricula, making it necessary to explore policy-level changes that facilitate more agile reforms.

The role of faculty development and institutional support is another critical factor in sustaining academic change. Studies confirm that continuous professional development is essential for educators to remain effective in dynamic learning environments. The Technological Pedagogical Content Knowledge (TPACK) framework underscores the importance of integrating technology, pedagogy, and subject expertise. The Academic CHANGE Model recognizes this by emphasizing structured training programs and faculty collaboration mechanisms to improve teaching quality. However, a key challenge remains: resource allocation. Institutions must ensure adequate investment in technological infrastructure and faculty incentives to sustain long-term educational change.

## Sustaining Academic Change through Human Resources

The research confirms that teacher capacity and institutional support mechanisms are critical components in achieving effective academic change. Professional development came out to be the major issue expressed by participants, and many shared their views that teachers should be continuously trained in line with emerging pedagogical techniques and digital tools. The study emphasizes the need to develop a collaborative culture among the teaching fraternity, one that promotes knowledge-sharing and contributes towards solving collective problems. It is also institutional, therefore, because investment in faculty incentives, workload management, and career advancement opportunities should be taken seriously by the institution to sustain educators' motivation and commitment. Without these mechanisms, reforms in education are likely to remain incomplete, with differences in the quality of teaching varying from one institution to another.

The findings also highlight that institutional leadership plays a crucial role in facilitating sustainable academic change. Strong leadership fosters an environment where faculty members feel empowered to adopt innovative teaching methods and continuously improve their professional skills. Furthermore, peer mentoring and cross-disciplinary collaboration were identified as strategies that enhance knowledge-sharing and build collective expertise within institutions. Future research could explore how leadership styles influence faculty adaptability to academic change and how these dynamics impact overall institutional effectiveness.

Despite highlighting the significance of teacher capacity and institutional support, a key limitation lies in the variability of faculty engagement across institutions. Some educators may be resistant to change due to workload pressures, lack of incentives, or insufficient training opportunities. Additionally, disparities in professional development resources between well-funded and underfunded institutions may limit the scalability of this model. Future research should investigate the feasibility of institutional policies that promote equal access to training and career development while addressing potential financial constraints that hinder long-term sustainability.

## Assessments and Assimilation: A Move Beyond Rote Learning

The main challenges identified in the study included the dominance of traditional assessment methods that focus on memorization rather than critical thinking and problem-solving. The findings indicate that institutions should incorporate formative assessments, project-based evaluations, and self-assessment mechanisms to offer a more holistic and valid measure of student learning. The study also emphasizes data-driven decision-making, where assessment results are systematically fed into pedagogical strategies. This helps in the adjustment of instructional approaches in line with student performance trends for continuous improvement in educational institutions. Besides, fairness and inclusiveness in assessments have remained paramount concerns, implying various evaluation techniques that best address different learning styles and abilities.

The study suggests that formative assessments and adaptive learning technologies should be more extensively incorporated to support individual learning trajectories. Adaptive assessments, which respond to student performance in real time, could ensure a more personalised learning experience and reduce disparities in student outcomes. Additionally, the role of artificial intelligence in streamlining assessment processes was briefly mentioned by participants, highlighting a potential area for further exploration in the evolving landscape of academic evaluation.

While the findings advocate for a shift towards formative and project-based assessments, a major limitation is the practical implementation challenges associated with large student populations. Institutions with high enrolment rates may struggle to provide continuous feedback and personalised assessments due to resource constraints, faculty workload, and technological accessibility. Additionally, reliance on data-driven decision-making assumes that institutions have access to robust data collection and analysis systems, which may not be universally available. Further research is needed to explore scalable and cost-effective strategies for integrating alternative assessments, particularly in resource-limited settings.

## Novelty as Driver for Creativity and Institutional Adaptability

The results show that institutions of learning should strike a balance between innovation and academic rigour. While novelty encourages creativity in teaching practices and curriculum design, it has to be implemented in a manner that does not erode the traditional values of education. It was also argued that one of the main drives for pedagogical transformation consists of digital platforms, virtual learning environments, and artificial intelligence-powered tools. A parallel view concerned over-reliance on technology at the cost of essential human interactions in the learning environment. It therefore supports the hybrid approach where the use of digital tools supplements, rather than completely replaces, conventional teaching.

While digital tools and artificial intelligence were found to be instrumental in educational transformation, there was also a call for a balanced integration that preserves the integrity of traditional pedagogical methods. Hybrid models that blend face-to-face instruction with technology-enhanced learning were preferred by many educators, as they provide flexibility without diminishing the personal engagement essential for deep learning. This raises an important question regarding how institutions can maintain academic rigour while fostering innovation, a theme that future studies could investigate in greater detail.

While innovation is crucial in modern education, a key limitation identified is the risk of over-reliance on digital tools. Some institutions may prioritise technological advancements without adequate consideration of their pedagogical effectiveness, potentially leading to superficial learning rather than deep conceptual understanding. Furthermore, while digital transformation is encouraged, not all educators and students have equal access to technological infrastructure, creating a risk of widening the digital divide. This suggests that future studies should investigate inclusive innovation strategies that ensure equitable access to digital learning resources without compromising academic integrity and traditional educational values.

## Curriculum and Its Changing Face

The discussions of curriculum development brought out one thing very clearly: relevance and adaptability are crucial in educational design. The stakeholders kept reiterating the needs for interdisciplinary learning and experiential approaches-a resonance of larger trends in higher education. Any curriculum that is not able to incorporate industry-relevant skills and current knowledge will surely turn obsolete and limit the students in their preparedness toward real challenges. These findings confirm the literature on modularising curriculum structures to allow flexibility and individualised learning pathways. Such insights also imply that curricula must be regularly reviewed to ensure that they reflect changes in technology, pedagogy, and changing workforce requirements.

However, the results also found that curriculum tends to be rigid and difficult to change rapidly. This is usually owing to the reluctance of the educational body of the central government to allow for rapid changes in the content being delivered. In some countries such as the United Kingdom and the United Arab Emirates, there are institutions which are licensed but maintain a level of flexibility when it comes to the curriculum of the various courses they have on offer.

The validated contextual framework has indicated a need for regular curricular reforms, but the micro and macro external environments do not allow for rapid changes. Future research should look at making curricular changes rapid and smoothly to allow for the new changes in the business landscape to be integrated into the world of academia. This will in turn help to prepare the leaders of tomorrow to lead organisations which operate differently than those described in the traditional business curriculum.

An additional challenge emerging from the findings is the disparity between curriculum design and industry expectations. While academic institutions strive to provide students with theoretical foundations, industry stakeholders often express concerns regarding graduates' job readiness. This highlights the need for more robust university-industry partnerships, where curriculum designers work closely with employers to ensure that academic content remains relevant and aligned with real-world demands. Research into best practices for fostering such collaborations could be instrumental in bridging this gap.

The findings underscore the necessity for curricular flexibility and adaptability, yet a significant limitation is the institutional and regulatory rigidity that often prevents rapid curriculum reforms. Many higher education institutions are governed by centralised accrediting bodies that impose strict guidelines on course structures, making it difficult to swiftly integrate industry-relevant skills and interdisciplinary approaches. Additionally, while modularised curricula are proposed as a solution, challenges remain in ensuring coherence and depth in academic content. Further research could examine policy-level changes that facilitate more agile curriculum reform while maintaining academic rigour and credibility.

## Engaging Students into Meaningful Educational Experiences through Gamification

Gamification was highly expected to be able to foster active student participation and motivation. The participants stressed the importance of interactive learning elements, such as point-based systems, leaderboards, and collaborative challenges, in increasing student engagement. However, there were concerns about unequal access to gamified learning environments, particularly because not all students have digital literacy or the necessary technology. Furthermore, while competition can foster motivation, if the focus is mostly on rankings and performance metrics of individual players, it may engender avoidable stress or disengagement for students. This would be a risk, but collaborative gamification methods, whose focus is more on teamwork rather than competition, were suggested as one avenue to more inclusive and equitable gamification.

Beyond gamification as a motivational tool, the findings suggest that its role in cognitive development warrants further investigation. Some participants pointed out that game-based learning fosters problem-solving skills and critical thinking, particularly in disciplines requiring high levels of analytical reasoning. However, more empirical evidence is needed to determine the long-term impact of gamification on learning retention and academic achievement. Future studies could examine different gamification frameworks to assess their effectiveness across diverse learning environments and subject areas.

Although gamification is recognised as an effective tool for enhancing student engagement, its implementation faces several challenges. One major limitation is that not all students respond positively to gamified learning—some may perceive it as distracting or trivialising complex subjects. Additionally, access to gamified tools is not uniform across institutions, as financial and technological constraints may hinder their adoption. Furthermore, competition-based gamification can inadvertently create stress and disengagement for some learners, particularly those who struggle in competitive environments. Future research should investigate adaptive gamification approaches that are inclusive, accessible, and tailored to diverse student needs.

## Student Inclusion and Engagement

The research findings affirm that student engagement is multi-dimensional in nature: cognitive, emotional, and behavioral. Active learning strategies, project-based learning, and problem-solving exercises were observed to be deemed effective across boards to create a deeper sense of engagement among students. Besides, the research has identified that engagement is closely related to inclusivity; students being valued and respected in their learning environments. Institutions that focused on student voice, feedback mechanisms, and flexible learning options had higher levels of participation and retention. Digital tools were also seen as instrumental in expanding accessibility, allowing students to engage with learning materials at their own pace. However, the research warns against over-dependence on technology, which, if not carefully managed, may lead to disengagement rather than deeper learning.

In addition to digital tools, the study found that fostering a sense of community significantly enhances student engagement. Institutions that prioritised inclusive classroom environments, peer learning opportunities, and mentorship programmes reported higher levels of student satisfaction and retention. This underscores the importance of not only technological advancements but also social learning dynamics in shaping meaningful educational experiences. Research into the interplay between social belonging and academic performance could provide further insights into optimising student engagement strategies.

While the research confirms the multidimensional nature of student engagement, a key limitation is that engagement strategies often assume homogeneity in student experiences. Factors such as socio-economic background, learning disabilities, and cultural diversity significantly influence how students engage with learning materials and institutional structures. Additionally, while digital tools can enhance accessibility, they may not always foster meaningful interactions, particularly in fully online environments. This suggests that a blended approach, combining technology-enhanced learning with strong social and community-building elements, may be more effective. Future studies should explore how different student demographics respond to engagement strategies and whether certain interventions disproportionately benefit specific groups over others.

## Interconnectivity of the Academic CHANGE Model Components

Most of all, an important insight arises from this interdependence of these six components that make up the Academic CHANGE Model. An excellent curriculum requires the best teachers to deliver it. Assessments lead to information on how teaching methodology can be formed to support the students in further improvement. Innovations and gamifications are the facilitators and help in retaining the interest of the students while engagement is a broader objective for all these interventions. It is strong because the model is designed holistically, and institutions can affect change systematically to ensure all elements work in concert for better educational outcomes.

While the Academic CHANGE Model presents a holistic framework for educational transformation, one limitation is that its effectiveness is context dependent. Institutions in different geographical regions or educational systems may face distinct challenges that limit the model's applicability. Additionally, while comparisons with Michael Fullan's Model, the TPACK framework, and the SAMR model demonstrate conceptual alignment, empirical evidence on the practical integration of these models remains limited. Future research should test the Academic CHANGE Model in diverse educational settings to identify potential adaptations required for different institutional and cultural contexts.

## Implications and Future Directions

The research study provides powerful empirical support for the Academic CHANGE Model as an effective framework for driving educational innovation. However, several challenges still lie ahead, particularly regarding resource allocation, resistance to change, and integrating digital tools without compromising traditional academic values. For future directions, institutions must adopt a phased implementation strategy that allows time for faculty adaptation, curriculum refinement, and iterative feedback cycles.

Long-term impacts of the Academic CHANGE Model on student performance, faculty development, and institutional outcomes could be investigated in future studies. Comparisons could be made to see how this model works in various educational settings: primary and secondary education, vocational training, online learning platforms. The continuous updating of the model by adding evidence provided could make teaching and learning in higher education relevant, effective, and efficient toward meeting global academic standards.

The findings suggest that the Academic CHANGE Model provides a feasible and scalable mechanism for the transformation of academic institutions. The model incorporates curriculum development, faculty engagement, assessment improvements, innovation, gamification, and student-centered learning to ensure learning institutions remain relevant and forward-looking yet firmly based on pedagogical excellence. Embracing challenges and strategic innovation will enable institutions to create learning environments that are adaptive, inclusive, and future-fit.

The study's findings suggest that the successful implementation of the Academic CHANGE Model requires a nuanced approach that considers both internal institutional factors and external societal influences. Policymakers and academic leaders should explore strategies for balancing educational tradition with innovation, ensuring that reforms enhance rather than disrupt the learning experience. Additionally, comparative studies across different educational contexts—such as public versus private institutions or Western versus non-Western academic systems—could provide a broader understanding of the model's adaptability and impact.

While the study highlights the potential impact of the Academic CHANGE Model, a significant limitation is the lack of long-term data on its effectiveness. The findings provide a strong conceptual basis, but longitudinal studies are needed to assess how the model influences student outcomes, faculty development, and institutional success over extended periods. Additionally, the study does not fully explore the financial and policy implications of implementing the model at a national or international level. Future research should address these gaps by conducting comparative studies across multiple institutions and assessing the cost-benefit ratio of adopting the model on a larger scale.

There is a need for cross-institutional studies to examine how the model performs in varied cultural and regulatory environments, ensuring its applicability across different education systems. Additionally, longitudinal studies should evaluate the long-term impact of curriculum adaptability, gamification, and faculty training programs on student performance and institutional success.

Moreover, emerging technologies such as Artificial Intelligence (AI)-driven assessments offer new possibilities for personalized learning pathways, ensuring students receive real-time, data-driven feedback. Future research should explore scalable AI-driven evaluation tools that support both students and educators in adapting instructional strategies dynamically.

Finally, an essential area of investigation is the integration of equity-driven engagement strategies. As research indicates, student engagement strategies often assume homogeneity in learning experiences, overlooking socioeconomic and accessibility barriers. Future studies should examine how diverse student populations respond to gamification, active learning, and assessment strategies, ensuring inclusive and equitable educational reform.

While the Academic CHANGE Model offers a comprehensive framework for guiding educational innovation, it is not without limitations. One significant concern is the model's assumption of institutional capacity and readiness. Not all educational contexts possess the technological infrastructure, funding, or human capital to implement the full model effectively (Laurillard, 2016). In resource-constrained settings, the emphasis on digital transformation and gamification may risk reinforcing existing inequalities rather than resolving them. Future iterations of the model should incorporate adaptive pathways that account for varying levels of digital maturity and pedagogical readiness, allowing for differentiated implementation strategies aligned to institutional context.

Another limitation lies in the model's current treatment of cultural and contextual diversity. The framework presupposes a relatively homogeneous academic environment, yet educational institutions across regions operate under vastly different policy regimes, cultural norms, and value systems (Leask, 2015). For instance, pedagogical autonomy and curriculum flexibility may be supported in Western contexts but restricted in more centralised education systems. To enhance its global relevance, the model could integrate culturally responsive indicators or cross-cultural adaptability measures that allow for contextual calibration without compromising on its core principles.

A further area for refinement is the model's long-term sustainability. The literature on educational reform frequently highlights the difficulty of maintaining innovation once external funding or pilot-phase enthusiasm diminishes (Coburn, 2003). To ensure sustained impact, the model must go beyond implementation and include strategies for embedding change within institutional governance, budgeting cycles, and staff development plans. Longitudinal evaluation mechanisms, informed by both quantitative and qualitative indicators, would support continuous improvement and help institutional leaders respond to evolving challenges.

## CONCLUSION

This study has highlighted the potential of the Academic CHANGE Model as a comprehensive framework for improving the quality of education. By focusing on the interconnected elements of Curriculum, Human Resources, Assessments and

Assimilation, Novelty, Gamification, and Engagement, the model addresses the diverse and evolving challenges faced by educational institutions in today's rapidly changing world.

Through interviews with educators, administrators, and other stakeholders, it became clear that these six components play a vital role in creating learning environments that are inclusive, dynamic, and effective. A well-thought-out curriculum, delivered by skilled and motivated educators, supported by meaningful assessments, and enriched by innovative and engaging approaches, is essential for fostering academic excellence. The study also reinforced the importance of providing educators with ongoing professional development, ensuring the availability of resources, and cultivating a culture of collaboration and openness.

However, the journey towards implementing the Academic CHANGE Model is not without its challenges. Issues such as resistance to change, limited funding, and the need for sustained effort were highlighted. Tackling these barriers requires careful planning, phased implementation, and a collective commitment from all stakeholders. By addressing these challenges head-on, institutions can ensure that the full benefits of this model are realised.

At its heart, this study serves as a reminder of the importance of adaptability and innovation in education. The Academic CHANGE Model provides a roadmap for institutions striving to meet the needs of modern learners, preparing them for an unpredictable future while fostering a love for lifelong learning.

The insights gathered here offer valuable guidance for educators, leaders, and policymakers who are seeking to make meaningful improvements in education. The findings also pave the way for further exploration into how this framework can be adapted and refined across different contexts. By continuing this dialogue, we can ensure that education evolves to meet the demands of the times while remaining true to its core purpose—empowering learners to thrive and succeed.

## REFERENCES


Al-Freih, M., & Alkhalaf, S. (2021). Challenges of digital transformation in higher education: A case study in Saudi Arabia. *Education and Information Technologies, 26*, 7607–7626.

Barnett, R. (2000). *Realizing the University in an Age of Supercomplexity*. Open University Press.

Barrett, H. C. (2007). *Digital Portfolios: Powerful Tools for Promoting Professional Growth and Reflection*. Corwin Press.

Barron, B., & Darling-Hammond, L. (2008). Teaching for Meaningful Learning: A Review of Research on Inquiry-Based and Cooperative Learning. In Darling-Hammond, L., & Barron, B. (Eds.), *Powerful Learning: What We Know About Teaching for Understanding* (pp. 11–70). Jossey-Bass.

Beane, J. A. (1997). *Curriculum Integration: Designing the Core of Democratic Education*. Teachers College Press.

Bergmann, J., & Sams, A. (2012). *Flip Your Classroom: Reach Every Student in Every Class Every Day*. International Society for Technology in Education.

Bishop, J. L., & Verleger, M. A. (2013). The Flipped Classroom: A Survey of the Research. *ASEE National Conference Proceedings, 30*(9), 1–18. DOI: 10.18260/1-2--22585

Black, P., & Wiliam, D. (1998). Assessment and Classroom Learning. *Assessment in Education: Principles, Policy & Practice, 5*(1), 7–74. DOI: 10.1080/0969595980050102

Cabau, B. (2014). Higher Education Ambitions and Societal Expectations. *Athens Journal of Education, 1*(2), 143–154. DOI: 10.30958/aje.1-2-4

Coburn, C. E. (2003). Rethinking scale: Moving beyond numbers to deep and lasting change. *Educational Researcher, 32*(6), 3–12. DOI: 10.3102/0013189X032006003

Collaborative for Academic, Social, and Emotional Learning (CASEL). (2021). *SEL Framework*. https://casel.org

Cook-Sather, A. (2006). Sound, Presence, and Power: "Student Voice" in Educational Research and Reform. *Curriculum Inquiry, 36*(4), 359–390. DOI: 10.1111/j.1467-873X.2006.00363.x

Darling-Hammond, L., Hyler, M. E., & Gardner, M. (2017). *Effective Teacher Professional Development*. Learning Policy Institute. DOI: 10.54300/122.311

Deci, E. L., & Ryan, R. M. (1985). *Intrinsic Motivation and Self-Determination in Human Behavior*. Springer. DOI: 10.1007/978-1-4899-2271-7

Dede, C. (2009a). Comparing frameworks for 21st century skills. In J. Bellanca & R. Brandt (Eds.), *21st century skills: Rethinking how students learn* (pp. 51–76). Solution Tree Press.

Dede, C. (2009b). Comparing Frameworks for 21st Century Skills. *21st century skills: Rethinking how students learn, 20*, 51–76.

Deterding, S., Dixon, D., Khaled, R., & Nacke, L. (2011). From Game Design Elements to Gamefulness: Defining "Gamification." *Proceedings of the 15th International Academic MindTrek Conference: Envisioning Future Media Environments*, 9–15. DOI: 10.1145/2181037.2181040

Dewey, J. (1938). *Experience and Education*. Macmillan.

Doll, W. E. (2012). The Four R's—An Alternative to the Tyler Rationale. In *Curriculum: Toward New Identities* (pp. 267–287). Routledge.

Domínguez, A., Saenz-de-Navarrete, J., de-Marcos, L., Fernández-Sanz, L., Pagés, C., & Martínez-Herráiz, J. J. (2013). Gamifying Learning Experiences: Practical Implications and Outcomes. *Computers & Education, 63*, 380–392. DOI: 10.1016/j.compedu.2012.12.020

DuFour, R., & Eaker, R. (1998). *Professional Learning Communities at Work: Best Practices for Enhancing Student Achievement*. Solution Tree Press.

Durlak, J. A., Weissberg, R. P., Dymnicki, A. B., Taylor, R. D., & Schellinger, K. B. (2011). The impact of enhancing students' social and emotional learning: A meta-analysis of school-based universal interventions. *Child Development, 82*(1), 405–432. DOI: 10.1111/j.1467-8624.2010.01564.x

Eisner, E. W. (2002). *The Arts and the Creation of Mind*. Yale University Press.

Finn, J. D., & Zimmer, K. S. (2012). Student Engagement: What Is It? Why Does It Matter? In Christenson, S. L., Reschly, A. L., & Wylie, C. (Eds.), *Handbook of Research on Student Engagement* (pp. 97–131). Springer. DOI: 10.1007/978-1-4614-2018-7_5

Fredricks, J. A., Blumenfeld, P. C., & Paris, A. H. (2004). School engagement: Potential of the concept, state of the evidence. *Review of Educational Research, 74*(1), 59–109. DOI: 10.3102/00346543074001059

Fredricks, J. A., Filsecker, M., & Lawson, M. A. (2016). Student Engagement, Context, and Adjustment: Addressing Definitional, Measurement, and Methodological Issues. *Learning and Instruction*, *43*, 1–4. DOI: 10.1016/j.learninstruc.2016.02.002

Fullan, M. (2007). *The New Meaning of Educational Change* (4th ed.). Teachers College Press.

Fullan, M. (2011). *Change Leader: Learning to Do What Matters Most*. Jossey-Bass.

Fullan, M. (2016). *The new meaning of educational change*. Teachers College Press.

Fullan, M. (2016). *The new meaning of educational change* (5th ed.). Teachers College Press.

Gay, G. (2010). *Culturally Responsive Teaching: Theory, Research, and Practice* (2nd ed.). Teachers College Press.

Gay, G. (2010). *Culturally responsive teaching: Theory, research, and practice*. Teachers College Press.

Gee, J. P. (2003). *What Video Games Have to Teach Us About Learning and Literacy*. Palgrave Macmillan. DOI: 10.1145/950566.950595

Gorski, P. C. (2013). *Reaching and teaching students in poverty: Strategies for erasing the opportunity gap*. Teachers College Press.

Guskey, T. R. (2002). Professional Development and Teacher Change. *Teachers and Teaching*, *8*(3), 381–391. DOI: 10.1080/135406002100000512

Halili, S. H. (2019). Technological advancements in education 4.0. *The Online Journal of Distance Education and e-Learning : TOJDEL*, *7*(1), 63–69.

Hall, G. E., & Hord, S. M. (2011). *Implementing Change: Patterns, Principles, and Potholes*. Allyn & Bacon.

Hamari, J., Koivisto, J., & Sarsa, H. (2014). Does Gamification Work? A Literature Review of Empirical Studies on Gamification. *Proceedings of the 47th Hawaii International Conference on System Sciences (HICSS)*, 3025–3034. DOI: 10.1109/HICSS.2014.377

Hamilton, E. R., Rosenberg, J. M., & Akcaoglu, M. (2016). The Substitution Augmentation Modification Redefinition (SAMR) Model: A critical review and suggestions for its use. *TechTrends*, *60*(5), 433–441. DOI: 10.1007/s11528-016-0091-y

Hanus, M. D., & Fox, J. (2015). Assessing the effects of gamification in the classroom: A longitudinal study on intrinsic motivation, social comparison, satisfaction, effort, and academic performance. *Computers & Education*, *80*, 152–161. DOI: 10.1016/j.compedu.2014.08.019

Hargreaves, A., & Fullan, M. (2012). *Professional Capital: Transforming Teaching in Every School*. Teachers College Press.

Harlen, W. (2007a). *Assessment of Learning*. Sage Publications. DOI: 10.4135/9781446214695

Harlen, W. (2007b). *The Quality of Learning: Assessment Alternatives for Primary Education*. Routledge.

Harris, A., & Jones, M. (2018). Why leadership matters: The role of leaders in engaging and supporting student learning. *Asia Pacific Journal of Education*, *38*(2), 194–206.

Hattie, J. (2009). *Visible Learning: A Synthesis of Over 800 Meta-Analyses Relating to Achievement*. Routledge.

Holmes, W., Bialik, M., & Fadel, C. (2021). *Artificial Intelligence in Education: Promises and Implications for Teaching and Learning*. Center for Curriculum Redesign.

Imran, M. K., Iqbal, S. M. J., Aslam, U., & Fatima, T. (2019). Does social media promote knowledge exchange? A qualitative insight. *Management Decision*, *57*(3), 688–702. DOI: 10.1108/MD-05-2017-0477

Januszyk, R., Miller, E. C., & Lee, O. (2016). Addressing student diversity and equity. *Science and Children*, *53*(8), 28–31. DOI: 10.2505/4/sc16_053_08_28

Kapp, K. M. (2012). *The Gamification of Learning and Instruction: Game-Based Methods and Strategies for Training and Education*. Pfeiffer.

Kelly, A. V. (2009). *The Curriculum: Theory and Practice* (6th ed.). SAGE Publications.

Koehler, M., & Mishra, P. (2009b). What is technological pedagogical content knowledge (TPACK)? *Contemporary Issues in Technology & Teacher Education*, *9*(1), 60–70.

Koehler, M. J., & Mishra, P. (2009a). What Is Technological Pedagogical Content Knowledge (TPACK)? *Contemporary Issues in Technology & Teacher Education*, *9*(1), 60–70.

Kryukov, V., & Gorin, A. (2017). Digital technologies as education innovation at universities. *Australian Educational Computing*, *32*(1), 1–16.

Kuh, G. D. (2009). What Student Engagement Data Tell Us About College Readiness. *Peer Review : Emerging Trends and Key Debates in Undergraduate Education*, *11*(1), 4–8.

Laurillard, D. (2016). *Teaching as a design science: Building pedagogical patterns for learning and technology*. Routledge.

Leal Filho, W., Lange Salvia, A., Beynaghi, A., Fritzen, B., Ulisses, A., Avila, L. V., Shulla, K., Vasconcelos, C. R., Moggi, S., Mifsud, M., Anholon, R., Rampasso, I. S., Kozlova, V., Ili̇̌ko, D., Skouloudis, A., & Nikolaou, I. (2024). Digital transformation and sustainable development in higher education in a post-pandemic world. *International Journal of Sustainable Development and World Ecology*, *31*(1), 108–123. DOI: 10.1080/13504509.2023.2237933

Leask, B. (2015). *Internationalizing the curriculum*. Routledge. DOI: 10.4324/9781315716954

Lindeman, B. M., & Lipsett, P. A. (2016). Evaluation and feedback. In *Curriculum development for medical education* (pp. 121–167). Radcliffe Publishing.

Luckin, R., Holmes, W., Griffiths, M., & Forcier, L. B. (2016). *Intelligence Unleashed: An Argument for AI in Education*. Pearson.

Marsh, J. A., Pane, J. F., & Hamilton, L. S. (2006). *Making Sense of Data-Driven Decision Making in Education: Evidence from Recent Research*. RAND Corporation.

Meyer, A., Rose, D. H., & Gordon, D. (2014). *Universal Design for Learning: Theory and Practice*. CAST Professional Publishing.

Moore, S., & Kuol, N. (2005). Students evaluating teachers: Exploring the importance of faculty reaction to feedback on teaching. *Teaching in Higher Education*, *10*(1), 57–73. DOI: 10.1080/1356251052000305534

Nah, F. F.-H., Zeng, Q., Telaprolu, V. R., Ayyappa, A. P., & Eschenbrenner, B. (2014). Gamification of Education: A Review of Literature. *Proceedings of the International Conference on HCI in Business*, 401–409. DOI: 10.1007/978-3-319-07293-7_39

Niess, M. L. (2011). Investigating TPACK: Knowledge growth in teaching with technology. *Journal of Educational Computing Research*, *44*(3), 299–317. DOI: 10.2190/EC.44.3.c

OECD. (2020). *Education responses to COVID-19: Embracing digital learning and online collaboration*. OECD Publishing.

Paris, D., & Alim, H. S. (2017). *Culturally sustaining pedagogies: Teaching and learning for justice in a changing world*. Teachers College Press.

Pinar, W. F. (2012). *What Is Curriculum Theory?* (2nd ed.). Routledge.

Polly, D., & Brantley-Dias, L. (2009). TPACK: Where do we go now? *TechTrends, 53*(5).

Prensky, M. (2010). *Teaching Digital Natives: Partnering for Real Learning*. Corwin Press.

Prince, M. (2004). Does Active Learning Work? A Review of the Research. *Journal of Engineering Education, 93*(3), 223–231. DOI: 10.1002/j.2168-9830.2004.tb00809.x

Puentedura, R. R. (2013). *SAMR and TPCK: Intro to advanced practice.*

Qawasmeh, E. F., Alnafisi, S. Y., Almajali, R., Alromaih, B. S., & Helali, M. M., & Ismail al-lawama, H. (2024). The impact of human resources management practices on employee performance: A comparative study between Jordanian and Saudi Arabian Universities. *Migration Letters : An International Journal of Migration Studies, 21*(2), 243–257.

Raes, A., Detienne, L., Windey, I., & Depaepe, F. (2020). A systematic literature review on synchronous hybrid learning: Gaps identified. *Learning Environments Research, 23*(3), 269–290. DOI: 10.1007/s10984-019-09303-z

Redecker, C. (2017). *European framework for the digital competence of educators: DigCompEdu*. Publications Office of the European Union.

Reeve, J. (2012). A Self-Determination Theory Perspective on Student Engagement. In Christenson, S. L., Reschly, A. L., & Wylie, C. (Eds.), *Handbook of Research on Student Engagement* (pp. 149–172). Springer. DOI: 10.1007/978-1-4614-2018-7_7

Sadler, D. R. (1989). Formative Assessment and the Design of Instructional Systems. *Instructional Science, 18*(2), 119–144. DOI: 10.1007/BF00117714

Sailer, M., Hense, J., Mayr, S. K., & Mandl, H. (2017). How Gamification Motivates: An Experimental Study of the Effects of Specific Game Design Elements on Psychological Need Satisfaction. *Computers in Human Behavior, 69*, 371–380. DOI: 10.1016/j.chb.2016.12.033

Selwyn, N. (2016). *Education and Technology: Key Issues and Debates*. Bloomsbury Academic.

Selwyn, N. (2022). *Should robots replace teachers? AI and the future of education*. Polity Press.

Shepard, L. A. (2000). The Role of Assessment in a Learning Culture. *Educational Researcher, 29*(7), 4–14. DOI: 10.3102/0013189X029007004

Shin, T., Koehler, M., Mishra, P., Schmidt, D., Baran, E., & Thompson, A. (2009, March). *Changing technological pedagogical content knowledge (TPACK) through course experiences.* Society for Information Technology & Teacher Education International Conference, 4152–4159. Association for the Advancement of Computing in Education (AACE).

Spady, W. G. (1994). *Outcomes-Based Education: Critical Issues and Answers.* American Association of School Administrators.

Taylor, R. D., Oberle, E., Durlak, J. A., & Weissberg, R. P. (2017). Promoting positive youth development through school-based social and emotional learning interventions: A meta-analysis of follow-up effects. *Child Development, 88*(4), 1156–1171. DOI: 10.1111/cdev.12864

Thomas, J. W. (2000). *A Review of Research on Project-Based Learning.* Autodesk Foundation.

Toda, A. M., Valle, P. H. M., & Isotani, S. (2019). The dark side of gamification: An overview of negative effects of gamification in education. *Communications in Computer and Information Science, 1005*, 143–156.

Tyler, R. W. (1949). *Basic Principles of Curriculum and Instruction.* University of Chicago Press.

UNESCO. (2022). *Global Education Monitoring Report: Technology in Education – A Tool on Whose Terms?* UNESCO.

Wang, W., Schmidt-Crawford, D., & Jin, Y. (2018). Preservice teachers' TPACK development: A review of literature. *Journal of Digital Learning in Teacher Education, 34*(4), 234–258. DOI: 10.1080/21532974.2018.1498039

Wijnia, L., Noordzij, G., Arends, L. R., Rikers, R. M., & Loyens, S. M. (2024). The effects of problem-based, project-based, and case-based learning on students' motivation: A meta-analysis. *Educational Psychology Review, 36*(1), 29. DOI: 10.1007/s10648-024-09864-3

Williamson, B., & Hogan, A. (2020). *Commercialisation and privatisation in/of education in the context of COVID-19.* Education International Research.

Zhao, Y., Pugh, K., Sheldon, S., & Byers, J. L. (2002). Conditions for Classroom Technology Innovations. *Teachers College Record, 104*(3), 482–515. DOI: 10.1111/1467-9620.00170

Zyngier, D. (2008). (Re)conceptualising Student Engagement: Doing Education Not Doing Time. *Teaching and Teacher Education*, *24*(7), 1765–1776. DOI: 10.1016/j.tate.2007.09.004

# Chapter 2
# The Cognitive Intersection of Artificial Intelligence (AI) Usage and Academic Excellence

**Mei Peng Low**
https://orcid.org/0000-0002-3141-3081
*Universiti Tunku Abdul Rahman, Malaysia*

**Wie Jane Chin**
https://orcid.org/0009-0000-9174-6753
*Universiti Tunku Abdul Rahman, Malaysia*

## ABSTRACT

*Incorporating Artificial Intelligence into education has become a transformative force with new opportunities for learning and teaching. This chapter examines the two core dimensions of AI usage with six types of AI usage: routine, regular, efficient, extended, innovative, and reinforced for their impact on students' academic performance. Self-Determination Theory guided the study to investigate connections between these AI usage types and students' perceived and measured academic success. Data collected from Higher Education Institution students through a structured survey were analyzed using Partial Least Squares Structural Equation Modeling. Findings revealed that routine, efficient, innovative, and reinformed uses of AI positively influence academic performance, while regular and extended uses show no significant effect. These results underscore the importance of strategic approaches to AI adoption in education. The chapter concludes with recommendations for educators and policymakers on leveraging AI to enhance academic outcomes and offers directions for future research.*

DOI: 10.4018/979-8-3373-7523-6.ch002

# INTRODUCTION

## Research Background

Artificial Intelligence (AI) has transformed many industries, especially education. Utilizing AI technologies can significantly improve teaching and learning experiences. By facilitating personalized learning, AI can customize educational experiences to address individual student needs, adjusting content and pacing according to each learner's unique strengths and preferences Wang et al., 2020). This level of customization ensures that students engage with material that resonates with them, ultimately fostering deeper understanding and retention (Feng et al., 2021).

AI enables adaptive assessments that automatically adjust the difficulty of questions in real-time, offering educators valuable insights into student performance and identifying areas in need of extra support (Kumar & Sharma, 2021). This approach not only helps to identify students who may be struggling but also allows for timely interventions, ensuring that no learner is left behind (Ranjan & Kumar, 2020). Additionally, integrating AI with innovative teaching methods, such as augmented reality (AR) and virtual reality (VR) can create immersive learning environments to enhance student engagement and motivation (Bailenson, 2018).

With the increasing adoption of AI technologies, the global AI education market is expected to expand from $4.03 billion in 2023 to $16.72 billion by 2030, signaling a significant shift in educational institutions worldwide. Governments worldwide, including Malaysia, are recognizing this potential and have launched initiatives like "AI Untuk Rakyat" and the "AI Talent Roadmap for Malaysia 2024-2030." These initiatives aim to incorporate AI into educational systems, ensuring that students are well-prepared for a technology-driven future and trained with the fundamental skills to thrive in an increasingly digital world.

Despite these promising developments, current research predominantly focuses on the technical aspects of AI tools rather than their impact on student learning outcomes. Most studies tend to be limited to specific academic disciplines or educational levels, neglecting the broader implications of AI across Higher Education Institutions (HEIs). This limited perspective obstructs a thorough understanding of how AI can be effectively applied to improve educational practices in various contexts.

This chapter seeks to bridge this critical gap by exploring how various types of AI usage influence academic performance. By examining the interplay between AI technologies and student outcomes, the chapter aims to offer valuable insights for educators and policymakers. Grasping these dynamics is crucial for creating effective strategies that maximize the advantages of AI in education, ensuring every student can utilize these technologies to enrich their learning experiences and achieve academic success.

## Research Problem

While AI has introduced innovative methodologies for teaching and learning, its adoption in higher education remains nascent. Most current AI applications in education primarily focus on content presentation and comprehension assessment (Bates et al., 2020). Most of the published research in this field is conducted by computer scientists, who often develop learning models based on the operational principles of computers and networks. This emphasis on algorithmic validation and technological tools frequently overshadows a thorough investigation into AI's impact on learning outcomes. Although there is some enthusiasm for enhancing educational results, this enthusiasm often centres on validating algorithms rather than understanding their educational implications.

As AI continues to permeate educational settings, it is crucial to comprehend its nuanced effects on academic performance across higher education institutions (HEIs). Despite the introduction of novel AI-driven approaches to enhance learning, research focusing on the roles, impacts, and implications of AI in higher education remains limited. Specifically, it is unclear how AI algorithms are commonly utilized and how they influence educational outcomes (Ouyang et al., 2022).

Despite extensive research has been conducted on the opportunities and challenges that AI presents in higher education (Zawacki-Richter et al., 2019; Bates et al., 2020; Kuleto et al., 2021), there is a notable scarcity of studies examining its actual outcomes on university students' educational performance. Of the limited research available, nearly half focuses on specific fields such as language learning, engineering, and computer science, with most studies concentrating exclusively on undergraduate levels (Crompton & Burke, 2023). The rapid incorporation of AI into the educational environment raises critical questions about how the diversity and extent of AI usage may affect students' academic performance, particularly within higher education institutions (HEIs). To gain a comprehensive understanding of AI's influence on academic achievement, it is essential to investigate its application across various HEIs rather than focusing solely on particular departments or educational levels. There is an urgent need to evaluate the actual impact of AI on educational outcomes to inform future practices and policies in higher education.

## Research Questions and Objectives

Building on the previously discussed research background and research problems, the following research questions have been developed to investigate the relationship between various independent variables associated with AI usage and the dependent variable, which is the academic performance of students in higher education institutions. The general research question is: "Are the types of AI usages affecting the academic performance of students in Higher Education Institutions (HEIs)?" This question aims to explore how various AI usage might influence students' learning outcomes, particularly on overall academic success. It can lead to an investigation into specific AI usages and their effectiveness in enhancing educational experiences.

The six specific research questions to be addressed are as follows:

1. Is routine use of AI positively influencing the academic performance of higher education institution students?
2. Is regular use of AI positively influencing the academic performance of higher education institution students?
3. Is efficient use of AI positively influencing the academic performance of higher education institution students?
4. Is extended use of AI positively influencing the academic performance of higher education institution students?
5. Is innovative use of AI positively influencing the academic performance of higher education institution students?
6. Is reinformed use of AI positively influencing the academic performance of higher education institution students?

Following the general research question, the general research objective is to establish the correlation between the type of AI usage on HEIs student academic performance. Below are the corresponding specific research objectives:

1. To examine the relationship between routine AI usage and academic performance.
2. To investigate the impact of regular AI usage on academic performance.
3. To analyze the effects of efficient AI usage on academic performance.
4. To explore the connection between extended AI usage and academic performance.
5. To assess the influence of innovative AI usage influences academic performance.
6. To study the relationship between reinformed AI usage in academic performance.

## LITERATURE REVIEW

## Self-Determination Theory

Self-Determination Theory (SDT) provides a robust framework for understanding motivation and behavior in educational contexts. It posits that fulfilling three fundamental psychological needs, namely autonomy, competence, and relatedness, is essential for optimal functioning and performance. In this study, SDT underpins the investigation of how HEI students' AI usage influences their academic performance.

SDT has been supported by extensive research and is a widely recognized theory of human drive and psychological well-being (Ryan & Deci, 2017). This theory addresses the motivational elements of personality and interpersonal conduct by exploring the relationship between fundamental psychological needs and well-being, mental flourishing, and quality of life. It examines the factors that either encourage or undermine self-motivation, external drive, and mental well-being, all of which are particularly relevant in educational contexts (Ryan & Deci, 2017). SDT has long been utilized to predict students' academic performance by focusing on various forms of motivation that range from autonomous to regulated, thereby influencing outcomes such as performance, engagement, and psychological well-being (Sergis et al., 2018).

SDT posits that "need" represents both a desire and a fundamental requirement crucial for psychological and emotional well-being. Meeting these needs is essential for optimal individual and societal functioning, especially in higher education. SDT identifies three core psychological needs: autonomy, relatedness, and competence. Autonomy reflects the feeling of self-direction and intrinsic motivation during an activity; relatedness refers to the sense of connection with others; and competence involves believing in one's ability to achieve desired outcomes. AI's integration into higher education can profoundly influence these needs, ultimately affecting academic performance.

## Academic Performance

Academic performance is a crucial assessment metric in education, which is influenced by a myriad of factors, including the use of technology. Research indicates that technology can have dual impacts (i.e., positive and negative) on learning outcomes (Naik et al., 2020). For instance, tools such as natural language processing (NLP) have the potential to enhance academic performance; however, excessive or unstructured use can lead to distractions and diminished efficacy. In a similar vein, Zawacki-Richter et al. (2019) assert that AI-based technologies can benefit students, educators, and administrators throughout the student learning lifecycle. The incorporation of AI in the educational environment is vital, as it has the potential to significantly enhance instructional processes and foster knowledge building. As technological advancements continue, AI is poised to evolve into more sophisticated forms of smart learning and education (Zhao & Liu, 2019). This evolution positions AI as a transformative technology that influences societal and educational development, necessitating an examination of its potential to enhance student creativity and academic achievement (Wang et al., 2022). Thus, exploring the diverse ways in which AI influences academic performance is critical.

Student academic performance is a fundamental component of any educational institution (Jokhan et al., 2018). Numerous studies (Rashid & Asghar, 2016; Alshater, 2022; Wecks et al., 2024) have investigated the correlation between technology use and educational performance. Rashid and Asghar (2016) identified a negative yet negligible correlation between average technology use and students' academic outcomes. They suggested that while students are increasingly exposed to various technologies, they may not be optimizing these tools for educational purposes. Additionally, excessive use and multitasking can lead to distractions, ultimately resulting in reduced time available for academic assignments (Alshater, 2022; Wecks et al., 2024). Adding on, Alshater (2022) specifically examined the potential AI applications, particularly NLP, in enhancing academic achievement, with a focus on economics and finance. His findings indicate that AI can profoundly improve academic performance in these fields. Conversely, Wecks et al. (2024) revealed that the use of generative AI negatively impacts students' test performance. Although positive aspects, such as simplifying information and boosting learning motivation, may exist, they are often overshadowed by adverse effects. Their research highlights that while AI may appear to facilitate easier studying, it can paradoxically hinder academic achievement.

In this study, academic performance was evaluated using students' most recent cumulative grade point average (CGPA) and their perceived performance. Despite the well-established that AI influences academic performance; the extent to which different uses of AI positively affect academic outcomes remains uncertain. This study examines different modes of AI usage including routine, regular, efficient, extended, innovative, and reinforced use, to identify their impacts on academic performance.

## Reinforced Use and Varied Use

In the context of AI use, it can be classified into reinformed use and varied use to enhance the understanding of AI impacts in the pursuit of academic performance (Pan et al., 2017). Reinformed use refers to a structured and habitual engagement with AI tools, ensuring their consistent and efficient application in academic settings. This includes routine use, where AI is seamlessly integrated into daily educational activities, such as automated grading systems or AI-powered tutoring platforms; regular use, characterized by a sustained and predictable reliance on AI for tasks like plagiarism detection or personalized learning recommendations; and efficient use, where faculty and students maximize AI's capabilities to streamline administrative processes and enhance learning outcomes with minimal effort. In contrast, varied use signifies a more dynamic and exploratory engagement with AI, fostering adaptability and innovation. This encompasses innovative use, where educators experiment with AI-driven pedagogical strategies, such as adaptive assessments and interactive AI simulations; extended use, which involves broadening AI's role beyond conventional applications to areas like research assistance, automated literature reviews, and academic writing support; and reinformed use, where AI adoption evolves based on insights from previous experiences, leading to continuous refinement and optimization of AI-driven educational practices. Together, these patterns of AI use reflect the dual nature of technology adoption in higher education by balancing stability with innovation to enhance teaching and learning among HEI students.

## Routine Use

In the context of higher education, the routine use of AI tools could be applied for tasks such as automated scheduling and administrative processes that may have a neutral impact on SDT. Although these tools can enhance operational efficiency, they do not directly address the core psychological needs that underpin student motivation and academic engagement. Individual academic performance may fluctuate based on variations in how AI solutions are implemented and engaged with by students (Sun et al., 2019). As such, routinization refers to the incorporation of modern technologies within daily academic activities; however, it does not necessarily imply that students are fully leveraging these systems' capabilities (Sundaram et al., 2007). Instead, it highlights the extent to which AI features are embedded into students' scholarly routines. This regular use of AI technologies must occur alongside an understanding and utilization of their full potential in order to maximize academic benefit (Chen et al., 2020).

Routine use in higher education refers to the systematic and ongoing application of AI tools by students (Hu & Pan, 2023). It encompasses students engaging with information systems regularly to assist with tasks such as research, assignment completion, and resource management (Li et al., 2013). For students to incorporate AI into their academic lives routinely, they must initially express interest in using these technologies and follow through with consistent application. Increased interaction with AI tools fosters their acclimatization and encourages students to embrace technology, thereby enhancing their academic productivity (Sundaram et al., 2007). Moreover, routine engagement with AI is often grounded in rational decision-making reflecting purposeful academic goals, but emotional and cognitive influences can also shape students' willingness to continue using such technologies. Over time, consistent use can evolve into habitual behaviors, allowing proficient tasks to be carried out with little conscious effort (De Guinea & Marcus, 2009).

The landscape of higher education is rapidly evolving, with students frequently exposed to innovative educational technologies that can be routinely used. When students become proficient with these tools and perceive no need to change their approach, they tend to engage more deeply with the material (Bourrie et al., 2016).

## Regular Use

Regular use is described as the degree to which an individual consistently engages with technology over an extended period (Sundaram et al., 2007; De Guinea & Markus, 2009). It encompasses repetitive interactions with information systems characterized by predictable patterns of behavior (Pan et al., 2017). This regularity establishes specific behavioral habits that are consistent over time (Limayem et al., 2007). Ma et al. (2014) provide preliminary evidence suggesting that regular use, or consistency in information technology engagement, significantly enhances habitual behavior. This consistency not only reinforces current behaviors but also positively influences future actions, thereby supporting the establishment of regular behavioral practices.

Regular use of AI in higher education, particularly for personalized learning recommendations and feedback, can positively influence students' sense of competence and autonomy, potentially leading to improved academic performance (Eltahir et al., 2024). Nonetheless, the effectiveness of these systems largely depends on their design and implementation. Effective design and implementation of these systems are crucial for maximizing their positive impact. Regular and consistent engagement with such AI tools, in terms of both duration and frequency, can cultivate a sense of familiarity and integration into the learning process, akin to developing a social attachment.

The extent and regularity of technology use, encompassing both frequency and overall duration, contribute to the overall learning experience (Christoforakos et al., 2021). While HEI students' satisfaction with educational technology may develop independently of the frequency of use, the cumulative experience influences overall satisfaction. This suggests that HEI students can develop positive perceptions of AI tools even without constant use, but consistent engagement contributes to a more holistic and potentially more positive experience (Al-Zahrani et al., 2024). Importantly, HEI student satisfaction with technology has been linked to improved educational achievement and functional competence, further emphasizing the potential benefits of regular AI integration in higher education (Memon et al., 2022).

## Efficient Use

Burton-Jones and Grange (2013) emphasized that to fully capitalize on information systems, particularly in higher education, they must be used both efficiently and effectively. In this context, system usage encompasses a user, a system, and a task, where the task represents a goal-driven action (Burton-Jones & Straub, 2006). Efficient use of information systems involves strategically using technology, such as AI tools and platforms, to help individuals achieve specific educational goals. This approach shifts the focus from merely interacting with the system to actively leveraging it to attain desired academic goals (Burton-Jones & Grange, 2013).

Pan et al. (2017) define efficient use as the demonstration of efficiency in executing specified activities within information systems. In higher education, efficient use emphasizes the positive outcomes that arise from effective engagement with these systems, of which these outcomes transcend the basic manner in which they are used. Importantly, this efficiency is objectively evaluated rather than relying solely on students' or educators' perceptions of effectiveness (Burton-Jones & Grange, 2013). Accordingly, technological advancements, coupled with efficient technology use, can significantly impact performance (Kim & Park, 2024). Educators, administrators, and students recognize that technology use in educational settings positively shape future individuals' effectiveness and efficiency in using various technologies (Tang & Austin, 2009). Therefore, the focus on efficient use becomes even more vital in routing the complexities and opportunities presented by AI technologies in higher education.

## Extended Use

The concept of "extended use" is related to the term "deep usage" introduced by Schwarz and Chin (2007) which highlights the extent to which specific technological functions are engaged. Increasing levels of extended use can lead individuals to gain an in-depth understanding and appreciation of the system, leading to innovative applications of the technology. When users first encounter a new technology, they often struggle to identify how to implement it effectively in their tasks. Initially, they may only utilize a limited set of features, but as they gain experience, they tend to explore additional, beneficial functionalities (Robey et al., 2002).

In the context of higher education, extended use refers to the strategic harnessing of advanced features of technology, particularly AI to assist students in executing their academic tasks more effectively. This concept encompasses the optimal utilization of additional technological functions that extend beyond the initial capabilities offered by a system (Wang & Hsieh, 2006). Extended use emphasizes how students can leverage these advanced features to manage a broader range of academic activities and responsibilities, thereby enhancing their overall productivity and performance (Wang & Hsieh, 2006). Consequently, as students become more familiar with an information system or AI tools, their initial simplistic experiences evolve into more complex interactions. They may transition to what is termed the routine use phase as discussed earlier, where the novelty of the system diminishes (Hsieh & Wang, 2007). However, as familiarity grows, students are likely to explore additional features that can complement their academic work and help them tackle new challenges. For instance, when faced with unfamiliar assignments or complex research tasks, students may reflect on their use of AI tools and adjust extend the system's capabilities. This reflective practice enables them to utilize AI more effectively, ultimately leading to improved productivity and performance in their studies (Sun, 2012).

## Innovative Use

In general, innovative use refers to the creative applications of AI in solving academic problems that significantly enhance engagement and performance. In the current study, innovative use is defined as the point at which individuals explore an information system, such as AI technologies, and uncover new features to apply in novel ways (Pan et al., 2017). To use technology innovatively, students must first develop consistent utilization patterns before they can begin to explore and discover innovative applications (Wang et al., 2008). Wang et al., (2020) argued that innovating with technology is a crucial step towards achieving meaningful innovation. Individuals who actively seek to innovate can discover effective technological solutions that enhance their performance (Ahuja & Thatcher, 2005).

In the context of higher education, the innovative use of AI technologies can provide significant advantages and value to both students and institutions (Bayaga, 2024). While educational organizations invest heavily in sophisticated technologies, their full potential is often underutilized. Encouraging students to discover creative and innovative applications of these AI tools is crucial to maximizing the return on investment and enhancing academic outcomes (Bayaga, 2024).

## Reinformed Use

Reinformed use refers to continuous usage and intention to continue exploring AI technologies. This represents a pattern of behavior that demonstrates the sustained and habitualized use of these advanced systems by students (Limayem et al., 2007). At the individual level, this ongoing use of AI goes beyond conscious acts and becomes an integral part of the student's daily academic activities (Bhattacherjee, 2001). Reinformed use of AI technologies is an indicator of a student's tendency to be creative and committed to learning about emerging technologies and uncovering their hidden features (Wang et al., 2024). This intention to continue exploring reflects the student's internal motivation and goal to interact with the technology as it evolves (Maruping & Magni, 2015). The beliefs about how AI can impact the student's ability to accomplish academic tasks advantageously can influence this willingness to explore further (Magni et al., 2010).

Reinformed use which being the intention to continue exploring the usage of technology emphasizes a student's interests and eagerness to delve deeper into a particular AI technology for more effective use in their studies (Maruping & Magni, 2015). This sustained engagement and exploration can lead to long-term benefits and greater adaptability in utilizing AI to enhance their academic performance and learning experiences. Continuous exploration of AI capabilities by higher education students fosters long-term benefits and adaptability, empowering them to leverage these advanced technologies more effectively in enhancing their academic performance and learning experiences.

## Hypothesis Development

Empirical research suggests a positive relationship between the routine use of educational technologies and academic performance among higher education students. For instance, Librenjak et al. (2016) found that the consistent utilization of e-learning platforms significantly enhances language proficiency, with regular users improving their skills by an average of 20.3% per semester, while irregular users only achieved an 11.6% improvement. Beatson et al. (2020) reported that active engagement with Quitch, a game-based technological platform, led to improved academic success among business students in Accounting and Management courses. The continuous use of Quitch fostered increased student engagement with educational activities throughout the semester, thereby positively impacting academic performance. Additionally, Prieto-Latorre et al. (2022) indicated that regular use of the Internet, excluding social networking sites, correlates positively with enhanced academic outcomes. Their findings showed that students who routinely utilize the Internet as an educational resource achieve better learning results. Given this evidence, the following hypothesis is proposed:

H1: Routine use of AI positively affects the academic performance of students in higher education institutions.

Several studies (e.g., Pardo-Cueva et al., 2019; Nayak, 2018) have explored the correlation between regular technology use and academic performance in higher education. Wentworth and Middleton (2014) examined the correlation between students' regular use of technology and their academic outcomes, as measured by GPA, SAT scores, and time spent studying. Their findings indicated that while regular technology usage could enhance academic performance, excessive use, particularly for entertainment, it could have detrimental effects. For instance, Anthony et al., (2021) found that using interactive technology for more than two hours per day negatively impacted students' academic performance, whereas moderate usage was linked to improved learning outcomes. Similarly, Sanders (2009) reported that educational technology use led to better academic results. With this, the following hypothesis is formulated:

H2: Regular use of AI positively affects the academic performance of students in higher education institutions.

The effect of technology use on academic performance has dual effects; when it is used effectively and efficiently, it can lead to positive academic achievements and contribute favorably to student development (Navarro-Martinez & Peña-Acuña, 2022). Efficient use of technology, particularly in asynchronous learning environments like gamification, can improve student retention and engagement (Olelewe et al., 2019). Productive technology use has a substantial positive effect on students, enhancing their skills and abilities, which can be highly beneficial (Ishaq et al., 2020). Furthermore, the efficient integration of ICT into classroom activities boosts student engagement, motivation, and enthusiasm, leading to more effective knowledge absorption, retention, and comprehension (Ishaq et al., 2020). Based on the presented evidence that demonstrates the positive impact of efficient technology use on various attributes of performance, the following hypothesis is proposed:

H3: Efficient use of AI positively affects the academic performance of students in higher education institutions.

In the educational context, studies indicate that while technology used solely for delivering content may not significantly influence educational outcomes (Yueng et al., 2021), incorporating specific advanced features can enhance learning experiences. For instance, Ahmed et al. (2020) found that various technological features positively impact students' academic performance. Alshater (2022) further demonstrated that the extended use of generative AI tools like ChatGPT can significantly advance academic achievement. Comprehensive engagement with such AI tools can aid academics in analyzing and interpreting large datasets, creating realistic scenarios for theory evaluation, and effectively communicating results. Utilizing these advanced features can lead to substantial improvements in educational outcomes (Alshater, 2022). Given the demonstrated benefits of extended use of AI technologies in enhancing academic performance, the following hypothesis is formed:

H4: Extended use of AI positively affects the academic performance of students in higher education institutions.

More recently, studies have demonstrated the positive impact of innovative technology use on academic performance. Rashid and Asghar (2016) found that while the general use of technology had a minimal direct correlation with school performance, the innovative and creative application of certain technologies, such as social media, had a significant positive association. Furthermore, Çakıroğlu et al. (2017) revealed that the combined use of various features, including gamification elements, had a beneficial impact on student engagement, which in turn improved educational achievement. Similarly, Youssef et al. (2022) showed that the interactive, creative, and innovative use of technology increased the likelihood of students obtaining higher grades, as it enhanced the effectiveness of instructional approaches. Following the evidence supporting the positive influence of the innovative use of AI on academic performance in higher education, below is the proposed hypothesis:

H5: Innovative use of AI positively affects the academic performance of students in higher education institutions.

Research has demonstrated the positive impact of students' continuous exploration, i.e., reinformed use of technology on their academic performance. Park and Weng's (2020) studies found that students' academic results improve when they possess a sense of independence and intention in effectively adopting technology. This can be attributed to the fact that students who are more interested in technology are more inclined to participate in educational projects involving technology or the internet, and are more enthusiastic about learning through these means. Furthermore, Gómez-Fernández and Mediavilla (2021) reported that students who are more interested in continuously exploring technology achieve better results in science, mathematics, and language. This positive relationship between students' interest in exploring technology and educational outcomes is particularly pronounced among the lowest-performing students. With this, H6 is proposed as below:

H6: Reinformed use of AI positively affects the academic performance of students in higher education institutions.

Based on the above discussion, the research framework is developed as illustrated in Figure 1. AI usage is classified into two dimensions of which each has three constructs to further delve into the specific usage in influencing HEI students' academic performance.

*Figure 1. Presents the research framework of the study.*

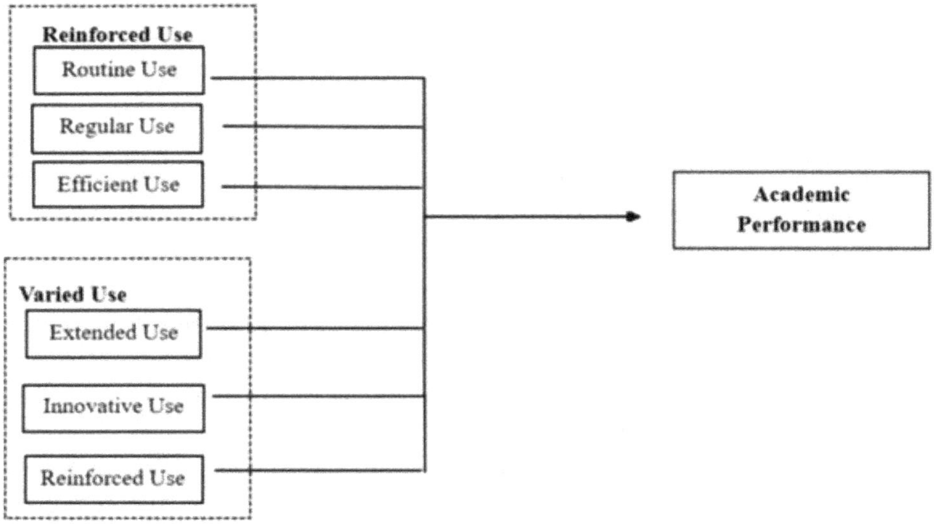


## METHODOLOGY

### Research Design

This study employed a quantitative, causal-predictive research design to investigate the correlation between AI usage types and academic performance among HEI students. Specifically, the research examined two main categories of AI use: reinforced use and varied use, and their impact on perceived academic performance. This explanatory approach aimed to clarify the specific interrelationships between these constructs, focusing on how different AI applications influence educational outcomes. The causal design allowed for the examination of cause-and-effect relationships, exploring how various AI uses affect student outcomes. Data were gathered through an online survey distributed to a diverse sample of HEI students, ensuring the representativeness of the target population.

### Sampling Technique and Data Collection Procedure

This study employed a non-probability sampling technique given that the sampling frame for HEI students with AI experiences is not available. More precisely, purposive sampling and snowball sampling were applied to recruit participants. The criteria for inclusion were being a student at a higher education institution, regardless of whether it was private or public, and having prior experience with using AI in their studies. Screening questions were used to ensure participants met these criteria. Additionally, diversity within the sample was prioritized by targeting representation across different majors and year levels. The questionnaire was distributed through various channels, including social media, word of mouth and student forums, over three months from June 2024 to September 2024. Ethical considerations were given careful attention throughout the study. Informed consent was obtained from all participants, and their data was anonymized and kept confidential. Stringent measures were implemented to ensure data security. For data analysis, Partial Least Squares Structural Equation Modeling (PLS-SEM) was used, which is a robust statistical technique for evaluating complex relationships between variables.

### Instrument

The survey instrument was carefully selected after involving the adaptation of existing established scales to measure specific constructs related to AI usage and academic performance. Pilot tests were performed to assess the validity and reliability of the survey. The questionnaire was structured to comprehensively capture the nuances of AI usage and its perceived impact on academic outcomes along with the CGPA of the students. There were two sections in the survey consisting of demographic questions using nominal scales and the other section covers items measuring the independent and dependent variables using the ordinal scale with responses recorded on a 7-point Likert scale.

### Sample Size

Guided by the recommendation of Memon et al. (2020) for a minimum sample size of 200 for structural equation modeling, and further validated by a G*Power analysis (effect size = 0.15, alpha = 0.05, power = 0.80, based on six predictors) suggesting a minimum of 146 participants, the study ultimately collected 301 complete responses, exceeding the required sample size for statistical significance.

## RESULTS

### Participants' Profile: Descriptive Analysis

The details of the participants are presented in Table 1. Most of them fell within the age range of 18 to 25, accounting for 88.7% of the sample. A smaller portion of the participants were aged 26 to 30 (8.31%), while only 2.32% were over the age of 30. Those below 18 years represented 0.66% of the sample. The gender distribution indicated a predominance of female participants, who made up 86.05% of the sample, whereas male participants represented 13.95%. The racial composition was dominated by Chinese respondents, who constituted 96.35% of the sample. In contrast, Malays and Indians were significantly underrepresented, comprising 1.99% and 1.66% respectively. The level of study among respondents showed that 77.41% were undergraduates, while 17.61% were postgraduate students. A smaller segment of the participants, 4.98%, were enrolled in foundation or diploma programs. Regarding the type of institution, 72.09% of participants attended private institutions, while 27.91% were enrolled in public institutions. Lastly, it is the GPA distribution, of which 46.18% of respondents achieved a GPA between 3.500 and 4.000, indicating a strong academic performance. A substantial 37.54% reported GPAs in the range of 3.000 to 3.499. Conversely, only a small fraction of participants had GPAs below 2.500, with 3.65% below 2.000, and 2.33% ranging from 2.000 to 2.499. 10.3% had GPAs between 2.500 and 2.999. The location of residence was predominantly urban, with 74.42% of respondents living in urban areas, while 25.58% resided in rural settings.

*Table 1.*

| **Profile** | **Number** | **Percentage (%)** |
|---|---|---|
| **Age** | | |
| Below 18 | 2 | 0.66 |
| 18 – 25 | 267 | 88.7 |
| 26 – 30 | 25 | 8.31 |
| Above 30 | 7 | 2.32 |
| **Gender** | | |
| Male | 42 | 13.95 |
| Female | 259 | 86.05 |
| **Race** | | |
| Chinese | 290 | 96.35 |
| Malays | 6 | 1.99 |
| Indian | 5 | 1.66 |
| **Level of Study** | | |
| Foundation/Diploma | 15 | 4.98 |
| Undergraduate | 233 | 77.41 |
| Postgraduate | 53 | 17.61 |

continued on following page

*Table 1. Continued*

| Profile | Number | Percentage (%) |
|---|---|---|
| **Type of Institution** | | |
| Private | 217 | 72.09 |
| Public | 84 | 27.91 |
| **GPA** | | |
| Below 2.000 | 11 | 3.65 |
| 2.000 - 2.499 | 7 | 2.33 |
| 2.500 - 2.999 | 31 | 10.3 |
| 3.000 - 3.499 | 113 | 37.54 |
| 3.500 - 4.000 | 139 | 46.18 |
| **Location of Residence** | | |
| Rural | 77 | 25.58 |
| Urban | 224 | 74.42 |
| Total | 301 | 100.00 |

## Measurement Model

The proposed research framework in Figure 1 was analyzed in two stages using PLS-SEM. First, the measurement model was evaluated, followed by the structural model in the second stage.

The first phase of the analysis focused on evaluating the measurement model to ensure the reliability and validity of the constructs. All measures utilized in this study were reflective, allowing for the assessment of internal consistency through Cronbach's alpha and composite reliability metrics. The results indicated strong internal consistency across all constructs, as evidenced by Cronbach's alpha values ranging from 0.815 to 0.907 and composite reliability values ranging from 0.825 to 0.929. Henceforth, the constructs Cronbach's alpha and composite reliability have surpassed the required threshold of 0.7 (Chin, 1998), further confirming their reliability.

Convergent validity was established through factor loadings and average variance extracted (AVE), with factor loadings for the items exceeding the threshold of 0.7 and AVE values ranging from 0.682 to 0.851, indicating acceptable convergent validity for each construct. The details are shown in Table 2.

*Table 2.*

| Construct | Item | Factor Loading | Cronbach's alpha | Composite reliability (rho_a) | Composite reliability (rho_c) | Average variance extracted (AVE) |
|---|---|---|---|---|---|---|
| Academic Performance | AAC1 | 0.885 | 0.883 | 0.888 | 0.919 | 0.74 |
| | AAC2 | 0.860 | | | | |
| | AAC3 | 0.871 | | | | |
| | AAC4 | 0.824 | | | | |
| Efficient Use | EFT1 | 0.852 | 0.815 | 0.82 | 0.89 | 0.73 |
| | EFT2 | 0.889 | | | | |
| | EFT4 | 0.820 | | | | |
| Extended Use | ETD1 | 0.893 | 0.885 | 0.885 | 0.929 | 0.812 |
| | ETD2 | 0.904 | | | | |
| | ETD3 | 0.906 | | | | |
| Innovative Use | INE1 | 0.823 | 0.907 | 0.908 | 0.928 | 0.682 |
| | INE2 | 0.813 | | | | |
| | INE3 | 0.831 | | | | |
| | INE4 | 0.842 | | | | |
| | INE5 | 0.834 | | | | |
| | INE6 | 0.810 | | | | |
| Regular Use | RGR1 | 0.924 | 0.825 | 0.825 | 0.919 | 0.851 |
| | RGR2 | 0.921 | | | | |
| Reinformed Use | RID1 | 0.876 | 0.854 | 0.857 | 0.911 | 0.774 |
| | RID2 | 0.883 | | | | |
| | RID3 | 0.880 | | | | |
| Routine Use | RUE1 | 0.901 | 0.876 | 0.878 | 0.924 | 0.801 |
| | RUE2 | 0.910 | | | | |
| | RUE3 | 0.874 | | | | |

Discriminant validity refers to the extent to which each latent variable is distinguished from other constructs within a model (Hair et al., 2014). In simpler terms, it measures how distinct the indicators are from one another across various constructs. Hair et al. (2019) recommend that researchers use the heterotrait-monotrait (HTMT) criterion for testing discriminant validity. This aligns with Henseler et al. (2015), who also suggest using the HTMT ratio of correlation for assessing discriminant validity. Henseler et al. (2015) further explained the establishment of discriminant validity, with the HTMT statistics not exceeding 0.90 or 0.85, dependent on whether the constructs are conceptually similar. As shown in Table 3, none of the HTMT values are greater than 0.90 (Henseler et al., 2015; Gold et al., 2001). Moreover, all the values of the confidence interval in Table 3 do not have a value of 1 in between, which suggests that all HTMT values are significantly different from 1 (Henseler et al., 2015). Hence, the discriminant validity for the present study is ascertained.

*Table 3.*

| Construct | 1 | 2 | 3 | 4 | 5 | 6 | 7 |
|---|---|---|---|---|---|---|---|
| **1. Academic Performance** | | | | | | | |
| **2. Efficient Use** | 0.529 (0.424, 0.632) | | | | | | |
| **3. Extended Use** | 0.432 (0.331, 0.538) | 0.831 (0.761, (0.895) | | | | | |
| **4. Innovative Use** | 0.607 (0.519, (0.688) | 0.665 (0.560, (0.762) | 0.622 (0.519, 0.720) | | | | |
| **5. Regular Use** | 0.388 (0.279, (0.502) | 0.739 (0.643, 0.826) | 0.735 (0.635, 0.824) | 0.551 (0.446, 0.655) | | | |
| **6. Reinformed Use** | 0.603 (0.501, (0.696) | 0.580 (0.469, (0.687) | 0.609 (0.497, 0.716) | 0.784 (0.703, 0.859) | 0.588 (0.477, 0.699) | | |
| **7. Routine Use** | 0.514 (0.403, (0.620) | 0.784 (0.709, (0.851) | 0.686 (0.589, 0.773) | 0.557 (0.451, (0.659) | 0.770 (0.675, 0.860) | 0.628 (0.516, 0.731) | |

Before continue with the structural model assessment, researchers must address the issue of collinearity present in the study (Diamantopoulos & Siguaw, 2006). This is done by using the variance inflation factor (VIF). The results exhibited in Table 4 that all the VIF values are below 3.3 concluding that collinearity is not a concern in this study.

*Table 4.*

| Constructs | VIF |
|---|---|
| Efficient Use | 2.586 |
| Extended Use | 2.441 |
| Innovative Use | 2.248 |
| Regular Use | 2.118 |
| Reinformed Use | 2.168 |
| Routine Use | 2.322 |

In the second stage of the analysis, an assessment of the structural model was carried out to evaluate the hypothesized relationships between constructs. The significance of these hypotheses was determined using a bootstrapping procedure with 10,000 resampling iterations (Becker et al., 2023). The results of the hypothesis testing are presented in Table 5, which shows that four hypotheses were supported: H1, H3, H5, and H6 with p values < 0.05 and t-statistics > 1.965. In contrast, two hypotheses, H2 and H4, were not supported, with p-values above 0.05 and t-statistics less than 1.965. To ensure the robustness of our findings, it was confirmed the results using the Confidence Interval Bias Corrected (CIBC) method, which indicated no zero values straddling the lower and upper bounds (Becker et al., 2023). Specifically, the results demonstrate that Routine Use, Efficient Use, Innovative Use, and Reinforced Use positively influence students' academic performance. On the other hand, Regular Use and Extended Use showed insignificant associations with academic performance.

*Table 5.*

| **Hypothesis Testing** | **β** | **T statistics** | **P values** | **CIBC** | | **Decision** |
|---|---|---|---|---|---|---|
| | | | | **5.00%** | **95.00%** | |
| **H1**: Routine Use -> Academic Performance | 0.182 | 2.276 | 0.011 | 0.057 | 0.322 | Supported |
| **H2**: Regular Use -> Academic Performance | - 0.092 | 1.538 | 0.062 | -0.189 | 0.003 | Not supported |
| **H3**: Efficient Use -> Academic Performance | 0.149 | 1.784 | 0.037 | 0.003 | 0.279 | Supported |
| **H4**: Extended Use -> Academic Performance | - 0.056 | 0.738 | 0.230 | -0.179 | 0.070 | Not supported |
| **H5**: Innovative Use -> Academic Performance | 0.280 | 3.636 | 0.000 | 0.151 | 0.403 | Supported |
| **H6**: Reinformed Use -> Academic Performance | 0.239 | 3.039 | 0.001 | 0.114 | 0.371 | Supported |

## PLSpredict

Shmueli et al. (2019) emphasized that PLS-SEM uses "causal predictive" approach with the ability to assess a path model's predictability. Consequently, PLSpredict was utilized, which involves separating training and holdout samples to estimate model parameters and evaluate the model's predictive power. The metrics used for evaluation included Root Mean Squared Error (RMSE) and Mean Absolute Error (MAE), chosen for their symmetrical nature in reflecting prediction errors in the existing data. The results presented in Table 6 show that PLS-SEM outperforms linear modeling (LM) across all indicators, with lower RMSE and MAE values compared to the naïve LM benchmark. Additionally, the Q values for the indicators of the PLS model exceeded those for the LM model ($Q^2 > 0$). These results suggest that the model used in this study demonstrates a high predictive power in representing reality and predicting academic performance.

*Table 6.*

| Academic performance | $Q^2$ | PLS-SEM_RMSE | PLS-SEM_MAE | LM_RMSE | LM_MAE | PLS-SEM_RMSE less LM_RMSE | PLS-SEM_MAE less LM_MAE |
|---|---|---|---|---|---|---|---|
| **AAC1** | 0.277 | 1.113 | 0.890 | 1.166 | 0.922 | -0.053 | -0.032 |
| **AAC2** | 0.279 | 1.053 | 0.811 | 1.110 | 0.856 | -0.057 | -0.045 |
| **AAC3** | 0.262 | 1.030 | 0.817 | 1.070 | 0.844 | -0.040 | -0.027 |
| **AAC4** | 0.184 | 1.132 | 0.861 | 1.178 | 0.907 | -0.046 | -0.046 |

## IMPLICATIONS OF THE STUDY

The findings of this study yield significant academic implications for policymakers and educators. First, the demonstrated positive relationship between routine AI use and academic performance highlights the need for educational institutions to integrate AI technologies into their curricula. AI-powered learning tools can enhance student performance by offering personalized learning experiences tailored to individual needs (Ellikkal & Rajamohan, 2024). Moreover, the effective and innovative deployment of AI not only boosts learning outcomes but also emphasizes the necessity for practical, inventive tools that encourage students to explore and engage deeply with content.

Educators should prioritize fostering the utilization of AI technologies that enhance student performance and support their academic journeys. However, the lack of significance associated with both regular and extended AI usage suggests that simply increasing AI utilization, without targeted educational objectives, may not yield beneficial results. As such, higher education institutions should focus on the meaningful application of AI rather than on its mere adoption. Additionally, an over-reliance on AI's extended functionalities, without specific academic goals, may hinder rather than promote student performance. Zhai et al. (2024) highlight that excessive dependence on AI can adversely affect cognitive abilities, as individuals may increasingly prefer instant responses over those that require thoughtful deliberation.

In light of these insights, both policymakers and educators should guide students in leveraging AI technologies to complement traditional learning methods while simultaneously nurturing critical thinking and problem-solving abilities. By emphasizing the integration of AI tools that align with educational objectives, educators can foster a more enriching learning environment. Policymakers must also invest in resources and training programs to facilitate innovative and effective AI use in higher education institutions.

## LIMITATIONS OF THE STUDY

This research provides valuable insights; however, it is essential to recognize its limitations. The first limitation is the number of variables examined was only limited to two dimensions (i.e., reinforced use and varied use) with six variables of AI use in relation to academic performance. Although this study focused on various uses of AI, it did not address other relevant factors such as students' digital competency, the accessibility of AI tools, and psychological aspects like interest and motivation. Additionally, other types of AI usage, such as personalized use, collaborative use, and assessment use, were not explored. Furthermore, this study utilized a cross-sectional design, meaning data was collected at only one specific point in time. Given that AI technologies and their integration into education are continuously evolving, students' usage behaviors may change over time. Lastly, the sample in this study primarily consisted of students from HEIs, limiting the generalizability of the findings to other groups, such as high school students or individuals in professional development programs. While these limitations are acknowledged, they do not undermine the significance of the findings; instead, they provide a solid foundation for future research.

## RECOMMENDATIONS FOR FUTURE RESEARCH

Following the limitation of the study, future researchers could expand the scope by investigating other additional factors to present a more comprehensive picture of how AI impacts student achievement. Longitudinal research is recommended to provide greater detail regarding AI's long-term impact on academic performance. In addition, expanding the demographic groups such as high-school students could provide further insight regarding how the different usage of AI impacts academic performance. Additionally, future research could address the concern of representativeness with the use of a weighted PLS (WPLS) method to attain better average population evaluations when a set of appropriate weights is accessible (Cheah et al., 2021; Low et al., 2021). Such attempts would make an important contribution to both academic research and the practical development of technology in education.

## CONCLUSION

This chapter highlights the transformative potential of artificial intelligence (AI) in reshaping education, contingent upon its strategic and innovative application. While the integration of AI technologies presents opportunities for enhanced learning experiences and improved academic outcomes, the realization of this potential depends on meticulous planning and implementation, with a focus on meaningful engagement with AI tools.

Future efforts should concentrate on key areas to effectively harness AI's capabilities. Future researchers are encouraged to explore the multifaceted role of AI in education, examining additional variables such as emotional intelligence, teacher training, and institutional culture. Additionally, investigating longitudinal impacts will provide insights into how sustained AI integration affects student learning and development over time. Moreover, examining diverse demographics can reveal differential effects, aiding in tailoring AI applications to varied learning needs and contexts. This involves scenario planning to envision how AI can address specific educational challenges, such as bridging achievement gaps in underprivileged communities or enhancing STEM education through immersive simulations. Ground-level implementation through pilot programs in diverse institutional settings, including rural schools and urban universities, is crucial to assess the practical feasibility and impact of AI-driven interventions. Iterative adaptation, involving the continuous refinement of AI tools and strategies based on real-world feedback and performance data, is essential to ensure alignment with evolving educational needs and standards. By expanding the scope of inquiry into these areas, researchers can provide a clearer understanding of how AI can be harnessed as a core component of educational design, rather than merely a supplementary tool. Such research will be invaluable in informing educators and policymakers about the best practices that maximize the beneficial impacts of AI in educational settings.

Ultimately, a comprehensive understanding of AI's role in education is vital for developing effective strategies that equip students with the skills necessary to thrive in an increasingly digital world. Moving forward, emphasis should be placed on creating adaptable, equitable, and impactful AI solutions that foster academic excellence and prepare students for the challenges and opportunities of a technology-driven future.

# REFERENCES


Al-Zahrani, A. M., & Alasmari, T. M. (2024). Exploring the impact of artificial intelligence on higher education: The dynamics of ethical, social, and educational implications. *Humanities & Social Sciences Communications*, *11*(1), 1–12. DOI: 10.1057/s41599-024-03432-4

Alshater, M. M. (2022). Exploring the Role of Artificial Intelligence in Enhancing Academic Performance: A Case Study of ChatGPT. *SSRN*. https://papers.ssrn.com/sol3/papers.cfm?abstract_id=4312358 DOI: 10.2139/ssrn.4312358

Anthony, W. L., Zhu, Y., & Nower, L. (2021). The relationship of interactive technology use for entertainment and school performance and engagement: Evidence from a longitudinal study in a nationally representative sample of middle school students in China. *Computers in Human Behavior*, *122*, 106846. Advance online publication. DOI: 10.1016/j.chb.2021.106846

Bailenson, J. (2018). *Experience on Demand: What Virtual Reality Is, How It Works, and What It Can Do*. HarperCollins.

Bates, T., Cobo, C., Mariño, O., & Wheeler, S. (2020). Can artificial intelligence transform higher education? *International Journal of Educational Technology in Higher Education*, *17*(1), 42. Advance online publication. DOI: 10.1186/s41239-020-00218-x

Bayaga, A. (2024). Leveraging AI-enhanced and emerging technologies for pedagogical innovations in higher education. *Education and Information Technologies*, •••, 1–28.

Beatson, N., Gabriel, C.-A., Howell, A., Scott, S., van der Meer, J., & Wood, L. C. (2020). Just opt in: How choosing to engage with technology impacts business students' academic performance. *Journal of Accounting Education*, *50*, 100641. Advance online publication. DOI: 10.1016/j.jaccedu.2019.100641

Becker, J. M., Cheah, J. H., Gholamzade, R., Ringle, C. M., & Sarstedt, M. (2023). PLS-SEM's most wanted guidance. *International Journal of Contemporary Hospitality Management*, *35*(1), 321–346. DOI: 10.1108/IJCHM-04-2022-0474

Bourrie, D. M., Jones-Farmer, L. A., & Sankar, C. S. (2016). Learning technologies: Bridging the gap between intention, adoption and routine use. *Technology*, *26*, 27.

Burton-Jones, A., & Grange, C. (2013). From Use to Effective Use: A Representation Theory Perspective. *Information Systems Research*, *24*(3), 632–658. DOI: 10.1287/isre.1120.0444

Çakıroğlu, Ü., Başıbüyük, B., Güler, M., Atabay, M., & Yılmaz Memiş, B. (2017). Gamifying an ICT course: Influences on engagement and academic performance. *Computers in Human Behavior*, *69*, 98–107. DOI: 10.1016/j.chb.2016.12.018

Cheah, J.-H., Roldán, J. L., Ciavolino, E., Ting, H., & Ramayah, T. (2021). Sampling weight adjustments in partial least squares structural equation modeling: Guidelines and illustrations. *Total Quality Management & Business Excellence*, *32*(13-14), 1594–1613. DOI: 10.1080/14783363.2020.1754125

Crompton, H., & Burke, D. (2023). Artificial intelligence in higher education: The state of the field. *International Journal of Educational Technology in Higher Education*, *20*(1), 1–22. DOI: 10.1186/s41239-023-00392-8

De Guinea, A. O., & Markus, M. L. (2009). Why Break the Habit of a Lifetime? Rethinking the Roles of Intention, Habit, and Emotion in Continuing Information Technology Use. *Management Information Systems Quarterly*, *33*(3), 433–444. DOI: 10.2307/20650303

Diamantopoulos, A., & Siguaw, J. A. (2006). Formative versus reflective indicators in organizational measure development: A comparison and empirical illustration. *British Journal of Management*, *17*(4), 263–282. DOI: 10.1111/j.1467-8551.2006.00500.x

Ellikkal, A., & Rajamohan, S. (2024). AI-enabled personalized learning: Empowering management students for improving engagement and academic performance. *Vilakshan – XIMB. Journal of Management.* Advance online publication. DOI: 10.1108/xjm-02-2024

Eltahir, M. E., & Babiker, F. M. E. (2024). The influence of artificial intelligence tools on student performance in e-learning environments: Case study. *Electronic Journal of e-Learning*, *22*(9), 91–110. DOI: 10.34190/ejel.22.9.3639

Feng, M., Heffernan, N. T., & Koedinger, K. R. (2021). Using Learning Analytics to Improve the Adaptive Learning Environment. *Journal of Educational Data Mining*, *13*(1), 1–20.

Gold, A. H., Malhotra, A., & Segars, A. H. (2001). Knowledge management: An organizational capabilities perspective. *Journal of Management Information Systems*, *18*(1), 185–214. DOI: 10.1080/07421222.2001.11045669

Hair, J. F., Sarstedt, M., & Ringle, C. M. (2019). Rethinking some of the rethinking of partial least squares. *European Journal of Marketing*, *53*(4), 566–584. DOI: 10.1108/EJM-10-2018-0665

Henseler, J., Ringle, C. M., & Sarstedt, M. (2015). A new criterion for assessing discriminant validity in variance-based structural equation modeling. *Journal of the Academy of Marketing Science*, *43*(1), 115–135. DOI: 10.1007/s11747-014-0403-8

Hu, Q., & Pan, Z. (2023). Can AI benefit individual resilience? The mediation roles of AI routinization and infusion. *Journal of Retailing and Consumer Services*, *73*, 103339. Advance online publication. DOI: 10.1016/j.jretconser.2023.103339

Ishaq, K., Mat Zin, N. A., Rosdi, F., Abid, A., & Ijaz, M. (2020). The Impact of ICT on Students' Academic Performance in Public Private Sector Universities of Pakistan. *International Journal of Innovative Technology and Exploring Engineering*, *9*(3), 1117–1121. DOI: 10.35940/ijitee.C8093.019320

Jokhan, A., Sharma, B., & Singh, S. (2018). Early warning system as a predictor for student performance in higher education blended courses. *Studies in Higher Education*, *44*(11), 1900–1911. DOI: 10.1080/03075079.2018.1466872

Kim, J. M., & Park, J. H. (2024). When is digital transformation beneficial for coupled open innovation? The contingent role of the adoption of industry 4.0 technologies. *Technovation*, *136*, 103087. DOI: 10.1016/j.technovation.2024.103087

Kuleto, V., Ilić, M., Dumangiu, M., Ranković, M., Martins, O. M. D., Păun, D., & Mihoreanu, L. (2021). Exploring Opportunities and Challenges of Artificial Intelligence and Machine Learning in Higher Education Institutions. *Sustainability (Basel)*, *13*(18), 10424. DOI: 10.3390/su131810424

Kumar, R., & Sharma, A. (2021). Adaptive Learning Systems: A Review and Future Directions. *Journal of Educational Technology & Society*, *24*(1), 1–15.

Librenjak, S., Kocijan, K., & Janjic, M. (2016). Improving Students' Language Performance Through Consistent Use of E-Learning: An Empirical Study in Japanese, Korean, Hindi and Sanskrit. *Acta Linguistica Asiatica*, *6*(2), 79–94. DOI: 10.4312/ala.6.2.79-94

Limayem, M., Hirt, S. G., & Cheung, C. M. K. (2007). How habit limits the predictive power of intention: The case of information systems continuance. *Management Information Systems Quarterly*, *31*(4), 705–737. DOI: 10.2307/25148817

Low, M. P., Cham, T. H., Chang, Y. S., & Lim, X. J. (2021). Advancing on weighted PLS-SEM in examining the trust-based recommendation system in pioneering product promotion effectiveness. *Quality & Quantity*, •••, 1–30. DOI: 10.1007/s11135-021-01147-1 PMID: 33879929

Magni, M., Susan Taylor, M., & Venkatesh, V. (2010). "To play or not to play": A cross-temporal investigation using hedonic and instrumental perspectives to explain user intentions to explore a technology. *International Journal of Human-Computer Studies, 68*(9), 572–588. DOI: 10.1016/j.ijhcs.2010.03.004

Maruping, L. M., & Magni, M. (2015). Motivating Employees to Explore Collaboration Technology in Team Contexts. *Management Information Systems Quarterly, 39*(1), 1–16. https://www.jstor.org/stable/26628338. DOI: 10.25300/MISQ/2015/39.1.01

Naik, G., Chitre, C., Bhalla, M., & Rajan, J. (2020). Impact of use of technology on student learning outcomes: Evidence from a large-scale experiment in India. *World Development, 127*, 104736. DOI: 10.1016/j.worlddev.2019.104736

Navarro-Martinez, O., & Peña-Acuña, B. (2022). Technology Usage and Academic Performance in the PISA 2018 Report. *Journal of New Approaches in Educational Research, 11*(1), 130–145. https://eric.ed.gov/?id=EJ1325570. DOI: 10.7821/naer.2022.1.735

Nayak, J. K. (2018). Relationship among smartphone usage, addiction, academic performance and the moderating role of gender: A study of higher education students in India. *Computers & Education, 123*, 164–173. DOI: 10.1016/j.compedu.2018.05.007

Olelewe, C. J., Agomuo, E. E., & Obichukwu, P. U. (2019). Effects of B-Learning and F2F on College Students' Engagement and Retention in QBASIC Programming. *Education and Information Technologies, 24*(5), 2701–2726. DOI: 10.1007/s10639-019-09882-7

Ouyang, F., Zheng, L., & Jiao, P. (2022). Artificial Intelligence in Online Higher education: A Systematic Review of Empirical Research from 2011 to 2020. *Education and Information Technologies, 27*(6), 7893–7925. DOI: 10.1007/s10639-022-10925-9

Pan, Z., Lu, Y., Wang, B., & Chau, P. Y. K. (2017). Who Do You Think You Are? Common and Differential Effects of Social Self-Identity on Social Media Usage. *Journal of Management Information Systems, 34*(1), 71–101. DOI: 10.1080/07421222.2017.1296747

Pardo-Cueva, M., Chamba-Rueda, L. M., Rios-Zaruma, J., & Gómez, A. H. (2019, June). Information and communication technologies and their relationship with academic performance in higher education. In *2019 14th Iberian Conference on Information Systems and Technologies (CISTI)* (pp. 1-6). IEEE. DOI: 10.23919/CISTI.2019.8760718

Ranjan, S., & Kumar, A. (2020). Artificial Intelligence in Education: A Review of the Current State and Future Directions. *International Journal of Educational Technology in Higher Education, 17*(1), 1–19.

Rashid, T., & Asghar, H. M. (2016). Technology use, self-directed learning, student engagement and academic performance: Examining the interrelations. *Computers in Human Behavior, 63*, 604–612. DOI: 10.1016/j.chb.2016.05.084

Robey, D., Ross, J. W., & Boudreau, M.-C. (2002). Learning to Implement Enterprise Systems: An Exploratory Study of the Dialectics of Change. *Journal of Management Information Systems, 19*(1), 17–46. https://www.jstor.org/stable/40398565. DOI: 10.1080/07421222.2002.11045713

Ryan, R. M., & Deci, E. L. (2017). *Self-Determination Theory: Basic Psychological Needs in Motivation, Development, and Wellness*. Guilford Press., DOI: 10.1521/978.14625/28806

Schwarz, A., & Chin, W. W. (2007). Looking forward: Toward an understanding of the nature and definition of IT acceptance. *Journal of the Association for Information Systems, 8*(6), 1–14. DOI: 10.17705/1jais.00123

Sergis, S., Sampson, D. G., & Pelliccione, L. (2018). Investigating the impact of Flipped Classroom on students' learning experiences: A Self-Determination Theory approach. *Computers in Human Behavior, 78*, 368–378. DOI: 10.1016/j.chb.2017.08.011

Shmueli, G., Sarstedt, M., Hair, J. F., Cheah, J. H., Ting, H., Vaithilingam, S., & Ringle, C. M. (2019). Predictive model assessment in PLS-SEM: Guidelines for using PLSpredict. *European Journal of Marketing, 53*(11), 2322–2347. DOI: 10.1108/EJM-02-2019-0189

Sun, H. (2012). Understanding User Revisions When Using Information System Features: Adaptive System Use and Triggers. *Management Information Systems Quarterly, 36*(2), 453–478. DOI: 10.2307/41703463

Sun, H., Wright, R. T., & Thatcher, J. B. (2019). Revisiting the Impact of System Use on Task Performance: *An Exploitative-Explorative System Use Framework. Journal of the Association for Information Systems, 20*(4), 398–433. Advance online publication. DOI: 10.17705/1jais.00539

Sundaram, S., Schwarz, A., Jones, E., & Chin, W. W. (2007). Technology use on the front line: How information technology enhances individual performance. *Journal of the Academy of Marketing Science, 35*(1), 101–112. DOI: 10.1007/s11747-006-0010-4

Tang, T. L.-P., & Austin, M. J. (2009). Students' perceptions of teaching technologies, application of technologies, and academic performance. *Computers & Education*, *53*(4), 1241–1255. DOI: 10.1016/j.compedu.2009.06.007

Wang, C., Wang, H., Li, Y., Dai, J., Gu, X., & Yu, T. (2024). Factors influencing university students' behavioral intention to use generative artificial intelligence: Integrating the theory of planned behavior and AI literacy. *International Journal of Human-Computer Interaction*, •••, 1–23.

Wang, F., Wang, Y., & Zhang, Y. (2020). Personalized Learning in the Era of Artificial Intelligence: A Review of the Literature. *Journal of Educational Technology Systems*, *48*(3), 309–331.

Wang, L., Qu, G., & Chen, J. (2022). Towards a meaningful innovation paradigm: Conceptual framework and practice of leading world-class enterprise. *Chinese Management Studies*, *16*(4), 942–964. DOI: 10.1108/CMS-12-2020-0536

Wang, W., & Hsieh, J. J. P.-A. (2006). Beyond Routine: Symbolic Adoption, Extended Use, and Emergent Use of Complex Information Systems in the Mandatory Organizational Context. *Computer Information Systems Faculty Publications*. https://scholarworks.gsu.edu/cis_facpub/8/

Wecks, J. O., Voshaar, J., Plate, B. J., & Zimmermann, J. (2024). Generative AI Usage and Academic Performance. *ArXiv*. https://doi.org//arXiv.2404.19699DOI: 10.48550

Wentworth, D. K., & Middleton, J. H. (2014). Technology use and academic performance. *Computers & Education*, *78*, 306–311. DOI: 10.1016/j.compedu.2014.06.012

Yeung, K. L., Carpenter, S. K., & Corral, D. (2021). A Comprehensive Review of Educational Technology on Objective Learning Outcomes in Academic Contexts. *Educational Psychology Review*, *33*(4), 1583–1630. DOI: 10.1007/s10648-020-09592-4

Youssef, A. B., Dahmani, M., & Ragni, L. (2022). ICT Use, Digital Skills and Students' Academic Performance: Exploring the Digital Divide. *Information (Basel)*, *13*(3), 129. DOI: 10.3390/info13030129

Zawacki-Richter, O., Marín, V. I., Bond, M., & Gouverneur, F. (2019). Systematic review of research on artificial intelligence applications in higher education – where are the educators? *International Journal of Educational Technology in Higher Education*, *16*(1), 39. Advance online publication. DOI: 10.1186/s41239-019-0171-0

Zhai, C., Wibowo, S., & Li, L. D. (2024). The effects of over-reliance on AI dialogue systems on students' cognitive abilities: A systematic review. *Smart Learning Environments*, *11*(1), 28. Advance online publication. DOI: 10.1186/s40561-024-00316-7

Zhao, Y., & Liu, G. (2019). How Do Teachers Face Educational Changes in Artificial Intelligence Era. *Proceedings of the 2018 International Workshop on Education Reform and Social Sciences (ERSS 2018)*. https://doi.org/DOI: 10.2991/erss-18.2019.9

## KEY TERMS AND DEFINITIONS

**Academic Achievement Criteria:** Standards or benchmarks used to evaluate the performance and success of students in educational settings.

**Academic Integrity:** Upholding ethical principles in academic work, including honesty and originality.

**Academic Performance:** The extent to which a student has achieved their educational goals, often measured through grades, test scores, and overall GPA.

**Adaptive Learning Platforms:** AI-driven systems that adjust content and assessments in real-time to suit learners' progress.

**Artificial Intelligence:** A branch of computer science focused on creating systems that can perform tasks typically requiring human intelligence, such as reasoning, learning, and problem-solving.

**Chat Generative Pre-training Transformer:** An advanced language model developed by OpenAI that utilizes deep learning techniques to generate human-like text based on input prompts.

**Digital Divide:** The gap between individuals with access to digital technologies and those without.

**Educational Equity:** Ensuring all students have access to quality education and resources, regardless of their background or circumstances.

**Efficient Use:** The use of resources, tools, or technologies in such a way that maximizes effectiveness while minimizing wasted effort or outcomes.

**Ethical AI:** The development and use of AI technologies in ways that align with ethical principles, such as fairness, transparency, and accountability.

**Extended Use:** A mode of utilization where technology or tools are employed for prolonged periods or in various contexts beyond their original intention.

**Generative AI:** A type of AI that creates content, such as text, images, or music, based on input data.

**Grade Point Average:** A numerical representation of a student's academic performance, calculated by assigning a value to their grades and averaging them over a specific period.

**Higher Education Institution:** Academic organizations, such as colleges and universities, that provide education and confer degrees at the post-secondary level.

**Information System:** A structured system designed to collect, manage, and disseminate information, often incorporating both technology and human resources.

**Information Technology:** The use of computers, software, and networks for processing, storing, and exchanging data and information.

**Innovative Use:** The application of new and creative approaches to utilizing technology or tools in educational settings to enhance learning outcomes.

**Natural Language Processing:** A field of AI that focuses on the interaction between computers and human language, enabling machines to understand, interpret, and respond to text or voice data.

**Personalized Learning:** Tailoring educational content and strategies to individual students based on their needs and preferences.

**PLS-SEM (Partial Least Squares Structural Equation Modelling):** A statistical technique used to analyze complex relationships among variables and assess structural models in research.

**Predictive Analytics:** The use of data, statistical algorithms, and AI to identify future outcomes based on historical data.

**Regular Use:** The consistent and frequent utilization of a technology or tool within its intended educational or practical context.

**Reinformed Use:** The mindful application of technology or tools in a way that is guided by enhanced understanding or improved strategies for achieving specific outcomes.

**Routine Use:** The habitual and systematic incorporation of technology or tools into daily practices or curricular activities in educational settings.

**Self-Determination Theory:** A psychological framework that emphasizes the role of intrinsic motivation and personal agency in driving human behavior, particularly in learning and development contexts.

# Chapter 3
# Blended and Hybrid Learning Approaches:
## Flexibility and Innovation in Business Colleges

**Mustafa Kayyali**
https://orcid.org/0000-0003-3300-262X
*Maaref University of Applied Sciences, Syria*

## ABSTRACT

*In the evolving landscape of business education, the line between physical and digital learning is no longer clear-cut. Blended and hybrid learning models have emerged not merely as logistical solutions, but as pedagogical innovations that prioritize adaptability, engagement, and learner autonomy. This chapter explores how these models are reshaping business colleges by bridging traditional classroom rigor with digital flexibility. Drawing on empirical observations, institutional practices, and theoretical insights, it highlights both the possibilities and the pitfalls of integrating online and face-to-face instruction. Rather than championing technology for its own sake, the discussion centers on intentional design—learning environments where method serves purpose. Ultimately, this chapter argues that the real promise of blended and hybrid learning lies not in convenience, but in cultivating more responsive, inclusive, and future-ready educational experiences.*

## INTRODUCTION

At no other time in recent memory has the traditional model of higher education faced such seismic disruption. While online learning platforms and educational technology had been steadily evolving for years, the global pandemic acted as a

DOI: 10.4018/979-8-3373-7523-6.ch003

catalytic force—compelling even the most conservative academic institutions to confront the limitations of lecture-driven, campus-bound education. Business colleges, often imagined as bastions of case studies, boardroom simulations, and group presentations, suddenly found themselves navigating an entirely new educational terrain (Jensen, 2024). Amid this disruption, two terms surged into the academic lexicon with renewed force: blended learning and hybrid learning. What began as emergency responses have since evolved into sustainable pedagogical models—ones that are not only functional but transformative in nature.

Yet, beneath the convenience of digital scheduling and modular course structures lies a more complex and pressing question: What kind of learning experience are we really trying to create? At their best, blended and hybrid learning approaches are not just about toggling between in-person and online modalities. They are about redefining engagement—about empowering learners to move between spaces, paces, and formats in a way that aligns with the realities of modern life and the demands of contemporary business practice. Flexibility, once viewed as a compromise, has become a catalyst for innovation.

The modern business school student is no longer a passive recipient of knowledge but a co-constructor of learning (Mnasri & Papakonstantinidis, 2023). With access to global information networks, digital collaboration tools, and asynchronous resources, students expect more than just lectures and exams—they seek relevance, immediacy, and the freedom to learn on their own terms. This generational shift challenges faculty to think beyond course content and reimagine their role as facilitators, mentors, and instructional designers.

Moreover, the business world itself has undergone radical transformation. The shift to remote work, the globalization of teams, and the rise of digital platforms demand graduates who are not only skilled in finance, marketing, or operations, but also digitally fluent, collaboratively agile, and comfortable with ambiguity. Traditional pedagogical models that privilege linear instruction and fixed classroom hours are increasingly mismatched with this reality (Strom & Martin, 2022). Blended and hybrid learning, when thoughtfully implemented, offer an opportunity to mirror the very environment that students will step into after graduation.

This chapter embarks on a reflective and evidence-informed exploration of how blended and hybrid learning approaches are transforming business education. It critically examines not only the technological frameworks and curricular adjustments that make these models feasible, but also the pedagogical philosophies and institutional strategies that determine their success. The discussion draws on case examples, faculty perspectives, and student experiences to illuminate both the promises and the paradoxes of this shift. What is at stake is more than just delivery mode. What we are witnessing is a reconfiguration of learning itself—a new architecture in which space, time, and interaction are no longer constrained by traditional academic calendars and physical classrooms. The task for business educators, then, is not simply to adopt new tools, but to craft learning experiences that are as dynamic, interconnected, and adaptive as the world they seek to prepare students for.

## RETHINKING PEDAGOGY IN BUSINESS EDUCATION: WHY FLEXIBILITY MATTERS

Something is shifting—quietly, sometimes messily, but undeniably—beneath the surface of business education. It isn't just about digital tools or redesigned syllabi or new learning management systems. It's something deeper, more philosophical: a slow but necessary unravelling of inherited pedagogical assumptions. For decades, business colleges have been built like banks of knowledge—structured, institutional, top-down (Lin, 2021). But today's learners don't want vaults. They want maps, windows, maybe even compasses. They want movement, agency, presence. And all of that, in one form or another, requires flexibility.

Now, let's pause for a moment and acknowledge how that word—*flexibility*—gets tossed around. It often sounds like a selling point on a brochure, or a convenience feature like curbside pickup. But in pedagogical terms, flexibility isn't about convenience. It's about power. The power to choose. To adapt. To move through content—and space and time—in ways that make learning more human, more livable, and paradoxically, more rigorous.

Think of it this way: The classroom, as we've known it, has been an unspoken contract. Students arrive on time, sit in a fixed space, absorb a curated lecture, respond to set questions, and leave (Hultquist, 2024). Professors, meanwhile, deliver content, moderate discussions, and assign grades. It's a model that worked, for a time—especially when knowledge was scarce, slow-moving, and geographically bound. But we're no longer there. We're in a world of information overload, microlearning, global teams, remote work, and shifting expectations of what it means to be educated. The old contract? It's expiring.

In this space of rupture, flexibility is not a luxury—it's a necessity. A reimagined pedagogical foundation that allows learners to navigate complexity without being crushed by rigidity. It doesn't mean chaos, or lack of structure. In fact, good flexibility is *designed*, not improvised. But it means loosening the grip on control. It means asking a different set of questions: *What if learning didn't have to happen in a fixed place? What if deadlines could stretch without compromising outcomes? What if students could show mastery through a portfolio instead of a multiple-choice test?*

This shift, of course, is easier said than done. Business schools, by their nature, often carry the burden of tradition. Many are still designed to simulate the formalities of the corporate world—suits, time slots, punctuality, hierarchies. There's an understandable desire to prepare students for that environment. But here's the paradox: the business world itself is changing faster than the schools that claim to prepare people for it. Companies are moving toward asynchronous collaboration, project-based work, self-directed learning, and dynamic leadership models. Shouldn't our classrooms reflect that same rhythm? Let's take a closer look at why flexibility matters so much—and why it's not just a trendy buzzword in pedagogy.

## 1. Cognitive Realism: Meeting Minds Where They Are

Learning is not a tidy, linear process. It's messy, uneven, recursive. Some students need time to reflect, while others thrive in fast-paced debate (Alarifi, 2023). Some digest information visually; others need to speak it out loud to understand it. When we insist that all learners move through content in the same way, at the same pace, in the same space, we don't create equity—we create friction. Flexibility, in this context, becomes a form of cognitive compassion. It allows students to revisit recorded lectures when their focus slipped. It lets them pause a simulation and rewatch a process without embarrassment. It gives the working parent time to study after the kids go to bed, instead of missing class altogether. In business education—where students often juggle internships, jobs, side projects, or entrepreneurial ventures—this kind of grace is not just appreciated. It's vital.

## 2. Cultural and Contextual Diversity: One Size No Longer Fits All

It's no secret that business education is increasingly international. Walk into any MBA or undergraduate business course today, and you'll likely find a mosaic of cultural backgrounds, learning traditions, and academic expectations. The standardized lecture model—anchored in Western, often Eurocentric traditions—doesn't always translate. What feels like active participation in one culture may feel like disrespect in another. What reads as silence to a professor might actually be a culturally conditioned form of deference. Flexible pedagogy allows space for this complexity (Du Plessis et al, 2024). It permits multiple forms of participation: written forums, video reflections, voice notes, peer teaching. It also respects that students may be navigating vastly different time zones, emotional realities, or access to resources. Pedagogical flexibility, then, becomes a kind of cultural fluency—a recognition that learning is never just about content, but about context.

## 3. Embracing the Organic Nature of Curiosity

There is something beautifully unruly about genuine curiosity. It doesn't obey schedules. It doesn't wait until week seven of the syllabus. It arises suddenly—often in the middle of a story, a case, a question. And the tragedy of rigid pedagogy is that it often shuts that curiosity down. *Stay on task. Stick to the objective. We'll cover that next semester.* But flexibility allows a different kind of pedagogical presence. One where the instructor can say, *That's an interesting tangent—let's explore it for five minutes.* Or where a student can propose an alternative case study because it mirrors a situation from their part-time job. Or where the learning outcomes emerge not just from the top down, but from the lived realities of the classroom community. This does not mean abandoning structure. It means creating structure with enough elasticity to bend toward curiosity rather than away from it.

## 4. Technology as a Portal, Not a Crutch

One of the most enduring misconceptions about flexible learning is that it's all about tech (Hermita et al, 2024). Just plug in a learning management system, record a few videos, throw in some discussion boards, and voilà—you have flexibility. But real flexibility is not about the platform. It's about the intent behind the design. Technology is only as liberating as the pedagogy that wields it. A poorly designed asynchronous course can feel more stifling than a bad in-person lecture. On the other hand, a thoughtfully curated hybrid experience—one that interweaves digital collaboration with live interaction, that gives students meaningful choices without overwhelming them—can be transformational. So, the question is not, *What tools are we using?* The real question is, *What experience are we trying to build?* And are we willing to revise, rebuild, or even dismantle that experience if it no longer serves our students?

## 5. Faculty as Learners: Redefining the Role of the Educator

To embrace flexibility is to relinquish the illusion of total control. That can be uncomfortable, especially for educators who were trained—and rewarded—for mastery, certainty, and authority. But in a flexible model, the instructor is less of a broadcaster and more of a facilitator, designer, co-learner. That shift is not about reducing the teacher's role, but elevating its complexity. This doesn't mean throwing out standards or academic rigor. Quite the opposite. Flexibility actually requires more intentionality, more responsiveness, more critical reflection from faculty (Barua & Lockee, 2024). You can't phone in a flexible course. It takes planning, experimentation, and a willingness to listen—to students, to peers, to your own discomfort. And sometimes it means failure. A new module flops. A discussion board stays empty. A student gets lost in the asynchronous maze. But that, too, is part of the pedagogy. Failure is feedback, and flexibility creates the space for that feedback to shape future iterations.

### 6. Business Education as a Mirror for the Future

Let's come full circle. Why should business schools care so deeply about pedagogical flexibility? Because business itself is now flexible—fluid, fast, global, ambiguous. Projects span time zones. Teams meet across Slack and Zoom. Decisions are made in real time, with partial data, under volatile conditions. The idea that students could be prepared for this kind of environment through fixed schedules, static lectures, and uniform assessments is not only naïve—it's negligent (Wormeli, 2023). Flexible pedagogy doesn't just accommodate new learners. It models the very mindsets and skills they will need to succeed: adaptability, self-regulation, digital fluency, critical thinking, and the ability to synthesize information from multiple sources across multiple modes. In other words, the way we teach may be the most powerful signal we send about what we value—and what we're preparing students for.

Flexibility, then, is not the easy road. It's not the lazy alternative to rigor. It's the harder path of pedagogical integrity—one that takes seriously the lived realities of learners, the demands of the global business landscape, and the shifting nature of knowledge itself. To rethink pedagogy is to admit that the old ways are no longer enough—and that something braver, messier, and more human is both possible and necessary. So, when we say flexibility matters, we are not advocating for the collapse of standards. We are calling for a deeper standard—one that prizes relevance over ritual, presence over posture, and transformation over tradition. And that is the beginning—not the end—of what business education can become.

## BLENDED AND HYBRID LEARNING: CONCEPTS, OVERLAPS, AND DISTINCTIONS

Walk into any faculty meeting these days and throw the terms *blended* or *hybrid* learning on the table. You'll get nods, raised eyebrows, a few affirming murmurs, and—if you're lucky—a debate. Everyone seems to be using the words, yet not everyone means the same thing (Kayyali, 2024). Sometimes, they're spoken interchangeably, tossed into institutional policy documents with the casual certainty of someone who's skimmed a pedagogical blog. Other times, they're guarded terms, laden with implications about workload, screen time, and how much "face-to-face" really matters anymore. The confusion isn't accidental. It's the result of fast-moving innovation colliding with slow-moving terminology. We're in a space where language is racing to catch up with practice—and where practice itself is constantly morphing. In this swirl, clarity becomes not just helpful, but necessary. Not to gatekeep, but to ground. To build a shared vocabulary for what's happening in our classrooms—and what might still be possible. So, what *do* we mean when we say "blended" or "hybrid"? What's the difference? Does it even matter? It does. Not just for semantics, but for intention, design, and expectation. Let's unpack this slowly, honestly, with all the nuance the subject deserves.

*Figure 1. Modality Mix In A Prototype Hybrid Course (Illustrative)*

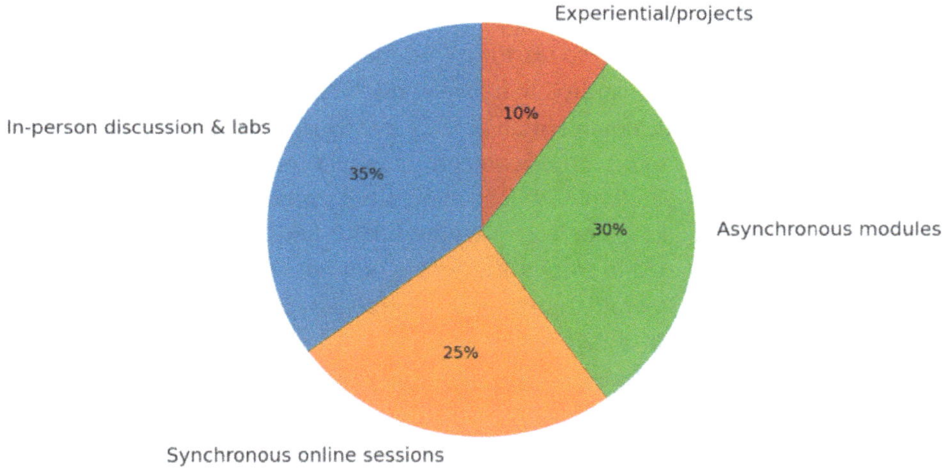


## Blended Learning: A Deliberate Weaving

Blended learning, in its truest sense, is not a haphazard mix of online materials and classroom time. It's a pedagogical approach that deliberately integrates digital and in-person learning in a way that leverages the strengths of both. It's not just a mix—it's a choreography. The face-to-face component might be used for discussion, collaboration, presentations—anything where human presence adds cognitive or emotional weight (Glazer, 2023). The online element, by contrast, might deliver readings, interactive quizzes, recorded lectures, or multimedia content that allows learners to pace themselves and revisit complex material. Done well, the two parts speak to each other. They echo. They reinforce. They are purposefully sequenced, not simply coexisting. What makes blended learning potent is this: it's not about splitting time—it's about integrating purpose. A lecture that's simply uploaded online is not blended learning (Kayyali, 2026). Nor is a face-to-face session that regurgitates what students already read in the LMS. The goal is not duplication but complementarity. If a concept can be better understood through discussion, it belongs in the room. If it can be mastered through self-paced practice, it thrives online. And there's another layer. Blended learning invites us to reconsider the very boundaries of learning time and space. It acknowledges that students may process information better in solitude, or at 11 p.m., or while commuting. It doesn't romanticize the classroom as the only site of learning. Instead, it treats it as one node in a broader ecosystem.

## Hybrid Learning: A Structural Innovation

Now, let's shift the lens. Hybrid learning is similar to blended learning, but it adds another layer—presence variability. In hybrid models, some students attend class in person while others join remotely, often at the same time. It's synchronous, and it's mixed—a dual-modality experience happening in real time. This structure became widespread during the pandemic, when universities scrambled to accommodate students in different locations or with varying health needs. Some sat masked in classrooms. Others Zoomed in from dorm rooms or across the globe. Suddenly, we had a model where physical and digital presence existed side by side—not alternated, but cohabiting. At its best, hybrid learning can be a marvel of inclusive design. It opens the classroom to students who otherwise couldn't attend—due to illness, disability, travel, or other commitments (Mastrogiacomi, 2021). It blurs geographic lines, enabling guest speakers from New York to join a lecture in Nairobi. It enables real-time collaboration across continents. But it also introduces real complications. Teaching to a hybrid class is twice the work, at least at first. You're managing in-room energy and digital engagement simultaneously. You're answering raised hands and chat box messages. You're keeping eye contact with students in front of you while glancing at the screen to see who's just unmuted themselves. The cognitive load on faculty is intense—and often underestimated by administrators who confuse tech access with pedagogical fluency. Students on either side of the screen can feel alienated. Those online may feel like observers rather than participants. Those in the room may sense a divided focus. Making hybrid learning work requires intentional design, not just a webcam and Wi-Fi. It calls for clear facilitation, tech-supported interactivity, and a deep understanding of how presence—digital or physical—affects perception, participation, and learning outcomes.

## Where the Lines Blur: Overlaps and Intersections

Here's where things get messier—and more interesting. The line between blended and hybrid learning is not always sharp. In fact, many educational experiences occupy a space somewhere between the two. A course might have a rotating hybrid model, where students alternate between in-person and remote attendance. Or it might include both asynchronous modules (a hallmark of blended learning) and synchronous remote sessions (common in hybrid). This is where design intention becomes more important than terminology. Instead of obsessing over labels, educators should be asking: *What are my goals for student learning? What is the best modality for each part of that process? How can I ensure that all students, regardless of format, feel equally seen, heard, and challenged?* That said, clarity matters—especially at the institutional level. Students need to know what they're signing up for. Is a course blended, with certain days online and others in person? Or is it hybrid, with an option to attend remotely at any time? These are not small distinctions. They affect planning, participation, and even equity. A student with unstable internet needs different accommodations than one who simply prefers asynchronous learning. Ambiguity around modality can breed frustration and disengagement. It also matters for assessment design. A hybrid classroom may require real-time discussion rubrics that account for both physical and virtual presence. A blended course might use portfolios that weave together outputs from both digital and in-person activities. The choice of modality has ripple effects across every aspect of course planning—from readings to grading to office hours.

## Beyond the Buzzwords: Pedagogical Responsibility

What gets lost in the flurry of buzzwords is the pedagogical core. Both blended and hybrid learning ask educators to step out of autopilot (Fisher et al, 2021). To interrogate the sacred cows of classroom culture. To ask, *Why am I doing it this way? Is this method serving my students—or just my habits?* This reflection is especially urgent in business education, where the content often mirrors real-world ambiguity. In a global marketing course, for example, students might analyze data asynchronously, then convene synchronously to craft strategy in real time. A hybrid structure allows a guest CMO to join from Tokyo. A blended structure lets students record their pitches and receive peer feedback before presenting live. The pedagogical decisions here aren't just logistical—they're philosophical. They speak to what we believe learning should look and feel like. Educators, then, become not just content experts, but learning architects. They build experiences, not just syllabi. They consider how time flows through a course. How energy shifts across formats. How students connect—or fail to—with each other and the material. This is not light work. It demands design thinking, empathy, agility, and self-awareness. And it often goes unrecognized in workload models that still measure teaching in credit hours, not complexity.

### The Learner's Perspective: Autonomy, Anxiety, and Everything In Between

For students, these models can feel liberating, confusing, or both. The ability to choose when and how to engage can foster a powerful sense of ownership. But it can also breed decision fatigue, especially for those unaccustomed to managing their own learning rhythms. Some students flourish in asynchronous settings, finding their voice in forum threads rather than in crowded classrooms. Others feel untethered without a strict routine. In hybrid settings, those online may struggle to feel seen, while those in the room may resent the divided attention. No format is neutral—each comes with benefits and blind spots. Educators need to make these trade-offs visible. To talk openly with students about format. To invite feedback early, not just at the end. To model flexibility—not just in schedule, but in mindset.

At the end of the day, blended and hybrid learning are not endpoints. They're waypoints in a larger pedagogical journey—toward more inclusive, responsive, and intentional education (Catthoor, 2023). They reflect a shift in how we understand presence, engagement, and what it means to "show up" in a classroom. They are not silver bullets. They will not solve all of education's equity gaps or engagement crises. But they are tools. And like all tools, their impact depends on how they're used. It's not about whether a course is called hybrid or blended. It's about whether that course feels alive, coherent, challenging, and human. Whether it allows students to bring their full selves. Whether it meets them where they are—and then invites them to go further. So yes, the terms matter. But only as long as they serve the learning. The moment they become boxes instead of bridges, they lose their value.

## FROM LECTURE HALLS TO LEARNING ECOSYSTEMS: INNOVATIONS IN PRACTICE

There was a time—not long ago—when the business school classroom looked almost identical around the world. Rows of seats. A podium. PowerPoint slides projected like gospel. The professor stood at the center, commanding attention with a voice honed by repetition. Students listened, scribbled, sometimes nodded, and when the bell rang, they scattered like petals in the wind. This model—the lecture hall as shrine to expertise—wasn't just dominant. It was sacred. Predictable. Orderly. But sacred things, when no longer questioned, become stale. Something began to fray around the edges. Slowly, quietly. Maybe it was the widening gap between what students experienced in class and what awaited them in the workplace. Maybe it was the fatigue of one-size-fits-all learning. Maybe it was the creeping suspicion—shared by students and educators alike—that education had become more about endurance than engagement. Then came the shockwave: a global disruption that emptied lecture halls overnight. For many, it felt like loss. But for others—for the curious, the restless, the pedagogically awake—it felt like an opening. A doorway. A prompt to reimagine not just where learning happened, but how it *lived*.

## Deconstructing the Lecture: Not Abandonment, But Reinvention

Let's be clear—this isn't an elegy for the lecture. At its best, a well-delivered lecture can still be electric: a compelling, high-wire act of storytelling, synthesis, and provocation. But the traditional lecture, in its static, one-directional form, has become insufficient for the learning demands of today's business world. In an economy powered by complexity, ambiguity, and collaboration, students need more than note-taking muscles. They need mental elasticity. They need to wrestle with ideas, not just receive them. And so, the lecture—if it remains—must evolve. It becomes part of a broader learning ecosystem. A piece, not the whole.

## What Is a Learning Ecosystem, Really?

The phrase may sound like another academic buzzword, but behind it is a genuine shift in how we conceive of education. A learning ecosystem isn't a classroom. It's a constellation. A dynamic web of tools, spaces, interactions, feedback loops, and experiences that work together to support learning (Kayyali, 2025). It's a course that includes video walkthroughs, real-world simulations, peer critiques, industry panels, Slack threads, virtual office hours, reflective journaling, and in-person labs. It's an environment where learning spills beyond the boundaries of time and space—sometimes asynchronously, sometimes live, sometimes in solitude, sometimes collaboratively. And here's the key: the learner is no longer a consumer but a participant, a node, a contributor. In a learning ecosystem, students don't just receive information—they help build it. Shape it. Sometimes even challenge it.

*Figure 2. Engagement Trend After Flexible Redesign (Illustrative)*

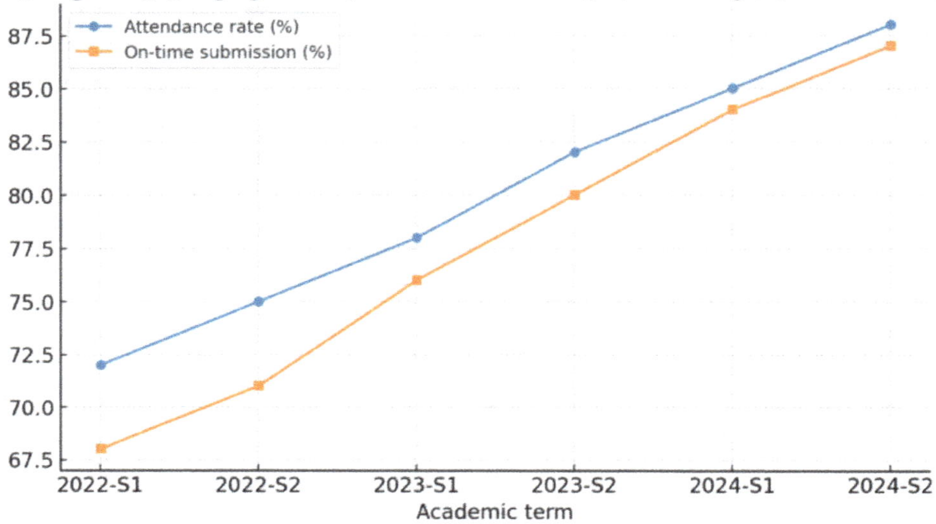


## Case Snapshot: The Negotiation Lab

At a mid-sized European business school, the traditional negotiation course was restructured into a hybrid, ecosystem-based format. Instead of just attending lectures on theory and tactics, students were immersed in a multi-modal experience:

- Pre-Class Microlearning: Short, scenario-based videos delivered key principles asynchronously. Students could pause, replay, or skip ahead—adapting to their own pace and prior knowledge.
- Live Role-Plays: In-person and virtual simulations where students negotiated with peers, role-playing as buyers, sellers, regulators, or stakeholders.
- Real-Time Feedback: A peer evaluation tool allowed immediate, structured feedback after each role-play, with prompts on communication style, emotional intelligence, and deal quality.
- Reflective Journaling: Students submitted short voice memos after each session, reflecting on strategy, bias, and lessons learned.
- Industry Immersion: A live session with a corporate negotiator from a global consulting firm offered applied insights and field stories, tying classroom theory to boardroom reality.

The result? Students reported greater confidence, deeper understanding, and improved adaptability. But more than that—they felt *seen*, *engaged*, and *responsible* for their learning arc. The course had shifted from content delivery to experience orchestration.

## The Rise of Modular, Self-Directed Pathways

One of the most significant innovations in learning ecosystems is modularity. In traditional lecture halls, time is fixed and content flows in one direction. Everyone moves at the same pace, regardless of interest or prior knowledge. Ecosystem models, by contrast, often use modular design: bite-sized learning blocks that can be assembled, sequenced, or revisited based on individual needs. In business education, this allows for personalization without sacrificing structure. A student who struggles with financial modeling can revisit foundational content before engaging in simulations. Another who already has Excel proficiency can skip ahead to strategic forecasting. This non-linear approach mirrors real-world learning, where people seek out knowledge as needed—Googling a formula, consulting a colleague, watching a tutorial—rather than waiting for it to arrive on a syllabus. Self-direction becomes not just a feature but a skill. And here, too, faculty roles shift. The professor becomes less of a gatekeeper and more of a curator, coach, and question-asker.

## Beyond the LMS: The Power of Informal Spaces

Traditional learning management systems (LMS) were designed to store content and manage grades (Bradley, 2021). But real learning ecosystems thrive in places less scripted—places that mimic how humans actually learn: informally, socially, sometimes accidentally. Innovative instructors are now integrating tools like Slack, Miro, Padlet, Discord, or even WhatsApp into their teaching—not as gimmicks, but as extensions of learning. A Slack channel becomes a hub for article sharing and spontaneous discussion. A Miro board evolves into a visual thinking map that charts the semester's conceptual journey. These aren't distractions; they're *learning habitats*—digital spaces where curiosity lingers, connections form, and learning breathes. Yes, these tools require boundaries. Not everything belongs in the social stream. But ignoring these spaces means ignoring a major dimension of student life. Meeting learners where they are doesn't mean pandering. It means designing with empathy.

## Emotional Architecture: Designing for Belonging and Vulnerability

Let's shift focus for a moment. Innovations in practice aren't just technological. Some of the most radical shifts are emotional. Learning ecosystems invite us to ask: *How does this environment make a student feel?* Do they feel safe to ask a "stupid" question? Do they feel challenged, but not overwhelmed? Do they feel like they matter? Some business schools are experimenting with intentional emotional design. Simple check-in rituals. Anonymous reflection tools. Collaborative grading contracts. Storytelling circles. Peer mentoring systems. These aren't soft extras—they're hardwired into the learning culture. One professor, noticing a lack of participation from international students in a strategy course, integrated "voice journals"—weekly, one-minute recordings where students could articulate what they were grappling with. Some were in English. Others, in their native language, accompanied by subtitles. The effect? Richer classroom dialogue, stronger peer empathy, and an embodied sense of being heard. Emotional innovation is subtle, but seismic. It's not about coddling. It's about creating the psychological infrastructure for deep learning.

*Table 1. Blended/Hybrid Course Design Matrix (12 weeks)*

| Week | Learning objectives | Modality | Learning activities | Assessment/Artifact | Tools |
|---|---|---|---|---|---|
| 1 | Diagnostic & foundations of the course | Async + F2F | Welcome video, LMS orientation; in room expectations workshop | Readiness quiz; learning contract | LMS, Quiz tool |
| 2 | Team formation & collaboration norms | Sync online + F2F | Live online icebreaker; in room team charter drafting | Team charter (pass/ fail) | Zoom/Teams, Docs |
| 3 | Case analysis methods | Async + F2F | Micro lectures; in room case discussion | Case memo #1 | Video, LMS |
| 4 | Data literacy for managers | Async + Sync online | Tutorial videos; live lab | Dashboard mini task | LMS, Analytics tool |
| 5 | Negotiation basics | F2F + Async | In room role play; reflection journal | Reflection (graded) | Classroom, LMS |
| 6 | Project scoping with industry mentor | Hybrid (F2F/ Remote) | Mentor briefing; Q&A | Project proposal | Video conf. |
| 7 | Design thinking sprint | F2F | Studio work; peer critique | Prototype v1 | Miro/ Whiteboard |
| 8 | Ethics & inclusivity in decision making | Async + Sync | Readings; live debate | Position paper | LMS, Video conf. |
| 9 | Analytics in action | Hybrid | Lab (room/remote); office hours | Prototype v2 | LMS, Analytics tool |
| 10 | Go to market strategies | Async + F2F | Flipped mini lectures; workshop | Pitch draft | Video, Classroom |

| Week | Learning objectives | Modality | Learning activities | Assessment/Artifact | Tools |
|---|---|---|---|---|---|
| 11 | Capstone rehearsals | Hybrid | Rehearsals with feedback panels | Pitch v2 + peer review | Video conf., Rubric tool |
| 12 | Capstone showcase & reflection | Hybrid | Public showcase; closing reflection | Final report & e portfolio | Showcase, LMS |

## Assessment as Feedback, Not Just Judgment

Old-school assessments were endpoints. You learned, you got tested, you moved on. But in a learning ecosystem, assessment becomes part of the learning process itself. It's iterative. It's formative. It *talks back*. Some educators are flipping the model entirely—inviting students to co-design rubrics, engage in self-assessment, or submit portfolios instead of exams. One business analytics course replaced its final test with a "Data Storytelling Festival," where students presented real-world case studies using Tableau dashboards and narrative arcs (Ryan, 2023). The assessment was public, performative, and reflective. It felt less like a judgment and more like a rite of passage. What's gained? Engagement. Creativity. Authenticity. What's lost? Memorization. Passive learning. Grade obsession. And yes, it's messier. But it's also more real. And isn't that the point?

## Barriers to Implementation: The Work Beneath the Work

We should be honest. These innovations sound exciting on paper. But they demand labor, time, trust, and institutional courage. Faculty need support—not just tech training, but philosophical space to rethink their role. Students need orientation—guidance on how to navigate freedom without floundering. Administrators need to rethink scheduling, credit systems, and evaluation models. This isn't a plug-and-play transformation. It's a cultural shift, and culture doesn't change through memos. It changes through lived experience, modeled behavior, and institutional storytelling.

## Learning Ecosystems as Mirrors of Complexity

Here's what it comes down to. The world we're preparing students for is not a lecture hall. It's a web of teams, tools, disruptions, deadlines, dilemmas. It's fast and slow, clear and ambiguous, stable and volatile. If our classrooms don't reflect that complexity, they risk becoming nostalgic theaters—beautiful, but irrelevant. Learning ecosystems—when done well—are messy. Sometimes frustrating. Always evolving. But they are alive. And that aliveness is what students remember.

Not just the content, but the *feeling* of learning: being stretched, seen, challenged, transformed. And that is something no PowerPoint can ever deliver.

## STUDENT EXPERIENCE AND FACULTY ADAPTATION: CHALLENGES AND OPPORTUNITIES

It begins quietly. A flicker in the eyes of a student who's drifted off-screen. The awkward pause in a breakout room no one wanted to enter. A professor staring into the lens, wondering if anyone is truly listening—or just logged in. Somewhere between innovation and intention, between best-laid plans and digital realities, there's an awkward middle space where learning either flourishes or fades. That space is the lived experience of blended and hybrid education—and it's where most of the story unfolds. We talk about pedagogical frameworks, platform integrations, curriculum redesigns. But strip it down, and what matters most are the people: students, trying to make sense of their role in a shifting world of learning, and faculty, adapting—sometimes clumsily, sometimes brilliantly—to a model no one fully trained them for. This chapter doesn't aim to idealize the process. It aims to explore it—with all the friction, fluidity, and forward motion that make blended and hybrid education as human as it is high-tech.

### The Student Side: Autonomy Meets Anxiety

Let's start with the learners. Blended and hybrid models are often praised for empowering students—giving them flexibility, agency, and access. And that's true, to an extent. But here's the nuance: freedom isn't always liberating. For some, it's disorienting. Like being handed the keys to a car before learning to drive. When students step into a blended environment, what they often encounter isn't just new tools—it's a new relationship with time, space, and responsibility. No longer bound by classroom schedules, they have to self-manage: when to watch the lecture, when to do the reading, how to reach out for help. Some thrive. Others spiral. One student I spoke to put it bluntly:

"It's like I'm in charge of building the bridge as I'm crossing it. There's no rhythm anymore."

That comment hit home. Because rhythm matters. In traditional classrooms, learning has a beat: Mondays at 10, quiz on Thursday, office hours on Friday. Remove that structure without replacing it with something intentional, and students drift. Not out of laziness, but out of uncertainty. Blended learning requires a new kind of academic rhythm—one that students often have to invent. And invention, while empowering, is also exhausting.

## Disconnection in a Connected World

The irony is thick. We've never had more tools to connect—Zoom, Teams, Slack, Padlet, Discord, you name it—and yet, many students describe feeling more isolated than ever. It's the paradox of presence: being logged in but not really *there*. Students in hybrid classrooms often describe a sense of "invisibility" when joining remotely (Hochuli & Jud, 2024). Their questions go unheard, their reactions unseen. When a professor turns toward the physical room, the screen-bound students become shadows. Even in blended models, where all students cycle between digital and physical formats, there's a challenge: continuity. The in-person discussion was electric. The online module? Disjointed. The conversation doesn't carry across formats. It's like living in two houses without a road between them. When educators fail to weave these formats together—not just administratively, but emotionally—students sense the fragmentation. They stop investing. They do what's required, nothing more. Engagement, once sparked by shared space and energy, flickers. And then there's the loneliness. Academic loneliness isn't just about being alone. It's about feeling unseen in the process of becoming. When students don't feel part of a learning community—when their insights aren't acknowledged, their questions hang in air—they don't just disengage. They shrink.

## But—When It Works, It Transforms

Let's not paint a bleak picture. When designed well, blended and hybrid experiences can be profound. Students have shared how asynchronous materials gave them the space to slow down, revisit, reflect—to learn without shame or speed. They've talked about the joy of learning across continents, collaborating with peers they never would've met in a traditional classroom. Some describe hybrid formats as a "lifeline," allowing them to continue learning despite illness, parenting responsibilities, or geopolitical constraints. The magic, though, isn't in the format. It's in the design, the intention behind the model. One student reflected: *"The course felt like a conversation, not a delivery. Like the professor was designing with me in mind, not just talking at a crowd."*

That's the heart of it. When students feel the structure was made for them—not just imposed on them—they rise to meet it.

*Figure 3. Student Satisfaction by Modality (Illustrative)*

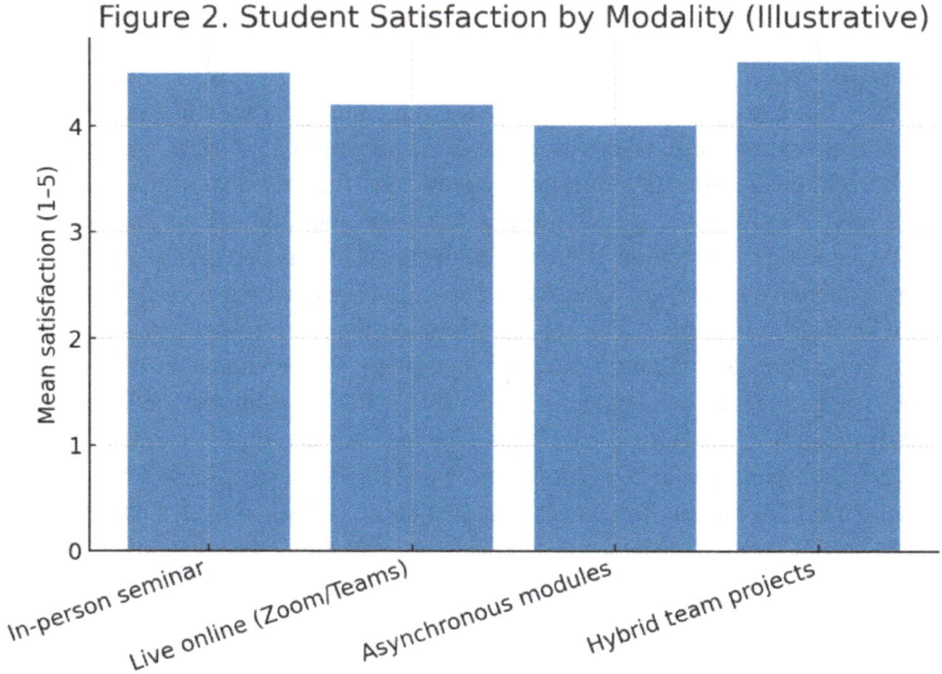


## The Faculty Side: Between Burnout and Breakthrough

Now let's switch sides. Because while student experience shapes the front-end of learning, faculty experience builds the back-end. And let's be honest: the shift to blended and hybrid learning has left many educators reeling (Kayyali, 2022). Some embraced the shift with excitement—finally, a chance to break free from the tyranny of the lecture slide. Others entered reluctantly, dragged into tech workshops and Zoom tutorials. A few resisted outright, seeing the entire movement as a threat to academic integrity or a corporate ploy. But whether willing or wary, one thing became clear: faculty are the nervous system of the learning ecosystem. If they aren't supported, energized, and listened to, no platform or pedagogy can succeed.

## The Emotional Labor of Adaptation

Faculty adaptation is more than mastering a new tool or uploading a syllabus (Swerzenski, 2021). It's emotional labor. It's rewriting how you think about presence, control, assessment, even expertise. Professors who once thrived on the energy of a live classroom now face silent black boxes on Zoom. Teachers who once prided themselves on Socratic discussion now juggle chat boxes, screen shares, and breakout rooms that feel more like limbo than dialogue. Many speak of performance fatigue—trying to animate a room while monitoring tech, timing, and engagement simultaneously. Others mention cognitive overload, managing two groups (online and in-person) with different needs in the same class session. Add to that the quiet grief of losing the rituals that once defined teaching: the pre-class banter, the spontaneous tangent, the unspoken rhythm of human bodies thinking together. This loss isn't trivial. It's a pedagogical identity crisis. And it deserves acknowledgment.

## But—There's Growth, Too

Amidst the fatigue, something else is happening. Faculty are reinventing themselves. Not out of trend-chasing, but out of necessity and care. Instructors are learning to be facilitators, not just deliverers. They're experimenting—often clumsily, but courageously—with flipped classrooms, asynchronous debates, student-generated content, collaborative grading. Some are even learning to say, *I don't know—let's find out together.* There's a humility in that. And a power. One professor shared how moving to a hybrid model forced her to rethink her entire course. *"I had to ask: what actually matters? What do I want students to feel when the course ends? What habits of mind am I cultivating?"* The result wasn't just a better course. It was a renewed sense of purpose. Faculty who embrace the messiness—who see adaptation not as a threat but as a craft—often emerge more connected, not less. Not just to students, but to their own values.

## The Equity Challenge

We must talk about equity. Blended and hybrid models often assume access: to devices, bandwidth, quiet spaces, digital literacy (Mulenga & Shilongo, 2025). But not all students—or faculty—begin on equal footing. Some students attend class from smartphones in crowded apartments. Some professors lack stable internet. Others juggle caregiving with course prep. One-size-fits-all digital learning exacerbates existing inequalities—unless deliberately countered. That means designing with inclusion in mind from the start, not as an afterthought. Offering multiple modes of participation. Being flexible with deadlines. Creating low-bandwidth alternatives. Checking in on emotional well-being. It also means retraining faculty not just on tools, but on trauma-informed pedagogy, universal design, and inclusive communication. Without equity, innovation becomes elitism. The learning gap widens. And the very models meant to empower become tools of exclusion.

## Opportunities: The Pedagogical Frontier

For all the tension and turbulence, this moment is ripe with possibility. Imagine business courses that mirror startup ecosystems—where students co-design the curriculum, respond to live market challenges, and receive feedback from real investors. Imagine hybrid classrooms that rotate roles: facilitator, note-taker, devil's advocate—so everyone engages from a different perspective. Imagine assessment as a conversation, not a score. Learning as relationship, not transaction. These aren't pipe dreams. They're already happening—in fragments, in pockets, in the margins of institutional inertia. The opportunity isn't just to use technology. It's to transform how we define teaching, learning, and the very shape of higher education.

At the end of the day, both students and faculty are navigating the same storm—albeit in different vessels. The success of blended and hybrid models won't depend solely on platforms or policies. It will depend on mutual empathy, shared reflection, and the courage to admit: *We're all still figuring this out.* Learning is not just about outcomes. It's about becoming. About finding voice in the chaos. About crafting meaning from fragments. In that sense, the real innovation isn't in technology—it's in the restoration of relationship as the foundation of education. And that—quiet, messy, luminous—is what makes this journey worthwhile.

# THE FUTURE OF BUSINESS LEARNING: TOWARD PURPOSEFUL INTEGRATION

If you asked me to sketch the future of business education, I wouldn't reach for a crystal ball. Instead, I'd listen to the whispers in the wind—the subtle shifts in how we gather, talk, argue, connect, and create knowledge. I'd watch how students rearrange their lives around fragmented attention spans, global crises, and digital noise. I'd watch how faculty wrestle with the impossible task of teaching ever-changing content in classrooms that can be anywhere and nowhere all at once. The future is not some tidy horizon. It's a swirling, unsettled space—a place of tension and promise, challenge and opportunity. It's a future where business learning refuses to be siloed, segmented, or static. Instead, it demands purposeful integration: of technology and humanity, theory and practice, presence and autonomy, tradition and transformation. Let me try to unpack what that means, as candidly and as fully as I can.

## Integration as an Act of Intent

The word "integration" often conjures images of smoothness—seamless platforms, polished workflows, and frictionless user experiences. But the integration

I'm talking about is messier. It's intentional, sometimes awkward, frequently iterative. It's a deliberate weaving of multiple strands that might otherwise pull apart. Purposeful integration isn't about shoehorning technology into existing pedagogies or layering on a virtual component for marketing purposes (Polymeropoulou et al, 2024). It's about rethinking from the ground up: what do we value in business learning? What are the core experiences and skills we want to cultivate? How can digital tools amplify—not replace—the human elements that matter most? Imagine a business school curriculum that is neither "face-to-face plus tech" nor "online plus content," but an ecosystem where the boundaries blur and bend: where asynchronous forums spark live debates; where data analytics projects feed real-time market simulations; where global cohorts collaborate on entrepreneurial ventures through virtual incubators; where AI tools scaffold creativity, not stifle it. This is integration that doesn't settle for coexistence. It demands synergy—a blending of modalities that creates something more than the sum of its parts.

*Table 2. KPI Dashboard for Blended/Hybrid Implementation*

| KPI | Definition | Baseline (2024) | Target (2026) | Data owner |
|---|---|---|---|---|
| Course completion rate (%) | Share of enrolled students who finish the course | 86 | 92 | Program QA Office |
| Mean student satisfaction (1 - 5) | End of course survey average across items | 4.1 | 4.5 | Institutional Research |
| LMS weekly engagement (min/student) | Median minutes spent in LMS content per week | 95 | 130 | LMS Analytics |
| Hybrid attendance coverage (%) | Percent of sessions with dual mode (room+remote) support | 62 | 95 | Scheduling/IT |
| Assessment turnaround (days) | Median days to return graded feedback | 10 | 5 | Course Team |
| Accessibility compliance (%) | Share of artifacts meeting UDL/ accessibility checks | 70 | 95 | Accessibility Office |
| DFW rate (%) | Drop/Fail/Withdraw percentage | 18 | 10 | Registrar/QA |

## Learner-Centered Futures: From Passive Recipients to Co-Creators

A key theme in envisioning the future is the transformation of the learner's role. The "sage on the stage" is giving way to the co-creator of knowledge. Business students won't simply consume frameworks or memorize models—they will be active agents shaping their learning paths, their cohorts, and even their fields. This co-creation requires flexibility and agency built into the curriculum's DNA. But it also requires new skills: digital literacy, critical reflection, self-regulation, and collaborative communication. These "meta-competencies" will be as essential as accounting or marketing know-how. One provocative question looms: can the future curriculum itself be modular and adaptive—responsive to individual learner trajectories, market shifts, and societal needs? Could students, in some cases, negotiate their learning outcomes with faculty or industry partners? Could portfolios, badges, or digital transcripts capture the richness of learning beyond grades? Such ideas challenge long-standing norms and administrative inertia. But they also hold the potential to humanize business education—making it more relevant, personalized, and alive.

## Technology as Partner, Not Puppet Master

Technological advancement is a given. AI, VR, blockchain, analytics—all will have their roles. But the question isn't what technology can do, but how we use it to serve pedagogical ends. Too often, tech adoption has been a race to novelty—chasing the next tool without deep reflection on its implications. The future demands more thoughtful integration. Think about AI tutors that provide personalized feedback, freeing faculty to focus on mentorship and critical dialogue. Imagine VR environments where students experiment with global supply chains or ethical dilemmas in immersive, embodied ways (Bernardo & Duarte, 2022). Picture blockchain-secured portfolios that enable seamless credentialing and lifelong learning. These are dazzling possibilities. But none of them can replace the intellectual courage, ethical grounding, and empathetic mentorship that define great business education. The future is about collaboration—between humans and machines, not competition.

## Bridging Theory and Practice in Real-Time

Business education has often struggled to keep pace with the rapid evolution of the business world. The traditional model—lecture, case study, exam—feels increasingly out of sync with entrepreneurial dynamism, digital disruption, and social complexity. Purposeful integration points toward real-time, project-based learning that connects theory with practice as a living dialogue, not a one-way transmission (Boss & Krauss, 2022). Imagine courses that partner with startups, NGOs, or social enterprises—where students tackle real challenges, iterate solutions, and reflect critically with faculty guidance. These projects don't just build skills; they cultivate adaptability, resilience, and ethical judgment. Such integration also demands agile assessment models—portfolios, reflective essays, peer reviews—that capture process, not just product.

## Equity, Access, and the Digital Divide

The future's brightest visions risk casting long shadows if they ignore the persistent inequalities in access to technology, stable internet, and supportive learning environments. Purposeful integration must be equity-centered. This means designing inclusive curricula and infrastructure from the start. It means acknowledging and addressing digital fatigue, socio-economic disparities, neurodiversity, and cultural difference. The future demands institutions committed to not only technological innovation, but also social justice.

## Faculty Development as Lifelong Practice

The future will belong to educators who see themselves as lifelong learners, experimenters, and collaborators. Faculty development can no longer be an annual checkbox workshop (Brode et al, 2025). It must be embedded in the culture—continuous, peer-supported, and reflective. Teaching in integrated environments requires not just technical skill, but emotional intelligence, cross-cultural competence, and an openness to ambiguity. Supporting faculty means valuing their labor, providing time and resources for innovation, and creating communities of practice where failure is reframed as feedback.

## Institutional Culture: The Soil for Innovation

Innovations will falter without fertile soil. Purposeful integration requires institutional cultures that reward risk-taking, collaboration, and student-centeredness. It demands flattening hierarchies that separate faculty from technologists from learners. It demands leadership willing to invest long-term, listen deeply, and embrace complexity. Institutions must become learning organizations themselves—reflective, adaptive, and humble.

## A Glimpse Toward the Horizon: The Learning Organization

Business schools of the future may look less like factories and more like living laboratories—where knowledge flows bi-directionally between students, faculty, industry, and society (Hazrat et al, 2023). Where courses evolve in response to feedback and global shifts. Where the boundary between learning and work, education and life, theory and practice dissolves. Where students graduate not just with degrees, but with the capacity to navigate uncertainty, co-create futures, and act ethically.

We're not waiting for a future to arrive. We're building it, moment by moment, in every course redesign, every faculty conversation, every student reflection. The promise of purposeful integration lies in its messiness. It resists tidy answers. It invites ongoing questioning: *Are we listening? Are we adapting? Are we centering the human in all this tech?* That question—humble, urgent, endlessly fascinating—is the pulse of the future of business learning. And it's one worth keeping close.

## CONCLUSION

As we reach the conclusion of this chapter, one truth becomes increasingly clear: blended and hybrid learning are no longer pedagogical novelties—they are the new normal. What began as makeshift solutions to an educational crisis have matured into robust, flexible models that are redefining the landscape of business education. But with this new normal comes a deeper responsibility. The challenge now is not simply to offer hybrid options, but to infuse them with meaning, intentionality, and pedagogical depth.

Throughout this chapter, we have examined how blended and hybrid models enable a level of customization and responsiveness that traditional classroom formats often struggle to achieve. We have seen how flexibility—once considered a logistical benefit—has evolved into a pedagogical virtue: allowing for asynchronous reflection, personalized pacing, and diverse engagement modes. These models encourage students to become active participants in their learning journeys, rather than passive note-takers bound by the rhythm of the lecture hall.

Yet the journey is far from complete. Flexibility must not come at the cost of coherence. One of the recurrent challenges in blended and hybrid learning environments is the fragmentation of experience—students juggling disjointed learning tools, unclear expectations, or uneven levels of instructor presence. To mitigate this, business colleges must invest not just in technology, but in instructional design, faculty training, and curriculum alignment. The hybrid model is not a plug-and-play solution; it requires careful orchestration—a choreography of tools, timelines, and touchpoints that together create a unified learning experience.

Another key insight is the transformative potential of faculty mindset. Instructors who see themselves as content transmitters may struggle to adapt, while those who embrace the role of facilitators, designers, and mentors are finding new ways to engage students meaningfully. This shift demands courage, continuous learning, and institutional support. Professional development should not be treated as an optional extra, but as a strategic priority for any business college serious about pedagogical innovation.

From the students' perspective, the hybrid model can be both empowering and overwhelming. The freedom to learn asynchronously or participate remotely comes with increased responsibility—and not all learners are equally equipped to manage that. Business schools must therefore build scaffolding structures—academic advising, tech support, peer communities—that help students thrive in flexible formats. Without such support, flexibility risks becoming a double-edged sword.

Looking ahead, the most promising horizon lies in intentional hybridity: learning ecosystems where digital and physical, synchronous and asynchronous, theoretical and applied are not seen as binaries to be toggled, but as interwoven dimensions of a cohesive whole. In such ecosystems, a virtual simulation might feed into an in-class case discussion; a live guest speaker might prompt an asynchronous debate on the forum; a team project might span continents, time zones, and technologies. This is not simply about method—it is about mirroring the complexity and interconnectedness of the real business world.

Finally, we must resist the temptation to treat blended and hybrid learning as endpoints. They are waypoints on a longer journey—markers of a deeper evolution in how we understand, facilitate, and value learning. If business education is to remain relevant in a volatile, uncertain, and digitized global economy, it must not only adapt to new formats but lead with vision, courage, and a commitment to meaningful transformation.

In the end, the question is not whether blended or hybrid learning is "better" than traditional learning. The question is: How can we create learning environments that serve our students' futures more faithfully than our pasts? That is the question that will shape the next era of business education—and it is one worth answering with care.

## REFERENCES


Alarifi, I. M. (2023). *Learning Limitless Knowledge: Transformative Learning Pathway to Unlocking and Harnessing the Endless Power of Knowledge*. Balboa Press.

Barua, L., & Lockee, B. B. (2024). A review of strategies to incorporate flexibility in higher education course designs. *Discover Education*, *3*(1), 127. DOI: 10.1007/s44217-024-00213-8

Bernardo, N., & Duarte, E. (2022). Immersive virtual reality in an industrial design education context: What the future looks like according to its educators. *Computer-Aided Design and Applications*, *19*(2), 238–255. DOI: 10.14733/cadaps.2022.238-255

Boss, S., & Krauss, J. (2022). *Reinventing project-based learning: Your field guide to real-world projects in the digital age*. International Society for Technology in Education.

Bradley, V. M. (2021). Learning Management System (LMS) use with online instruction. *International Journal of Technology in Education*, *4*(1), 68–92. DOI: 10.46328/ijte.36

Brode, E. C., Bernal, J. M., Cornes, S. B., Santhosh, L., Rivera, J. A., Kulkarni, S. A., Mandal, J. R., Henry, D. M., Bartz, K. S., & Van Schaik, S. M. (2025). Faculty Development for the People: Workplace-Based Solutions for Busy Clinicians. *The Clinical Teacher*, *22*(3), e70073. DOI: 10.1111/tct.70073 PMID: 40159456

Catthoor, L. (2023). THE FUTURE OF HYBRID AND BLENDED LEARNING (Doctoral dissertation, Ghent University).

Du Plessis, A. E., Küng, E., & du Plessis, E. (2024). Challenges for Pedagogical Effectiveness in an Ever-Changing Education Landscape: Conceptualisation of Pedagogical Mobility and Flexibility as a Context-Consciousness. *Education Sciences*, *14*(4), 349. DOI: 10.3390/educsci14040349

Fisher, D., Frey, N., Almarode, J., & Henderson-Rosser, A. (2021). *The quick guide to simultaneous, hybrid, and blended learning*. Corwin Press. DOI: 10.4135/9781071852644

Glazer, F. S. (Ed.). (2023). *Blended learning: Across the disciplines, across the academy*. Taylor & Francis.

Hazrat, M. A., Hassan, N. M. S., Chowdhury, A. A., Rasul, M. G., & Taylor, B. A. (2023). Developing a skilled workforce for future industry demand: The potential of digital twin-based teaching and learning practices in engineering education. *Sustainability (Basel)*, *15*(23), 16433. DOI: 10.3390/su152316433

Hermita, N., Alim, J. A., Putra, Z. H., Mahartika, I., & Sulistiyo, U. (2024). Hybrid learning, blended learning or face-to-face learning: Which one is more effective in remediating misconception? *Quality Assurance in Education*, *32*(1), 64–78. DOI: 10.1108/QAE-02-2023-0019

Hochuli, K., & Jud, J. (2024). No Place for Remote Students? Navigating Transitions of Hybrid Co-Presence in Seminar Rooms and Lecture Halls. In Navigating Transitions of Hybrid Co-Presence in Seminar Rooms and Lecture Halls. DOI: 10.2139/ssrn.4733524

Hultquist, B. L. (2024). Using Lecture in Active Classrooms. Innovative Teaching Strategies in Nursing and Related Health Professions, 115.

Jensen, K. (2024). *The Ethics of Entrepreneurship Education*. MIT Press. DOI: 10.7551/mitpress/15073.001.0001

Kayyali, M. (2022). The Importance of Faculty Development in Higher Education. *International Journal of Higher Education Policies and Leadership*, *1*(1), 1–9.

Kayyali, M. (2024). Quality Assurance in Online and Blended Learning Environments. In *Quality Assurance and Accreditation in Higher Education: Issues, Models, and Best Practices* (pp. 227–292). Springer Nature Switzerland. DOI: 10.1007/978-3-031-66623-0_5

Kayyali, M. (2025). E-Learning Platforms and Their Influence on Lifelong Learning. In Impact of Digitalization on Education and Social Sustainability (pp. 155-176). IGI Global.

Kayyali, M. (2026). Online and Blended Learning in Doctoral Studies: Opportunities and Challenges. Improving Doctoral Education and Research Development for Sustainability, 103-138.

Lin, S. R. (2021). Understanding university-industry collaboration on project-based learning in business education.

Mastrogiacomi, F. (2021, November). A hybrid teaching and learning toolkit for a creative and curious mindset. In Innovate Learning Summit (pp. 263-271). Association for the Advancement of Computing in Education (AACE).

Mnasri, S., & Papakonstantinidis, S. (2023). The teaching-learning dynamic from behaviourism to social constructionism: A communication-centred narrative. *International Journal of Learning and Change*, *15*(3), 312–327. DOI: 10.1504/IJLC.2023.130629

Mulenga, R., & Shilongo, H. (2025). Hybrid and blended learning models: Innovations, challenges, and future directions in education. *Acta Pedagogia Asiana*, *4*(1), 1–13. DOI: 10.53623/apga.v4i1.495

Polymeropoulou, P., Potsis, K., & Kameas, A. (2024). A MODEL FOR ASSESSING THE EFFECTIVE INTEGRATION OF TECHNOLOGY INTO EDUCATIONAL PRACTICE FROM A PEDAGOGICAL PERSPECTIVE. In INTED2024 Proceedings (pp. 3651-3658). IATED.

Ryan, L. (2023). *Visual Analytics Fundamentals: Creating Compelling Data Narratives with Tableau*. Addison-Wesley Professional.

Strom, K. J., & Martin, A. D. (2022). Toward a critical posthuman understanding of teacher development and practice: A multi-case study of beginning teachers. *Teaching and Teacher Education*, *114*, 103688. DOI: 10.1016/j.tate.2022.103688

Swerzenski, J. D. (2021). Why teaching technology must adapt to our teaching. *Communication Education*, *70*(2), 211–213. DOI: 10.1080/03634523.2020.1857414

Wormeli, R. (2023). *Fair isn't always equal: Assessment & Grading in the Differentiated Classroom*. Routledge. DOI: 10.4324/9781032681122

## KEY TERMS AND DEFINITIONS

**Asynchronous learning:** self-paced study (videos, readings, quizzes) that students complete on their own schedule.

**Blended learning:** a deliberate integration of online and face-to-face activities sequenced to complement each other.

**Flexible assessment:** portfolios, projects, and iterative feedback that allow multiple ways to evidence mastery.

**Hybrid learning:** real-time teaching where some learners attend in-room while others join remotely in the same session.

**Learning ecosystem:** an orchestrated mix of tools, spaces, and interactions (LMS, labs, studios, forums) that support learning.

**Synchronous learning:** live sessions (in-person or online) requiring simultaneous participation.

**Universal Design for Learning (UDL):** designing courses from the outset to be accessible and inclusive for diverse learners.

# Chapter 4
# Fostering Intrinsic Motivation and Self-Directed Learning Through Cooperative Learning in Blended Business Education

**Dorothea Lowes**
https://orcid.org/0009-0006-9811-1228
*North-West University, South Africa*

**Christo van der Westhuizen**
*University of Johannesburg, South Africa*

**Chantelle Bosch**
https://orcid.org/0000-0001-5743-1985
*North-West University, South Africa*

## ABSTRACT

*This chapter explores the transformative potential of cooperative learning (CL) in fostering intrinsic motivation (IM) and self-directed learning (SDL) within blended learning (BL) business education environments. Drawing on a design-based, mixed-methods study conducted at a South African TVET college, it presents the Cooperative–Self-Directed–Blended Learning (C–SD–BL) framework. The chapter unpacks theoretical foundations, empirical findings, and practical implications, demonstrating how structured CL strategies in BL contexts enhance learner engage-*

DOI: 10.4018/979-8-3373-7523-6.ch004

*ment, autonomy, and competence. Insights are drawn exclusively from the author's doctoral research, presenting a contextually grounded, theoretically rigorous contribution to active learning scholarship in business education.*

## INTRODUCTION

The business education landscape in South Africa's TVET College sector is undergoing transformation. Mandated to provide skills-oriented education to a diverse population, TVET Colleges must build a responsive and inclusive workforce. However, persistent challenges, such as low learner motivation, limited self-directed learning (SDL), and unequal digital access remain (Muhria et al., 2023; Namyssova et al., 2019). Despite policy efforts to implement blended learning (BL), many students lack foundational digital skills and face connectivity issues (Nhlongo, 2020), preventing SDL development (Bosch, 2017). In business education, these challenges are amplified by traditional instructor-led methods that hinder active learning, undermining 21st-century skill development requirements (Nhlongo, 2020). This chapter addresses these challenges by exploring the potential of cooperative learning (CL) in BL environments. Cooperative learning promotes positive interdependence, individual accountability, and social interaction, all conditions conducive to fostering intrinsic motivation (IM) and SDL (Johnson & Johnson, 2009; Deci & Ryan, 2000). Anchored in social constructivism and the Community of Inquiry (CoI) framework, this chapter introduces the C–SD–BL framework, developed through a design-based mixed methods study at a South African TVET College. The framework integrates CL-BL to support collaboration, reflection, and learner autonomy and responds to contextual barriers in motivation and digital access while promoting lifelong learning. The chapter further outlines the theoretical foundations of CL and SDL, followed by a literature review on, SDL, and IM in BL contexts. It presents the study's design-based methodology, key findings from the C–SD–BL framework implementation, and implications for curriculum reform and educator development, concluding with future research directions.

### Context and Relevance of the Study

South Africa's TVET sector, marked by diversity and limited resources, faces urgent demands for skills-based education (Mwale & Ntsobi, 2023). Many students begin with low academic confidence and little exposure to SDL, yet exhibit strong potential for autonomy and collaboration when supported appropriately (Du Toit-Brits, 2019; Gresham, 1986). The study found that CL significantly improved learner engagement, group collaboration, and academic performance in a BL environment. Interviews and focus groups revealed heightened IM when learning was social, relevant, and participatory. Educators observed stronger group dynamics and greater autonomy when BL tasks aligned with real-world business contexts (Bosch & Laubscher, 2022). These findings extend beyond South Africa, providing adaptable strategies for Higher Education Institutions (HEI's) seeking to expand BL models and foster 21st-century competencies (Khalid et al., 2020; Chiu, 2021).

## Target Audience

This chapter is intended for business educators, curriculum designers, administrators, EdTech developers and researchers in the fields of motivation, pedagogy, and digital education.

# THEORETICAL AND PEDAGOGICAL FOUNDATIONS

To contextualise the C–SD–BL framework, this chapter draws on four foundational theories: Social Constructivist Theory, Self-Determination Theory, Social Interdependence Theory, and the Community of Inquiry (CoI) framework. These theories inform the design principles of the framework without dominating the discussion.

## Social Constructivist Theory (SCT)

According to Social Constructivist Theory, learning occurs through social interaction (Vygotsky, 1978; Bruner, 1966). Cooperative learning within the C–SD–BL framework activates the Zone of Proximal Development (ZPD), where learners progress through support from more capable others (MKO) (Bosch, 2017; Bosch & Laubscher, 2022; Lowes, 2024). Through scaffolding of tasks, rotating roles and collaborative inquiry deeper cognitive engagement is promoted, fostering reflective learning, essential for SDL. Cooperative learning also addresses the psychological needs of autonomy, competence, and relatedness outlined in Self-Determination Theor (SDT) (Deci & Ryan, 2000). Social interaction develop learner agency, mastery, and connection to group goals, boosting IM and ownership of learning (Loh & Ang, 2020; Lowes, 2024; Ryan & Deci, 2017; Shimizu et al., 2022).

## Self-Determination Theory (SDT)

Self-Determination Theory (SDT) identifies autonomy, competence, and relatedness as core psychological needs, that when fulfilled, lead to IM (Deci & Ryan, 1985, 2000). CL strategies promote autonomy through meaningful role selection, competence through structured tasks, and relatedness through social interaction (Bosch, 2017; Mentz & Van Zyl, 2018), assisting learners' to transition from passive to active learners, increasing IM to engage deeply with content and peers (Ryan & Deci, 2020). By embedding SDT within cooperative and constructivist pedagogy, the framework promotes active participation and cultivates intrinsically motivated learners, that are capable of self-direction, and equipped with the cognitive and emotional capacities required for lifelong learning.

## Social Interdependence Theory (SIT)

Social Interdependence Theory (SIT) upholds that, positive interdependence and mutual goal alignment enhance learning outcomes and motivation (Johnson & Johnson, 2005, 2018). When individuals believe that they can reach their goals only if others do too, this interconnection promotes interaction, accountability, and persistence, key contributors to academic achievement and IM (Slavin, 1996). The C–SD–BL framework operationalises SIT through structured collaboration and clearly defined interdependent roles, supporting both cognitive development and the formation of social-emotional bonds (Gillies, 2004).The C–SD–BL framework incorporates peer collaboration, shared goals, and reciprocal feedback, enhancing accountability and SDL.

## Community of Inquiry (CoI)

The Community of Inquiry (CoI) framework integrates teaching, cognitive, and social presence to foster meaningful learning in BL environments (Garrison et al., 2000; (Harini et al., 2023). Within the C–SD–BL framework, teaching presence is shared among facilitators and learners, cognitive presence is sustained through inquiry and reflection, and social presence is established via peer collaboration and supportive digital tools like Moodle™ and synchronous activities, that fosters trust and belonging (Bosch & Laubscher, 2022). These presences collectively nurture SDL and IM in vocational contexts, aligning motivation, cognition, and collaboration for authentic learning (Ryan & Deci, 2020; Du Toit-Brits, 2019).

## Integration of the C–SD–BL Framework

The convergence of these theories underpins the C–SD–BL framework. Cooperative learning is positioned as transformative approach that links psychological motivation with cognitive autonomy in BL environments (Adebiyi, 2019; Nafis & Nasri, 2024; Vygotsky, 1978). Cooperative learning integrates instructional practice with the psychological drivers of IM and the behavioural strategies of SDL.

Unlike passive traditional methods, CL fosters active and engaged co-construction of knowledge, mutual responsibility, and dialogic interaction. In BL settings prone to isolation, structured interdependence supports relatedness within SDT (Deci & Ryan, 2000; De Bruijn-Smolders & Prinsen, 2024; Elrayah,& Sadiq, 2025), while rotating leadership and collaborative tasks promote autonomy and competence. Additionally, CL enhances SDL by encouraging learners to co-plan, reflect, and assess progress (An et al., 2024; Shi, 2021). Activities like peer teaching, digital collaboration, and co-assessment build both metacognitive and motivational skills, essential for lifelong learning (Aboderin & Havenga, 2024). Structured CL involves scaffolding, role rotation, and reflection, balancing cognitive demand with emotional and instructional guidance.. Its strength lies in its structured yet responsive design, which allows educators to align cooperative structures with technological tools and motivational supports. Through this alignment, the framework addresses both systemic and pedagogical gaps, empowering learners to thrive in blended, collaborative, and digitally mediated environments.

## LITERATURE REVIEW

### Definitions and Theoretical Underpinnings of Intrinsic Motivation and Self-Directed Learning

Reimagining business education in the 21st century demands an instructional paradigm that develops autonomy, motivation, and digital fluency(Magagula & Awodiji, 2024). The C–SD–BL framework is a response to this demand, underpinned by a convergence of CL, SDL, and IM. These three dimensions form a mutually reinforcing triad in which CL provides the interactive foundation, SDL fosters autonomy and self-regulation and IM sustains engagement through personal relevance and satisfaction.

- ***Intrinsic motivation*** is defined as the internal desire to engage in learning due to interest or inherent satisfaction, rather than external rewards (Deci & Ryan, 1985). Intrinsic motivation has been shown to drive deeper learning and sustained effort, especially in vocational settings where learners must apply knowledge in real-world contexts (Ryan & Deci, 2000). In TVET colleges, where students often encounter complex socio-economic barriers, IM is essential for persistence, curiosity, and the development of lifelong learning dispositions.
- ***Self-directed learning*** involves taking initiative in diagnosing learning needs, setting goals, identifying resources, selecting strategies, and evaluating out-

comes (Knowles, 1975). In BL environments, SDL becomes indispensable. Learners must manage asynchronous content, interact with peers online, and monitor their own progress. These skills, requires a high degree of metacognitive awareness and motivational commitment (Garrison, 1997).

- ***Cooperative learning*** acts as a bridge between IM and SDL, promoting social interaction, accountability, and shared goal orientation, creating a climate where learners feel supported and are more willing to assume ownership of their learning (Johnson & Johnson, 2009). Within the C–SD–BL framework, these dynamics are activated through task interdependence, structured group roles, peer feedback, and collaborative inquiry. As students engage with their peers and negotiate meaning in digital spaces, they cultivate the autonomy and self-regulation essential in SDL.

Cooperative learning bridges IM and SDL by promoting shared responsibility and co-regulated learning. In BL contexts, CL reduce isolation through joint problem-solving and perspective-sharing, enhancing engagement (Johnson & Johnson, 2009; Chim et al., 2024; West et al., 2024). Strategies like task interdependence, peer scaffolding, and feedback support autonomy and competence (Johnson & Johnson, 2017; Schippers et al., 2020; Reeve, 2016; Ryan & Deci, 2020; Sukkamart et al., 2023). In addition, reflective dialogue and peer assessment foster metacognitive growth and learner autonomy (Aporbo, 2023; Gillies, 2016; Hanafi et al., 2023). Within the C–SD–BL framework, CL, SDL, and IM enhance learner engagement and lifelong learning (Lowes, 2024).

## Cooperative Learning: Promoting Autonomy and Engagement

Cooperative learning, forms the instructional backbone of the C–SD–BL framework, fostering autonomy, active participation, and social interdependence in BL environments. Grounded in Johnson and Johnson's (2009) five principles: positive interdependence; individual accountability; promotive interaction; group processing, and interpersonal skills, CL structures facilitate learner engagement and support the development of self-regulation in learning.

- **Positive interdependence** ensures that learners perceive their success as part of the group success. The C–SD–BL framework operationalises this principle through shared goals, co-assessment, and team-based problem-solving, promoting both accountability and mutual support. This structure not only drives collaboration but also enhances motivation as learners recognise the value of contributing meaningfully to a shared outcome (Slavin, 1995).

- **Individual accountability** is maintained by assigning specific roles and using peer evaluations and rotating responsibilities. This limits free-riding and ensures that each learner remains actively involved. Such practices build competence and support SDL (Gillies, 2004), by reinforcing the learner's role in managing their own contributions towards group tasks
- **Promotive interaction**, whether in face-to-face or online settings, provides learners with opportunities to explain concepts, challenge perspectives, and offer encouragement. These reciprocal exchanges enhance understanding, reflection, and social presence (Garrison et al., 2000). As learners engage in this dialogic process, they are not only co-construct knowledge but also deepen their IM through meaningful interpersonal connection.
- **Group processing** is enhanced by structured reflection on group functioning, encouraging learners to evaluate collaboration, identify areas for growth, and make shared decisions for improvement. This reflective practice is integral to metacognitive development and reinforces SDL (Johnson & Johnson, 2009).
- **Interpersonal skills**, such as communication, leadership, and conflict resolution, are explicitly cultivated through scaffolded teamwork and continuous facilitation. These skills improve group effectiveness and also prepare learners for the collaborative demands required in the modern workplace (Juniar et al., 2023;Thaibah, 2023).

Within the TVET context, where students often face low engagement and fragmented digital exposure, CL offers a structured pathway toward developing core academic and social competencies. Activities such as collaborative case studies, peer feedback, and co-constructed artefacts enable learners to practise autonomy within supported group settings. As learners become more confident in managing their responsibilities and navigating group dynamics, SDL and IM improve. The implementation of CL-BL fosters a learning environment where learners are both challenged and supported. This interplay of structure and autonomy aligns with the psychological conditions required for IM and positions learners as active agents in their own development.

## Think-Pair-Share: A Strategy for Promoting Motivation and Engagement

Among the CL techniques used in the C–SD–BL framework, Think-Pair-Share (TPS) stands out for its simplicity and effectiveness in engaging all learners. This method, entails individual reflection, peer discussion, and finally share with the group, fosters autonomy, competence, and relatedness, the core drivers of IM in SDT (Deci & Ryan, 2000; Niemiec & Ryan, 2009; Ismail et al., 2023; Nafis & Nasri, 2024).

Structured engagement (Vaughan et al., 2013) enhances independent thinking, ideas expression and meaningful peer interaction, enhancing SDL. Think-pair-share reinforces promotive interaction, by offering a safe, collaborative space for mutual knowledge construction and cognition (Lyman, 1985; Lyman et al., 2023; Sari & Susiani, 2021; Aisma, 2024). In both face-to face (f2f) and online settings, learners participated in group-based tasks, case-based collaboration, peer review, and mutual knowledge construction using tools like Moodle™ forums. These activities-maintained accountability and engagement through asynchronous interaction, and embedded learning in authentic, socially meaningful contexts. As a result, learners developed IM together with cognitive and regulatory competencies essential for self-direction in learning.

## Blended Learning Environment as Enabler of Self-Directed Learning and Active Learning

Blended learning provides the digital and structural conditions required to support SDL and IM in the C–SD–BL framework. By combining f2f instruction with synchronous and asynchronous online elements, BL empowers learners with flexibility, choice, and increased control (Garrison & Vaughan, 2008), key requirements for developing SDL and IM.

The blended modality utilized in the study centred around Moodle™, which served as the learning management system (LMS) for content delivery, interaction, and assessment. Within this platform, learners accessed multimedia lectures, digital readings, discussion forums, quizzes, and collaborative tasks. In addition, asynchronous features such as self-paced modules, resource banks, and threaded discussions supported self-regulation and time management (Garrison, 1997). These tools allowed learners to revisit content and reflect on their learning in their own time (Deci & Ryan, 2000), essential elements of SDL (Garrison, 1997).

Importantly, digital interaction was scaffolded using CL strategies that reinforced accountability and collaboration. For instance, peer-led workshops, collaborative document editing, and forum-based debates required one-on-one and collaborative content engagement. This type of activity created cognitive presence while supporting social presence, being two of the three dimensions in the Community of Inquiry (CoI) framework (Garrison et al., 2000). Blended learning also enabled the integration of formative assessments and self-evaluation tools. Timed quizzes, instant feedback mechanisms, and self-marking rubrics helped learners monitor their progress and adjust strategies accordingly. These tasks promoted metacognitive growth and IM by providing immediate reinforcement and a sense of accomplishment.

Within the C–SD–BL model, BL tools were intentionally aligned with CL structures to build community, foster engagement, and strengthen learner agency. Learners collaborated asynchronously and synchronously, planned and reflected on their progress, and engaged in peer feedback, contributing to a sense of ownership and relevance, increasing their IM to persist and succeed. Ultimately, BL served as a powerful enabler in the development of SDL and IM, especially for learners in under-resourced environments. It created a space where digital tools, when aligned with cooperative pedagogy, could overcome traditional limitations and empower students to take an active role in their learning journey.

## Bridging the Digital Divide: Challenges in South African TVETC's

Despite the promise of BL, digital inequity remains one of the most pressing challenges in the South African TVET sector. Many students, particularly in rural or underserved communities, lack access to digital devices, stable internet connections, and foundational digital literacy (Mwale & Ntsobi, 2023; Mayisela & Govender, 2024). These limitations directly impact learners' ability to engage in SDL and experience the motivational benefits of BL environments.

To address these disparities, the C–SD–BL framework incorporated low-bandwidth tools and leveraged peer scaffolding as a strategy for inclusive participation. By emphasising digital collaboration as both a skill and a learning outcome, learners were not only introduced to digital tools but supported in their use. Digital literacy was gradually developed through contextually embedded tasks such as group editing, online peer feedback, and guided navigation of the LMS (Du Toit-Brits, 2019; Gillies, 2004). Students with stronger digital skills acted as peer mentors, modelling tool use and helping peers troubleshoot in real-time, which reduced digital anxiety and supported the development of competence and relatedness—two psychological needs central to IM (Deci & Ryan, 2000). Over time, digital confidence increased and empowered students to navigate and contribute meaningfully to asynchronous forums, group submissions, and individual reflections.

The framework's inclusive design demonstrates that with strategic scaffolding and intentional peer support, the digital divide can be narrowed within existing infrastructural constraints. Rather than viewing digital access as a precondition for learning, the C–SD–BL approach positioned it as a learning goal in itself, achievable through cooperative engagement and iterative practice. The framework not only mitigated barriers to participation, but actively contributed to digital equity and learner empowerment, reaffirming the potential of CL-BL integration in enhancing learner engagement and SDL (Laubscher & Bosch, 2025).

## Educator Roles in Supporting Intrinsic Motivation and Self-Directed Learning in Online and Blended Environments

Educators play a pivotal role in enhancing IM and SDL within the C–SD–BL framework. In BL contexts, their responsibilities extend beyond content delivery to include designing structured learning environments, facilitating group dynamics, and cultivating autonomy-supportive conditions. Four predominant teacher roles to enhance IM are challenge, curiosity, control, and fantasy. These approaches align with SDT and constructivist learning theory and are embedded throughout CL tasks and digital interactions.

- *Challenge* acts as a catalyst for personal goal setting and cognitive growth. Tasks that are demanding, yet achievable engage learners in metacognitive processes such as planning, monitoring, and evaluating their learning, promoting self-regulation and problem-solving abilities. Feedback, concerns the belief in one's ability to succeed, integral to challenging tasks, enhance progress, reinforce effort, and builds self-efficacy (West & Witt, 2020). This sense of efficacy strengthens motivation and supports sustained persistence and performance.
- *Curiosity*, an innate human trait, plays a vital role in prompting learner engagement. Environments that nurture inquiry and stimulate intellectual interest, encourage active exploration and sustained attention. These settings promote deeper learning by aligning with self-motivation to understand and make sense of the world (Duan et al., 2020). Curiosity flourishes in intrinsically motivating contexts (Kanellopoulou & Giannakoulopoulos, 2020), fostering proactive cognitively invested learners who engage meaningfully with content (Westerhout et al., 2019).
- *Control*, particularly as perceived choice, is essential in enhancing IM. When learners have autonomy and choice over their learning, selecting topics, modes of engagement, or assessment types, they develop ownership of the process. This autonomy supports SDL by encouraging initiative, decision-making, and responsibility. The ability to make meaningful choices reinforces IM by fulfilling the psychological need for autonomy (Kanellopoulou & Giannakoulopoulos, 2020).
- *Fantasy*, often overlooked, powerfully enhances IM by allowing learners to transcend daily realities. Imaginative scenarios enable learners to explore future possibilities and adopt new perspectives, promoting introspection and reflection, vital to both SDL and IM. Fantasy enriches the learning experience and engages learners emotionally and cognitively. According to Purnomo et

al. (2019) and West and Witt (2020), fantasy has the ability to creating emotionally resonant, personally relevant contexts, enhancing IM.

These teacher roles facilitated structured group tasks, fostered emotionally safe environments that encouraged learner voice and experimentation, modelled reflective questioning, and provided formative feedback to guide learning. Tools, such as Moodle™ journals, collaborative documents, and self-assessment rubrics supported educators in maintaining presence and guided learners' through SDL processes. By shifting from traditional instruction to facilitation and scaffolding, educators helped students develop reflective thinking, resilience, and ownership of learning. Teacher roles were central in sustaining the psychological conditions that support IM, while also enabling the procedural and cognitive practices foundational to SDL.

## Implications for Curriculum Responsiveness to 21st-Century Competencies

The demand for 21st-century competencies, such as critical thinking, digital literacy, collaboration, creativity, and adaptability necessitates urgent curriculum reform in South African TVET Colleges. Traditional, content-heavy instruction often fails to prepare learners for the digital and global workforce (Department of Higher Education and Training, 2013). To address the Fourth Industrial Revolution (4IR), reforms must prioritize learner autonomy, digital fluency, and lifelong learning capabilities (Du Toit-Brits, 2019; Exter & Ashby, 2022).

Despite reform efforts, many students still lack access to devices, connectivity, and foundational digital skills (Bosch & Laubscher, 2022). To bridge this gap, digital literacy must be embedded as a transferable skill across curricula, with ITC integrated in content delivery and assessment practices (Kalenskyi et al., 2023; Scott & Ivala, 2019). Low-bandwidth, and mobile-friendly tools like Moodle™ has the ability to enhance access for under-resourced learners. The C–SD–BL framework addresses these challenges by embedding CL into BL contexts, promoting collaboration, learner agency, and reflection. Cooperative learning characteristics, such as interdependence and accountability enhance digital and cognitive skills, promoting SDL and IM (Du Toit-Brits, 2019). These competencies are vital to support teamwork and adaptability in the modern workplace (Johnson & Johnson, 2009).

Curricula must emphasize digital collaboration, higher-order thinking, and reflective practices, while assessments should focus on real-world applications and portfolio-based evaluations (Esposito & Virili, 2014; Ferguson-Patrick, 2018). The C–SD–BL framework demonstrates that with intentional design, even digitally constrained environments can foster the competencies required for participation in dynamic, evolving economies. Its growth capacity and adaptability make it a viable strategy for embedding 21st-century skill development in TVET and similar post-school settings.

## METHODOLOGICAL ORIENTATION

### Design-Based-Mixed Methods Research

This study employed a Design-Based Research (DBR) approach to develop, test, and refine the C–SD–BL framework within the real-world constraints of a South African TVET college. Design-Based Research was selected for its flexibility and capacity to iteratively improve interventions in complex educational environments (Li et al., 2022). The context-sensitive nature of DBR allowed the framework to evolve in response to local challenges, such as resource limitations, variable digital literacy, and differing levels of student motivation.

Quantitative tools included the Intrinsic Motivation Inventory (IMI), Self-Directed Learning Instrument (SDLI), and Cooperative Learning Application Scale (CLAS), which assessed learner engagement and the impact of CL structures (Deci & Ryan, 2000; Du Toit-Brits, 2019; Khalid et al., 2020). The CoI survey further evaluated teaching, social, and cognitive presence in the BL environment (Garrison et al., 2000), linking these directly to motivational and self-regulatory development.

Qualitative data were gathered via focus groups, interviews, and open-ended questionnaires, capturing learner experiences of autonomy, reflection, and collaboration. Themes like agency, accountability, and relevance emerged as critical to understanding how the C–SD–BL model fostered IM and SDL. Collectively, this integrated research design enabled a robust exploration of the C–SD–BL framework's capacity to support meaningful, context-sensitive learning transformation. The combination of DBR and mixed methods provided the depth, flexibility, and theoretical grounding necessary to evaluate the framework's impact on motivation and SDL in the TVET environment (Mwale & Ntsobi, 2023; Lowes,2024).

### Research Context

Participants were approximately 60 Level 3 Business Practice students, selected for their curricular alignment with the C–SD–BL framework. They were purposively divided into an experimental group, which received the intervention, and a control group, which followed traditional, teacher-centred instruction. Convenience sampling ensured demographic diversity in socioeconomic status, and digital literacy, capturing a broad range of learner experiences and challenges (Bosch & Laubscher, 2022; Du Toit-Brits, 2018). The intervention integrated structured

CL strategies into Moodle-based BL environments. Learners in the experimental group engaged in scaffolded digital tasks designed to improve engagement, peer support, and metacognitive awareness. Activities included role assignments, collaborative problem-solving, peer assessment, and structured reflection; aligned with SDL principles to develop both cognitive and social competencies (Garrison & Vaughan, 2008). Pre- and post-intervention tools measured shifts in SDL, IM, CL engagement, and the dimensions of the CoI framework. Quantitative data were triangulated with qualitative reflections and interview responses to build a holistic understanding of learner transformation, particularly in autonomy, metacognitive control, and interdependence. Results affirmed the framework's effectiveness in fostering lifelong learning dispositions within digitally supported, collaborative educational environments.

## Data Collection Methods

Data collection took place over a 10-week period, aligning with the phased implementation of the C–SD–BL framework, enabling continuous documentation of instructional strategies and learner engagement. Pre-intervention, validated quantitative tools were used to establish baseline levels of SDL and IM, distributed to the control and experimental groups. These included the IMI, which measured perceived competence and enjoyment; and the SDLI, assessing goal-setting, self-monitoring, and motivation (Khalid et al., 2020). Pre-and-post-test instruments(IMI and SDL) assessed shifts in IM and SDL behaviours before and after the intervention. In addition to the IMI and SDLI, post-tests the experimental group received a CLAS questionnaire, for capturing engagement with CL structures (Du Toit-Brits, 2019), and the CoI questionnaire for evaluating teaching, cognitive, and social presence in the BL environment (Garrison et al., 2000). This pre- and post-assessment approach enabled comparative analysis and ensured methodological triangulation across quantitative and qualitative data analysis (Du Toit-Brits, 2018).

## Thematic Analysis and Methodological Triangulation

Following quantitative data collection, qualitative data were gathered through semi-structured interviews and open-ended questionnaires with students from the experimental group. These instruments were designed to elicit detailed, reflective accounts of students' experiences with the C–SD–BL intervention. Qualitative data were coded using ATLAS.ti™ 24. Codes were derived deductively from theory (autonomy, competence, relatedness) and inductively from participant narratives. Themes were grouped into families and categories, allowing analysis of cognitive, emotional, and social dimensions of the learner experience.

## FINDINGS AND DISCUSSION

The implementation of the C–SD–BL framework produced notable shifts in learner engagement, autonomy, and motivation. These outcomes were captured through both quantitative data and rich thematic analysis, providing a comprehensive understanding of how CL in BL contexts fosters IM and SDL.

*Figure 1. A proposed community of inquiry and technology integration matrix framework for implementing cooperative learning in a blended learning environment in a technical and vocational education and training college to promote intrinsic motivation and self-directed learning. (Author's own contribution)*

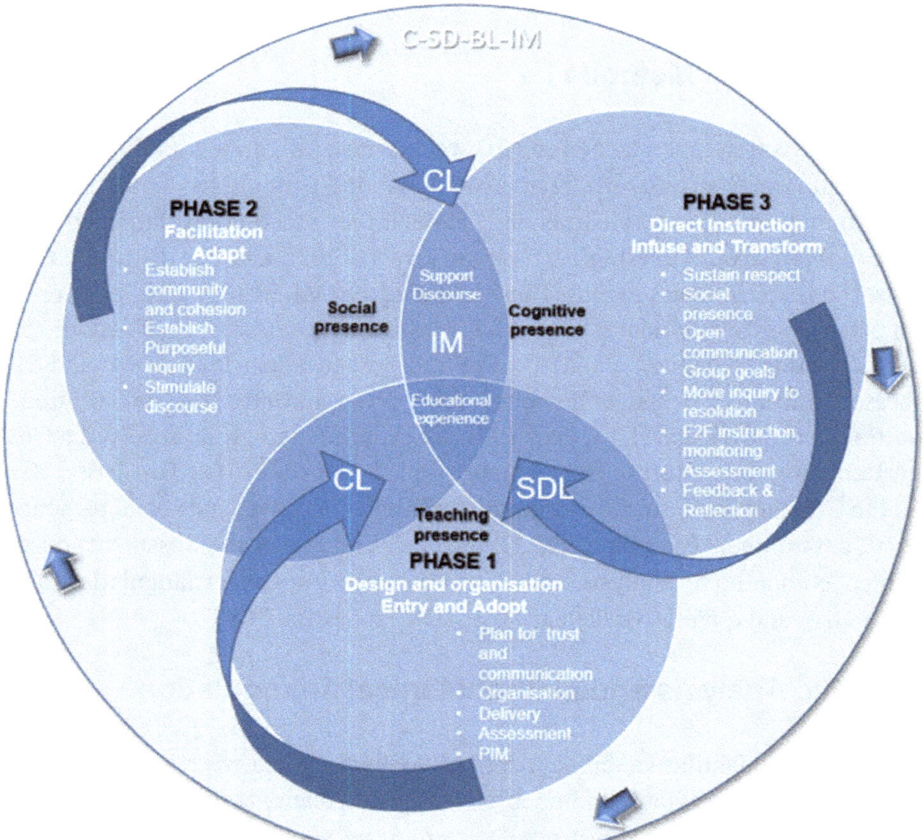


Figure 1 outlines three phases that build teaching, social, and cognitive presence through CL, peer collaboration, and scaffolded inquiry. Each phase integrates CL and SDL strategies, grounded in Self-Determination Theory (SDT) to support motivation.

Four core themes emerged from the qualitative analysis:

1. **Learner Engagement and Peer Collaboration**-Structured CL groups enhanced learner participation and responsibility. Students reported feeling more engaged when tasks required joint problem-solving and mutual accountability. Role rotations, peer feedback, and collaborative submissions fostered trust, encouraged timely participation, and improved persistence, hallmarks of SDL. Educators observed that when learners shared responsibility to reach outcomes, they became more invested in both the task and their peers' success.
2. **Digital Competence and Equity**-The use of low-bandwidth digital tools and scaffolded digital collaboration helped close access gaps. Students initially lacking digital skills were supported by peers through task-based mentoring. Over time, these learners demonstrated greater confidence in navigating Moodle™, contributing to forums, and using collaborative platforms. Digital competence thus emerged as both a prerequisite and an outcome of participation, reinforcing motivation and enabling continued self-directed behaviour.
3. **Autonomy and Agentic Learning**-Learners increasingly demonstrated ownership over their learning through self-initiated role delegation, reflection, and decision-making. Activities such as choosing project directions or managing group dynamics led to greater awareness of personal learning strategies. These behaviours reflected key elements of IM—namely, acting with a sense of volition and purpose—and solidified SDL through practice.
4. **Facilitator Support and Motivation**-Facilitators played a central role in creating autonomy-supportive environments. By offering choice, constructive feedback, encouragement and reflection, cultivated competence and relatedness amongst group members. Students reported feeling "seen" and "respected," which translated into greater effort and confidence. Facilitator presence was essential to sustaining motivation and ensuring that learners felt supported yet independent.

The thematic analysis confirmed that the C–SD–BL framework functioned as an interdependent system: Cooperative learning practices motivated engagement, digital tools enabled flexible learning, and facilitator strategies reinforced psychological needs for autonomy, competence, and relatedness. Together, these variables produced a positive shift in learners' ability to engage, reflect, and regulate their learning processes in ways that are sustainable beyond the intervention. By aligning CL strategies with motivational supports and digital scaffolding, the framework addressed the multi-dimensional challenges of the TVET environment. The findings underscore that enhancing IM and SDL requires not only pedagogical redesign but also an intentional focus on social and emotional dimensions of learning, specifically relevant in digitally constrained contexts.

## Role of Structured Cooperative Learning in Fostering Self-Directed Learning and Intrinsic Motivation

Structured CL within the C–SD–BL framework proved essential in fostering both SDL and IM. Structure in this context refers to deliberately planned learning experiences that include clear roles, timelines, scaffolding, and collaborative expectations. These structured elements facilitated meaningful peer interaction and consistent task engagement, which were critical for building autonomy, competence and IM (Hassan et al., 2024; Lowes, 2024; Ryan & Deci, 2020). By assigning interdependent roles such as summariser, timekeeper, and peer reviewer, learners developed accountability and felt valued in their group contributions (Li, Kao, Tang & Kaiser, 2024; Tran et al., 2019), enhancing relatedness and IM. Simultaneously, the predictability and clarity of structured tasks, created a psychologically safe environment for learners to take risks and explore new strategies, supporting SDL.

Learners engaged in co-planning, peer assessment, and reflection sessions, encouraging metacognition. These experiences enabled students to monitor their learning, adjust approaches, and build confidence in their ability to manage complex tasks. The repeated practice of these behaviours helped internalise SDL habits, making them transferable to future learning contexts. Structured CL also allowed learners to experience autonomy through guided choices, such as selecting group strategies, defining task parameters, or role rotation. Task design included the systematic scaffolding of CL tasks to promote learner autonomy, and control. This balance between support and freedom was key to sustaining engagement and motivation.

Ultimately, structured CL enabled learners to experience ownership, collaboration, and growth, while simultaneously addressing psychological needs and academic goals. Cooperative learning became the mechanism through which IM and SDL were consistently developed and reinforced across the BL cycle.

## Educator Facilitation Practices Aligned with Constructivist and SDL-Supportive Pedagogy

Educators shifted from traditional content delivery to facilitation, fostering autonomy, collaboration, and metacognitive growth. Peer teaching, rotating leadership, and structured group debriefings supported co-construction of knowledge and accountability (Du Toit-Brits, 2019; Gillies, 2016). Moodle™ tools and reflective journals were used for goal-setting and self-monitoring, promoting SDL. Autonomy-supportive strategies, such as offering meaningful choices and acknowledging learner input enhanced IM and learner engagement (Deci & Ryan, 2000). In addition, timely, feedback promoted competence, and peer recognition supported relatedness. These educator practices established teaching presence as vital to sustaining IM and SDL within blended TVET settings (Garrison et al., 2000; Lowes, 2024).

## Empirical Alignment with Theoretical Frameworks

The empirical data confirm the theoretical coherence of the C–SD–BL framework, particularly its grounding in *constructivist* theory. Practices observed during the intervention, such as learner-led dialogue, peer mentoring, and group problem-solving demonstrated the framework's emphasis on knowledge co-construction in collaborative settings (Du Toit-Brits, 2017). These strategies engaged learners within their ZPD, enhancing cognitive presence and promoting sustained reflection and inquiry.

Cooperative learning structures supported by SIT, including task interdependence and role negotiation, encouraged individual accountability and shared goals (Johnson & Johnson, 2009). These, in turn, reinforced autonomy, competence, and relatedness through cooperative engagement, strengthening learners' SDL skills (Du Toit-Brits, 2019). Autonomy increased as students made choices about task division and leadership; competence grew through feedback and mastery-focused assessments; and relatedness was promoted in socially supportive groups (Deci & Ryan, 2000; Lowes, 2024). These motivational conditions underpinned the development of SDL behaviours and sustained IM across the BL environment.

The CoI framework was particularly effective in the online components of the C–SD–BL model. Unlike traditional f2f settings, a BL environment requires deliberate cultivation of social and cognitive presence to prevent isolation. The synergy of CoI's three presences promoted interaction, cognition and motivation. Collectively, these frameworks provided a cohesive lens to explain the C–SD–BL framework's impact on learner autonomy, motivation, and collaborative inquiry in TVET business education (Lowes, 2024).

## Contextual Relevance: Bridging Theory and Practice in the TVETC Sector

The implementation of the C–SD–BL framework demonstrated how structured CL can be adapted to the socio-economic and infrastructural realities of South African TVET Colleges, translating theory into impactful pedagogy. In resource-constrained, contexts, where learners often face limited access to connectivity, devices, and digital literacy CL fostered engagement, resilience, and equity (Jonker et al., 2020; Lin et al., 2019; Sutarman et al., 2019; Lowes, 2024). Key design features such as mobile-accessible content, asynchronous collaboration on Moodle™, and peer-led tasks addressed logistical barriers while enabling active participation. These elements reflected an intentional alignment of CL with *constructivist* and *motivational theory* (Lowes, 2024). The integration of CL within BL not only scaffolded digital skills and social presence, but also deepened SDL and IM. By promoting task ownership, collaborative inquiry, and contextual relevance, the framework developed competencies vital for lifelong learning and employability. The study confirms the value of CL–BL as more than a support strategy, being a core instructional approach that bridges theory and practice in under-resourced vocational settings. Each theme affirms how CL enriched learner interaction, digital engagement, and development of SDL and IM, validating the framework's effectiveness in cultivating responsive, learner-centered pedagogy in TVETC.

## IMPLICATIONS FOR POLICY AND PRACTICE

The implementation of the C–SD–BL framework offers key strategic insights for policymakers and practitioners in South African TVETC. Institutions continue to face structural challenges, declining student engagement, limited development of SDL, and low IM, issues further enhanced by digital inequities and outdated teaching models.

Current curricula often lack alignment with the digital and collaborative competencies demanded by the modern workforce, particularly 21st-century skills such as problem-solving, digital fluency, and adaptability. A shift toward learner-centered, inquiry-based, and socially constructed pedagogy is essential. The C–SD–BL framework directly addresses this need by embedding CL into blended curricula, creating structured pathways to foster SDL and IM, aligning pedagogy with motivational theory, which enables institutions to modernize instruction without heavy reliance on advanced infrastructure. At a policy level, curriculum design should prioritize collaborative and blended strategies that embed digital literacy, teamwork, and reflective learning. Educators need professional development in CL strategies, digital facilitation, and autonomy-supportive pedagogy to implement these changes effectively. This model encourages flexible learning ecosystems that promote equity, agency, and skill transferability, supporting both national goals for vocational transformation and broader global workforce readiness.

## Recommendations for Embedding Cooperative Learning in TVET Blended Curricula

Cooperative learning should be institutionalized as a foundational component of curriculum design within BL frameworks. In South Africa's TVET sector, persistent challenges, such as learner disengagement, low autonomy, and poor retention can be addressed through CL's emphasis on interdependence, accountability, and reflective inquiry (Johnson & Johnson, 2009; Du Toit-Brits, 2017).

Structured CL strategies such as peer-led problem solving, rotating roles, TPS, and reciprocal teaching promotes dynamic, participatory learning where students co-construct knowledge (Gillies, 2004). The C–SD–BL framework shows how integrating CL enhances both cognitive and social skills essential for SDL and IM.

Through authentic tasks and defined roles, learners develop SDL competencies: goal setting, self-monitoring, and reflection (Du Toit-Brits, 2019). This approach shifts instruction from passive content delivery to active, collaborative engagement. Institutional adoption should include training educators in CL pedagogy and aligning assessments with collaborative, inquiry-driven outcomes. These efforts will help embed lifelong learning competencies and promote learner-centered education aligned with national and global priorities.

## Strategies to Enhance Digital Equity and Infrastructure in Under-Resourced Institutions

Bridging the digital divide in South African TVET Colleges is a critical policy and pedagogical imperative (Kalenskyi et al., 2023; Scott & Ivala, 2019). Many students lack reliable internet, access to digital devices, and supportive home learning environments, all barriers that limit engagement in BL and constrain the development of digital and SDL skills (Gaffoor & Van der Bijl, 2019; Magut & Kihara, 2019; Lowes, 2024).A coordinated response is required.

Policymakers should invest in broadband infrastructure (Muhria et al., 2023; Namyssova et al., 2019), implement device subsidies and adopt mobile-friendly, low-bandwidth platforms like Moodle™ to improve accessibility (Lowes, 2024). Pedagogically, blended curricula should not assume digital fluency but instead build it incrementally through integrating CL strategies that support peer scaffolding (Kalenskyi et al., 2023; Scott & Ivala, 2019).

Public-private partnerships, NGOs, and donor agencies can supplement institutional capacity by supporting educator training, learner digital literacy, and provision of resources that promote SDL and IM through inclusive, context-aware design (Lowes, 2024). These strategies are essential not only for promoting equity, but also for ensuring that digital transformation in TVET is sustainable, scalable, and socially just. Enhancing infrastructure is thus foundational to curriculum reform and learner empowerment in 21st-century vocational education.

## Professional Development for Educators to Promote Intrinsic Motivation and Self-Directed Learning

Professional development is essential for equipping educators to foster IM and SDL within CL-BL environments. Many TVET educators were trained in traditional didactic methods and may lack the pedagogical tools to support autonomy, metacognition, and digital facilitation (Du Toit-Brits, 2019; Garrison & Vaughan, 2008). Training programs should focus on autonomy-supportive teaching strategies, formative assessment, and the integration of CL structures that promote learner agency, peer interaction, and reflective inquiry (Johnson & Johnson, 2009; Deci & Ryan, 2000). Educators must be supported in designing tasks that offer choice, scaffold digital skills, and cultivate co-regulated learning practices (Lowes, 2024).

Ongoing communities of practice and blended professional development formats, such as online modules, peer observation, and action research is required, to help educators internalize and apply SDL and IM as supportive pedagogy. Investing in educator capacity is thus pivotal for ensuring that innovations like the C–SD–BL framework are implemented effectively and sustainably across diverse vocational contexts. By equipping educators with the pedagogical and digital competencies necessary to support IM and SDL, institutions create the conditions for scalable, sustainable change. This investment in educator development is foundational to embedding CL-BL approaches that foster meaningful learner transformation.

## Curriculum Redesign Considerations to Meet 21st-Century Skill Demands

TVET curricula must evolve to meet the realities of a digitised, innovation-driven economy. Traditional models that prioritise rote content and passive learning do not prepare students for the adaptability, problem-solving, and collaborative work expected in modern workplaces. The C–SD–BL framework offers clear principles and practices for designing curriculum that promotes SDL, IM, and essential 21st-century skills.

- *Curriculum design* should emphasise transferable competencies such as collaboration, critical thinking, digital literacy, and communication. These skills should be scaffolded across modules through structured CL experiences and project-based tasks that reflect real-world business challenges.

- *Learning outcomes* should reflect behavioural and cognitive competencies alongside content mastery. Goals should include evidence of self-regulation, learner reflection, and peer interaction. Tasks must be designed to foster these outcomes, using role-based activities, co-assessment, and learner choice.
- *Assessments* should move beyond summative exams. Authentic assessments, such as group portfolios, case studies, digital artefacts, and process journals allow learners to demonstrate growth in SDL and IM and encourage deeper engagement and knowledge application.
- *Curriculum redesign* should consider the integration of low-cost, scalable technologies that support blended and cooperative delivery. Tools like Moodle™, and open educational resources (OER) can be harnessed to create engaging, accessible, and collaborative learning environments.
- *Cross-disciplinary integration* is essential. Embedding cooperative strategies and digital tools in subjects beyond business studies ensures that SDL and IM become embedded learning dispositions across the curriculum.

Redesigning TVET curricula through the lens of the C–SD–BL framework ensures relevance, resilience, and responsiveness and empowers learners with the cognitive, emotional, and social competencies vital for lifelong learning and workforce readiness.

## Policy Integration and Innovation

Policymakers should f recognize DBR as a catalyst for educational innovation. Supporting pilot programmes, iterative curriculum development, and scalable models such as the C–SD–BL framework can help align TVET with national priorities, including those in the White Paper for Post-School Education and Training (Bosch, 2017). These reforms are essential for addressing equity gaps, meeting international skill standards, and advancing inclusive, learner-centered systems that promote lifelong learning. Cooperative learning must be central, not peripheral in blended curricula, fostering inquiry, dialogue, and interdependence as consistent pathways for SDL in vocational education.

*Digital Equity:* Policymakers must prioritize the development of digital infrastructure and equitable access to technology in under-resourced colleges. Bridging the digital divide requires targeted investment in connectivity, hardware, and digital literacy programs that empower both learners and educators.

*Professional Development:* Capacity building initiatives must equip educators with facilitation strategies rooted in constructivist pedagogy and SDL promotion. Training programs should emphasize the creation of autonomy-supportive environments, scaffolding techniques, and formative assessment practices that motivate learners.

*Policy Integration:* Broader education policy must acknowledge the role of BL in fostering lifelong learning and workforce adaptability. Policies should incentivize flexible, learner-centered curricular approaches and recognize the legitimacy of design-research as a vehicle for ongoing innovation.

These recommendations underscore the need for systemic support to foster SDL and IM, ensuring TVET institutions are aligned with the demands of a digital, knowledge-driven economy.

## CONCLUSION AND FUTURE RESEARCH DIRECTIONS

The C–SD–BL framework has demonstrated its potential to address persistent challenges in TVET education, specifically low motivation, limited digital access, and underdeveloped self-regulation. By embedding structured CL into BL environments, the model fosters both IM and SDL, preparing students for adaptive success in the 21st century.

Empirical evidence from the study affirms that this framework is both expandable and adaptable to digitally constrained, socioeconomically diverse settings. It operationalises key learning theories through context-responsive practices and offers a blueprint for curriculum reform, educator training, and institutional innovation.

Future research should explore longitudinal effects of C–SD–BL on learner retention, graduation outcomes, and workplace readiness. Comparative studies across disciplines and institutions would further refine the model's generalisability. Additionally, more work is needed to understand how to institutionalise and scale such models sustainably, particularly through system-wide policy adoption and cross-sector collaboration.

In conclusion, the C–SD–BL framework is more than a pedagogical model; it is a strategic response to systemic barriers in vocational education. Through its emphasis on collaboration, reflection, and digital inclusion, it lays the foundation for an education system that nurtures autonomy, resilience, and lifelong learning in every student.

## REFERENCES


Aboderin, O. S., & Havenga, M. (2024). Essential skills and strategies in higher education for the Fourth Industrial Revolution: A systematic literature review. *South African Journal of Higher Education, 38*(2), 24–43. https://www.researchgate.net/publication/379843842_Essential_skills_and_strategies_in_higher_education_for_the_Fourth_Industrial_Revolution_A_systematic_literature_review. DOI: 10.20853/38-2-5430

Adebiyi, D. R. (2019). The role of social interaction in learning: A Vygotskian perspective.

Aisma, N. H. (2024). *The influence of using cooperative learning (think pair share technique) towards students writing ability at the first semester of the eighth grade at SMP Negeri 19 Bandar Lampung in academic year of 2023/2024* (Doctoral dissertation). https://repository.radenintan.ac.id/32749/1/PERPUS%20PUSAT%20BAB%201%20DAN%202.pdf

An, F., Xi, L., & Yu, J. (2024). The relationship between technology acceptance and self-regulated learning: The mediation roles of intrinsic motivation and learning engagement. *Education and Information Technologies, 29*(3), 2605–2623. DOI: 10.1007/s10639-023-11959-3 PMID: 37361728

Aporbo, R. J. (2023). Impact of cooperative learning strategy on students' academic productivity. *Journal of Student and Education, 1*(1), 16–26.

Bosch, C. (2017). Promoting self-directed learning through the implementation of cooperative learning in higher education blended learning environment. (Doctoral thesis). http://dx.doi.org/DOI: 10.13140/RG.2.2.22135.11687

Bosch, C., & Laubscher, D. (2022). Cooperative learning in blended environments: Challenges and prospects in South African TVET colleges. *South African Journal of Education, 42*(2), 1–12.

Bruner, J. S. (1966). *Toward a theory of instruction*. Harvard University Press.

Chim, H. Q., Dolmans, D. H., Oude Egbrink, M. G., & Savelberg, H. H. (2024). Experiences of face-to-face and online collaborative learning tutorials: A qualitative community of inquiry approach. *Education and Information Technologies, 29*(14), 1–29. DOI: 10.1007/s10639-024-12533-1

Chiu, T. K. (2021). Digital support for student engagement in blended learning based on self-determination theory. *Computers in Human Behavior, 124*, e106909. DOI: 10.1016/j.chb.2021.106909

De Bruijn-Smolders, M., & Prinsen, F. R. (2024). Effective Student Engagement with Blended Learning A systematic review. *Heliyon, 10*(23), e39439. DOI: 10.1016/j.heliyon.2024.e39439 PMID: 39687123

Deci, E. L., & Ryan, R. M. (1985). *Intrinsic motivation and self-determination in human behavior*. Springer. DOI: 10.1007/978-1-4899-2271-7

Deci, E. L., & Ryan, R. M. (1985). The general causality orientations scale: Self-determination in personality. *Journal of Research in Personality*, *19*(2), 109–134. DOI: 10.1016/0092-6566(85)90023-6

Deci, E. L., & Ryan, R. M. (2000). The" what" and" why" of goal pursuits: Human needs and the self-determination of behavior. *Psychological Inquiry*, *11*(4), 227–268. DOI: 10.1207/S15327965PLI1104_01

Department of Higher Education and Training (DHET). (2013). White Paper for Post-School Education and Training: Building an expanded, effective and integrated post-school system. Pretoria: Department of Higher Education and Training.

Du Toit-Brits, C. (2017). Towards a transformative and holistic continuing professional teacher development (CPTD) through self-directed learning. *South African Journal of Higher Education*, *31*(2), 54–72.

Du Toit-Brits, C. (2018). Towards a transformative and holistic continuing self-directed learning theory. *South African Journal of Higher Education*, *32*(4), 1753–5913. DOI: 10.20853/32-4-2434

Du Toit-Brits, C. (2019). A focus on self-directed learning: The role that educators' expectations play in enhancing student motivation. *South African Journal of Education*, *39*(2), 1–11. DOI: 10.15700/saje.v39n2a1645

Duan, H., Fernández, G., Van Dongen, E., & Kohn, N. (2020). The effect of intrinsic and extrinsic motivation on memory formation: Insight from behavioral and imaging study. *Brain Structure & Function*, *225*(5), 1561–1574. https://link.springer.com/article/10.1007/s00429-020-02074-x. DOI: 10.1007/s00429-020-02074-x PMID: 32350643

Esposito, M., & Virili, F. (2014). Improving student success with the goal setting theory: A literature review. In *XI conference of the Italian chapter of AIS, Genova* (pp. 1-14). http://www.itais.org/proceedings/itais2014/pdf/17.pdf

Exter, M., & Ashby, I. (2022). Lifelong learning of instructional design and educational technology professionals: A heutagogical approach. *TechTrends*, *66*(2), 254–264. DOI: 10.1007/s11528-021-00657-x

Ferguson-Patrick, K. (2018). The importance of teacher role in cooperative learning: The effects of high stakes testing on pedagogical approaches of early career teachers in primary schools. *Education 3-13, 46*(1), 89-101.

Gaffoor, A., & Van der Bijl, A. (2019). Factors influencing the intention of students at a selected TVET college in the Western Cape to complete their National Certificate (Vocational) Business Studies programme. Journal of Vocational. *Adult and Continuing Education and Training*, *2*(2), 23–42. DOI: 10.14426/jovacet.v2i2.70

Garrison, D. R. (1997). Self-directed learning: Toward a comprehensive model. *Adult Education Quarterly*, *48*(1), 18–33. DOI: 10.1177/074171369704800103

Garrison, D. R., Anderson, T., & Archer, W. (2000). Critical inquiry in a text-based environment: Computer conferencing in higher education. *The Internet and Higher Education*, *2*(2–3), 87–105.

Garrison, D. R., & Vaughan, N. D. (2008). *Blended learning in higher education: Framework, principles, and guidelines*. Jossey-Bass.

Gillies, R. M. (2004). The effects of cooperative learning on junior high school students during small group learning. *Learning and Instruction*, *14*(2), 197–213. DOI: 10.1016/S0959-4752(03)00068-9

Gillies, R. M. (2016). Cooperative learning: Review of research and practice. *The Australian Journal of Teacher Education*, *41*(3), 39–54. DOI: 10.14221/ajte.2016v41n3.3

Gresham, F. M. (1986). Conceptual and definitional issues in the assessment of children's social skills: Implications for classifications and training. [REMOVED HYPERLINK FIELD]. *Journal of Clinical Child Psychology*, *15*(1), 3–15. DOI: 10.1207/s15374424jccp1501_1

Hanafi, A. G., Ahmad, H. H., Mansor, M. F., & Mustafa, W. A. (2023). An integrated approach in empowering technical and vocational education and training (TVET) for Malaysian Asnaf in the IR4.0 era. *Journal of Advanced Research in Applied Sciences and Engineering*

Harini, E., Islamia, A. N., Kusumaningrum, B., & Kuncoro, K. S. (2023). Effectiveness of e-worksheets on problem-solving skills: A study of students' self-directed learning in the topic of ratios. *International Journal of Mathematics and Mathematics Education*, *1*(2), 150–162. DOI: 10.56855/ijmme.v1i02.333

Ismail, F. A., Bungsu, J., & Shahrill, M. (2023). Improving students' participation and performance in building quantities through think-pair-share cooperative learning. *Indonesian Journal of Educational Research and Technology*, *3*(3), 203–216. DOI: 10.17509/ijert.v3i3.50348

Johnson, D., & Johnson, R. (2017). The use of cooperative procedures in teacher education and professional development. *Journal of Education for Teaching, 43*(3), 284–295. DOI: 10.1080/02607476.2017.1328023

Johnson, D. W., & Johnson, R. T. (2009). An educational psychology success story: Social interdependence theory and cooperative learning. *Educational Researcher, 38*(5), 365–379. DOI: 10.3102/0013189X09339057

Johnson, D. W., & Johnson, R.T. (2018). Cooperative learning: The foundation for active learning. DOI: 10.5772/intechopen.81086

Johnson, D. W., & Johnson, R. T. (2018). The impact of cooperative learning on achievement and engagement. In Slavin, R. E. (Ed.), *Cooperative learning: Theory, research, and practice* (pp. 23–37). Allyn and Bacon.

Juniar, D. T., Suherman, A., Tarigan, B., & Mahendra, A. (2023). Effects of project-based learning model and cooperative learning model in improving student social skills in physical education. *Jurnal Pendidikan Jasmani dan Olahraga, 8*(1), 49-57.

Kalenskyi, A., Gerliand, T., Kravets, S., Homeniuk, D., & Nagayev, V. (2023). Dual educational system of professional training of future skilled workers. In Ivanov, V., Trojanowska, J., Pavlenko, I., Rauch, E., & Piteľ, J. (Eds.), *Advances in Design, Simulation and Manufacturing VI. DSMIE 2023. Lecture Notes in Mechanical Engineering* (pp. 369–378). Springer Nature. DOI: 10.1007/978-3-031-32767-4_35

Kanellopoulou, C., & Giannakoulopoulos, A. (2020). Engage and conquer: An online empirical approach into whether intrinsic or extrinsic motivation leads to more enhanced students' engagement. *Creative Education, 11*(02), 143–165. DOI: 10.4236/ce.2020.112011

Khalid, M., Bashir, S., & Amin, H. (2020). Relationship between self-directed learning (SDL) and academic achievement of university students: A case of online distance learning and traditional universities. *Bulletin of Education and Research, 42*(2), 131–148. https://files.eric.ed.gov/fulltext/EJ1281053.pdf

Khalid, M. S.. (2020). Measuring self-directed learning skills: Development and validation of the SDL instrument. *Education + Training, 62*(2), 1–15.

Knowles, M. S. (1975). *Self-directed learning: A guide for learners and teachers*. Association Press.

Laubscher, D. J., & Bosch, C. (2025). Promoting Student Engagement and Self-Directed Learning in a Blended Learning Environment Using Cooperative Learning. In *Case Studies on Blended Learning in Higher Education: Design, Development, and Delivery* (pp. 157–174). Springer Nature Singapore. DOI: 10.1007/978-981-96-0722-8_9

Li, J., Luo, H., Zhao, L., Zhu, M., Ma, L., & Liao, X. (2022). Promoting STEAM education in primary school through cooperative teaching: A design-based research study. *Sustainability (Basel)*, *14*(16), 10333. DOI: 10.3390/su141610333

Loh, R. C. Y., & Ang, C. S. (2020). Unravelling cooperative learning in higher education: A review of research. *Research in Social Sciences and Technology*, *5*(2), e2395–e6518. DOI: 10.46303/ressat.05.02.2

Lowes, D. (2024). The effect of cooperative self-directed blended learning on intrinsic motivation in a Technical Vocational Education and Training college. [Unpublished doctoral dissertation]. North-West University.

Lyman, F. T. (1985). *Think-Pair-Share (Mimeograph).* University of Maryland.

Lyman, F. T., Tredway, L., & Purser, M. (2023). Think-pair-share and Thinktrix: Standard bearers of student dialogue. In R. M. Gillies, M. Millis, & N. Davidson (Eds.), *Contemporary Global Perspectives on Cooperative Learning: Applications across educational contexts* (pp. 124-143). Routledge.

Magagula, M. M., & Awodiji, O. A. (2024). The implications of the fourth industrial revolution on technical and vocational education and training in South Africa. *Social Sciences & Humanities Open*, *10*(100896), 1–11. DOI: 10.1016/j.ssaho.2024.100896

Magut, C. K., & Kihara, A. (2019). Influence of student retention strategies on performance of TVETs in Nairobi County, Kenya. *Journal of Business and Strategic Management*, *4*(1), 1–24. DOI: 10.47941/jbsm.279

Mayisela, T., & Govender, S. (2024). *Open learning as a means of advancing social justice: Cases in post-school education and training in South Africa*. African Books Collective.

Mentz, E., & Van Zyl, S. (2018). The impact of cooperative learning on self-directed learning abilities in the computer applications technology class. *International Journal of Lifelong Education*, *37*(4), 482–494. DOI: 10.1080/02601370.2018.1513426

Muhria, L., Supriatna, N., & Nurfirdaus, N. (2023). Students' challenges of blended learning model in higher education. *Journal Corner of Education, Linguistics, and Literature*, *2*(3), 223–233. DOI: 10.54012/jcell.v2i3.123

Mwale, B. J., & Ntsobi, M. (2023). Trends in access and success at Gert Sibande Technical and Vocational Education and Training (TVET) College. *Journal of Education and Practice*, *14*(19), 34–55. DOI: 10.7176/JEP/14-19-05

Nafis, S. A. B. M., & Nasri, N. B. M. (2024). The effectiveness of cooperative learning towards low-achieving students in class: A concept paper. *International Journal of Academic Research in Progressive Education and Development*, *13*(1).

Namyssova, G., Tussupbekova, G., Helmer, J., Malone, K., Mir, A., & Jonbekova, D. (2019). Challenges and benefits of blended learning in higher education. *International Journal of Technology in Education*, *2*(1), 22–31. http://nur.nu.edu.kz/handle/123456789/4494

Nhlongo, A. H. (2020). *University lecturers' perspectives of Moodle usage in teaching postgraduate modules: a case study of the School of Education* (Doctoral dissertation). https://researchspace.ukzn.ac.za/items/e9092741-b45e-4ac5-8b1f-137ef0d6f866

Niemiec, C. P., & Ryan, R. M. (2009). Autonomy, competence, and relatedness in the classroom: Applying self-determination theory to educational practice. *Theory and Research in Education*, *7*(2), 133–144. DOI: 10.1177/1477878509104318

Reeve, J. (2016). Autonomy-supportive teaching: What it is, how to do it. In Liu, W. C., Wang, J., & Ryan, R. M. (Eds.), *Building autonomous learners* (pp. 129–152). Springer. DOI: 10.1007/978-981-287-630-0_7

Ryan, R. M., & Deci, E. L. (2000). Intrinsic and extrinsic motivations: Classic definitions and new directions. *Contemporary Educational Psychology*, *25*(1), 54–67. DOI: 10.1006/ceps.1999.1020 PMID: 10620381

Ryan, R. M., & Deci, E. L. (2017). *Self-determination theory: Basic psychological needs in motivation, development, and wellness*. Guilford Press. DOI: 10.1521/978.14625/28806

Ryan, R. M., & Deci, E. L. (2020). Intrinsic and extrinsic motivation from a self-determination theory perspective: Definitions, theory, practices, and future directions. *Contemporary Educational Psychology*, *61*, e101860. https://psycnet.apa.org/doi/10.1016/j.cedpsych.2020.101860. DOI: 10.1016/j.cedpsych.2020.101860

Sari, I. P., & Susiani, S. (2021). The effects of Jigsaw, Student Teams Achievement Divisions (STAD), and Think-Pair-Share (TPS) techniques in writing narrative text. *Journal of Educational Sciences*, *5*(1), e2581–e2203. DOI: 10.31258/jes.5.1.p.66-79

Schippers, M. C., Morisano, D., Locke, E. A., Scheepers, A. W., Latham, G. P., & De Jong, E. M. (2020). Writing about personal goals and plans regardless of goal type boosts academic performance. *Contemporary Educational Psychology*, *60*, e101823. https://www.sciencedirect.com/science/article/pii/S0361476X1930428X. DOI: 10.1016/j.cedpsych.2019.101823

Scott, C. L., & Ivala, E. N. (2019). Moving from apartheid to a post-apartheid state of being and its Impact on transforming higher education institutions in South Africa. In Scott, C. L., & Ivala, E. N. (Eds.), *Transformation of higher education institutions in post-apartheid South Africa*. Routledge. DOI: 10.4324/9781351014236-1

Shi, H. (2021). Examining college-level ELLs' self-efficacy beliefs and goal orientation. *Journal of Comparative and International Higher Education*, *13*(2), 2380–9205. https://www.ojed.org/index.php/jcihe/article/view/2978. DOI: 10.32674/jcihe.v13i2.2978

Shimizu, I., Matsuyama, Y., Duvivier, R., & Van der Vleuten, C. (2022). Perceived positive social interdependence in online versus face-to-face team-based learning styles of collaborative learning: A randomized, controlled, mixed-methods study. *BMC Medical Education*, *22*(1), 567. DOI: 10.1186/s12909-022-03633-y PMID: 35869477

Slavin, R. E. (1995). *Cooperative learning: Theory, research, and practice* (2nd ed.). Allyn and Bacon.

Slavin, R. E. (1996). Research on cooperative learning and achievement: What we know, what we need to know. *Contemporary Educational Psychology*, *21*(1), 43–69. DOI: 10.1006/ceps.1996.0004

Sukkamart, A., Pimdee, P., Leekitchwatana, P., Kongpiboon, W., & Kantathanawat, T. (2023). Predicting student-teacher self-directed learning using intrinsic and extrinsic factors: A theory of planned behavior adoption. *Frontiers in Psychology*, *14*, 1211594. DOI: 10.3389/fpsyg.2023.1211594 PMID: 37780149

Sutarman, S., Sunendar, D., & Mulyati, Y. (2019). Investigating cooperative learning model based on interpersonal intelligence on language learners skill to write article. *International Journal of Instruction*, *12*(4), e201–e218. DOI: 10.29333/iji.2019.12413a

Thaibah, H. (2023, December). Cooperative learning to improve social skills in acceleration students. In *Proceedings of the 6th International Conference on Learning Innovation and Quality Education (ICLIQE 2022)* (pp. 1151-1164). Atlantis Press. DOI: 10.2991/978-2-38476-114-2_106

Tran, V. D., Nguyen, T. M. L., Van De, N., Soryaly, C., & Doan, M. N. (2019). Does cooperative learning may enhance the use of students' learning strategies? International Journal of Higher Education, 8(4), Article e.

Vygotsky, L. S. (1978). *Mind in society: The development of higher psychological processes* (Cole, M., John-Steiner, V., Scribner, S., & Souberman, E., Eds.). Harvard University Press.

West, B. K., & Witt, A. (2020). Challenge, fantasy, and curiosity: Activating students' intrinsic motivation within information literacy sessions. The Journal of Creative Library Practice. https://knightscholar.geneseo.edu/library-research/6?utm_source=knightscholar.geneseo.edu%2Flibrary-research%2F6&utm_medium=PDF&utm_campaign=PDFCoverPages

West, H., Hill, J., Abzhaparova, A., Cox, W., & Alexander, A. (2024). Pandemic pedagogies: Reflecting on online learning using the community of inquiry framework. *Journal of Geography in Higher Education*, *48*(2), 157–176. DOI: 10.1080/03098265.2023.2190962

Westerhout, E., Drijvers, P., & Bakker, A. (2019). The impact of a mathematics game programming project on student motivation in grade 8. In Eleventh Congress of the European Society for Research in Mathematics Education,25, Freudenthal Group; Freudenthal Institute; ERME. https://hal.archives-ouvertes.fr/hal-02410276

# Chapter 5
# Engaging Minds With Hybrid Models in Business Education:
## Insights From India's B-Schools

**Pravin Kumar**
https://orcid.org/0009-0008-9393-7324
*Brainware University, India*

## ABSTRACT

*This chapter examines the use of hybrid learning models as a means of improving the level of student engagement in a business learning context, taking the Indian institutions as an example. With its roots in a mixed-methods design, the study will supplement the quantitative survey design to quantify the characteristics of the sample with the qualitative interview-based design to understand individual personality and challenges faced by them. The pedagogical practices used by the methodology include case methods, simulations, role-plays, active learning strategies, and the usage of hybrid tools. The research demonstrates that the combination of technology and participatory pedagogy ensures a significant margin of emotional, behavioral, and cognitive involvement, which results in enhanced learning, positive knowledge results, and satisfaction, being one of the brightest innovations of higher education.*

DOI: 10.4018/979-8-3373-7523-6.ch005

# INTRODUCTION

## Evolution of Learning Models in Business Education

Over the past few decades, the business learning environment has witnessed a revolutionary change in terms of the changes in the educational paradigm, technological innovations, and the changing industry needs globally. Traditionally pedagogically oriented, business programs were once strictly face-to-face with a lot of lectures, chalkboard-based explanations, and case studies discussed in the classroom. Starting with the rapid growth of globalization along with the incorporation of digital technology and the adoption of experiential learning, the pedagogical implications of the specific management-related tools, techniques, and practices gained a new implication among the business schools (Aparicio et al., 2017). The business education of the current age should develop along with industry, attract the active participation of learners, and combine real-life situations, starting graduates on the way to the leading positions. In addition to knowledge transfer, contemporary management programs will, ideally, nurture critical thinking, problem-solving, negotiation, and interpersonal competencies that are currently required by the contemporary competitive business environment. This change has made room to accommodate blended and hybrid ways of learning that are partially classroom-based and partially digital since they address the professional skills as well as academic requirements of the student (Bedenlier et al., 2020). Considering that, virtual delivery subsequently transformed into blended learning because there was increased demand for more flexible, accessible, and customizable delivery, and hybrid learning is no different since it is a systematic pedagogical method in business learning.

## The Digital Turn: Rise of Hybrid and Blended Approaches

The onset of the 21st century saw technology transforming the field of management education using Learning Management Systems (LMS), video conferencing tools, virtual simulation, and artificial intelligence-driven analytics. Such sources enabled teachers to make each learning process unique, keep track of student progress on an ongoing basis, and introduce more flexible approaches to instruction (Baber, 2021). In business education, hybrid learning is being used as a strategic way to blend live interactive sessions necessary in teaching using the case method instruction, negotiation games, and group projects with learning activities that are individual and involve students using an independent digital environment through simulation-based exercises in strategy games and market study assignments. The hybrid model also retains the advantages of face-to-face communication and uses the advantages of digital resources to increase accessibility, speed, and variety of different types of experiences (Beatty, 2019). In the Indian and international management institutions, hybrid course curricula incorporate both web-based and face-to-face courses to develop industry-specific skills. Instruction of finance, marketing classes via flipped-classroom, team-based consulting assignments managed through collaborative platforms, and multimedia case databases to equip students with the solutions to modern business issues is also encouraged among teachers (Bedenlier et al., 2020). Notably, the mixed mode enables business students to balance their time and still enjoy face-to-face networking and mentoring activities, which are important elements of professional development in management education. These achievements have been accompanied by concerns regarding academic involvement and learning results at the particular business schools. What are the quantifiable improvements of the development of business skills related to which hybrid instructional designs? What are their barriers, either technological, pedagogical, or institutional, to success? The above issues characterize the realm of existing studies on engagement as applied to the hybrid approach to business teaching.

## Engagement: The New Standard

The act of participating in business education is closely associated with improved understanding, improved retention of ideas and concepts, as well as being in a position to implement the ideas learned professionally (Deci & Ryan, 2000). It is critical not to leave students intellectually and emotionally disengaged during case discussions, simulation games, or collaborative problem-solving games. The importance of such engagement increases when the courses are conducted both online and offline (Aparicio et al., 2017). Learners could log out during an online session without the real-time communication and instant guidance of peers and faculty during the online sessions, thus minimizing the success of the hybrid model. As a result, management courses need to deliberately plan instructions so that they can maintain interest and fit the career-oriented ambitions of business learners. Guided business simulation games and financial modeling tasks, role-playing negotiation exercises, industry-based webinars, and capstone projects involving multiple processes can be implemented to merge theoretical knowledge and practice with the support of hybrid methods (Bedenlier et al., 2020). The risks of learning passivity can be solved by embedding these experiences in hybrid courses and also developing a dynamic, practice-oriented learning environment.

## Post-Pandemic Disruptions and the New Normal

The call to action represented by the COVID-19 pandemic in the year of 2020 was a catalyst driving a fast and unprecedented transformation of business education delivery across the world (Agarwal & Kaushik, 2020). Swiftly, management institutes switched to an entirely online schedule, exposing the power of online education as well as its weaknesses (Basilaia & Kvavadze, 2020). Access to technology issues, pedagogical adjustment, and equity among the students emerged as well, but the crisis increased new tools and delivery methodologies adoption and adoption. The future of management education is no longer replaced by hybrid learning as an emergency solution but experienced as a strategic choice that business schools voluntarily make after the pandemic (Baber, 2021). The status quo thus lends itself as a key point in revisiting not just the way the content is presented, but also how it accords to the ethos of business competencies, industry requirements, and lifelong learning. In the current scenario, the management colleges are developing learning ecologies that integrate technology with adaptability, inclusivity, and interactivity (Beatty, 2019). In this emerging paradigm, the current research paper will examine how to use hybrid learning methods to improve the participation, motivation, and skills training of students in business-related education to ensure that technology adoption does not undermine but supplements the quality and relevance of management education.

## Statement of the Problem

### Challenges in Maintaining Engagement

Although hybrid learning looks like a good solution for changing business education, one issue is yet to be solved: keeping students involved in both physical and online classes. Student engagement also describes how much time every student invests in learning and how seriously they determine their knowledge, and it's known to be a reliable predictor of achievement and satisfaction at school. It becomes very challenging to keep hybrid classrooms active and meaningful. Asynchronous online learning often includes distractions, few interactions with others, and no quick feedback, leaving students without enough motivation and exhausted from using the computer. Furthermore, how well learners adapt to hybrid learning depends on their ability to use technology, stay disciplined, and have access to it, making the situation even more detailed.

### Misalignment Between Technology and Pedagogy

There is also a problem when the tools teachers use in hybrid learning do not fit with how they are teaching students. Many times, people become more concerned with using technology instead of making sure the instruction is well-designed. If pedagogy is not well prepared, digital tools could only add little value to students' education. As real-world simulations, collaboration, and decision-making play important roles in business education, technology needs to support learners in engaging in those tasks. But many educators cannot move beyond information dissemination, which means students and their teachers develop different expectations. Not only does this negatively impact student outcomes, but it also causes people to lose faith in the value of hybrid learning.

### The Need for Evidence-Based Hybrid Models

Even though more schools are adopting hybrid learning, there is not much research on how it affects students' involvement in business teaching. There are many papers about using technology in the classroom, but not many studies look at how a mix of in-person and virtual learning affects students' participation, teamwork, and performance. Currently, it is very important to address this gap since schools are trying to use data to improve student success in mixed learning environments. If there is no basis in evidence, hybrid learning could become uneven and ineffective, missing the chance to provide engaging business education to learners.

## Objectives

The reason for this study is to review the impact of hybrid models on student involvement in business programs. Since technology is radically changing the way learning happens, educational institutions should concentrate on developing useful and engaging learning activities. It highlights mixing online instruction with classroom instruction as a main way to succeed in this area. Such a model plans to respond to the new needs of business education by encouraging students to work together in active and hands-on ways. Understanding engagement as an activity and a result, the study tries to connect what is studied with what happens in schools. It examines how hybrid learning affects students' progress in school and also builds their motivation, feelings, and working together skills, all of which are necessary for business education. Thus, the study outlines different goals: to determine the effects of hybrid settings on cognitive, emotional and behavioral engagement in business education; to define good learning strategies like flipped classes, game-based approaches, virtual team exercises and online simulations; to examine challenges related to keeping students interacted in hybrid learning; to suggest useful approaches to increase student participation; and to improve scientific studies by focusing on student engagement when measuring the success of hybrid learning in business programs.

# THEORETICAL FRAMEWORK

## Constructivist Learning Theory in Practice

In hybrid learning, it is most important that students are actively involved in the learning process (Halverson et al., 2014). In the Constructivist Learning Theory, the main idea is that learners play a part in their education by exploring, teaming up, and reflecting on what they learn. Constructivists suggest that knowledge is formed by experience, communicating with others, and solving issues (Deng et al., 2019).

Hybrid business education uses constructivist theory very effectively (Keržič et al., 2019). With the use of hybrid learning, students can study when and how they want and also get the benefits of interacting with others face-to-face. Applying techniques like flipped classroom, case-based discussions, project-based learning, and role-plays allows students to put the things they learn into practice and understand them better (Huang et al., 2020).

Hybrid learning settings are ideal for constructivist pedagogy because students can look at content again, join forces on online projects, and engage in conversations that offer many standpoints (Hodges et al., 2020). Students in hybrid environments are expected to work together to generate knowledge that reflects the philosophy of constructivism. By using this approach, students can learn concepts that make sense to them and support their plans, which is especially necessary in business education (Adedoyin & Soykan, 2023).

## Self-Determination Theory (SDT): Autonomy, Competence, and Relatedness

SDT gives important information about what causes students to actively participate in learning when in hybrid environments. Deci and Ryan created SDT, and they believe that satisfaction of autonomy, competence, and relatedness is important for human motivation.

- Autonomy means how the learners experience themselves in control of their educational course. The freedom given to the students to choose when and how to complete asynchronous materials creates an independent feeling. They have shown that this autonomy has served to increase intrinsic motivation and accountability.
- Competency means a learner's belief in the ability to succeed and master tasks. The need is met by hybrid learning that promotes self-paced learning, frequent formative assessments, and interactive tools, which are quizzes and

simulations that provide immediate feedback. This makes sure the students monitor their progress and have a sense of achievement and confidence.

- Relatedness is defined as the degree of relationship of the learner to his peers, faculty, and the wider academic community. Online learning has often been critiqued regarding the isolating nature of online learning, but hybrid models that are well-designed can allow for community forming through discussion forums, peer review activities, collaborative projects, and synchronous class interaction. When other students are capable of having their feelings, respect, and ideas honored, these elements make them feel valued and supported, which reinforces their emotional investment in learning.

If hybrid business education is based on these three aspects, it leads to a climate where people find it easy to stay committed and involved. Therefore, SDT makes it easy to study what leads students to participate and how the school builds those motivations (Agarwal & Kaushik, 2020).

## Relevance to Business Education and Hybrid Environments

These two theories complement each other well in terms of engagement to enhance student engagement in hybrid business education (Halverson et al., 2014). Learning for business usually involves the application of theory into practice, which involves not only knowledge but also motivation, autonomy, and collaboration (Deng et al., 2019). Learners are encouraged to question and investigate in constructivist teaching approaches, while SDT is used to determine that motivation is influenced by psychological needs that are contextualized in specific situations (Keržič et al., 2019).

These theories are applied while developing engaging experiences for students who are in hybrid conditions, i.e., becoming up and down between face-to-face classes and online access to the course site (Huang et al., 2020). Thus, in a flipped marketing class, students could watch lecture videos by themselves, play online games to practice setting prices, and engage in group teamwork for their pitch assignments (Hodges et al., 2020). All of these theories together recommend that learning environments should offer information along with empowerment, engagement, and a sense of community (Adedoyin & Soykan, 2023).

Embracing these educational frameworks by business schools makes it easier to use modern teaching methods, turning hybrid learning into a valuable resource for educational progress.

## CONCEPTUAL FRAMEWORK

### Key Constructs and Variables

This study is predicated upon the understanding, outside of a systems context, of the whole in terms of its component elements of educational technology components in a hybrid and business learning environment. The four key constructs for this framework are: hybrid tools, active learning strategies, student engagement, and learning outcomes. These are the constructs with which engagements of hybrid learning models can be examined to see how they influence engagement in business education.

- ***Hybrid Tools***: Hybrid Tools are mixed synchronous and asynchronous technological solutions such as Learning Management Systems (LMS), videoconferencing, discussion forums and forums, distance digital and digital collaboration tools, and virtual simulations. These are tools of enabling hybrid learning: access, communication, content delivery, and real-time interaction.
- ***Active Learning Strategies:*** Pedagogical strategies to encourage student participation, including flipped classroom, problem-based learning, gamification, case method teaching, and peer-reviewed projects, are the common practices in modern teaching. Through these strategies, learners are encouraged to apply knowledge, to think reflectively, to collaborate, and to function independently.
- ***Student Engagement***: This construct is multidimensional and includes such aspects as emotional engagement (interest, motivation), behavioral engagement (participation, persistence), and cognitive engagement (critical thinking, problem solving). Instructional design is mediated by engagement, which is what we care about.
- ***Learning Outcomes***: The end goal of hybrid business education is to have academic performance, critical thinking, teamwork skills, real-world readiness, and student satisfaction. Apart from being measurable, these outcomes indicate instructional success.

The idea behind this approach is that teaching using active strategies and hybrid tools together boosts how involved students are, which improves their performance in learning.

Figure 1 is a conceptual visualization of the hybrid learning concept in business education, which links four main constructs, i.e., Hybrid Tools, Active Learning Strategies, Student Engagement, and Learning Outcomes. It shows how technological tools such as learning management systems, video conferencing, discussion forums, as well as virtual simulation, and pedagogy such as flipped classrooms, gamification, problem-based learning, and case method instructions can all be used as a form of engagement facilitators. The theory of student engagement has three dimensions: emotional, behavioral, and cognitive, which have a combined effect on important learning, such as academic levels, critical thinking, teamwork abilities, ability to live in the real world, and general student satisfaction. The cause-and-effect dyad flow here is by means of tools and strategies to engagement and eventually, better educational outcomes as reflected by this visual representation.

*Figure 1. Conceptual Framework of Hybrid Learning in Business Education*

*Source: Author's illustration*

## LITERATURE REVIEW

### Historical Perspectives on Hybrid and Blended Learning

Hybrid and blended learning are rooted in the early 20th century, when educators started to implement technology in classroom teaching (Crawford et al., 2020). To date, blended learning has been mostly perceived as a mixture of face-to-face and technology-based learning (Bozkurt & Sharma, 2020). High internet speeds and educational technologies allowed the use of several strategies that allowed self-paced and easily accessible education (Dhawan, 2020). Hybrid learning was pre-dated by distance learning, which came in the form of correspondence courses and the academic study on television broadcasts (Hodges et al., 2020). Nevertheless, blended programs were systemically introduced into educational institutions only at the beginning of the 2000s when comprehensive Learning Management Systems (LMS) and, in particular, Moodle and Blackboard became widely available (Bhat et al., 2018).

NPTEL and SWAYAM have promoted the advent of blended learning in India (Almaiah et al., 2020). Hybrid learning is based on blended learning, but its introduction allowed the development of an inseparable connection between in-person classes and online resources (Hew et al., 2020). In contrast to the previous ones, which occasionally divided in-person and digital elements as two different things, hybrid learning focused on the pedagogical integrity (Gelles et al., 2020). The reason behind its increased popularity is that learners want flexibility, personalization, quality, and high academic standards. Back in their early days, hybrid models in business education were mostly applied to niche MBA courses and executive education (Dumford & Miller, 2018), which were focused on working professionals who needed to have their education structured flexibly (Ansari & Khan, 2020). However, as time went on, business schools realized the possibility of integrating the essential pedagogical innovations like the use of the Harvard case method, live business simulations, and role-play games of leadership and negotiation into hybrid systems. Historically, physical (classroom) location of use of such practices is inaccessible and scaleable in comparison to its digital implementation in virtual breakout rooms, interactive case repositories, and AI-driven simulation tools (Bond et al., 2020). As a result, hybrid education has shifted towards a more traditional process, with hybrid education becoming a standard method of delivery in the most distinguished business schools across the globe (Kahu, 2013).

## Student Engagement Theories and Metrics

Engagement has been described as the levels of degrees of participation, effort, participation, engagement, responsiveness, and cognitive involvement with the learning. This becomes particularly relevant in business education, where active learning proves to be the determining factor of the extent to which the ideas are applied in the complex environments of the real world. Constructivist theory thinks that students are not supposed to learn, but that they should be able to create knowledge using simulations, analysing cases, and group work. In the case of business schools, this will entail designing hybrid classes in such a way that they allow learners to participate in digital strategy games, virtual market research stories, and cloud-based team consulting tasks.

A Self-Determination Theory (SDT) provides the hypothesis that engagement has the capacity to blossom when learners can self-motivate themselves through a feeling of freedom, ability, and attachment. In a hybrid design, the asynchronous instruction naturally supports autonomic development, and the synchronous courses, whether live role-play negotiations or interactive financial modeling workshops, prove a source of feedback and collaborative facility to build confidence and social connectedness. Business schools all over the world have used SDT to create hybrid courses that recreate high-engagement modes of learning, such as academic debates of the Harvard-style case studies in online classrooms or international entrepreneurship initiatives to be taken and finished online.

Engagement has changed in the sense of measurement of hybrid learning. The traditional parameters encompassing attendance and verbal contribution have been replaced with data analytics, which can be obtained via the LMS platform, which not only gives information on the duration of which students take to accomplish assignments but also includes the paths of browsing and the nature of interaction between students. In India, nowadays most B-schools have started using these analytics not merely to track engagement but also to dynamically adjust instruction in courses such as finance, marketing, and even some entrepreneurship courses where instructors want to optimize student engagement in hybrid courses.

## Hybrid Education in Business Schools: Global Trends

Business schools worldwide have incorporated hybrid learning to address the changing demands of the workforce and learners. Management courses in North America and Europe increasingly involve pre-recorded lectures, online discussions, face-to-face case debriefs, virtual simulation activities, and multi-modal assessments. The most common version of a blended course asks participants to participate in fundamental course content online before meeting in-person to learn more advanced applications of the material via case analysis, simulation, or design-thinking workshop sessions. This will be especially useful in courses related to finance, marketing, and entrepreneurship since applied problem-solving is fundamental to these courses.

The Top institutions have already trained on immersive virtual reality simulation of a supply chain, the use of artificial intelligence that is able to tailor case content to individual learner needs, and team projects across multiple regions around the world via online team collaboration spaces. Post-pandemic, the Indian B-schools (IIMs, XLRI, and major privately funded schools, among others) and national digital infrastructure (SWAYAM and DIKSHA) have opted to employ modular hybrid formats. These enable presenting theoretical materials digitally to give classroom time to more experiential learning, as well as mock boardroom negotiations, investment pitches, and cross-disciplinary capstone projects. There are still challenges, such as the hindrances in the infrastructure, the faculty's preparedness, and the equal representation.

## Gaps in Existing Research

Although hybrid models are becoming entrenched in business education, a knowledge gap still exists. Most of the literature addresses hybrid learning across the entire field of higher education or science, technology, mathematics, and engineering rather than its exact effects on the teaching needs of business schools. Business education is highly dependent on discussion-based learning and applied-practice pedagogical components of industry integration that necessitate special arrangements in hybrid settings. The impact of hybrid models on such skills as teamwork, decision-making, and strategic communication is under-researched, in particular, in the Indian domain.

The current literature will also draw on scant literature of the long-term effects that hybrid learning has had as regards workplace readiness, flexibility, and commitment to lifelong learning, qualities highly coveted in management graduates. Also, a majority of hybrid work does not, according to some observers, fail due to technology but rather due to instructional design and the absence of faculty education. Further research has to then look at the pedagogical and operational, multi-year and multi-method research designs that explore how digital implementation of case-based, simulation-based, and role-play pedagogies affects learning outcomes in business education.

# METHODOLOGY

The sequential mixed methods study design was applied in this research in an attempt to adequately understand the impact of hybrid learning models on student engagement in the learning sector, business education. The proposed study was set in the Indian context of higher learning and limited to the management programs, which are Master of Business Administration (MBA), Post Graduate Diploma in Management (PGDM), and executive education courses. The selection was based on the fact that the samples cover the entire range of business education delivery in India, full-time academic programs that traditionally have high pedagogical standards, industry-specific diploma programs, and shorter-format offerings that provide professional growth to executives in the workplace.

## Research Design and Rationale

The **sequential mixed-methods approach** was chosen to capture both the breadth of experiences through quantitative measures and the depth of insights through qualitative exploration. The first phase involved a **structured survey** to collect standardized data on engagement levels, perceived learning outcomes, and challenges in hybrid learning. The second phase comprised **semi-structured interviews** to probe deeper into specific pedagogical practices used in business education, such as the Harvard case method, live business simulations, role-play negotiations, and consulting projects, and to explore how these practices were adapted for hybrid delivery.

This design was appropriate because business education, unlike many other disciplines, relies heavily on interactive, experiential, and applied learning activities. Capturing the subtleties of how these activities translate into a hybrid environment required both quantitative generalizability and qualitative nuance.

## Population and Sampling

The research focused on both students and faculty to measure the opinions of both sides, learners and educators. In the study, 6 business schools of India were used, three publicly funded (including the Indian Institutes of Management), two autonomous and privately owned B-schools, and a university with an associated management institute.

The **student sample** consisted of 248 respondents:

- 152 full-time MBA students,
- 64 PGDM students, and
- 32 participants enrolled in executive education programs.

The sample size of the faculty amounted to 26 members of key business disciplines, namely, marketing, finance, strategic management, operations, and organization behavior. Faculty who took direct part in conducting hybrid courses during the period of data collection were chosen.

The stratified purposive sampling method was put to good use to make the sample diverse in terms of the type of programs, institutional governance (public/private), and geographic regions of India. This was because this would help put the findings into perspective based on delivery modes, infrastructural capabilities, and student demographics that are distinctive of Indian business schools.

## Data Collection Instruments

### Quantitative Survey

The survey instrument contained 42 items organized into five constructs:

- *Cognitive Engagement:* E.g., attention in hybrid courses, the capacity to use the coursework in the business environment, critical thinking problem solving.
- Engagement in Discussions Behavioral Engagement: involvement in discussions of hybrid cases, role-playing, and team-consulting projects.
- Motivating: self-motivation.Technological Readiness: the desire to use LMS systems, collaborative working tools, and simulators, e.g., Capsim or Marketplace Live.
- Perceived Learning outcomes: Learning of skills in business-related areas such as innovation in business decision making, negotiation, and learning of skills in financial modeling.

It surveyed previous models of engagement (Fredricks et al., 2004; Dixson, 2015) and added a domain-specific setting by offering examples of the answers to the business school setting. The answers were noted on a five-point Likert scale anchored at Strongly Disagree or Strongly Agree.

### Qualitative Interviews

Semi-structured interviews were conducted with 24 students (eight were in MBA, eight in PGDM, and eight in executive education) and 18 faculty members. When I read the interesting interview guide –

- Adaptations of the classic pedagogies of business schools to a hybrid environment,
- Barriers to emulating the classroom environment using the internet,
- How important was the technology in terms of either enabling or preventing participation?
- Beliefs about the ability to apply skills in the working environment.

The interviews took place on Zoom and Microsoft Teams, and each lasted between 45 and 60 minutes. Transcription: The interviews (with consent) were recorded and transcribed to be analyzed.

## Data Collection Procedures

The questionnaire was available through two online lanes of Google Forms and institutional LMS notifications. The links were also shared through email and

WhatsApp groups dedicated to specific programs in order to encourage participation. The community was followed within four weeks.

The participants in the interviews were selected among those who responded to the survey, and they were willing to give a follow-up interview. Faculty interviews were carried out according to teaching commitments, and student interviews were taken into account, including lectures, academic deadlines, and placement activities.

## Data Analysis

### Quantitative Analysis

The analysis of data was conducted with the help of SPSS v27. Descriptive statistics enabled a representation of the engagement levels, whereas inferential statistics, such as independent-sample t-tests and ANOVA, represented the differences between types of programs and students and faculty. Pearson correlations investigated the relationships between constructs of engagement and learning outcomes that have been perceived by students.

### Qualitative Analysis

Thematic analysis followed Braun and Clarke's (2006) six-step approach: familiarization, coding, theme development, reviewing, defining, and reporting. NVivo 12 was used to manage data and ensure systematic coding. Themes emerged around: (1) instructional strategies in hybrid business education, (2) enabling technologies and infrastructural gaps, and (3) the effectiveness of hybrid adaptations of interactive pedagogies.

### Validity, Reliability, and Ethical Considerations

To enhance instrument reliability, the survey was pre-tested on 18 students of the MBA and four faculty members of a non-sample institute. The alpha Cronbach varied between 0.78-0.91, per construct, and they were strong in internal consistency. When performing a qualitative analysis, inter-coder reliability was determined by using two independent researchers who coded 20 per cent of the transcripts and reached an agreement of 87 per cent.

In all the participating institutions, ethical approvals were sought. All participants signed informed consent and were assured that a certain level of confidentiality would be maintained through the use of anonymized identifiers. The information was kept on secure devices that were encrypted and will be held for five years, after which they are to be deleted securely. The respondents participated voluntarily and were allowed to withdraw at any step that they wanted without any punishment.

## Limitations of the Methodology

Although the purposive sampling warranted representation of most of the important types of programs, the conclusion might not be relevant to every single business school in India, specifically those with lesser infrastructure in technology. Also, self-reported engagement is prone to a response bias, and the accuracy of the interview depends on the participant's memory, which could have affected the study. However, the credibility of the results was increased by the triangulation of survey and interview data.

By combining the quantitative width and qualitative depth and by tapping MBA, PGDM, and executive education program students and faculty publicly and explicitly, the methodology places a crisp yet multidimensional face on hybrid learning at India-based business schools. The presence of pedagogies specific to business, case method (pedagogy) teaching, simulations, and role-plays on the methods of Darcy et al. makes the research highly imbued with the realities of management education and yet able to contribute to the general understanding of technology-enhanced learning.

The methodology chosen in the study is visually presented in Figure 2 and specifies the order of actions required to define research objectives to deliver recommendations. It starts by explaining the aim and scope of the study before it constructs a comprehensive framework that fits the context of hybrid learning in Indian business schools. The second phases entail a variety of participants, creating adequate instruments, e.g., surveys and interview protocols, as well as data collection, both quantitative and qualitative. It is then followed by systematic analysis whereby a statistical method and thematic codings are applied in order to identify recognitions and patterns. Completion of these steps entails synthesis of findings to give recommendations that can be used; thus, the methodology applied is broad in scope whilst being rooted in the roots of management teaching.

*Figure 2. Mapping the Path: Step-by-Step Research Process*

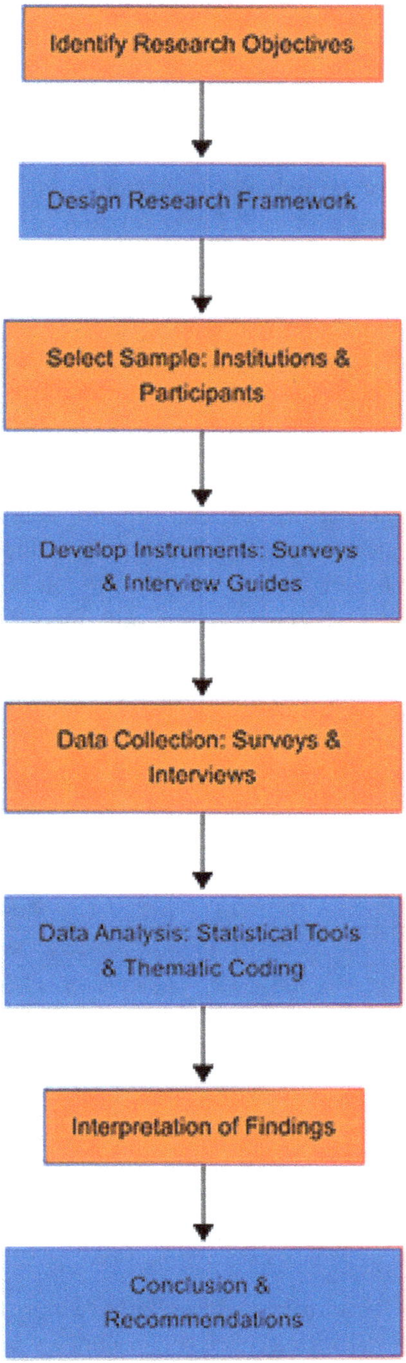


*Source: Author's illustration*

## Data Analysis

### Quantitative Findings: Engagement Scores, Usage Metrics

Some interesting trends emerged from the survey's data regarding how students participate in hybrid classes, based on the data from the survey of approximately 300 students and 60 faculty members in 10 business schools.

A five-point Likert scale was used for evaluation of the cognitive, emotional, and reactive aspects of engagement. The engagement score for all three dimensions was 3.87, so the majority of participants reported that they engaged in the study. Students were most engaged cognitively with an average score of 4.02 in the three areas assessed. There were 3.81 points for emotional engagement, and a score of 3.78 for behavioral engagement, including attendance, assignment completion, and involvement in the class.

The way hybrid tools were used varied significantly depending on the course being taught and the amount of institutional support received by the student body. The students who have attended the university were using Learning Management Systems most often (89% every week) and then video conference platforms like Zoom or Google Meet (82%). More than three-quarters of students stated that they use recorded lectures, forums, and quizzes at least three times per week.

The following table summarizes the average engagement ratings and tool usage frequencies:

*Table 1.*

| Engagement Type | Mean Score (out of 5) | Most Influential Factors |
|---|---|---|
| **Cognitive Engagement** | 4.02 | Flipped classes, self-paced content |
| **Emotional Engagement** | 3.81 | Teacher feedback, peer collaboration |
| **Behavioral Engagement** | 3.78 | Class attendance, participation in discussions |
| **Tool/Platform Used** | **Frequency of Use** | **Student Satisfaction (%)** |
| **LMS** | High | 85% |
| **Video Conferencing Tools** | High | 79% |
| **Discussion Forums** | Moderate | 64% |
| **Online Quizzes** | Moderate | 72% |
| **Virtual Simulations** | Low | 68% |

Besides, taking part in learning tasks was related to more flexible and technology-aware courses. Those who reported more self-reliance when managing their work and timetable generally stayed more involved in their studies.

The descriptive statistics of the student engagement scores as per several hybrid learning strategies established in business schools surveyed are summed up in Table 2. The measurement of engagement was done using a five-point Likert scale with its lowest tar (1= Very Low Engagement) and highest tar (5 = Very High Engagement). Findings show that flipped classrooms received the overall highest average engagement score, with virtual simulations and gamification-based methods having the next-best performance.

Table 2 shows the average student engagement according to the standard deviation of the different hybrid learning strategies achieved, and which ranked by order of student engagement as the best engagement scores. The greatest part of the interaction was in the Flipped Classroom variable (4.32, SD = 0.61), and then in Virtual Simulations (4.05, SD = 0.74) and Gamification (3.88, SD = 0.82). Blended Lecture Discussion (M=3.72, SD = 0.69), Offline (M=4.03, SD = 0.62) and Online Case Analysis (M=3.65 to SD = 0.77). The findings indicate that interactive and student-based approaches, specifically the Flipped Classroom and Virtual Simulations, have shown greater engagement of students in hybrid learning settings.

*Table 2. Student Engagement Scores by Hybrid Learning Strategy*

| Hybrid Learning Strategy | Mean Engagement Score (M) | Standard Deviation (SD) | Rank |
|---|---|---|---|
| **Flipped Classroom** | 4.32 | 0.61 | 1 |
| **Virtual Simulations** | 4.05 | 0.74 | 2 |
| **Gamification** | 3.88 | 0.82 | 3 |
| **Blended Lecture-Discussion** | 3.72 | 0.69 | 4 |
| **Online Case Analysis** | 3.65 | 0.77 | 5 |

## Qualitative Themes: Motivation, Collaboration, Barriers

The investigation of faculty interviews and student comments from the survey produced 3 main themes: motivation, the value of working together, and barriers faced.

Getting motivated became the most important factor that drove workers to be involved. It was observed that students felt more engaged with their studies when activities like Q&A, business simulation, and assignments reviewed by others were added to the course. Students showed they preferred modules infused with game elements and real-world discussions, which kept their studies lively and interesting.

Ten students mentioned that group work was a significant way to become more engaged in learning. Some faculty mentioned how breakout rooms, group projects, and students looking at each other's work online helped to bring student groups together. Students revealed that synchronous and asynchronous collaboration helped them stay in touch and made them responsible. It was noted that students preferred doing planning and online discussions, and having their presentations and feedback in person.

The lack of engagement was caused by difficulties with both the environment and the mind. The challenges that were talked about most often were:

- Having limited or unstable internet access, especially in Tier-II and Tier-III cities.
- Long asynchronous sessions or recordings of lectures that are not well organized will only add to "digital fatigue".
- And, especially courses with little synchronous interaction, lack real-time feedback.
- The faculty members showed an inconsistent digital skill level, which negatively influenced the implementation of the hybrid tool.

They admitted to struggling with an advanced digital platform learning curve and expressed a preference for professional development and peer learning forums to create instructional confidence in hybrid contexts.

## Case Highlights: Flipped Classrooms, Gamification, Virtual Simulations

The case studies demonstrated that different hybrid strategies helped increase student involvement in learning. The approaches in every case showed unique creativity in planning and fully utilized available technology.

One famous B-school in India turned the marketing course into a 'flipped classroom,' in which videos on marketing topics were provided for review at any time, while actual classroom sessions were for debate, questions, and applying the knowledge to available case studies. The number of students in live classes increased by 35%, and 84% confirmed that the program prepared them better and involved them more.

The course materials in a European management institute included gamification features in each week's assignment, such as quizzes and a leaderboard. Most participants said they became more motivated and recalled better. In addition, the students in this class improved their scores on concept-based tests by 12% more than those in regular classes. Students were noticed by faculty to persist more, since they completed optional bonus activities regularly.

A university in India incorporated virtual simulation into its operations management module. Students were required to go into teams to respond to new and changing business situations, and a significant proportion of students (92%) turned their assignments in on time, according to faculty, and student participation in debriefing also improved. The tasks were enjoyed by students since they reflected actual business scenarios.

These examples proved that getting learners to act, reflect, and work with others is best done in places that are both organized and adaptable. Furthermore, those institutions that spent on faculty training, educational design assistance, and technological equipment were more likely to have successful hybrid teaching.

# DISCUSSION

## Aligning Results with Constructivist and SDT Theories

This study's findings support the fundamental tenets of Constructivist Learning Theory and SDT and reinforce the trends identified in other institutions.

The constructivist theory further indicates that students who learn experientially and interactively fare well in flipped classrooms, simulations, and group work (Katsaris & Vidakis, 2021). Students doing a hybrid model reported greater levels of thinking activity than students using only one learning model. As a result, we can see that constructivist ideas are right in saying that students are active and engaged as they learn (Anthonysamy et al., 2020). The students in the flipped marketing course had access to all lessons and cases online, and together they applied their thinking and shared ideas through live discussions.

Also, all of SDT's psychological needs, autonomy, competence, and relatedness, were cited as main factors in student engagement (Kocdar et al., 2018). Asynchronous course students experienced more autonomy in their schedules, thus increasing their internal motivation (Dziuban et al., 2018). Internal motivation was also facilitated by formative assessments that provided immediate feedback and engagement opportunities (e.g., quizzes and simulations) (Picciano, 2021). Course resources provided students an opportunity to monitor their progress and build confidence in their ability to learn (Kumar & Nanda, 2019). Because students were able to collaborate and participate in real-time group projects with their instructor, Relatedness developed, helping them feel connected to others while learning remotely (Bond et al., 2021).

Specific students were also noted to be more engaged with their thoughts and emotions; these students generally liked learning through all of SDT's principles. These findings suggest that the experience of instruction matters more than just the content in instruction (Rasheed et al., 2020).

## Effective Strategies for Hybrid Engagement

It demonstrated numerous approaches that engaged students in hybrid business education (Liu et al., 2020). Each of the effective practices shared some common themes: they engaged students, were learner-centered, and incorporated technology with educational objectives.

Multiple studies showed that Flipped Classrooms work (Katsaris & Vidakis, 2021). Putting lectures on demand and conducting real discussions and exercises at the same time made learners more involved and better prepared for classes. It also helped with being organized and learning on one's own, which are useful in business jobs.

As it turned out, gamification was an absolute success. It caused evaluations to shift into being interesting tasks that give rewards, feedback, and enable people to compare themselves with others (Picciano, 2021). Therefore, students who were taught in a gamified manner were more motivated to study, memorization was better, and they participated in extra tasks that showed they were eager to learn outside the regular activities.

In operations and supply chain management, Virtual Simulations excelled in bridging the gap between student learning in a classroom setting and reality (Kumar & Nanda, 2019). The students were presented with opportunities to make business decisions and experience the outcomes, all in a safe environment. They facilitated aspects of teamwork, leadership, and critical thought, all key elements of student learning in business.

The most impactful part was being part of the teamwork, especially with students from other colleges of study or study areas (Anthonysamy et al., 2020). Team-based exercises forced students to utilize communication and collaboration skills. Hybrid platforms allowed students to respond to the assignments based on their time and also allowed them to participate in live presentations, exposing them to multiple ways of learning and exchanging ideas (Dziuban et al., 2018).

Additionally, the use of tools such as LMS dashboards, discussion boards, and peer reviews allowed learners to remain engaged in their lessons, both cognitively and emotionally (Kocdar et al., 2018). The most important action to achieve success was identifying how the tools aligned with students' learning objectives and expectations.

## Critical Reflections on Implementation Challenges

Even if hybrid learning is beneficial, some instructional and organizational difficulties still need to be solved to maintain students' participation (Rasheed et al., 2020).

A significant concern is called digital fatigue. Some students mentioned they felt mentally overwhelmed due to spending lots of time in front of screens, going through the same lessons remotely, and not having many ways to do their work. Lectures that are only recorded and have no feedback become dull for students (Picciano, 2021). It makes clear that having a mix of activities in class and short breaks is essential for students.

Many students also worried about Delayed Feedback, mainly in courses with numerous enrollees or limited time spent by teachers with students (Kumar & Nanda, 2019). Much of the value came from the swift feedback provided by machine testing, classmates' opinions, and educational instructors. Late feedback led to students' motivation decreasing and a feeling that there was less value in their work. Institutions need to discover ways to conduct low-stakes assessments automatically and to provide feedback systems for feedback that work for many students without being impersonal (Liu et al., 2020).

It was difficult for students from Tier-II and Tier-III cities to use technology and access the internet. Because many people used mobile devices, limited bandwidth made it hard for them to take part and achieve their best results (Dziuban et al., 2018). Such a gap made it difficult for students to stay connected, and this sometimes meant either missing a session or feeling uncomfortable about participating online. They should focus on including people in the digital world by setting up resource centers, lending out electronic devices, or offering downloadable materials for use at home.

It was found that having faculty ready to use technology was a barrier (Rasheed et al., 2020). A lot of instructors weren't trained in digital teaching and struggled with the difficulties of using the tools. As a result, course designs became unpredictable, and the platforms were used in ways that were not very effective. They liked using hybrid tools for classes, but became irritated when instructors did not use everything available or gave them similar content twice (Bond et al., 2021). In shifting to hybrid classes, institutions should make investing in faculty development a top concern.

How many students could manage themselves also made a big difference in their involvement (Katsaris & Vidakis, 2021). Students will have different success factors in strategies for time management, information management/assessment online, and independent study behaviours. Even in hybrid designs for learning in which students learn at different paces, they require some explicit orientation and peer mentors to assist with the learning (Anthonysamy et al., 2020).

This dictates that hybrid designs rely on everything in the ecosystem, including, but not limited to, technologies, environments, training the faculty, course design, course delivery, and student support.

Within the profession of business education, the discussed hybrid approaches of engagement can be connected with discipline-based pedagogical traditions that equip learners with the practice of managing professional issues in real life. Beyond business programs, flipped classrooms may be used to their advantage in preparing students through complex case studies, as in the Harvard style of discussion, where students break down complex market situations to understand the problem prior to in-class discussions and strategy-making exercises. The concept of gamification can be used to implement competitive business simulations, thereby enabling students to generate and experiment with strategies to enter the market in a risk-free, interactive simulation that reflects competition within the industry. Engineering courses in operations and supply chains often provide virtual simulations ideal to confront crisis management situations like demand shake-ups or supply chain incidents, where the student might get to engage in quick decision-making, resource allocation, and intergroup coordination under pressure. Beyond maintaining interest, hybrid learning makes it possible to explicitly develop valuable managerial skills because they are embedded right in the heart of pedagogical business school curricula.

## IMPLICATIONS

The results have important consequences for theories, leadership in business schools, and the way business topics are taught in classes. The greater use of hybrid learning means these insights help guide how a school is taught, the job description of educators, and the creation of inclusive classrooms.

### Theoretical Implications

#### Contribution to Engagement-Focused Learning Theory

The research demonstrates that student engagement in hybrid environments depends on their autonomy and the design features used. This research contributes to the multifaceted perspective by showing that hybrid learning engages every one of these essential aspects even more, having all of the important pedagogical and technological elements active together.

The analysis expands our knowledge of learning theories by proving that hybrid learning prompts students to use content on their own, think about the ideas, and meet with others for collaborative work. This repetitive pattern underlines that engagement changes and does not follow a basic step-by-step approach. As a result, the study provides greater insight into how learning environments affect students' ability to pay attention, become motivated, and engage in activities.

### Validation of Hybrid-Active Learning Connections

The research proved that using both approaches is very suitable for effective learning. Flipped classrooms, gamification, and simulations were proven effective to engage students more, let them understand the lessons better, and motivate them to be more involved in their classes. With these approaches, students could actively build up their knowledge in line with the values of constructivist theories.

Linking these active learning methods to SDT's basic needs of autonomy, competence, and relatedness gives more insight into why such environments support learning motivation. If intentionally designed with interaction, feedback, and independence in mind, hybrid models play a key role in improving education, going beyond just using technology.

## Managerial Implications

### Insights for Academic Administrators

For those in charge of academics and administration, the study gives clear guidelines for shaping and carrying out engagement-focused hybrid teaching. The fact is, relying only on digital tools does not mean learners will engage. Institutions, on the other hand, should make sure that their digital infrastructure, methods of instruction, and teachers' skills are all aligned as a whole.

It is suggested that engagement indicators ought to be recognized as important measures, together with regular completion data or test outcomes. LMS data helps administrators watch how students use the system, notice if anyone is losing interest, and offer help promptly to address it. Additionally, it would be helpful for schools to start "hybrid learning units" that assist with course design, assist teaching, and monitor instructional quality, to maintain uniformity among departments.

### Faculty Development and Instructional Redesign

One of the most useful points for a manager is that faculty should be helped to develop all the time. Such inconsistency was mostly the result of instructors not being familiar with how to teach in this environment or not applying the digital tools effectively. For this reason, institutions have to build reliable faculty development programs that include ongoing and effective learning activities.

People teaching should learn to create modular review lessons, make interactive content, add simulations, and follow students' engagement with feedback through analytics. Besides, faculty members can join professional circles where they can exchange ideas and develop new approaches. Making the workload more manageable and adding incentives for teachers who want to revise their courses for hybrid learning should also be part of managerial support.

## Practical Implications

### Scalable Hybrid Teaching Practices

This research also highlights teaching practices that institutions can use and repeat for students. Applying structured flipped classrooms, organized content, peers working in groups, and slow-release activities has worked well to raise engagement. They don't require much time or effort, and they can be adjusted for teachers with many students or diverse subjects.

Additionally, the study urges educators to rely on engagement diagnostics such as simple check-ins, pulse surveys, or engagement dashboards to support prompt changes in their teaching. Reflective questions placed in self-study sections and being responsible for groups can help students stay attentive to their learning.

Implementation is important and starts with using design thinking: build a student journey map, see where people might leave the course, and place reminders, small achievements, or quick feedback to motivate them.

### Recommendations for Inclusive, Tech-Enabled Learning Environments

Designing hybrid systems that include and are equitable is what the research highlights. The availability of stable internet, devices, or digital literacy was identified as a major barrier. So, practical reforms to ensure digital inclusion must focus on:.

- Offering course materials for download via offline use.
- It is also important to provide platforms that are mobile-friendly and have low data usage.
- Also, learning resource centers can be established on campuses and in communities.
- Emphasizing having multilingual and culturally sensitive content.

Peer mentoring, training for using technology, and time management sessions should be included in the overall environment. Students relying on self-paced lessons and those who find it hard to keep going need these support tools.

Moreover, those who design or teach hybrid courses should follow UDL standards, so that course materials are accessible to students from different backgrounds and with any preferred method of learning.

Therefore, these findings represent many aspects. They help build theory in academia, provide templates for the implementation of hybrids, and provide educators with grounded advice on incorporating technology into classroom practices. Further, the findings documented here are necessary findings concerning hybrid learning, as it will shape business education shortly. The findings create a strong foundation for transformational change, available to anyone and transferable between contexts.

## RECOMMENDATIONS

Recommendations based on the research findings and real-world observations of Indian and international business schools for student engagement in the hybrid learning environment are provided below.

### Policy-Level Recommendations

A national education authority, regulatory bodies such as the University Grants Commission (UGC), All India Council for Technical Education (AICTE), etc., must standardize and promote hybrid learning as a mainstream pedagogical model for business education at the policy level. This requires:

- Policy measures on digital equity, requiring institutions to make provisions for students from underserved geographies with provisions of infrastructure such as community digital labs or device lending schemes.
- Hybrid engagement metrics (frequency of student interaction, responsiveness to feedback, and usage of adaptive tools for teaching) into the accreditation frameworks for assessing a hybrid engagement model.
- Funding innovation and inclusion, including grants for hybrid course creation, tech-powered classroom model, and faculty certification programs in instructional design.
- National repositories of hybrid learning best practices: encouraging knowledge sharing among institutions by publishing examples of best practices and course structure design, lesson plans, and faculty testimonials on open, accessible platforms.

The aim of these recommendations is for hybrid learning quality standards to become institutionalized so that they can be widely adopted and last.

## Institutional and Pedagogical Suggestions

Hybrid learning implementation has to be viewed as a structural transformation, not a way to work around the issue in the interim, for educational institutions and their leadership teams. In this regard, B-schools need to think of:

- Establishing dedicated units for instructional design to serve as partners in departments to facilitate hybrid curriculum development, content (perhaps open) digitization, and formative assessment integration.
- To institute hybrid pedagogy training in faculty development programs that not only teach technical training, but also learning theory, engagement analytics, and development of interactive digital tools.
- Rather, it involves sewing digital navigational skills, collaborative tool usage, and time management skills into onboarding programs for students.
- Audits of the hybrid learning environments through faculty feedback, LMS engagement logs, and student pulse surveys to continuously improve the design.

Learning has to be transformed from content delivery to delivery of experiences if it is of pedagogical effect. It is involved in instructional planning.

- In this context, the structuring of learning in modular blocks is built in moments of interaction and self-assessment.
- Developing blended group activities that start online and end with a face-to-face reflection.
- The gamified tasks or competitive elements that increase engagement without the need for expensive platforms.

## For Educators and Digital Designers

Engagement is sustained by educators. Tutors and digital content creators should emphasize the following, according to the results from the study.

- Asynchronous content prioritization in clarity, brevity, and interactivity. Embedded questions, short videos, and real-world business case applications can help digest ideas and make them meaningful.

- Having a tiered feedback model, for example, auto-evaluated quizzes providing instant reinforcement and open-ended reflections, considered in weekly live sessions or forums.
- Part of course content creation should take advantage of Universal Design for Learning (UDL) principles, multiple means of representation (video, text, audio), flexible submission modes, and multilingual support where possible.
- It comprises forming a feedback culture, whereby students can express preferences and course administrators make timely changes to the course.

Finally, educators should be encouraged to form a community of practice where they share tools, techniques, and challenges related to the hybrid engagement with one another regularly. And innovation can be fostered and collective confidence and leadership built through peer mentoring and team teaching in hybrid settings.

## FUTURE DIRECTIONS

The hybrid movement is expected to continue reshaping the geography of business education, and therefore, sustained inquiry and adaptive strategies will have to continue. This study lays the foundation for engagement in hybrid models, leaving multiple avenues for further research and practice to obtain broader, deeper, and more inclusive engagement.

### Need for Cross-Disciplinary and Longitudinal Studies

There is a need for research projects that connect different fields and trace how gamers' habits change with time. Most of the studies performed, including this one, investigate only short or immediate areas of interest. Still, it may take a while for the full influence of hybrid learning to be seen in students' motivation, skills, and career preparation. Following cohorts over the years will show how prolonged use of hybrid settings affects students' learning progress, capacity to adapt, and what they eventually remember.

Likewise, when perspectives from education, behavioral science, technology, and management are merged through interdisciplinary research, the results tend to be more significant and helpful. By bringing together educational psychology and data analytics, we may discover that some actions usually lead to dropping out. This would help to address the problem sooner. For this reason, combining ideas from cognitive science, organizational behavior, and design thinking could form improved hybrid engagement models for business education.

## Addressing Cultural and Regional Variations in Hybrid Adoption

Scholarship also needs to direct more attention to how different cultural contexts and geographic regions adapt to and succeed in hybrid models. Factors in the way students are engaged in learning are their home environment, language differences, online access, and the perception of education by their cultural context. To learn more about South Asia and India, current studies should examine how different types of cultural contexts impact hybrid learning outcomes.

We need to have local studies that recognize the inequalities that exist in digital skills and school practices in urban, semi-rural, and rural locations. A study looking into hybrid learning at vernacular language colleges, community colleges, and regional business schools would provide a deeper understanding of the challenges and opportunities that hybrid education practice exists in other than in the most elite programs.

## Exploring Learning Outcomes Beyond Engagement

While engagement greatly matters in education, we should also investigate what other effects hybrid learning can have on learners. Depending on the role, business education needs critical thinking, the ability to work well with teams, good leadership skills, a focus on business, and knowledge of using technology. Further investigation of hybrid learning and its impact on these competencies can benefit educators and education policymakers. Beyond looking at students' job readiness, job market readiness, and alumni point of view about a program, we may look at how hybrid learning contributes to their overall success after leaving a program is equally of consideration. Accessing data from alumni, employers, and the outcomes of internships could inform the relationship between academic learning and professional practice. If the field embraces these new directions, hybrid business education can evolve into a full, data-driven, and flexible model that is beneficial to students in every corner of the world.

# CONCLUSION

The main purpose of this research chapter was to find out if hybrid models can help improve student engagement in business education. The study revealed the main ways in which learners use their minds, feelings, and actions in schools and online by using different research techniques. Flipped classroom, gamified learning, and virtual simulations became popular ways to teach, but challenges such as tiredness from using technology, weak feedback, and teachers' confidence in using online resources remained issues to address. Those findings confirmed that using hybrid models can address important aspects of students' motivation and the way they develop their knowledge.

In today's business education, students' engagement is necessary and cannot be ignored. This chapter points out that using both models is more than responding to events—it allows for the creative development of learning by focusing on interaction, independence, and using prior knowledge. When carefully built, hybrid education boosts students' love for learning, helps them build relationships with others, and encourages a more confident experience for all learners.

The examination points out that involving students in learning is an ongoing process affected by course design, instruction methods, and how prepared the institution is. Environments that include real tasks, immediate assistance, and group work can strongly boost both learning results and students' satisfaction. Similarly, institutions are required to invest in their faculty's growth and build settings that are welcoming to all learners.

With changes in business education, the course should be updated by centering on hybrid teaching and investing in the student. Institutions should adjust their approach by regarding technology as an active contributor to students' learning. The information from engagement metrics helps to revise the course, and faculty members should be helped to use innovative ways of teaching.

Business education will reach success if it renews its approach, accepts everyone, and continues to encourage its students. Nowadays, teachers use hybrid interaction to stir their students' interest in the topic and encourage them to take action in their studies.

In addition to increased student participation, hybrid approaches in business education offer ideal systems to develop those competencies most prized in the international business community. Based on the combination of real-time collaboration, data-driven critical analysis, and hands-on learning activities, the models empower students to grow to think strategically, adapt to challenges related to problem-solving, communicate effectively, and form cross-cultural cooperation. The experience of simulations, case-based projects, and teamwork supported by technology reflects the demands of the modern business setting and trains graduates to operate in conditions of uncertainty, innovate in a stressful context, and manage diverse teams. In this sense, hybrid learning is not a pedagogical experiment; it is a business strategy capable of creating industry-ready and business-flexible leaders that can deliver to the bottom line of business institutions in the ever-fickle business environment.

With hybrid models, tomorrow's business leaders can get more involved, notice their needs, and apply lessons to real-life situations.

## REFERENCES


Adedoyin, O. B., & Soykan, E. (2023). Covid-19 pandemic and online learning: The challenges and opportunities. *Interactive Learning Environments, 31*(2), 863–875. DOI: 10.1080/10494820.2020.1813180

Agarwal, S., & Kaushik, J. S. (2020). Student's perception of online learning during COVID pandemic. *Indian Journal of Pediatrics, 87*(7), 554–554. DOI: 10.1007/s12098-020-03327-7 PMID: 32385779

Almaiah, M. A., Al-Khasawneh, A., & Althunibat, A. (2020). Exploring the critical challenges and factors influencing the E-learning system usage during COVID-19 pandemic. *Education and Information Technologies, 25*(6), 5261–5280. DOI: 10.1007/s10639-020-10219-y PMID: 32837229

Ansari, J. A. N., & Khan, N. A. (2020). Exploring the role of social media in collaborative learning the new domain of learning. *Smart Learning Environments, 7*(1), 9. DOI: 10.1186/s40561-020-00118-7

Anthonysamy, L., Koo, A. C., & Hew, S. H. (2020). Self-regulated learning strategies and non-academic outcomes in higher education blended learning environments: A one decade review. *Education and Information Technologies, 25*(5), 3677–3704. DOI: 10.1007/s10639-020-10134-2

Aparicio, M., Bacao, F., & Oliveira, T. (2017). Grit in the path to e-learning success. *Computers in Human Behavior, 66*, 388–399. DOI: 10.1016/j.chb.2016.10.009

Baber, H. (2021). Modelling the acceptance of e-learning during the pandemic of COVID-19-A study of South Korea. *International Journal of Management Education, 19*(2), 100503. DOI: 10.1016/j.ijme.2021.100503

Basilaia, G., & Kvavadze, D. (2020). Transition to online education in schools during a SARS-CoV-2 coronavirus (COVID-19) pandemic in Georgia. *Pedagogical Research, 5*(4).

Beatty, B. (2019). *Hybrid-flexible course design*. EdTech Books. DOI: 10.59668/33

Bedenlier, S., Bond, M., Buntins, K., Zawacki-Richter, O., & Kerres, M. (2020). Facilitating student engagement through educational technology in higher education: A systematic review in the field of arts and humanities. *Australasian Journal of Educational Technology, 36*(4), 126–150. DOI: 10.14742/ajet.5477

Bhat, S., Raju, R., Bikramjit, A., & D'Souza, R. (2018). Leveraging e-learning through google classroom: A usability study. *Journal of Engineering Education Transformations*, 129-135.

Bond, M., Bedenlier, S., Marín, V. I., & Händel, M. (2021). Emergency remote teaching in higher education: Mapping the first global online semester. *International Journal of Educational Technology in Higher Education*, *18*(1), 50. DOI: 10.1186/s41239-021-00282-x PMID: 34778537

Bond, M., Buntins, K., Bedenlier, S., Zawacki-Richter, O., & Kerres, M. (2020). Mapping research in student engagement and educational technology in higher education: A systematic evidence map. *International Journal of Educational Technology in Higher Education*, *17*(1), 2. DOI: 10.1186/s41239-019-0176-8

Bozkurt, A., & Sharma, R. C. (2020). Emergency remote teaching in a time of global crisis due to CoronaVirus pandemic. *Asian journal of distance education*, *15*(1), i-vi.

Crawford, J., Butler-Henderson, K., Rudolph, J., Malkawi, B., Glowatz, M., Burton, R., ... & Lam, S. (2020). COVID-19: 20 countries' higher education intra-period digital pedagogy responses. *Journal of applied learning & teaching*, *3*(1), 1-20.

Deci, E. L., & Ryan, R. M. (2000). The" what" and" why" of goal pursuits: Human needs and the self-determination of behavior. *Psychological Inquiry*, *11*(4), 227–268. DOI: 10.1207/S15327965PLI1104_01

Deng, R., Benckendorff, P., & Gannaway, D. (2019). Progress and new directions for teaching and learning in MOOCs. *Computers & Education*, *129*, 48–60. DOI: 10.1016/j.compedu.2018.10.019

Dhawan, S. (2020). Online learning: A panacea in the time of COVID-19 crisis. *Journal of Educational Technology Systems*, *49*(1), 5–22. DOI: 10.1177/0047239520934018

Dumford, A. D., & Miller, A. L. (2018). Online learning in higher education: Exploring advantages and disadvantages for engagement. *Journal of Computing in Higher Education*, *30*(3), 452–465. DOI: 10.1007/s12528-018-9179-z

Dziuban, C., Graham, C. R., Moskal, P. D., Norberg, A., & Sicilia, N. (2018). Blended learning: The new normal and emerging technologies. *International Journal of Educational Technology in Higher Education*, *15*(1), 3. DOI: 10.1186/s41239-017-0087-5

Gelles, L. A., Lord, S. M., Hoople, G. D., Chen, D. A., & Mejia, J. A. (2020). Compassionate flexibility and self-discipline: Student adaptation to emergency remote teaching in an integrated engineering energy course during COVID-19. *Education Sciences*, *10*(11), 304. DOI: 10.3390/educsci10110304

Halverson, L. R., Graham, C. R., Spring, K. J., Drysdale, J. S., & Henrie, C. R. (2014). A thematic analysis of the most highly cited scholarship in the first decade of blended learning research. *The Internet and Higher Education, 20*, 20–34. DOI: 10.1016/j.iheduc.2013.09.004

Hew, K. F., Jia, C., Gonda, D. E., & Bai, S. (2020). Transitioning to the "new normal" of learning in unpredictable times: Pedagogical practices and learning performance in fully online flipped classrooms. *International Journal of Educational Technology in Higher Education, 17*(1), 57. DOI: 10.1186/s41239-020-00234-x PMID: 34778516

Hodges, C., Moore, S., Lockee, B., Trust, T., & Bond, A. (2020). The difference between emergency remote teaching and online learning. *EDUCAUSE Review, 27*(1), 1–9.

Huang, R. H., Liu, D. J., Tlili, A., Yang, J., Wang, H., & Zhang, M. (2020). Handbook on facilitating flexible learning during educational disruption: The Chinese experience in maintaining undisrupted learning in COVID-19 outbreak. *Beijing: Smart Learning Institute of Beijing Normal University, 46*.

Kahu, E. R. (2013). Framing student engagement in higher education. *Studies in Higher Education, 38*(5), 758–773. DOI: 10.1080/03075079.2011.598505

Katsaris, I., & Vidakis, N. (2021). Adaptive e-learning systems through learning styles: A review of the literature. *Advances in Mobile Learning Educational Research, 1*(2), 124–145. DOI: 10.25082/AMLER.2021.02.007

Keržič, D., Tomaževič, N., Aristovnik, A., & Umek, L. (2019). Exploring critical factors of the perceived usefulness of blended learning for higher education students. *PLoS One, 14*(11), e0223767. DOI: 10.1371/journal.pone.0223767 PMID: 31751345

Kocdar, S., Karadeniz, A., Bozkurt, A., & Buyuk, K. (2018). Measuring self-regulation in self-paced open and distance learning environments. *International Review of Research in Open and Distance Learning, 19*(1). Advance online publication. DOI: 10.19173/irrodl.v19i1.3255

Kumar, V., & Nanda, P. (2019). Social media in higher education: A framework for continuous engagement. [IJICTE]. *International Journal of Information and Communication Technology Education, 15*(1), 97–108. DOI: 10.4018/IJICTE.2019010107

Liu, Q., Geertshuis, S., & Grainger, R. (2020). Understanding academics' adoption of learning technologies: A systematic review. *Computers & Education, 151*, 103857. DOI: 10.1016/j.compedu.2020.103857

Picciano, A. G. (2021). Theories and frameworks for online education. *A guide to administering distance learning, 21*(3), 166-190.Rasheed, R. A., Kamsin, A., & Abdullah, N. A. (2020). Challenges in the online component of blended learning: A systematic review. *Computers & Education*, *144*, 103701.

Chapter 6

# Blended and Hybrid Learning Approaches in Business Education:
## Innovating Flexible and Interactive Pedagogy

**Surjit Singha**
https://orcid.org/0000-0002-5730-8677
*Kristu Jayanti University, India*

## ABSTRACT

*This chapter explores integrating blended and hybrid learning models in business education to enhance flexibility, accessibility, and engagement. Grounded in constructivist, sociocultural, and cognitive load theories, it presents the FOT Model—Flexible Instructional Design, Outcomes-Focused Pedagogy, and Technology-Enabled Interaction—as a framework for optimal hybrid learning. Drawing on case studies from Harvard Business School, IIM Bangalore, Wharton, IE Business School, and Kristu Jayanti (Deemed to be University), it showcases best practices in aligning pedagogy, technology, and assessment to create scalable, inclusive, and active learning environments. Benefits like personalization, real-world skill development, and scalability are discussed alongside challenges like digital equity, faculty readiness, and instructional quality. The chapter concludes by examining emerging trends—AI, immersive technologies, and predictive analytics—and proposing future research directions to strengthen the sustainability and effectiveness of hybrid learning for industry-ready graduates.*

DOI: 10.4018/979-8-3373-7523-6.ch006

## INTRODUCTION

Higher education has experienced a tremendous shift in recent years due to new technologies, globalization, and changes in learner expectations. No place is that shift more intense than in business education, a growing number of whose students are being reached with blended and hybrid learning solutions to meet the needs of varied, tech-savvy, career-focused learners (Means et al., 2014). These pedagogical innovations represent a promising alternative to conventional classroom teaching by harnessing the potential of face-to-face interaction and combining it with the convenience and scalability of digital media (Garrison & Vaughan, 2008).

Blended learning, by definition, is a structured amalgam of face-to-face and online instruction that allows students to experience synchronous instruction and learning in a classroom while working through asynchronous digital content (Graham, 2006). Hybrid learning (often synonymous with the term blended learning, which is subtly different) is distinguished by including synchronous online experiences in combination with face-to-face or asynchronous work in an adaptable, learner-centred approach (Moore, 2013). These strategies enable personalized learning, expand access and promote increased student voice — attributes that are becoming more important in today's volatile, uncertain, complex and ambiguous (VUCA) business environment.

The COVID-19 pandemic accelerated the demand for hybrid models and exposed the promise and pitfalls of technology-enabled teaching and learning (Crawford et al., 2020). Higher education institutions with a prior investment in digital infrastructure and faculty development were in a position to scale more quickly. In contrast, those with limited resources were on steep learning curves with unequal student impacts (Allen & Seaman, 2017). Therefore, business education and the various options of delivery modes are now in a new era, and they are taking a fresh look at the direction, structural design, and how education is delivered to meet the demands for skills and competencies in the Fourth Industrial Revolution (World Economic Forum, 2020).

Moreover, this is true in business education, too; the move towards blended and hybrid flexibility is part of the broader orientation to active learning and outcomes- or metrics-based education. Business Schools are tasked to develop students not only to have IT knowledge but also soft skills, ethical thinking, multicultural teamwork and the ability to make data-driven decisions (Kolb, 1984). Such learning objectives demand a more dynamic pedagogy that supports learning through experience, peer interaction, and immediate feedback—all facilitated by a hybrid format.

Furthermore, the shift towards flexible and equitable digital learning models has made hybrid approaches essential to enable non-traditional learners to access higher education (e.g. working adults, international learners, and those in remote areas) (UNESCO, 2023). Blended and hybrid learning models can promote inclusivity, decrease student attrition rates, and develop a stronger, more robust educational environment (Garrison et al., 2000).

In designing blended and hybrid business education models, incorporating values-based frameworks such as mindfulness, compassion, and Ubuntu can further enhance learner engagement and social connectedness. Mindfulness cultivates present-moment awareness, improving focus and reflective capacity; compassion deepens empathy and ethical responsibility; and Ubuntu reinforces community interdependence and collaborative learning. Embedding these principles into hybrid learning design promotes academic achievement and fosters moral development, intercultural competence, and socially responsible leadership—qualities essential for thriving in diverse, globalized business environments (Singha, 2024).

Incorporating mindfulness and meditation practices within blended and hybrid learning frameworks can significantly enhance students' cognitive performance, emotional regulation, and sustained attention. These approaches contribute to improved academic outcomes and build resilience, intrinsic motivation, and social competence—traits vital for navigating complex business environments. When educators model mindfulness themselves, they reinforce a culture of reflective, balanced, and holistic learning. Such integration aligns with learner-centred design principles, ensuring that hybrid education supports intellectual growth and overall well-being, preparing students for adaptive, future-oriented leadership roles (Singha, 2025).

This chapter investigates the theoretical underpinnings, practical implementation and possible future development of blended and hybrid teaching in a business context. Based on case studies of existing models, institutional case examples, and best practices, it explores how these models are developed and implemented to support student engagement, instructional quality, and graduate employability. The chapter also considers the barriers to the transition - including faculty willingness, technology availability, and quality control - to provide practical solutions to teachers, administrators, and policy-makers.

This chapter adds to the emerging educational debate confronting transformation in the digital world by deconstructing the hybrids from pedagogical perspectives and anchoring them in business education objectives. It argues for a new paradigm that makes flexibility, interactivity , and learner-centredness central to instructional design, not as a temporary accommodation but as a fundamental strategy for the future of higher education.

## Background

The evolution of digital technology and its integration into higher education has been a significant catalyst for pedagogical innovation. The acceleration in blended and hybrid learning models in business education has come about by a convergence of factors such as globalization, the diversification of student demographics, and increased demand for lifelong learning opportunities (Allen & Seaman, 2017). These instructional models combine the best of both worlds: the traditional face-to-face interaction with digital asynchronous content delivery and student interaction capabilities that can extend across institutions and provide access to a broader and more diverse population of learners (Garrison & Vaughan, 2008).

The COVID-19 pandemic reiterated the need for robust digital readiness and potential to pivot to online or hybrid formats gracefully without compromising the quality of education provided (Crawford et al., 2020). Those business schools that had already invested in digital infrastructure and supported some online pedagogies found it much easier and quicker to adapt. Consequently, hybrid learning is not conceptualized as an optional supplement but as the foundation of educational resilience (UNESCO, 2023).

Additionally, the rise of Industry 4.0 and an ongoing digital transformation across sectors have helped shape curriculum development in business education. Today, employers require graduates who understand business basics and are agile with digital technologies, virtual collaboration tools, and data-supported decision-making processes (World Economic Forum, 2020). Good blended learning and hybrid learning models are authentic learning experiences that mirror many realities in the workplace (Moore, 2013).

According to institutional studies, hybrid learning adoption is positively linked with higher student performance, student retention, and student satisfaction (Means et al, 2014). Nevertheless, to realize aspiration and utilize such models, accompanying institutional support regarding faculty development, learning technologies, and pedagogical frameworks is necessary (Ibrahim & Nat, 2019). Faculty must also change from content deliverer to a learning facilitator, representing a fundamental re-conception of course design and student involvement.

Blended learning is a transparent approach to bridging education gaps, like those from the global south, where the spatial predisposition is referred to as areas with poor access to higher education. Mobile learning, low-bandwidth content, and open educational resources (OERs) are used to maintain equity of access to quality business education (Selwyn, 2020). Although problems such as the digital gap remain, progress in the direction of hybrid studying implies a longer-term change to the design and supply of enterprise education.

Integrating technological, institutional and social changes propels blended and hybrid learning in business education. They are responsive modifications to previous models in times of crisis and proactive approaches for simulating innovation, accessibility and innovation in a fast-paced, continually changing world.

Before 2020, blended and hybrid learning in business education was a gradual evolution, with many initiatives being trialed as complementary to more traditional delivery. It was the trend of globalization, growth of adult learning and slow convergence of the LMS platforms which fostered adoption, but uptake was patchy. COVID-19 was an inflexion point: academic institutions were forced to pivot rapidly, so hybrid delivery went from a niche complement to a strategic imperative. Amid — and likely partly due to — the pandemic, surveys show that more than half of faculty and students now anticipate hybrid modalities to be included in standard offerings. Such a transition uncovered broader issues — low levels of digital literacy, unequal access to bandwidth, lack of expertise in designing hybrid curricular materials, and obstacles to maintaining student engagement online. Overcoming these challenges will ultimately require an institutional-level coordinated approach: faculty development, IT infrastructure investment, student orientation, and continuous evaluation to ensure hybrid teaching maximizes equitable and engaging academic rigor.

## Theoretical Framework

Theoretical constructs of learning regarding interaction, engagement and knowledge construction gave rise to blending and flipping in business education. Among these is Constructivist Learning Theory, which posits that as the learner learns, they construct knowledge for themselves as a result of training (Piaget, 1952; Vygotsky, 1980). When teaching and learning are saturated online, constructivist teaching and learning emphasize the belief that students learn in meaningful ways through opportunities to make choices and explore, collaborate, and apply content in various digital and face—to—face environments.

Vygotsky's sociocultural theory especially emphasizes the role of social interactions in cognitive development. It introduces the concept of the Zone of Proximal Development (ZPD), which posits that learning is optimized when one is being led by someone more knowledgeable (Vygotsky, 1980). In many instances, blended and hybrid learning contexts fall into this framework, with peer learning, group projects, and teacher facilitation stitched together in digital and physical spaces.

Another model that builds on constructivism is Community of Inquiry (CoI) (Garrison et al., 2000), which has increasingly been used to inform the design of online and hybrid courses. The CoI model has three core components: cognitive presence– the extent to which learners can create and validate meaning through critical reflection and discourse; social presence – the ability of learners to project themselves socially and emotionally in a community of inquiry, openly communicate in a trusting environment, and develop interdependence with other participants in the process of learning; and teaching presence – the design, facilitation, and direction of cognitive and social processes in a way that realizes personally meaningful and educationally worthwhile learning outcomes (Garrison, Anderson, & Archer, 2000).

In hybrid education models, these presences dynamically converge, producing a collaboration-rich learning space.

Cognitive load theory (Sweller, 1988) also helps explain how learners manage information in multimedia settings. This would mean that by regulating intrinsic, extraneous, and germane cognitive load, faculty members could create hybrid learning experiences that would promote retention and transfer of learning. This theory is also highly relevant concerning digital spaces, where students might be flooded with multimedia or other chaotically arranged postings.

These theoretical bases create a rich soil for blended or hybrid instruction design. Both tend to highlight a learner-centered approach to pedagogy, the role of dialogue, and the judicious structuring of content and activities in promoting meaningful learning.

## CONCEPTUAL FRAMEWORK

The theoretical foundations for adapting blended or hybrid learning to business education is steeped in three integrated dimensions: flexible instructional design, technology-enabled learning interaction, and outcome-focused pedagogy. These dimensions are consistent with modern educational goals of active learning, student agency, and real-world relevance.

Hybrid and blended models also emphasize customizing course content and delivery for varied student groups (i.e., a flexible instructional design). Flexibility in time and modality is displayed through asynchronous content delivery, curriculum structures, and flexible assessment types (Moore, 2013). This technique allows students to proceed with learning individually and enables faculty to utilize differentiated instructional practices (Means et al., 2014).

Use of Technology to Enhance Learner Engagement The effective use of technology to engage learners in a participatory digital learning environment is about engaging students in the dialogue and testing the dialogue for questions, interrogating both the question and the answer, and engaging in the process of questioning in a manner which is critical, creative, reflective, and challenging (Williams, & Bower, 2025; Cornell University, 2025). Discussion forums, simulators, real-time polling and virtual whiteboards enable the communication process and the active engagement of participants in higher-order thinking tasks (Hrastinski, 2009). LMS integration also means instructors can access analytics to track student engagement and respond accordingly (Martin et al., 2020).

Outcomes-Based Pedagogy: Team-Based Learning (TBL) and hybrid or online courses are well-suited for mapping conceptual design to specific competencies in the real world. Business education specifically profits from experiential learning activities, including simulations, project-based learning, or case studies. These activities equip students with the skills to operate within ambiguous business environments, work in teams, and apply theoretical learning in industrial settings (Kolb, 1984).

These three dimensions, in combination, develop a composite framework that facilitates personal and engaging as well as relevant learning experiences in business education. It also offers a strategic tool for examining blended and hybrid models' design, development, and operational success in varying educational settings.

*Figure 1. Conceptual Framework for Blended/Hybrid Learning in Business Education:*

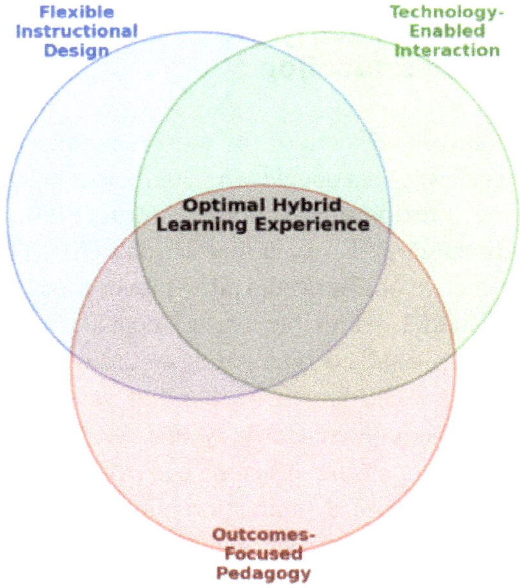


Flexible Instructional Design (FID), Outcomes Focused Pedagogy (OFP), Technology Enabled Interaction (TEI), Optimal Hybrid Learning Experience (OHLE)

Proposed conceptual perspective on blended/hybrid learning in business education, integrating three domains: Flexible Instructional Design, Technology-Enabled Interaction, and Outcomes-Focused Pedagogy (i.e., the center indicates the optimal hybrid learning experience). Centre overlapping is optimal blended/hybrid learning, where delivery invocations (i.e., Flexible delivery, Rich digital engagement, and Competency-based pedagogy) perfectly fit into each other, giving rise to personalized, interactive, and career-relevant learning experiences.

This 3D integration is captured in a TPACK-like (Elmaadaway & Abouelenein, 2023) Venn diagram. In TPACK, the intersection of Technological, Pedagogical, and Content Knowledge enveloped by three intersecting circles symbolizes the best possible teaching competence that is achieved when all three domains are aligned for the best effect. Thus, the Flexible Instructional Design, Technology-Enabled Interaction, and Outcomes-Focused Pedagogy correspond to equivalent positions in this model, and the point of intersection in the center—(C)— (Optimal Hybrid Learning Experience) conveys the result of balanced synthesis between these dimensions. Like the integrated zone of TPACK, this center overlap tends to be where technology, pedagogy, and content instructional capacity come together to yield the highest quality business education outcomes.

## The FOT Model for Blended/Hybrid Learning in Business Education

Following the framework of some of the most recognized integrative models, such as TPACK (Elmaadaway & Abouelenein, 2023), the chapter introduces a new model, the FOT model (Flexible Instructional Design (FID), Outcomes-Focused Pedagogy OFP, and Technology-Enabled Interaction (TEI). These three key areas are the essentials of effective business education blended and hybrid learning. The three pillars of the FOT model — Flexible Instructional Design, Outcomes-Focused Pedagogy and Technology-Enabled Interaction — are represented in the bottom row of the architecture, as each domain is its pillar yet interdependent. Flexible Instructional Design allows content delivery and assessment to be bifurcated; Outcomes-Focused Pedagogy ensures learning activities align with business competencies; and Technology-Enabled Interaction allows multi-faceted digital tools to stimulate active participation. The optimal hybrid learning experience (OHLE) resides in the perfect overlap of these three areas – the intersection of flexibility, engagement, and competency alignment. Similar to the overlaid region of the TPACK knowledge model, deeper learning environments in the FOT model, characterized by OHLE, reflect the most integrated levels of synergistic knowledge, occurring when learner, educator, and technology co-create unique, interactive, experiential or career-oriented, and individualized pedagogical environments. The framework offers a schematic that helps educators visualize a hybrid course at the pedagogical and technological levels.

## RESEARCH PROBLEM

Business education is using blended and hybrid learning models with increasing frequency. But they need to do much better about focusing on the problems of implementing and sustaining such initiatives and evaluating their effects on student learning. However, one of the biggest challenges is the lack of a standardization tool that could seamlessly combine face-to-face and online formats. Many schemes have been attempted to integrate our domains, yet these efforts tend to be limited and very different from the approach to design, implementation, and assessment of the integration (Boelens et al., 2017).

Common barriers are faculty preparedness and institutional support. There may be insufficient professional development in instructional design and educational technology to help faculty design interactive and student-centered hybrid courses (Porter et al., 2014). In addition, the absence of infrastructure support — including access to IT tools, instructional design support, and ongoing capacity-building — in several institutions complicates the move to hybrid modes (Moore,2013).

Another trend is the growing debate around the digital divide and how discrepancies in technology access can affect students' participation and achievement. Though hybrid delivery models are praised for their flexibility, students from disadvantaged socio-economic backgrounds or rural placements may be disadvantaged by low internet access, low digital literacy, or an inappropriate learning environment (Van Dijk, 2019). These factors can dramatically impact learning equity and the inclusivity of hybrid learning strategies.

In addition, there is a dearth in the extant literature that empirically explores the lasting effects of hybrid learning in business education—most studies look at short-term outcomes, such as student satisfaction and course completion rates. It has also been recommended to conduct a longitudinal study on the effect of hybrid learning on skill set, employability, and career readiness (Bernard et al, 2009; Means et al, 2014).

For this reason, the research question focuses on identifying practices for designing, developing and evaluating the hybrid learning models in business education. Understanding that will be vital to confirming that these methods bring about better academic attainment, greater equality of opportunity and sustained employment success.

## UNDERSTANDING BLENDED AND HYBRID LEARNING

Blended and hybrid learning share much terminology and may be almost synonymous, but they possess different formal and pedagogical parameters guiding learning design and the student experience. Blended learning has historically been used to describe the joining of face-to-face and online instructional approaches in a complementary fashion. Students are usually required to attend class meetings at specific times, with additional student time spent on asynchronous online activities (Graham, 2006). On the other hand, hybrid learning combines synchronous and asynchronous learning in a responsive medium where students can attend face-to-face or participate online concurrently, affording them much flexibility (Means et al., 2014).

However, one of the greatest strengths of both models is that they work in multiple teaching situations. For example, business studies regularly call for experiential learning through simulations, presentations and group work. Hybrid and blended formats are ideal for these usages because real-time collaboration can be integrated (e.g., Zoom, Microsoft Teams) along with asynchronous discussion forums (e.g., Canvas, Moodle) (Bryson & Andres, 2020; Allen & Seaman, 2017). The concurrent model allows for immediate interaction and feedback, and the time-separated aspect allows students to utilize material at their convenience to enhance deeper learning (Hrastinski, 2009).

The effectiveness of these learning models is also highly dependent on teaching design. One common approach to blended learning, the flipped classroom model, involves having students absorb lectures and readings before class to enable them to spend time together in class working on collaborative, constructivist, problem-based activities as a class (Bishop & Verleger, 2013). This model supports active learning by enabling class time for meetings, discourse, and hands-on learning. Several studies have found a higher level of retention, increased scores, and better satisfaction in flipped or hybrid classrooms than in traditional classrooms (O'Flaherty & Phillips, 2015).

In addition, hybrids have demonstrated potential for enhancing access for "non-traditional" students, including adult and part-time students and those with family caregiving obligations. These models mitigate geographic and time constraints so students can access them from different locations and times, contributing to educational equality (Van Dijk, 2019). However, this flexibility also comes with issues associated with self-regulation, digital literacy, and social presence, which all need to be accounted for by carefully designed e-learning systems and support for learning (Boelens et al., 2017).

From an institutional standpoint, blended or hybrid learning depends on the technology and culture. Faculty training, curricular redesign, and administrative infrastructure are necessary to implement these learning models on a larger scale (Porter et al., 2014). Institutions that have effectively introduced these teaching models report higher student enrollments, lower drop-out rates and greater engagement of students (Bernard, 2009; Moore, 2013).

Blended and hybrid learning is the path to innovation in education. These models manifest 21st-century teaching and learning (versus the previous century's model of the teacher at the front of the class, imparting knowledge to students), one that stresses student-directed learning, flexible learning, and authentic teaching and learning. As schools negotiate post-pandemic shifts, hybrid and blended models will likely continue to be a focus for the strategic direction of business education.

## ROLE OF TECHNOLOGY

Technology is a game-changer for blended and hybrid learning in business education. It supports flexible content delivery and gains interactivity, personalization, assessment and data-driven decision-making. Appropriate use of learning technologies can yield better student learning outcomes and institutional effectiveness if adapted to pedagogical goals (Martin et al., 2020).

A central aspect of hybrid learning is the Learning Management System (LMS), including platforms like Moodle, Canvas, or Blackboard. LMS systems are key to delivering a course, from a centralized repository of materials to a place where students go to read/watch/listen to materials, turn in work, have discussions, and see where they stand in the course. These tools in LMS platforms enable formative and summative assessments (e.g., grade books, quizzes, rubrics and analytics dashboards) (Al-Fraihat et al., 2020).

Hybrid learning systems increasingly incorporate AI and machine learning technology to help personalize the learning experience. Intelligent tutors, adaptable quizzes, and chatbots assist in diagnosing disease-based targeting feedback and guidance (Holmes et al., 2019). These systems use learner data to personalize teaching and learning for each student, tailoring learning to close gaps and maintain motivation. Predictive analytics allows educators to get involved with at-risk students early in their education for better retention and success rates (Ifenthaler & Yau, 2020).

Another vital aspect is collaborative technologies. Video conferencing apps like Zoom, Google Meet, and Microsoft Teams have facilitated synchronous activities—like taking a class, participating in a breakout session, or viewing a live video. Such asynchronous technologies as discussion forums, Wikis, and Padlets enable reflective thought and the construction of community between lessons (Hrastinski, 2009). LABS, Journalspace.com 11 technology tools can positively impact cognitive, social, and teaching presence, with these incorporated tools assisting the Community of Inquiry model (Garrison et al., 2000).

Leaderboards, badges, and progress indicators are examples of gamification to improve motivation and engagement in blended courses. Coupled with learning objectives, these aspects motivate achievement and promote peer competition and cooperation (Deterding et al., 2011). Likewise, VR and AR provide immersive experiences that can simulate real-life organizations and allow learners to get hands-on practice in a safe way where businesses can be emulated (Radianti et al., 2020).

## Pros and Cons of Technology in Hybrid Learning

Table 1: Summary of benefits and challenges of EdTech integration in business education

| Pros | Cons |
|---|---|
| Flexibility of access for diverse learners | Unequal access to devices/internet (digital divide) |
| Interactive tools increase engagement and collaboration. | Faculty/student training needs |
| Learning analytics enable personalization and early interventions | Risk of technical failures disrupting learning |
| Gamification and simulations enhance motivation. | Potential reduction in social presence if not designed intentionally |

Digital tools also support an ongoing and multimodal assessment. E-portfolios, simulations, digital badges and quizzes currently assist in assessing students' work for the school and their use. Platforms like Kahoot! and Socrative promote active learning through teachers receiving instant feedback to assess student involvement and adjust teaching during in-session (Bicen & Kocakoyun, 2018).

However, the effective use of EdTech in hybrid teaching depends on institutional capability and digital equity. Faculty need clear training in how to incorporate and use technology in teaching. Students must, however, have equal access to dependable internet service and devices and be adequately supported to effectively avail themselves of the benefits of digital restructuring (UNESCO, 2023). If these fundamental needs are not met, the promise of technology to democratize education might not be fulfilled.

Technology underpins blended or hybrid learning rather than being an add-on. Technology improves access, equity, and engagement in business education when coordinated with sound instructional design and policy.

# DESIGNING ACTIVE LEARNING STRATEGIES

Active learning forms the core of the blended or hybrid learning experience, particularly in business education, where the emphasis is on the applied and the critical. Active learning approaches advocate for students' involvement in the learning process by using discussion, problem-solving, teaching of peers, case studies, simulations, and group learning projects (Bonwell & Eison, 1991). These models of instruction differ from traditional lectures because they transfer the responsibility of learning from teacher to student and activate deeper cognitive processing and longer-term retention (Freeman et al., 2014).

The flipped classroom model is one of the most popular active learning strategies. In this approach, students come to class having encountered content through videos, readings, or interactions and then use class time to practice with concepts by doing problems, engaging in debates, and having discussions (Bishop & Verleger, 2013). This approach has proven effective in business disciplines—finance, marketing, and management—where applied learning is critical. Their meta-analyses, such as that of Strelan et al. (2020), showed that flipped classrooms lead to significantly better learning outcomes than conventional methods.

Another good way is through case-based learning, which is especially common within a business school. Case Studies – These can provide students with real-life scenarios or simulated business problems where they have to pinpoint the issue, provide solutions, and give reasons for the solutions. Through a case-centric method, we develop problem-solving skills and an understanding of the many facets of the business world (Herreid & Schiller, 2013). With their hybrid implementation, case discussions could be introduced asynchronously through LMS forums and synchronously through video conferencing, allowing for reflection and participation among all parties.

Another effective active learning strategy we have utilized is simulations and role-plays. Business simulations allow students to oversee a simulated company, react to market conditions, and compete against other classmates in a shifting environment. These experiential learning activities support risk-free trial and error and strategic approaches (Salas et al., 2009). Tools like Harvard Business Publishing's simulations or Capsim have been adapted into these hybrid models to offer these experiences virtually.

Approaches that leverage collaborative learning—like group projects, peer review, and problem-based learning— work exceptionally well in a hybrid setting. Cloud-based applications, including Google Workspace, Miro and Microsoft Teams, allow students to co-create content and share real-time feedback. According to the literature, students engaged in collaborative learning online are more satisfied and learn better group work skills (Laal & Ghodsi, 2012; Hrastinski, 2009).

Active learning techniques can only work if there is a high degree of structured support and regular feedback. Formative assessment tools such as low-stakes quizzes, reflective journals, and peer assessments allow students to track their individual performance progress and identify weaknesses. Online tools like Kahoot! Quizlet and Edpuzzle can support teachers in gamifying tests and giving immediate feedback, thus enhancing engagement and motivation among pupils (Grier, 2021).

In addition, active learning activities must consider Universal Design for Learning (UDL) principles. UDL promotes multiple ways of engaging, representing, and expressing to reach all learners (including those with disabilities) across diverse cultural backgrounds (CAST, 2024). Implementing UDL in hybrid models allows all students to engage in relevant and equitable ways.

Practical strategies for active learning in blended and hybrid learning environments must be designed with pedagogy and technology integrated well. These approaches encourage academic success and help business students learn how to navigate a complex world of work by promoting interaction, cooperation and critical analysis.

## ADVANTAGES

Blended and hybrid learning has many benefits that can increase teaching efficacy, learner engagement, and institutional flexibility. These potentials become relevant for business education, which values experiential teaching, skill development, and multi-disciplinary approaches that resemble the workplace (Brown et al., 2020).

**Flexibility and accessibility:** Blended and hybrid models allow plenty of flexibility for learners and teachers; this is one of their key advantages. They allow students to access class material from anywhere, anytime, accommodating students' different schedules and learning styles (Means et al., 2014), which is quite simply where part-time working and career students can find support. Additionally, hybrid models are inclusive since they eliminate the barriers for learners from remote or disadvantaged backgrounds (Van Dijk, 2019).

**Personalized Learning:** Using digital tools and analytics, hybrid learning enables a more personal learning experience. AI systems, in which the system does not deliver the content itself but serves as a means for personalizing content based on student progress, preferences and performance, can make the learning environment more interactive and adaptive (Ifenthaler & Yau, 2020). This personalized learning strategy promotes learner independence and allows differentiated instruction suitable for mixed-ability classrooms.

**Increased Student Engagement:** Evidence suggests that learning in these blended environments—including “flipped” lessons where the introduction of content occurs outside of class time before in-class activities incorporating the technology-supported active learning strategies—leads to increased student engagement in the classroom (Freeman et al., 2014). Multimodal presentation elements—such as video lectures, interactive simulations, live discussions, and interdisciplinary collaboration—address diverse learning styles and promote cognitive and affective engagement. Apps for polling, live chatting, and breakout rooms promote active engagement and peer interactions.

**Increased Learning:** Multiple meta-analysis studies have indicated that the likelihood of more learning (based on student achievement scores) is greater when students are provided instruction in a blender or hybrid model as compared to direct instruction in a traditional face-to-face or fully online class (Bernard et al., 2009; Means et al., 2014). Combining asynchronous and synchronous elements enables the student to master and use the content in real-time, promoting deeper and stronger knowledge retention.

**Scalable and sustainable delivery:** Blended and hybrid delivery are both eminently scalable, allowing institutions to continue to increase the number of students they teach without adding to physical footprint or infrastructure costs. Digital content can be reused, modified, and repurposed for broader dissemination over sustained periods, which renders them cost-efficient in the long term (Moore, 2013). Hybrid instruction also decreases the need for physical space, which is advantageous, particularly in urban or resource-limited contexts.

**Gain Real-World Skills:** Hybrid learning environments mirror today's workplace, where students learn to communicate digitally, work together remotely, manage time wisely and deliver presentations via digital meetings. These authentic experiences reflect the real business world while enabling learners to develop employability skills such as digital literacy, communication, teamwork and self-directed learning (World Economic Forum, 2020).

## CHALLENGES AND LIMITATIONS

Now that the pros and cons of blended and hybrid learning are clear, note that they are not without a particular set of challenges and limitations. Overcoming these barriers, which can be technical, pedagogical, social and institutional, is essential for successful FOSS deployment. Failure to address these challenges can lead to ineffective learning outcomes, student alienation, and a lack of access.

**Digital Divide and Access Inequity:** A critical issue with hybrid learning is the issue of the digital divide. Poor or rural students may lack regular internet access, sufficient digital devices, and secure and silent learning spaces (Van Dijk, 2019; UNESCO, 2023). This lack of equality restricts their access and capacity to participate within a hybrid learning model, which compromises the model's claim to inclusivity and flexibility.

**Faculty readiness and resistance:** Educators may not be trained or feel confident enough to use technology in the classroom. Flipping into hybrid instruction necessitates educators to have training in online pedagogy, instructional design, and digital tools (Porter et al., 2014). Faculty resistance to change, mainly when faculty use lecture-based methodologies, hinders improvement and the hybrid learning model (Moore, 2013).

**Increased Workload and Burnout:** Creating, implementing, and maintaining hybrid courses tends to be more labor-intensive than traditional ones. Teachers must juggle online and in-person lessons, prepare multimedia content, give continuous feedback and deal with technical hiccups. Stress and burnout. However, this extra workload can also lead to stress and burnout, especially in an organization which lacks good support (Boelens et al., 2017).

**Retention of student motivation and engagement:** Hybrid learning environments demand learner autonomy and self-regulation. "Students need to be more active with their time and interact with content via asynchronous delivery. However, most students lack motivation, especially in distance learning or when not in a face-to-face situation with their mates and teachers. Without thoughtful design, students can feel sidelined or disinterested.

**Integrity and Quality Maintenance of Assessment and Feedback:** Academic integrity in online assessment is still hard. Online proctoring tools also worry educators about privacy and equity, and open-book exams and take-home assignments often fail to test real learning. Furthermore, offering personalized, timely feedback in large hybrid courses can be challenging, potentially impacting student learning and satisfaction (Bolliger & Halupa, 2012).

**Technical Support and Reliability:** The backbone of hybrid learning, technology is also fallible. Such system crashes, issues with software compatibility and internet failures can derail learning and cause frustration. Unresponsive IT support also contributes to the issue, especially in schools with a confined IT infrastructure (Al-Fraihat et al., 2020).

Overcoming these challenges necessitates investment in curricular planning, infrastructure, and professional development through a student-centered lens. Institutions must also be proactive in mapping out support systems and just-in-case plans so that the new blended and hybrid learning model lives up to its promise of being accessible, engaging, and academically rigorous.

## CASE STUDIES AND BEST PRACTICES

To showcase how the application of blended learning and hybrid learning in business education can be practical, reviewing specific case studies and instructional strategies that have taken place can be helpful as a model for potential discoveries. These cases demonstrate how technology and pedagogical advances support better learning outcomes, student satisfaction and Scale.

## Harvard Business School (HBS) – HBX and its Online Business Education:

An example of such prestigious institutions doing so without diluting their brand value is the HBX initiative of Harvard Business School (renamed Harvard Business School Online). Their most popular course, CORe (Credential of Readiness), combines business fundamentals with case-based learning in a dynamic, online setting. Through social learning tools and ' cold calls' within video modules, the course mimics classroom discussion and involves asynchronous and real-time deadlines to guarantee engagement. Results indicate high engagement and high completion rates, which indicate that well-designed hybrid approaches may allow for a rigorous approach with greater reach (Harvard Business School, 2025; Harvard Business School. (2025a)

## Indian Institute of Management Bangalore (IIMB) – MOOCs and Blended Initiatives:

There is another fine example in the MOOCs of IIM Bangalore on the edX and SWAYAM platforms. These courses are both freestanding for self-study and used as blends in on-campus programs. IIMB has applied a blend to its Post Graduate Program in Management, where MOOCs have been used as pre-or post-work, with face-to-face intensive sessions. Their analysis indicates gains in the preparedness of students as well as classroom interaction (Indian Institute of Management Bangalore, 2025).

## The Wharton School – Wharton Online:

Wharton has also expanded its MBA and Executive Education programs through Wharton Online, using simulations, discussion boards, and group projects to accommodate hybrid formats. The school values data-driven feedback as a tool to improve how instruction is designed. Faculty interventions and personalization of support include the use of learning analytics for video engagement, quiz performance, and forum activity (The Wharton School, 2025)

## IE Business School, Spain – Liquid Learning Model:

'Liquid Learning', only at IE Business School, unites online and offline learning periods in one cohesive experience. Real-time flexibility is built into this model so students can seamlessly transition in person or remotely. Virtual campus tours and augmented reality add to the experience. Learner satisfaction, engagement, and perceived career readiness value improved in learner surveys (IE University, 2025).

## Kristu Jayanti (Deemed to be University), Bengaluru – KJLMS and Hybrid Pedagogical Integration

Kristu Jayanti (Deemed to be University), a renowned university, has innovatively integrated blended learning into its business education curriculum through the Kristu Jayanti Learning Management System (KJLMS). Designed as a digital platform for collaborative and flexible learning, KJLMS supports business and management courses' synchronous and asynchronous delivery, empowering faculty to combine lectures, case studies, discussion forums, and assessments within a unified ecosystem. The Business Administration department leverages KJLMS for pre-class content delivery, including lecture videos, readings, and reflection prompts, which students review before engaging in live class discussions. This flipped classroom approach improves comprehension and prepares students for application-based problem-solving activities during contact sessions. The college emphasized multimodal teaching in hybrid modes, especially during and post-COVID, where physical classes are simultaneously streamed or recorded for later access. Evaluation data from internal surveys showed improved learner satisfaction, digital competency, and adaptability among faculty and students. The administration employs analytics tools embedded in the LMS to monitor login patterns, participation levels, and quiz performance, leading to timely academic interventions and tailored mentoring. (Kristu Jayanti (Deemed to be University), 2025)

Several best practices come out in these case studies:

**Align Technology and Pedagogy:** Tools should be productive to explicit learning goals and active learning methods (Garrison & Vaughan, 2008).

**Support Faculty Development:** Training ensures instructors can go from content deliverers to facilitators (Porter et al., 2014).

**Use Learning Analytics:** Real-time data can facilitate personalized learning paths for early interventions (Ifenthaler & Yau, 2020).

**Facilitate Social Learning:** Interaction with peers in forums, breakout rooms, and the collaborative platform is a condition of engagement (Hrastinski, 2009).

**Scalability and accessibility are key:** From mobile optimization to multilingual content, reach expands to geographies and learning styles.

**Assessment and Revision:** Regular feedback from students and faculty fosters ongoing improvement (Means et al., 2014).

Business schools can model these best practices and invoke them in adapting to their administration, such as a hybrid learning format that is sustainable, scalable, and impactful, and that prepares students for the complexity of the globalized economy in which they will one day compete.

## IMPLEMENTATION FRAMEWORK

Blended and hybrid learning – a structured approach to business education. There is a need for a structured, incremental approach to implementing blended and hybrid learning in business education, which is closely aligned with pedagogy, technology and the institution. A practical implementation strategy includes more than just instructional design; it should also consider the involvement of stakeholders, resource appropriation, and the development of an ongoing improvement process. Below is a four-phase structure outlining some essential methodologies for deploying hybrid learning at Scale.

### Stage 1: Design and consultations with interested parties

In the planning phase, the institution's goals, the needs of the learners, and the current technological infrastructure are assessed. A needs analysis with surveys, focus groups, and a curriculum review can help establish the initiative's needs and goals (Moore, 2013). Including all stakeholders (faculty, IT, administrative, and students) leads to buy-in and guarantees that multiple perspectives contribute to the design process (Porter et al., 2014). Strategic integration with accreditation standards and industry requirements is also essential at this stage.

### Stage 2: Instructional Design and Course Construction

This is the stage in which ID and faculty work together to design the course blueprint. This involves identifying learning objectives, deciding on the type of activities used (synchronous or asynchronous), and the tools used for delivery, interaction, and evaluation (Boelens et al., 2017). Course development should be informed by the Universal Design for Learning (UDL) to accommodate all learners (Centre for Applied Special Technology, 2018). Courses should use active learning methods like flipped teaching, case-based education, and simulations to keep students engaged.

### Step 3: Pilot Implementation and Support Systems

Before expanding, institutions ran pilot programs to perfect their hybrid courses. Pilot courses enable troubleshooting, feedback collection, and early results assessment (Al-Fraihat et al., 2020). Faculty will need training in digital pedagogy and the ability to have ongoing support from instructional technologists/IT support. Student orientation for the hybrid model and platforms are also critical.

### Phase 4: Analysis and Iteration of Program/ Value-Added Assessment

The last step includes the examination of the actual effectiveness of hybrid instruction across student indicators such as interaction, completion, and satisfaction. Tools like LMS analytics, surveys, and learning portfolios can yield valuable data (Ifenthaler & Yau, 2020). The door of institutional monitoring: Institutional review boards or quality assurance units should spearhead iterative quality improvements by identifying deficits and prescribing correctives. Peer reviews, faculty self-reflection, and alums voices also foster a culture of continuous improvement.

### Case Illustration – Kristu Jayanti (Deemed to be University)

Implemented in four phases: needs analysis with stakeholder input; instructional redesign using flipped methods on KJLMS; pilot roll-out with faculty training and IT support; and continuous improvement using LMS analytics to adjust content and target interventions. Outcomes included improved student satisfaction, digital competency, and faculty confidence in hybrid delivery.

A well-structured and flexible deployment plan is required to successfully adopt and diffuse blended and hybrid learning in management education. With the correct sequencing, higher education institutions can manage risks, maximize resources, and provide students with a high-quality, student-centric education.

## ANALYTICAL INSIGHTS AND EMERGING TRENDS

Data from post-pandemic cohorts show hybrid learning has shifted from a contingency measure to a core delivery mode in business education. Demand remains strong, with enrolment growth in hybrid MBA and executive programmes. The design quality is critical: poorly structured hybrids risk cognitive overload, while well-designed models consistently yield higher engagement and satisfaction. Institutions are moving towards optimization—balancing synchronous and asynchronous elements, embedding active learning, and using analytics for continuous improvement.

## Recommendations and Solutions

Recommendations and Implementation Strategies Drawing on a critical analysis of the state of blended and hybrid learning business education, key recommendations and suggestions for overcoming challenges with the design, delivery, and sustainability of such instructional models are presented here. These process lines cut across policy, pedagogy, technology, and organizational design.

## Invest in faculty development and support.

Successful hybrid learning starts with the instructors being well-prepared. Higher education institutions should offer systematic training for faculty in online instruction, instructional design, and educational technology (Porter et al., 2014). Ongoing professional learning opportunities, peer mentorship, and communities of practice can promote shared learning for teachers. Institutions should also provide access to instructional designers and IT support during every course phase.

## Advocate for the use of Universal Design for Learning (UDL)

Hybrid learning needs to be grounded in inclusive pedagogy. However, learning materials and activities are developed to cater to all students, no matter their abilities or learning styles (CAST, 2024). Faculty should be trained in the design of multiple means of representation (videos and transcripts), expression (written and oral options) and engagement (self-paced tasks and live discussions).

## Prepare technology and make it available.

A strong tech backbone is key to hybrid learning. We will need more LMS to accommodate the higher demand due to quarantine, as the schools are closing. Cloud-based systems and mobile and multilingual support enhance usability and accessibility (Al-Fraihat et al., 2020). Compliance with data privacy and security is also key, and increasingly, it is likely to become relevant with more use of AI learning tools.

## Employ data analytics for ongoing improvements.

Learning analytics must be used to improve teaching and learning and support learning. Engagement patterns can be revealed by indicators such as login frequency, assignment submissions and forum activity (Ifenthaler & Yau, 2020). Institutions must create dashboards and predictive models to detect at-risk students and deliver interventions matched to the specific population. This usage-meets-science approach enables the personalization of learning and increases retention.

## Integrate Active Learning into the Hybrid Design

Hybrid programmes should promote interactive methods like problem-based and project-based learning, simulations and projects. These approaches link theory and practice successfully and promote student autonomy (Freeman et al., 2014). Instructors must be prepared to weigh synchronous and asynchronous modalities for participation and reflection.

## Centralize Student Support Services

A central help desk or one-stop service for academic advising, IT help, mental health counselling and library support is essential. Orientation sessions and how-to guides can help students establish effective practices in hybrid spaces (Garrison & Vaughan, 2008).

## Involve stakeholders and Scale Slowly.

Taking society as a whole, A whole-of-society approach is necessary if we want to bring about institutional change that will engage administrators and faculty, students and industry. Iteration based on regular consultations, feedback loops, and pilot projects can help shape the scaling process. Service research and evidence-based policy. Service research needs to consider quality assurance standards, incentives for faculty innovation, program impact indicators, and policy-level indicators of success (Boelens et al., 2017).

They reinforce the recommendations for helping institutions develop scalable, equitable and pedagogically effective hybrid learning environments. With the pace of digital transformation increasing, these pre-emptive steps will ensure that business schools remain nimble, learner-focused and futureproofed.

# FUTURE RESEARCH DIRECTIONS

Despite significant strides in knowledge and practice regarding the respective blended and hybrid learning models, several issues need to be addressed by further research. This section identifies several lines of future research that would inform and advance the improvement, development, and localization of hybrid learning within business education.

## Extended Effects on Learning and Employability

Hybrid learning has been researched mainly based on short-term measures, such as student satisfaction, engagement, and grades. Longitudinal studies may also need to examine how hybrid learning affects graduate employability, work performance and lifelong learning (Means et al., 2014). Following cohorts longitudinally allows us to examine the effects of hybrid learning experiences on professional pathways and career achievement.

## Cross-Cultural and Comparative Studies in the Context of Culture and Economy

Most of the literature tends to reflect Western-based experiences and does not pay enough attention to hybrid models in low and middle-income countries. Cross-national research has the potential to enlighten understanding of whether and how cultural context, digital infrastructure, and institutional preparedness influence the adoption and impact of hybrid provision (Selwyn, 2020). These insights are essential when working on more inclusive global educational strategies.

## Role of AI and Disruptive Technologies

Education delivery is fast evolving through artificial intelligence (AI), augmented reality (AR), and virtual reality (VR). They are likely to promote the integration of these technologies in hybrid models to achieve a more personalized learning experience to engage in immersion and real-time assessment (Holmes et al., 2019)—empiric evaluations examining their cost-effectiveness, ethical considerations, and learner outcomes will drive evidence-based implementation.

## Psychological and Emotional Aspects of Hybrid Learning

The psychological aspects of hybrid learning, including, among others, student well-being, social isolation, motivation, and anxiety, also need to be investigated as they are under-researched (Bolliger & Halupa, 2012). Research into emotional intelligence, mindfulness, and resilience in digital learning environments can contribute to models of holistic learner support.

## Innovations in Pedagogy and Staff Development

Effective models of faculty development should also be a subject of further research. Research could investigate the most effective training modes, workshops, peer coaching, or online modules to develop instructor efficacy for hybrid instruction (Porter et al., 2014). Further, newer teaching methods, transdisciplinary integration, project-based learning, and global virtual teams require rigorous testing in hybrid settings.

## Learning Analytics predictive modelling

Advanced analytics and machine learning offer prospects for individualizing learning and predicting student success. Future studies may design and test predictive models to detect at-risk learners and suggest timely interventions (Ifenthaler & Yau, 2020). Privacy, ethics , and transparency must be paramount in this quest.

The future of BHL in business education is ripe with opportunities to engage in interdisciplinary research. By studying these contexts, researchers can construct more adaptive, equitable, and data-informed learning ecosystems designed to prepare learners for the realities of the contemporary workplace.

# DISCUSSION

The increasing use of blended and hybrid methodologies in business education is a transformative move away from traditional pedagogy. This technological transformation represents an underlying transformation like knowledge generation, propagation, and application in the 21st-century learning environment (Garrison & Vaughan, 2008). Hybrid programs provide a synergy of flexibility, access, and creativity, but success is contingent on the successful triangulation of technology, pedagogy, support, and presence.

A critical lesson from the review is the importance of deliberate instructional design. Writing classroom instruction in a digital format does not cut it for hybrid learning. Instead, it demands a curricular redesign that emphasizes active learning, aligns with learning objectives, and encourages cooperation (Bonk & Graham, 2005). Faculty act as agents of change with instructional innovation, and the institutions must offer professional development to facilitate that changing role (Porter et al., 2014).

It also discusses equity and inclusion. In short, hybrid models can democratize education by targeting more geographically and economically widespread populations. However, they can further exacerbate inequalities if access to technology and support structures is not guaranteed (Van Dijk, 2019; UNESCO, 2023). Practices such as Universal Design for Learning, mobile-friendly resources, and multilingual support are paramount to narrowing this digital gap (CAST, 2024).

Furthermore, adaptable learning paths are available in the hybrid education context, supported by learning analytics and Artificial Intelligence (AI). Such capabilities enable educators to identify the needs of learners as they happen and then make timely interventions (Ifenthaler & Yau, 2020). However, ethical issues such as privacy, consent and bias must be addressed for responsible innovation (Holmes et al. , 2019).

Another key element for the success of hybrid learning is institutional preparedness. Universities must have strong infrastructure, digital libraries, cloud-based platforms, and centralized student support systems (Al-Fraihat et al., 2020). Cross-departmental collaboration—academic, IT, and student affairs—is crucial to creating a comprehensive ecosystem conducive to teaching and learning.

Curriculum-wise, the real world through simulations, case studies, and group projects allows students to deal with the changes and a fast-paced global business environment. When digital tools accompany such experiential learning, they can develop students' critical thinking, problem-solving, and decision-making (Freeman et al., 2014). This conversation is a reminder that hybrid learning is not a concession nor a temporary solution—it is a pedagogical breakthrough that does justice to the complex demands on learners and educators in the school and the workplace of the twenty-first century.

Finally, wide-scale adoption of blended and hybrid models also requires a culture of continual assessment and incremental change. Colleges and universities that develop a culture of innovation are more likely to reshape courses and school policies based on feedback from students, faculty, and industry partners (Moore, 2013). This way, hybrid learning will continue to be timely, robust, and adaptable, and help meet the changing needs of learners and society.

## CONCLUSION

Blended and hybrid learning models represent a paradigm shift in business education, moving from teacher-centred delivery to learner-centred, technology-enabled pedagogy. When thoughtfully designed and grounded in active learning principles, these approaches offer flexibility, inclusivity, personalization, and real-world skill development, aligning closely with the demands of Industry 4.0. The Flexible Instructional Design, Outcomes-Focused Pedagogy, and Technology-Enabled Interaction (FOT) Model proposed in this chapter lays out a flexible roadmap for designing large-scale hybrid learning that is engaging while maintaining pedagogical integrity. Yet fully capitalizing on technology in education goes beyond the pandemic; it has long demanded overcoming ongoing hurdles in digital equity, faculty readiness, and institutional sustainability. It requires investment in professional development, learner support systems, and evidence-based instructional design. While hybrid learning should not be considered a stopgap, as educational ecosystems change, it offers a transformational and future-oriented strategy to increase access, improve quality, and equip graduates for success in a globalized, technology-centric business setting.

## REFERENCES


Al-Fraihat, D., Joy, M., & Sinclair, J. (2020). Evaluating E-learning systems success: An empirical study. *Computers in Human Behavior*, *102*, 67–86. DOI: 10.1016/j.chb.2019.08.004

Allen, I. E., & Seaman, J. (2017). Digital learning compass: Distance education enrollment report 2017. Babson Survey Research Group. https://onlinelearningsurvey.com/reports/digtiallearningcompassenrollment2017.pdf

Bernard, R. M., Abrami, P. C., Borokhovski, E., Wade, A., Tamim, R., Surkes, M., & Bethel, E. (2009). A meta-analysis of three types of interaction treatments in distance education. *Review of Educational Research*, *79*(3), 1243–1289. DOI: 10.3102/0034654309333844

Bicen, H., & Kocakoyun, S. (2018). Perceptions of students for gamification approach: Kahoot as a case study. *International Journal of Emerging Technologies in Learning*, *13*(2), 72–93. DOI: 10.3991/ijet.v13i02.7467

Bishop, J. L., & Verleger, M. A. (2013). The flipped classroom: A survey of the research. 2013 ASEE Annual Conference & Exposition, 1–18. https://peer.asee.org/22585

Boelens, R., De Wever, B., & Voet, M. (2017). Four key challenges to the design of blended learning: A systematic literature review. *Educational Research Review*, *22*, 1–18. DOI: 10.1016/j.edurev.2017.06.001

Bolliger, D. U., & Halupa, C. (2012). Student perceptions of satisfaction and anxiety in an online doctoral program. *Distance Education*, *33*(1), 81–98. DOI: 10.1080/01587919.2012.667961

Bonk, C. J., & Graham, C. R. (2005). *The Handbook of blended learning: Global perspectives, local designs*. Pfeiffer., https://www.wiley.com/en-us/The+Handbook+of+Blended+Learning%3A+Global+Perspectives%2C+Local+Designs-p-9780787977580

Bonwell, C. C., & Eison, J. A. (1991). *Active Learning: Creating Excitement in the Classroom* (ASHE-ERIC Higher Education Report No. 1). Washington, DC: The George Washington University, School of Education and Human Development. Available from ERIC ED336049: https://eric.ed.gov/?id=ED336049

Brown, M., McCormack, M., Reeves, J., Brooks, D. C., & Grajek, S. with Alexander, B., Bali, M., Bulger, S., Dark, S., Engelbert, N., Gannon, K., Gauthier, A., Gibson, D., Gibson, R., Lundin, B., Veletsianos, G., & Weber, N. (2020). *2020 EDUCAUSE Horizon Report: Teaching and learning edition*. EDUCAUSE. https://library.educause.edu/-/media/files/library/2020/3/2020_horizon_report_pdf.pdf

CAST. (2024). Universal Design for Learning guidelines version 3.0. http://udlguidelines.cast.org

Cornell University. (2025). *Engaging students in discussions*. Cornell University. https://teaching.cornell.edu/teaching-resources/engaging-students/engaging-students-discussions

Crawford, J., Butler-Henderson, K., Rudolph, J., Malkawi, B., Glowatz, M., Burton, R., & Lam, S. (2020). COVID-19: 20 countries' higher education intra-period digital pedagogy responses. *Journal of Applied Learning & Teaching*, *3*(1), 1–20. DOI: 10.37074/jalt.2020.3.1.7

Deterding, S., Dixon, D., Khaled, R., & Nacke, L. (2011). From game design elements to gamefulness: Defining 'gamification'. *Proceedings of the 15th International Academic MindTrek Conference*, 9–15. DOI: 10.1145/2181037.2181040

Elmaadaway, M. A. N., & Abouelenein, Y. A. M. (2023). In-service teachers' TPACK development through an adaptive e-learning environment (ALE). *Education and Information Technologies*, *28*(7), 8273–8298. DOI: 10.1007/s10639-022-11477-8 PMID: 36571083

Freeman, S., Eddy, S. L., McDonough, M., Smith, M. K., Okoroafor, N., Jordt, H., & Wenderoth, M. P. (2014). Active learning increases student performance in science, engineering, and mathematics. *Proceedings of the National Academy of Sciences of the United States of America*, *111*(23), 8410–8415. DOI: 10.1073/pnas.1319030111 PMID: 24821756

Garrison, D. R., Anderson, T., & Archer, W. (2000). Critical inquiry in a text-based environment: Computer conferencing in higher education. *The Internet and Higher Education*, *2*(2–3), 87–105. DOI: 10.1016/S1096-7516(00)00016-6

Garrison, D. R., & Vaughan, N. D. (2008). *Blended learning in higher education: Framework, principles, and guidelines*. John Wiley & Sons., DOI: 10.1002/9781118269558

Grier, D., Lindt, S. F., & Miller, S. C. (2021). Formative assessment with game-based technology. *International Journal of Technology in Education and Science*, *5*(2), 173–187. DOI: 10.46328/ijtes.97

Harvard Business School. (2025). *Harvard Business School Online*. https://online.hbs.edu/

Harvard Business School. (2025a). *Executive education*. https://www.exed.hbs.edu/

Herreid, C. F., & Schiller, N. A. (2013). Case studies and the flipped classroom. *Journal of College Science Teaching*, *42*(5), 62–67. https://eric.ed.gov/?id=EJ1011743

Holmes, W., Bialik, M., & Fadel, C. (2019). Artificial intelligence in education: Promises and implications for teaching and learning. Center for Curriculum Redesign. https://curriculumredesign.org/wp-content/uploads/AI-in-Education.pdf

Hrastinski, S. (2009). A theory of online learning as online participation. *Computers & Education*, *52*(1), 78–82. DOI: 10.1016/j.compedu.2008.06.009

Ibrahim, M. M., & Nat, M. (2019). Blended learning motivation model for instructors in higher education institutions. *International Journal of Educational Technology in Higher Education*, *16*(1), 12. DOI: 10.1186/s41239-019-0145-2

Ifenthaler, D., & Yau, J. Y. K. (2020). Utilizing learning analytics to support study success in higher education: A systematic review. *Educational Technology Research and Development*, *68*(4), 1961–1990. DOI: 10.1007/s11423-020-09788-z

Indian Institute of Management Bangalore. (2025). *IIMBx*. https://iimbx.iimb.ac.in/

Jayanti, K. (Deemed to be University). (2025). *KJLMS*. https://www.kristujayantiexamlms.com/login/index.php

Kolb, D. A. (1984). Experiential learning: Experience as the source of learning and development. Prentice-Hall. https://www.researchgate.net/publication/235701029_Experiential_Learning_Experience_As_The_Source_Of_Learning_And_Development

Laal, M., & Ghodsi, S. M. (2012). Benefits of collaborative learning. *Procedia: Social and Behavioral Sciences*, *31*, 486–490. DOI: 10.1016/j.sbspro.2011.12.091

Means, B., Toyama, Y., Murphy, R., Bakia, M., & Jones, K. (2014). *The effectiveness of online and blended learning: A meta-analysis of the empirical literature*. U.S. Department of Education. https://tech.ed.gov/files/2013/10/impacts-of-online-learning.pdf

Moore, M. G. (Ed.). (2013). *Handbook of distance education* (3rd ed.). Routledge., DOI: 10.4324/9780203803738

Piaget, J. (1952). *The origins of intelligence in children*. W. W. Norton & Company., DOI: 10.1037/11494-000

Porter, W. W., Graham, C. R., Spring, K. A., & Welch, K. R. (2014). Blended learning in higher education: Institutional adoption and implementation. *Computers & Education*, *75*, 185–195. DOI: 10.1016/j.compedu.2014.02.011

Salas, E., Rosen, M. A., Held, J. D., & Weissmuller, J. J. (2009). Performance measurement in simulation-based training: A review and best practices. *Simulation & Gaming*, *40*(3), 328–376. DOI: 10.1177/1046878108326734

Selwyn, N. (2020). Should robots replace teachers? AI and the future of education. Polity Press. https://www.wiley.com/en-se/Should+Robots+Replace+Teachers%3F%3A+AI+and+the+Future+of+Education-p-9781509528967

Singha, R. (2024). Cultivating holistic learning environments in higher education: Mindfulness, compassion, and Ubuntu philosophies. In Omona, K., & Kayi O'dama, M. (Eds.), *Global perspectives on micro-learning and micro-credentials in higher education* (pp. 174–194). IGI Global., DOI: 10.4018/979-8-3693-0343-6.ch011

Singha, R. (2025). Empowering students through mindfulness and meditation practices. In Gonçalves, S. P. (Ed.), *Nurturing student well-being in the modern world* (pp. 141–170). IGI Global., DOI: 10.4018/979-8-3693-1455-5.ch006

Strelan, P., Osborn, A., & Palmer, E. (2020). Student satisfaction with courses and instructors in a flipped classroom: A meta-analysis. *Journal of Computer Assisted Learning*, *36*(3), 295–314. DOI: 10.1111/jcal.12421

Sweller, J. (1988). Cognitive load during problem-solving: Effects on learning. *Cognitive Science*, *12*(2), 257–285. DOI: 10.1207/s15516709cog1202_4

The Wharton School. (2025). *Wharton Interactive*. The University of Pennsylvania. https://interactive.wharton.upenn.edu/

UNESCO. (2023). *Global education monitoring report: Technology in education—A tool on whose terms?* https://www.unesco.org/gem-report/en/publication/technology-education

University, I. E. (2025). *Liquid learning*. https://www.ie.edu/liquid-learning/

Van Dijk, J. (2019). The digital divide. Polity. https://www.politybooks.com/bookdetail?book_slug=the-digital-divide--9781509534449

Vygotsky, L. S. (1980). Mind in society: The development of higher psychological processes. Harvard University Press. https://www.hup.harvard.edu/books/9780674576292

Williams, D., & Bower, M. (2025). The impact of technology-mediated dialogue on critical thinking in the secondary English classroom. *Education and Information Technologies*. Advance online publication. DOI: 10.1007/s10639-025-13680-9

World Economic Forum. (2020). *The future of jobs report 2020*. https://www.weforum.org/reports/the-future-of-jobs-report-2020

## KEY TERMS AND DEFINITIONS

**Active Learning:** A teaching approach that encourages student involvement in learning from activities such as discussion, problem-solving, or group work.

**Blended Learning:** A teaching model is used to mix a virtually mediated course/lab design with traditional face-to-face teaching to provide greater flexibility and access.

**Business Education:** The theory and practice of business, management, and economics prepare individuals to lead and succeed in business.

**Digital Equity:** Equitable access to technology, internet access and digital skills are necessary for effective online and hybrid learning participation.

**Educational Resilience:** The ability of schools and their students to innovate and survive during disruptions such as pandemics or technological innovation.

**Flexible Pedagogy:** Where the teaching mode is adaptable and responsive to diverse learning styles, timetables, locations and demands through technology.

**Hybrid Learning:** A teaching modality that combines synchronous and asynchronous components, where students are typically allowed to participate in person or remotely.

**Instructional Design:** Unfortunately, the thoughtful design and implementation of educational activities with associated objectives, activities, and assessment methods are not conducive to student success.

# Chapter 7
# Collaborative Learning and Peer Instruction:
## Fostering Critical Business Skills in Modern Education

**Surjit Singha**
https://orcid.org/0000-0002-5730-8677
*Kristu Jayanti University, India*

## ABSTRACT

*This chapter examines how collaborative learning and peer instruction improve critical business skills in postsecondary education. As business conditions are subject to frequent changes, educational orientation should also change to develop students' abilities for the future. Pedagogies of partnership strengthen communication, leadership, decision-making, and cultural intelligence. This chapter develops a rich framework for integrating these practices with technology use, diversity in groups, and integrating the real world into the classroom setting. This framework offers practical guidance for educators and institutions on developing students' job-ready skills through active learning.*

## INTRODUCTION

Business education has changed in the last couple of decades. Institutions now increasingly emphasize modes of teaching and learning that promote critical thinking, teamwork, flexibility, and lifelong learning. Active, student-centered pedagogies like collaborative learning and peer instruction replace traditional lecture-style instruction. The effects of these methods are to engage students more

DOI: 10.4018/979-8-3373-7523-6.ch007

directly in learning and developing vital skills for today's world and global business environment (Prince, 2004; Michaelsen & Sweet, 2008).

Collaborative learning is a method of education that combines at least two team members to achieve a shared academic objective. It helps students to become more responsible, respect each other, and gain better intercommunication skills. Peer-based learning activities such as peer instruction, which encourages conceptual thinking and structured peer discussions, have also been well-received for supporting deeper learning and enhancing student outcomes (Crouch & Mazur, 2001). Such models are consistent with the constructivist or active learning theories, which underpin the teaching of these five functions, which form the basis for some genuine engagement and development amongst students.

Business schools have followed suit as they prepare students for the competencies and demands of a rapidly moving global economy. In such a context, learning strategies must do more than transmit content; they must enable students to acquire cross-cutting leadership competencies such as innovation and moral reasoning (Freeman et al., 2014). Such competencies are developed, for instance, in learning communities and peer instruction teaching methods where collaboration mimics real-world settings that necessitate problem-solving in teams, negotiation, and strategic decision-making.

As the digital revolution continues, blended and online learning formats have become widely accepted. This shift offers an opportunity to integrate collaborative tools (real-time editing, video conferencing, discussion forums, etc.) into everyday education (Hrastinski, 2008), making learning accessible anywhere, anytime for everyone.

There is a growing desire for experiential and project-based educational experiences in business education. Collaborative pedagogy and peer instruction offer realistic learning environments within which students can reflect on their practice, apply theory to their practice, and receive feedback promptly. If done well, these strategies can dramatically improve outcomes and help develop future leaders in their chosen arena of professional practice.

Recent research underlines that peer instruction is fundamentally a form of collaborative learning that leverages student discussion to deepen understanding (Amri et al., 2024). For instance, a business education study found that students who participated in peer instruction achieved significantly greater engagement and higher performance than those in traditional lectures. Likewise, peer-learning strategies (e.g. structured discussions and peer review) have been shown to promote cooperation and increase students' emotional investment in the learning process (Wu & Yu, 2025). These findings reinforce the synergy between collaborative learning and peer instruction in fostering critical skills in modern education.

## BACKGROUND

The move away from traditional lecture-based teaching business education is driven by the realization that passive lecturing methodologies are not serving learners. As the world of work becomes increasingly interdisciplinary, international, and digital, educators have to accommodate the way they teach likewise (Bonwell & Eison, 1991).

Collaborative learning is a phenomenon that can be traced back to the philosophies of Socrates and John Dewey, in that both men promoted dialogic, inquiry-based, and experiential models of learning. Dewey, for example, particularly highlighted the value of experiential learning, where students learn by doing and reflecting on experience to create meaning (Dewey, 1938). These early concepts established the foundation for contemporary models of collaborative learning.

Such theoretical development in the 20th century has crystallized the principles of collaborative learning even more. The Zone of Proximal Development (ZPD) proposed by Lev Vygotsky stressed that social interaction is critical to learning and that a learner develops cognitively most efficiently in the company of others – peers and mentors (Vygotsky, 1978). This theory supports the notion that learning is a social endeavour and underscores the power of interaction in a group setting.

The 1980s and 1990s were a time of what some call the "cooperative turn in ELT methodology", especially strong in North America. Educators such as David and Roger Johnson developed structured techniques such as Jigsaw Classroom, Think-Pair-Share, and Group Investigation, which were designed to foster positive interdependence, individual accountability and interpersonal skills (Johnson & Johnson,1989).

These models became particularly popular in management education by solving the problem between theory taught in an academic environment and that experienced in the workplace. Business schools introduced simulations, case-based material, and project teams into their teaching at this time so that students could face real-world problems in the safety of the classroom. Employers' preference for graduates with strong, soft skills, such as communication, adaptability, and working collaboratively (NACE, 2023), is also a factor in this change.

The internet has enabled even greater richness and effectiveness in collaborative learning Harasim, 2017). The development of online learning environments and educational technology in recent years has enabled Collaborative Learning to reach even more pupils and students. Web-based instruments, learning systems, and collaborative software, including tools like Google Apps for Education, Slack, and MS Teams, could be used by students for co-creation, resource sharing, and communication between geographical locations (Hrastinski, 2008).

These developments represent a turning point in how education is presented and experienced. Collaborative learning is not only a face-to-face activity in business and management education and training – the approach has now spread globally and become multi-faceted with new technology —it extends to learners' cognitive, social, emotional and vocational development.

## REVIEW OF LITERATURE

Reuter et al. (2022) explored the role of gamification, game-based learning, and serious games as tools for enhancing motivation and collaboration in organizational and training contexts. The study highlighted that elements making games appealing—such as clear goals, feedback loops, challenges, and rewards—can be adapted to professional and educational environments to improve intrinsic and extrinsic motivation. The authors argued for its potential in fostering collaboration and skill development by examining how gamification impacts teamwork and engagement. However, they noted that group-based game learning remains underutilized in workplace training, calling for greater awareness and adoption. In the context of collaborative learning and peer instruction in business education, gamification offers a complementary strategy for creating interactive, motivating, and socially engaging environments. Integrating game-based mechanics into collaborative projects and peer instruction cycles can enhance active participation, sustain motivation over time, and provide immediate feedback—key elements for developing critical business skills. Such approaches align with experiential learning principles by embedding challenge-driven tasks within real or simulated business scenarios, linking cognitive engagement with social and emotional interaction.

Yu et al. (2023) examined the dynamics of online collaborative learning within the broader context of distance education, emphasizing that successful collaboration requires systematic activation and sustained regulation of cognitive, motivational, behavioural, and emotional processes among group members. Drawing on a review of scholarly publications, the study identified prevailing trends, challenges, and strategies for practical online group work. Key challenges included unequal participation, limited engagement, and difficulties fostering trust in virtual settings. The chapter proposed strategies such as straightforward role assignment, structured tasks, technology-mediated interaction, and instructor facilitation to improve collaborative outcomes in online environments. These insights closely align with collaborative learning and peer instruction goals in business education, especially in technology-enhanced or blended delivery modes. The emphasis on sustained motivation, structured interaction, and emotional engagement parallels the principles outlined in active learning frameworks, where peer instruction cycles and group projects depend on equitable participation and consistent engagement. The findings reinforce the importance of intentional design and facilitation in creating online learning communities that foster critical business skills such as teamwork, leadership, and reflective practice.

Singha (2024) examined the integration of mindfulness, compassion, and Ubuntu within higher education, particularly in microlearning and micro-credential frameworks. The study emphasized that mindfulness cultivates present-moment awareness, compassion fosters empathetic engagement, and Ubuntu—an African philosophy centred on interconnectedness—promotes a sense of shared humanity and collective responsibility. When embedded in curriculum design, pedagogical strategies, and cultural practices, these principles contribute to moral development, social responsibility, and leadership capacity. These findings directly relate to collaborative learning and peer instruction in business education. Collaborative environments require interpersonal trust, cultural intelligence, and empathetic communication—attributes that mindfulness, compassion, and Ubuntu actively cultivate. Embedding such values into group-based projects, peer mentoring, and reflective discussions can deepen student engagement and enhance interaction quality, thereby improving cognitive and socio-emotional learning outcomes. The study also reinforces the importance of integrating diverse cultural philosophies into active learning strategies to prepare students for leadership roles in globalized business contexts.

Thomas et al. (2024) investigated the factors shaping student attitudes and usage behaviours toward learning management systems (LMS) in higher education. Using the Unified Theory of Acceptance and Use of Technology (UTAUT) and the Extended Expectation–Confirmation Model (ElAM), the authors surveyed 363 students from urban, semi-urban, and rural Karnataka over five months. Structural equation modelling and path analysis revealed that perceived usefulness, ease of use, social influence, and facilitating conditions significantly influenced engagement with LMS platforms. The study presented an integrated model that merged established technology acceptance theories with original insights into student engagement patterns. The findings are particularly relevant to technology-enabled collaborative learning and peer instruction. LMS platforms are often the central infrastructure for facilitating group projects, peer discussions, and collaborative content creation in business education. By identifying the key determinants of LMS adoption and sustained use, this research informs strategies to improve the effectiveness of digital tools in supporting structured cooperation, timely feedback, and equitable participation. Such insights strengthen the technological foundation for embedding collaborative learning and peer instruction into face-to-face and blended learning environments.

Singha & Kanna S. (2025) explored the role of Intentional Learning Communities (ILCs) in supporting educators experiencing challenges such as addiction. The study integrated psychometric assessment through the Multidimensional Addiction Behaviour Scale (MABS) to evaluate psychological, biological, social, and environmental influences, cognitive and behavioural patterns, and motivation for change. The authors found that ILCs—characterized by structured, empathetic, and collaborative environments—enhanced mental health and professional development. Although the study focused on educator well-being, its findings are relevant to collaborative learning in business education. The ILC model parallels structured collaborative learning environments in that both rely on intentional group formation, shared goals, and reflective practice. By fostering trust, accountability, and mutual support, ILCs provide a blueprint for creating educational settings where participants can engage meaningfully, develop resilience, and transfer skills to their professional roles. These insights align with the principles of peer instruction and collaborative learning, suggesting that structured peer engagement can have far-reaching benefits for participants' cognitive, emotional, and social growth. The study further underscores the importance of institutional support in sustaining such communities, which mirrors the infrastructure needed to implement effective collaborative pedagogies in higher education.

Matongo & Goronga (2025) examined innovative teaching methods in higher education that integrate collaborative learning as a core pedagogical approach. The chapter critically analyzed the benefits, challenges, and strategies for implementing collaborative methodologies, emphasizing that such approaches promote active participation, mutual assistance, and the co-construction of knowledge in inclusive and emancipatory learning spaces. By framing collaborative learning as both a pedagogical and epistemological tool, the authors argued that it enhances learner engagement, fosters critical dialogue, and nurtures interpersonal skills essential for professional success. These findings directly reinforce the principles of collaborative learning and peer instruction in business education. Both methods rely on participatory engagement, equitable contribution, and supportive peer interaction to achieve deep learning outcomes. The emphasis on creating "emancipatory epistemological spaces" parallels the need for culturally inclusive and psychologically safe environments where business students can develop leadership, communication, and teamwork competencies. Additionally, the study's practical strategies for implementation align with structured cooperation models that underpin effective peer instruction cycles.

The reviewed literature demonstrates that collaborative learning and peer instruction are strengthened when supported by diverse pedagogical strategies, technological tools, and inclusive values. Approaches such as gamification, online collaborative learning frameworks, mindfulness-based practices, intentional learning communities, and innovative cooperative methodologies all contribute to deeper engagement, sustained motivation, and the development of critical business skills. Technology, particularly LMS platforms, is a key enabler, while culturally responsive and empathetic environments ensure equitable participation.

These studies highlight that effective implementation of collaborative learning and peer instruction in business education requires intentional design, structured cooperation, reflective practice, and strong institutional support to prepare students for the complexities of professional and global contexts. Building on these insights, the following Theoretical Framework section outlines the educational and psychological paradigms—such as constructivism, social interdependence theory, and cognitive load theory—that provide the conceptual underpinnings for integrating collaborative learning and peer instruction into modern business curricula.

## THEORETICAL FRAMEWORK

The theoretical base of CL and PI is grounded in numerous educational and psychological paradigms, each of which grants unique perspectives on how students learn, accept and process information in a collaborative domain. These theories are crucial in informing how we teach in business education, which seeks academic capabilities and practical, interactive, and leadership skills.

The theory of constructivism constitutes the foundation of collaborative learning. Grounded in the thinking of both Jean Piaget and later developed by Seymour Papert and Lev Vygotsky, constructivism suggests that learners construct knowledge and meaning of the world around them. Zone of Proximal Development (ZPD) – The concept developed by Vygotsky determines that the Zone of Proximal Development is the distance between the actual development level as determined by independent problem-solving and the level of possible development as determined through problem-solving under adult guidance or in collaboration with more capable peers (Vygotsky, 1978). In business classrooms, group-based assignments such as case studies, simulations, and peer mentoring help learners develop their learning through social interaction and collective problem-solving.

Another useful lens is the social interdependence theory, initially developed by Morton Deutsch and later elaborated by Johnson and Johnson (1989). This theory classifies interdependence based on whether it is positive, negative or neutral, with positive interdependence being particularly well-suited to cooperative learning. In business team projects, which are appropriately designed, students view their performance as being dependent on their team members. These qualities create a trust, accountability, and human support-based system essential in learning and working within a group environment.

Also applicable is Albert Bandura's (1986) Social Learning Theory, which focuses on learning via observation, imitation and modelling. Peer instruction -the idea that students should teach each other – is an excellent example of Bandura at work. By explaining their thinking, students strengthen their comprehension and demonstrate ways of thinking and acting to their peers, each learning in the process.

Cognitive load theory, founded by John Sweller (1988), provides a cognitive psychology understanding of instructional design. It implies the limited capacity of the working memory for learners, and lecture materials should be organized to minimize the extraneous load while facilitating the maximization of the germane load of the mental effort students spend on processing, constructing and automating schemas. When accustomed to collaborative and peer-teaching environments, splitting work between students' tasks or complex problems into its solvable pieces minimizes the cognitive burden and provides some deep learning.

Students from business studies learning from each other have been reported to contribute to higher education engagement and comprehension. For instance, Woodward and Pattinson (2023) found that peer learning occurs among business degree students, contributing to students' skill development and learning. Working in groups on projects that demand assertion, analytical, and leadership skills engages students at all levels of Bloom's taxonomy, from comprehension to creation.

These theories come together, providing a solid pedagogic base. It tells us that not only are collaborative learning and peer instruction ways of teaching, but they are also evidence-based principles based on solid research, which reflects a much deeper understanding of how human beings learn and engage socially with one another. These constructs underpin the transition from passive to active learning and participative engagement in preparing students for the challenges of the modern business world.

## CONCEPTUAL FRAMEWORK

The framework of this chapter combines collaborative learning and peer instruction into a single model representing the vision of active business learning. This model assumes that education, skill development and professional identity development are most successful when learners interact meaningfully with peers and instructors.

At the core of this model are the three principles of experiential involvement, structured partnership and ongoing reflection. Hands-on engagement is defined as real-life problems, which are project-based tasks similar to those in the business environment. They are the building block of learning, requiring respondents to collaborate, negotiate, resolve differences and evaluate results (Kolb, 1984).

Structured cooperation is promoted with intentionally designed group formation, explicit task roles, and assisted peer interaction. This tactic will ensure that all pupils are engaged and that the collaborative process is fair and successful. The role of the recognized expectations, scaffolding and providing the group dynamics does not lead to social loafing and domain on the part of students is crucial (Oakley et al., 2004).

Peer instruction is embedded in the model to support further explanations and reflect metacognitively. Cognitive elaboration occurs when students teach or explain what they have learned to their peers, a particularly effective method that has been found to increase retention and transfer (Chi et al., 1989). This feature also encourages peer accountability and mutual support in the classroom, whereby students feel responsible for their learning and others' learning.

A cross-cutting enabler in this framework is technology. Accompanying tools, including forums, wikis, voting, and video conferencing, help break down the walls of the classroom and support a more flexible engagement. These digital devices facilitate access, enable immediate feedback, and offer analytics to guide instruction (Means et al., 2013).

Lastly, the model strongly emphasizes reflection via self-assessment, peer feedback, and teacher scaffolding. Reflection helps reinforce learning and develop transferable soft skills such as empathy, leadership and resilience – all vital in today's business world.

If this concept is applied effectively, it also becomes a dynamic, interactive, and student-centred learning experience. It integrates learning tactics and professional readiness, producing well-informed professionals who are not merely present but ready to tackle new challenges and build effective relationships.

## RESEARCH PROBLEM

Despite widespread advocacy for collaborative learning and peer instruction, their implementation in business education remains limited and inconsistent. Many programs still emphasize content coverage over skill development, leaving little room for teamwork or peer teaching; as a result, students may graduate with theoretical knowledge but insufficient practice in leadership, communication, and teamwork. Furthermore, existing studies focus mainly on short-term engagement gains, with little examination of how active learning affects equity, inclusion, or long-term career preparedness. Institutional barriers—such as faculty accustomed to lecture-based methods, large class sizes, and rigid curricula—hinder the adoption of these student-centred approaches.

While the literature espousing the use of collaborative learning and peer instruction is vast, the practice of these pedagogical methods in business education is inconsistent and generally shallow. Although educators and institutions are paying more attention to student-centred pedagogy, they often lack clear goal-setting and institutional dimensions to realize student-centred pedagogy outcomes (Tiwari et al., 2014).

One such barrier involves the mismatch of curricular design and the real educational aim of business education. The structure of many conventional curricula frequently emphasizes content coverage at the expense of skill acquisition, providing little scope for collaborative work and peer teaching. Consequently, students may leave with the theoretical underpinnings for leadership, communication, and teamwork skills, as recently identified by employers (NACE, 2023).

A further challenge is the absence of detailed objective information concerning the effects of collaborative learning and peer instruction on the various facets of student output. For instance, although some studies describe increased engagement and critical thinking (Freeman et al., 2014), few have asked how active learning pedagogies influence equity, inclusion, and long-term professional preparedness. There is also an inadequate investigation that contrasts different collaboration models (e.g., structured versus informal group work) or tests the efficacy of technology-mediated peer learning employing hybrid or fully online designs.

In addition, the resistance from faculty members can become a barrier to adaptation. Faculty who have availed themselves of the lecture-based teaching model might be ill-prepared or unwilling to take on the facilitative roles required by collaborative pedagogy. As an additional barrier, institutional obstacles (e.g., large numbers of students, limited time and assessment workload) discourage trial and error using active learning techniques (Prince, 2004).

Based on these deficiencies, this chapter aims to answer the following research question: How can collaborative learning and peer instruction be designed in business education to foster students' critical skills and enhance their learning outcomes? The chapter presents systems, technologies, and good practices supporting this integration and discusses how these approaches relate to the current academic and professional landscape.

## UNDERSTANDING COLLABORATIVE LEARNING IN BUSINESS EDUCATION

In business education, collaborative learning is not simply a teaching device but an essential strategic move in response to an increasingly complex and cross-disciplinary context in which business challenges are met. Whether it is known as collaborative learning (CL), a pedagogy that involves students working in groups to accomplish a learning goal as opposed to working as individuals, it is recognized as a strategy in which students' cognitive, social, and personal skills are developed in light of recent workplace demands and expectations (Laal & Ghodsi, 2012).

This cooperative learning engagement model is based on positive interdependence, individual accountability, face-to-face promotive interaction, social skills, and group processing (Johnson, Johnson, & Smith, 2007). These practices guarantee that all students collaboratively contribute, learn from their peers, and practice the skills of teamwork and professionalism that are so important in careers. In business education, which features many case studies, project-based learning and entrepreneurial simulations, collaborative learning changes the classroom into an active learning lab.

Collaborative learning itself originated as a response to traditional lecture formats. In the 1960s and 70s, educational researchers and practitioners started to push for more student-centred methodologies. As guided by the Johnson brothers, the cooperative learning movement in the U.S.A. produced formalized models that were later incorporated into business and management education classes (Johnson & Johnson, 1989). Their studies showed that students who studied collaboratively learned more, understood the material more deeply and retained it longer than students who studied individually.

Contemporary collaborative learning combines aspects from these historical roots and recent tendencies. Today, in business classrooms, that means tools such as role-playing, group presentations, strategic planning simulations and consulting-style projects. The students are challenged to use theoretical knowledge and apply leadership, problem-solving and ethical decision-making under time-based urgencies.

The diversity of collaborative learning groups is another important factor. Heterogeneous grouping—of academic ability, cultural background, or communication style—also improves learning and critical thinking by creating an environment with multiple perspectives (Brindley et al., 2009). Students learning and working in an increasingly multicultural environment will undoubtedly gain from such exposure. Institutions dedicated to inclusive group formation practices and culturally competent training will ensure that collaborative learning serves equity and excellence.

To understand collaborative learning in business education, it is necessary to consider its theoretical ground, pedagogical applications, and emancipatory opportunities. Done well, it is a link between knowing and doing — an essential launching pad for the business leaders of tomorrow.

## PEER INSTRUCTION: A COMPLEMENTARY STRATEGY

Peer instruction, in addition to cooperative learning, also encourages valuable peer-to-peer discussion, which leads to conceptual understanding, critical thinking, and metacognition. Originating in undergraduate physics courses at Harvard University and popularized by Eric Mazur during the 1990s, peer instruction has been implemented in various disciplines, including business education (Mazur, 1997).

Peer instruction consists of a structured procedure: the instructor poses a conceptual question (often multiple-choice), and students think and vote. Then, they discuss their reasoning with each other and then reconsider and revise. This process clarifies misconceptions and supports understanding by expressing and defending one's ideas (Crouch & Mazur, 2001).

Peer teaching opportunities in business education are endless – from ethics discussions to financial analysis, marketing planning and case study appraisals. It is a method of promoting involving participation, particularly in large classes where learners may be passively engaged. Peer instruction encourages an environment where reasoning becomes visible, and the classroom becomes a learning community that works together to solve problems.

As opposed to the typical collaborative learning experience that tends to be for long-duration projects, where the peer instruction is brief and happens in cycles during a lecture or seminar, this immediacy, in turn, provides numerous opportunities for feedback and amendment. It also democratizes the classroom by allowing every student to have a voice irrespective of background and existing knowledge, not being new (Porter et al., 2011).

Studies have shown that peer instruction can help students more effectively and actively—for instance, in a population-based study, Freeman et al. (2014) reported that students who take courses in which they learn via active learning—often using peer instruction—show nearly half a standard deviation higher learning gains than students who take courses with traditional lectures. These benefits might be rephrased in the business world as more powerful analysis, precise understanding and sharper questioning.

Peer instruction has since been extended to have more technical power. Platforms such as Poll Everywhere, Mentimeter, Socrative, and LMS-provided toolsets (e.g., Moodle's quiz modules) support asking questions, obtaining real-time responses and learning analytics. These tools generate participation and provide rich data that can be used for formative assessment and adaptive teaching.

Peer instruction augments collaborative learning by offering structure, clear guidance, and real-time feedback to the active learning experience. Whereas cooperative learning focuses on permanent cooperative group intertwining, peer instruction focuses on teaching that activates immediate cognitive work, and it guarantees that students are not only "participating" but are learning from one another.

## DEVELOPING CRITICAL BUSINESS SKILLS THROUGH GROUP WORK

Collaborative learning within business education serves as an essential incubator for the necessary 21st-century workplace skills. Using interdisciplinary team projects and student-led exercises, participants gain experiential knowledge of leadership, decision-making, communication, and cultural intelligence skills essential to excelling in globalized, diversified work settings (Day et al., 2014).

One of the first advantages of working in a group is the development of leadership skills. They actively rotate roles—facilitator, timekeeper, evaluator—because it keeps students thinking about what it means to practice different forms of leadership. These defined roles enable each individual to develop skills which can be far-reaching in psychological terms, like managing team dynamics, conflict and strategic decision-making in a supported learning environment (Oakley et al., 2004). This way, learners enhance their self-confidence in expressing their ideas, working in teams, and influencing others.

Decision-making and negotiation skills are also developed. Students confront different views in a group context, learning to decide through consensus. This represents typical business settings where coordinated negotiation is needed to discover strategic solutions. Through working together with constraints—with less than perfect information or a limited time frame—students learn to assess options, calculate risks, and make decisions based not on faith but on evidence and analysis (Kaufman et al., 2000).

In addition, group work enhances cultural intelligence. Teams with individuals from different cultures, countries, educational backgrounds, or work experience are fertile ground for learning about different communication methods, decision-making norms, and value priorities (Earley & Mosakowski, 2004). Such experiences foster empathy and global awareness, which are increasingly important in today's multinationals and start-ups.

Articulation efforts of business education programs so frequently replicate actual corporate endeavours. For example, a class may create a business plan, analyze a market, or solve an ethical problem. Such simulations also serve to inculcate professionalism in students (such as responsibility for and time management with clients) and reinforce academic content.

Skill progress is also reinforced through measurement techniques. Peer review, reflective journals and group debriefing offer students clear ways to self-evaluate and learn through feedback. These metacognitive strategies promote emotional intelligence, adaptability, and resilience, thus valuable attributes across academic and professional domains (Brindley et al., 2009).

When group work is intentionally planned and efforts are taken to facilitate its smoothness, it transforms into something greater than a learning appliance. It serves as a kind of trial by fire, leaving the students with the values of cooperation, social skills and problem-solving necessary to be successful managers.

## THE ROLE OF TECHNOLOGY IN FACILITATING PEER LEARNING

Technology is transformative in enabling and amplifying peer learning in business education. Additionally, with the growing presence of digital tools in the classroom, instructors now have greater opportunities to promote collaboration, feedback, and engagement in real time or at their convenience (Hrastinski, 2008).

A technology that significantly impacts peer learning is the Learning Management System (LMS), the most widely used technology for employee development. Examples include discussion forums, peer-review assignments, Moodle, Blackboard or Canvas group workspaces. These tools enable students to exchange resources, comment on each other 's work, and participate in the scaffolded discussion, which is a vital component of peer instruction and collaborative knowledge creation.

Video conferencing platforms such as Zoom, Google Meet and Microsoft Teams have also become essential innovations in a hybrid or fully online learning model. These features all support virtual breakout rooms that allow small groups to discuss topics reflective of the face-to-face collaborative learning experience. Studies show that good online conversations can be at least as good as face-to-face ones if well moderated (Brindley et al., 2009).

Real-time polling and quizzing apps like Kahoot!, Poll Everywhere and Mentimeter are increasingly being applied as a tool for peer instruction. With these tools, teachers can ask conceptual questions and promptly obtain a response. More significant is the sharing of answers, which allows challenged children to compare results, discuss differences, and modify their interpretations during peer dialogue. This cyclic feedback loop is essential to peer instruction, enhancing retention and understanding (Mazur, 2001).

Students can co-author presentations, reports, and business plans with collaborative document tools like Google Docs, Microsoft OneNote, Living Atlas, and Notion. These tools are tools for tracking contributions, open collaboration, and open accountability. Commenting, suggesting edits, and replying in real time will also help kids gain communication and project management skills.

New technologies, from artificial intelligence to analytics tools, provide new opportunities to make learning more personalized and monitor engagement. For example, AI could offer insights into participation patterns in group work, recommend optimal group compositions according to learning preferences and interaction history, or provide personalized feedback to help improve students' contributions.

Another page-turner is gamification. Educational platforms incorporating game elements can motivate students and promote friendly competition, encouraging more peer-to-peer interaction. Platforms such as Classcraft and Edmodo Gamify also provide structured paths to integrate peer learning within a motivational framework (Deterding et al., 2011).

At the macro level, technology does not just back peer learning; it extends it, amplifies its effectiveness and weaves it with the digital competencies mandated in a contemporary business atmosphere. Teachers who wisely leverage technology for peer learning practices become more effective educators in their ability to engage students, build community, and ensure equitable participation and access.

## CHALLENGES AND MITIGATION STRATEGIES IN COLLABORATIVE LEARNING

Although there are many advantages to cooperative learning and peer instruction, there are also various difficulties that can detract from the optimal use if they are not tended to carefully—understanding these obstacles and developing strategies to address them are critical to the effective integration of business education.

a. Unequal Participation and Free-Riding:

The issue of unequal participation is reported most commonly in group work. Some learners dominate the conversation, while others may be passive or less talkative. This inequality may result in frustration, lower motivation and worse learning outcomes for all group members (Oakley et al., 2004).

Mitigation strategies are to make roles explicit within groups, make peer evaluations part of the grading scheme, and employ collaborative tools that record contributions (e.g., Google Docs version history). Switching instructors is also recommended to establish team norms and conduct check-ins on team processes early.

b. Interpersonal Conflict and Group Tension:

Cross-functional teams can also experience conflict when team members have different ways of communicating, working, or cultural expectations. Such tensions may undermine cooperation without appropriate means for conflict resolution (Brindley et al., 2009).

One way is to provide teachers with communication and conflict resolution training. There needs to be a safe space established for students to feel comfortable raising concerns. Structured reflection exercises and tools for anonymous feedback can also surface issues and address them easily.

c. Lack of Preparation or Understanding of Group Work:

Not all students know what collaborative learning and peer instruction are. Others might have had a bad experience or a misunderstanding of what the role requires, which can lead to a lack of enthusiasm or an inability to follow directions (Laal & Ghodsi, 2012).

So, pre-task briefings, orientation modules, and practice drills can develop student readiness. The purpose, process, and outcomes of group activities and peer instruction should be explained by faculty early on.

d. Assessment Challenges:

Assessing group work can be tricky. Teachers must evaluate both the group work and the contribution of each student. Without transparency or fairness, PAT can lose legitimacy as an assessment exercise.

Adopting multi-facet assessment approaches (e.g., incorporating peer assessment, self-assessment, instructor assessments and project deliverables) may increase fairness. Rubrics must be shared in advance so students know what is expected.

e. Technology Barriers:

Technology allows for collaboration but can also create inequality, technical issues and digital fatigue. Some students might have trouble getting the hang of different platforms or be slowed down due to internet connectivity problems.

Institutional responsibility is required to ensure digital equity through training, technical assistance, and access to needed resources. Instructors should exercise flexibility with deadlines and offer an option for alternative modes of participation.

f. Faculty Resistance and Lack of Training:

Educators are often reluctant to try active learning because it is unknown and time-consuming, and there are questions about its effectiveness (Prince, 2004).

Professional development programs, peer mentoring, and organizational recognition for innovative teaching can bring about the adoption. Sharing templates, toolkits, and best practices can also boost faculty confidence.

Although controversial debates are part and parcel of any pedagogical innovation, they are not destined to derail curriculum reform. With proactive planning, continued support, and responsive pedagogical design, collaborative learning can be successful in varied, complex, and technologically mediated learning environments.

## FRAMEWORKS FOR IMPLEMENTING COLLABORATIVE PEDAGOGIES IN BUSINESS CURRICULA

The effective infusion of collaborative learning and peer instruction into business instruction demands deliberate planning, systematic delivery, and constant improvement. Fads to be adopted should be grounded in evidence-based pedagogical parameters and concomitantly support the institution while having the flexibility to adapt to student and faculty needs.

a. Curriculum Alignment:

This pedagogy of collaboration needs to be integrated into the central design of the business curriculum, not limited to electives and extracurricular programs. To the extent that teamwork, communication, and ethicalreasoning are targeted learning objectives, they should beexplicit in syllabi, assessment criteria, and accreditation (Michaelsen & Sweet, 2008). Alignment is necessary to maintain consistency among teaching methods and skills employers value.

b. Course Design and Sequencing:

Work should be spread out in courses to scaffold collaborative complexity from semester to semester. Elementary classes can focus on the basics of teamwork. At the same time, advanced courses emphasize strategic teamwork, such as simulations, live case projects, and capstone experiences, which are slow but steady progressions of confidence and competence.

c. Team Formation Strategies:

Great teamwork begins with great teams. Random assignment can foster diversity, but more often, strategic grouping around complementary skills, learning styles, or cultural backgrounds leads to greater productivity. Some organizations also use surveys and or algorithms to maximize group chemistry.

d. Structured Group Processes:

The collaborative activity needs to be designed with specific objectives, schedules, planning and role assignments, and explicit outputs from the collaboration. Curriculum models such as Team-Based Learning (TBL) and Problem-Based Learning (PBL) provide evidence-based scaffolding in engaging the learner and driving accountability. These models allow for peer review, self-assessment and instructor feedback during the learning process (Brame & Biel, 2015).

e. Assessment and Feedback Mechanisms:

A solid model encompasses multidimensional measures that evaluate the collaboration process and product. Rubrics, peer evaluations, reflective journals, and progress reports allow for comprehensive and fair grading. These actions can be automated through digital platforms, delivering immediate insights.

f. Faculty Training and Support:

Teachers who want to support collaborative learning successfully need continuous support. Institutions must train faculty on group facilitation, conflict resolution, or digital pedagogy. Additionally, it is possible to support large classes by using teaching assistants and peer facilitators so that small groups can be effectively managed (Freeman et al., 2014).

g. Integration of Technology:

The enabling technology infrastructure should also enable collaboration. That ranges from LMS capabilities and cloud workspaces to video conferencing tools and analytics snapshots. Blended models, a combination of face-to-face and online tasks, are also frequently associated with the highest levels of engagement and flexibility (Means et al., 2013).

h. Continuous Improvement and Feedback Loops:

Iterative evaluation is necessary for successful implementation. Institutions should track student engagement, outcomes, and satisfaction measures to see how these become more mature over time. Best practices and reflection through the teaching community should be encouraged among the faculty.

By embracing a whole-school deployment model, business schools can incorporate collaborative learning and peer instruction within the DNA of business education, equipping students to be able, enthusiastic, and collaborative leaders in a complex society.

## DISCUSSION

The conclusions and insights offered throughout previous sections show us that cooperative learning and peer teaching are not just pedagogical alternatives that could support students toward producing the competencies needed in today's business settings. Educational theory, digital technology, and real-world business demands are the powerful forces that collide to make these strategies relevant and necessary.

One critical insight that is uncovered is the ripple effect of partnering. It deals with cognitive, affective, and behavioural learning areas. Students retain and understand information better and develop social skills, confidence and ethical judgment. These elements are becoming increasingly part of corporate recruitment plans, with soft skills such as emotional intelligence, flexibility, and collaborative problem-solving topping the chart for desired competencies (NACE, 2023).

Peer instruction addresses the much-neglected formative assessment and in-time conceptual feedback. Peer explanation and discussion allow the reader to transition from passive knowledge absorption to active comprehension. It is also inclusive in that it respects students' perspectives regardless of achieving or not achieving, being fluent in or not being fluent in the target language, and regardless of their culture (Crouch & Mazur, 2001).

When the technology is integrated, the rewards are even greater. Collaborative tools and digital learning spaces. Collaborative tools and online learning environments provide an open, flexible and scalable setting for peer interaction. Learning analytics can provide actionable information regarding participation patterns that can be used to take more effective action and to provide tailored support from educators. As discussed above, digital inclusion and accessibility must take precedence to avoid perpetuating new forms of inequality.

Conversation serves as a reminder that intention is crucial, as well. Throwing a project or discussion at them does not mean you are doing collaborative learning. Teachers need to set tasks with clear objectives, roles and assessments. Investment in faculty development, institutional support and curricular coherence is necessary for these strategies to succeed.

These strategies may not be universally successful across all settings. Cultural and disciplinary differences and institutional factors affect the effectiveness of collaborative and peer-based approaches. These strategies require a flexible, sensitive, evidence-based response to align them with the local context.

Peer discussion affirms the importance of co-learning and peer-to-peer instruction as building blocks of a new business educational model—one that educates students not to compete but to learn to collaborate and lead with empathy, critical thought and resilience.

## RECOMMENDATIONS AND SOLUTIONS

Following the comprehensive investigation of collaborative learning and peer instruction in business education, practical measures can be suggested to enhance their usefulness and effectiveness. These approaches were developed for educators, leaders, instructional designers, and policymakers seeking to build stronger, more inclusive, and future-ready learning environments.

a. Embed Collaborative Pedagogy into Learning Outcomes:

Those responsible for curricular development should see that competencies in teamwork, communication, and decision-making are reflected in program-level goal statements and directly tied to course-level student learning outcomes. Rubrics, assessments, and in-class activities should be connected to these goals to promote alignment and consistency.

b. Provide Ongoing Faculty Training and Mentorship:

Institutions should invest in robust faculty development beyond content mastery to encompass collaborative facilitation, assessment design, conflict resolution, and digital pedagogy. The sharing of best practices and support among faculty members as they move into active learning formats can be facilitated through peer mentorship and communities of practice (Michaelsen & Sweet, 2008).

c. Utilize Technology to Enhance Participation and Accountability:

Use collaborative platforms incorporating features like versioning, peer commenting and real-time interaction. Transparent tools like Slack, Google Workspace, or LMS-integrated peer review systems permit instructors to watch contributions and step in if necessary (Hrastinski, 2008).

d. Structure Group Work Around Realistic Business Scenarios:

The projects should work with real business challenges. e.g., market entry dilemmas, ethical dilemmas or stakeholder negotiation. These simulations encourage real-world interaction and experiential learning based on classroom theory.

e. Encourage Diverse Group Composition and Inclusivity:

The group projects should immerse students in genuine business challenges (e.g. market entry strategy, ethical dilemmas, or stakeholder negotiations). Where possible, incorporate real industry data or live case problems to increase authenticity. These practical experiences and simulations promote hands-on, experiential learning grounded in classroom theory, requiring students to apply concepts in real time and reflect on their solutions (Brindley et al., 2009).

f. Implement Peer and Self-Assessment as Standard Practice:

Use structured peer and self-assessment in both formative and summative assessment. These "tools" help men to be accountable and reflective, as well as help develop metacognition. When you work in a team, anonymous feedback websites can provide psychological safety and candid feedback (Oakley et al., 2004).

g. Address Resistance Proactively Through Institutional Support:

Acknowledge and confront apprehension of sceptical faculty with data, success stories and bite-size pilot projects. Incentivizing with teaching awards, redesign grants, or reduced teaching for innovation efforts may drive adoption.

h. Establish Feedback Loops and Iterate:

Collect student and faculty feedback at intervals during the semester. Conduct surveys, reflection journals and focus groups to find strengths and pain points. Adjust in light of this feedback to keep growing and stay relevant.

i. **Leverage Industry Partnerships for Experiential Projects:**

Encourage collaboration with businesses and organizations to bring real-world projects into the curriculum. For example, courses can include a consultancy project with a local company, a business plan competition, or an internship-like project component. Such partnerships enable students to apply classroom knowledge to live problems, enhancing the authenticity of learning (Rao et al., 2024)

This approach not only reinforces theory-through-practice but also improves employability by exposing students to industry expectations and teamwork in professional settings.

Following these guidelines, institutions can escape superficial adoption and establish an enduring, active, collaborative learning ecology. These are the networks necessary to ensure that graduates are grounded in content and the ability to be emotionally and socially intelligent, capable of adaptation, and prepared for leadership in the fast-paced world of dynamic systems.

## FUTURE RESEARCH DIRECTIONS

Although much has been accomplished concerning understanding and implementing collaborative learning and peer instruction in business education, some under-explored aspects remain. Subsequent studies allow future investigations to gain a more detailed understanding, test theoretical models, and develop applications for improving pedagogical practices in various settings.

a. Longitudinal Impact on Career Outcomes:

Although prior work provides evidence for the short-term academic advantages of social learning, more longitudinal research is required to evaluate the impact of such experiences on career paths, collaborative skills in the workforce, leadership, and job satisfaction after college completion.

b. Comparative Studies Across Disciplines and Institutions:

Future research should examine how collaborative and peer learning strategies function in other academic disciplines and types of institutions (e.g., public vs. private, liberal arts vs. business school). Such studies can contribute to informing factors of context that affect efficacy and adoption.

c. Cross-Cultural and International Perspectives:

More studies should consider the role of cultural and social norms and communication styles in collaborative learning within the multilingual classroom. A comparative analysis advanced as a part of global research can help identify patterns of best practices for how groups are formed, managed, and resolve conflict in various educational settings (Earley & Mosakowski, 2004).

d. Role of Artificial Intelligence and Learning Analytics:

AI and analytics are revolutionizing education. Future work should also investigate the potential of machine learning for optimizing matchmaking, participation monitoring, group success prediction, and feedback personalization. Ethical issues, such as privacy and bias, should also be explored.

e. Collaborative Learning for Underrepresented and Neurodiverse Students:

What is the nature of peer instruction and group work for students with disabilities, neurodiverse learners, and students from marginalized backgrounds? Further inquiry should explore design principles to promote equity in such collaborative environments.

f. Faculty Experience and Pedagogical Transformation:

Not much is known about the teacher's history of working with collaborative pedagogy. There is a need to study faculty motivation, faculty burnout, and professional identity transformation in moving from a lecturing to a facilitative teaching model (Prince, 2004).

g. Digital Platforms and Engagement Patterns:

More research is required on how specific tools (e.g., asynchronous forums versus real-time chats) influence the quality and depth of peer interaction. Insights from the user experience can inform the design of more user-friendly, pedagogically oriented platforms.

Through a detailed examination of these, scholars can help the development of a stronger, broader and more evidence-based collaborative and peer learning model. Such findings enable educators, curricula developers and policymakers to develop better teaching methodologies that meet the changing needs of learners and industries.

## CONCLUSION

This chapter has discussed the crucial importance of collaborative learning and peer instruction in business education innovation. To this end, it has provided a comprehensive indie covering theoretical bases, practical patterns, technical improvements, implementation guidelines, and future research. In today's global environment, business partners often must share information across time zones, organizational boundaries, and digital platforms; therefore, educational solutions should incorporate real-world learning experiences to prepare students for these realities

Students participating in collaborative learning create a deeper understanding of knowledge and develop leadership, critical thinking, and active communication skills by engaging in authentic, meaningful, and active team-based experiences. This is supplemented with peer instruction, in which conceptual learning is built up through reflection dialogue and peer teaching. Both strategies move business education from passive information consumption towards active socially mediated knowledge creation and professional growth.

Digital technology has increasingly amplified the scope and impact of collaborative pedagogies. Technology allows more flexible participation, immediate feedback, and performance monitoring to provide more inclusive and adaptive learning environments. However, successful integration depends upon institutional investment, thoughtful curricular planning and, most importantly, ongoing faculty development. Unequal participation, cultural challenges, and faculty resistance are real but not insurmountable. Educators can address these challenges through careful planning, clear assessment, and robust feedback culture and promote trust, equity, and motivation in student groups. Collaborative learning and peer learning are not the endgame but rather a means by which students are taught how to lead, work together, and continue learning in today's increasingly fast-paced world. As such, business education must shift beyond traditional pedagogy to focus on lively, experiential and student-centred pedagogy.

Collaborative learning and peer teaching are essential instruction tools for future business educators. However, to be sure, their value is neither simply their impact on educational outcomes nor upon resilient and inventive professionals of tomorrow. Institutions that embrace these practices are more likely to be able to face the special problems of the 21st century head-on and develop a generation of leaders who are as practised in strategy as in cooperation, communication, and ethical action.

## REFERENCES


Amri, M., Prasetyo, J., Halim, C., & Adhimas, Y. B. (2024). Assessing the influence of peer collaboration, classroom management, and assessment practices on student motivation in secondary education. *International Journal of Business, Law, and Education, 5*(2). Advance online publication. DOI: 10.56442/ijble.v5i2.660

Bandura, A. (1986). *Social foundations of thought and action: A social cognitive theory*. Prentice-Hall.

Bonwell, C. C., & Eison, J. A. (1991). Active learning: Creating excitement in the classroom (ASHE-ERIC Higher Education Report No. 1). The George Washington University, School of Education and Human Development. https://files.eric.ed.gov/fulltext/ED336049.pdf

Brame, C. J., & Biel, R. (2015). Test-enhanced learning: The potential for testing to promote greater learning in undergraduate science courses. *CBE Life Sciences Education, 14*(2), es4. DOI: 10.1187/cbe.14-11-0208 PMID: 25999314

Brindley, J. E., Blaschke, L. M., & Walti, C. (2009). Creating effective collaborative learning groups in an online environment. *International Review of Research in Open and Distance Learning, 10*(3). Advance online publication. DOI: 10.19173/irrodl.v10i3.675

Chi, M. T. H., Bassok, M., Lewis, M. W., Reimann, P., & Glaser, R. (1989). Self-explanations: How students study and use examples in learning to solve problems. *Cognitive Science, 13*(2), 145–182. DOI: 10.1207/s15516709cog1302_1

Crouch, C. H., & Mazur, E. (2001). Peer instruction: Ten years of experience and results. *American Journal of Physics, 69*(9), 970–977. DOI: 10.1119/1.1374249

Day, D. V., Fleenor, J. W., Atwater, L. E., Sturm, R. E., & McKee, R. A. (2014). Advances in leader and leadership development: A review of 25 years of research and theory. *The Leadership Quarterly, 25*(1), 63–82. DOI: 10.1016/j.leaqua.2013.11.004

Deterding, S., Dixon, D., Khaled, R., & Nacke, L. (2011). From game design elements to gamefulness: Defining 'gamification'. In *Proceedings of the 15th International Academic MindTrek Conference: Envisioning Future Media Environments* (pp. 9–15). DOI: 10.1145/2181037.2181040

Dewey, J. (1938). Experience and education. *Macmillan*. https://www.schoolofeducators.com/wp-content/uploads/2011/12/EXPERIENCE-EDUCATION-JOHN-DEWEY.pdf

Earley, P. C., & Mosakowski, E. (2004). Cultural intelligence. *Harvard Business Review, 82*(10), 139–146. https://hbr.org/2004/10/cultural-intelligence PMID: 15559582

Freeman, S., Eddy, S. L., McDonough, M., Smith, M. K., Okoroafor, N., Jordt, H., & Wenderoth, M. P. (2014). Active learning increases student performance in science, engineering, and mathematics. *Proceedings of the National Academy of Sciences of the United States of America, 111*(23), 8410–8415. DOI: 10.1073/pnas.1319030111 PMID: 24821756

Harasim, L. (2017). *Learning theory and online technologies* (2nd ed.). Routledge., DOI: 10.4324/9781315716831

Hrastinski, S. (2008). Asynchronous and synchronous e-learning. *EDUCAUSE Quarterly, 31*(4), 51–55. https://er.educause.edu/articles/2008/11/asynchronous-and-synchronous-elearning

Johnson, D. W., & Johnson, R. T. (1989). *Cooperation and competition: Theory and research.* Interaction Book Company.

Johnson, D. W., Johnson, R. T., & Smith, K. A. (2007). The state of cooperative learning in postsecondary postsecondary and professional settings. *Educational Psychology Review, 19*(1), 15–29. DOI: 10.1007/s10648-006-9038-8

Kaufman, D. B., Felder, R. M., & Fuller, H. (2000). Peer ratings in cooperative learning teams: What do they tell us? Proceedings of the 2000 Annual ASEE Meeting, St. Louis, MO. https://www.researchgate.net/publication/2450650_Peer_Ratings_in_Cooperative_Learning_Teams

Kolb, D. A. (1984). Experiential learning: Experience as the source of learning and development. *Prentice-Hall.* https://www.learningfromexperience.com/images/uploads/process-of-experiential-learning.pdf

Laal, M., & Ghodsi, S. M. (2012). Benefits of collaborative learning. *Procedia: Social and Behavioral Sciences, 31*, 486–490. DOI: 10.1016/j.sbspro.2011.12.091

Matongo, M., & Goronga, P. (2025). Embracing collaborative learning: Innovative teaching methods at tertiary level. In Burris-Melville, T. S., & Burris, S. T. (Eds.), *Developing effective and high-performing teams in higher education* (pp. 187–216). IGI Global., DOI: 10.4018/979-8-3693-3852-0.ch007

Mazur, E. (1997). *Peer instruction: A user's manual.* Prentice Hall., https://www.pearson.com/en-us/subject-catalog/p/Mazur-Peer-Instruction-A-User-s-Manual/P200000006892?view=educator

Means, B., Toyama, Y., Murphy, R., Bakia, M., & Jones, K. (2013). The effectiveness of online and blended learning: A meta-analysis of the empirical literature. *Teachers College Record.* https://eric.ed.gov/?id=EJ1018090

Michaelsen, L. K., & Sweet, M. (2008). The essential elements of team-based learning. *New Directions for Teaching and Learning*, *2008*(116), 7–27. DOI: 10.1002/tl.330

National Association of Colleges and Employers. (2023). Job Outlook 2023. https://www.naceweb.org

Oakley, B., Felder, R. M., Brent, R., & Elhajj, I. (2004). Turning student groups into effective teams. *Journal of Student-Centered Learning*, *2*(1), 9–34.

Piaget, J. (1954). *The construction of reality in the child.* Basic Books. DOI: 10.1037/11168-000

Porter, L., Bailey Lee, C., Simon, B., & Zingaro, D. (2011). Peer instruction: Do students really learn from peer discussion in computing? *Proceedings of the Seventh International Workshop on Computing Education Research,* 45–52. DOI: 10.1145/2016911.2016923

Prince, M. (2004). Does active learning work? A review of the research. *Journal of Engineering Education*, *93*(3), 223–231. DOI: 10.1002/j.2168-9830.2004.tb00809.x

Rao, S. S. P., Sekhar, S. C., Yadav, T. C. S., Kumar, V. P., & Haran, H. B. M. (2024). Implementing experiential learning strategies for enhanced business education in India: Challenges and opportunities. Journal of Innovations in Educational Research, 4(3). https://jier.org/index.php/journal/article/view/1301

Reuter, J., Dias, M. F., & Sousa, M. J. (2022). Collaborative learning: Increasing work motivation through game-based learning. In Bernardes, O., Amorim, V., & Moreira, A. C. (Eds.), *Handbook of research on cross-disciplinary uses of gamification in organizations* (pp. 277–292). IGI Global., DOI: 10.4018/978-1-7998-9223-6.ch013

Singha, R. (2024). Cultivating holistic learning environments in higher education: Mindfulness, compassion, and Ubuntu philosophies. In Omona, K., & O'dama, M. K. (Eds.), *Global perspectives on micro-learning and micro-credentials in higher education* (pp. 174–194). IGI Global., DOI: 10.4018/979-8-3693-0343-6.ch011

Singha, R., & Kanna, Y. S. (2025). Supporting educators with addiction: Intentional learning communities in higher education. In Velliaris, D. M. (Ed.), *Academic support services and strategies in higher education* (pp. 171–192). IGI Global., DOI: 10.4018/979-8-3693-4175-9.ch007

Sweller, J. (1988). Cognitive load during problem-solving: Effects on learning. *Cognitive Science, 12*(2), 257–285. DOI: 10.1207/s15516709cog1202_4

Tiwari, R., Arya, R. K., Bansal, M., & Bansal, A. (2014). Application of collaborative learning in business education. *International Journal of Advanced Research in Management and Social Sciences, 3*(11), 134–145.

Vygotsky, L. S. (1978). *Mind in society: The development of higher psychological processes*. Harvard University Press.

Woodward, R., & Pattinson, N. (2023). Informal peer learning of diverse undergraduate students: Some learners make meaning through collaborative activity. *Practitioner Research in Higher Education, 15*(1), 72–85. https://files.eric.ed.gov/fulltext/EJ1409406.pdf

Wu, J., & Yu, X. (2025). The influence of formative assessment on academic performance: Exploring the role of teachers' emotional support. *Frontiers in Psychology, 16*, 1567615. DOI: 10.3389/fpsyg.2025.1567615 PMID: 40271370

Yu, C., Walsh, J., & Boone, J. (2023). Optimizing online collaborative learning: Challenges and strategies in online teaching and learning. In Keengwe, J. (Ed.), *Handbook of research on facilitating collaborative learning through digital content and learning technologies* (pp. 20–43). IGI Global., DOI: 10.4018/978-1-6684-5709-2.ch002

## KEY TERMS AND DEFINITIONS

**Active Learning:** Active learning is a student-centred approach to instruction that allows students to participate in their learning through engaged activities and critical reflection. Instead of being passive listeners, the students participate in discussions, problem-solving, and case studies and undertake various activities (Bonwell & Eison, 1991). It is also about student input and responsibility in creating knowledge.

**Business Education:** Business education involves academic programs that prepare students for careers in business and instructional practices that prepare students for business careers. It covers general management, marketing, finance, entrepreneurship, and organizational behaviour and strives to build technical and soft skills, such as leadership and teamwork.

**Collaborative Learning:** Collaborative learning is an instructional approach in which students work in groups to accomplish shared learning goals. This method encourages the co-construction of knowledge, mutual help, and the socialization of interpersonal skills. It was founded on a constructivist overview of mutual accountability and interdependence (Johnson & Johnson, 1989).

**Peer Instruction:** Peer instruction is a method of teaching students by having them explain the material to one another, often after the instructor has posed a conceptual question. It facilitates comprehension in dialogue with class peers, promotes the skill of critical thinking and eradicates any misunderstanding (Mazur, 1997).

**Critical Business Skills:** Critical business skills are the hard, operational skills without which businesses cannot function today. These range from leadership to decision-making/ negotiation, communication, cultural intelligence, and strategic thinking. The knowledge of these languages is more than theoretical but also experiential.

**Experiential Pedagogy:** Experiential pedagogy is a philosophy of teaching and learning that focuses on learning by doing and reflection. It is based on the models of Dewey (1938) and Kolb (1984) and advocates for active, applied tasks in the real world, simulations, internships, and projects that connect theory to practice.

**Group Dynamics:** The term group dynamics is a system of behaviours and psychological processes occurring within a social group (intragroup dynamics) or between social groups (intergroup dynamics). Contributing to group effectiveness and learning outcomes are roles, communication patterns, power sharing, conflict management, and cohesiveness (Forsyth, 2014), which are also present in educational settings.

**Technology-Enhanced Learning:** Technology-enhanced learning uses digital tools and platforms to improve and enable learning. Examples are collaboration simulation Analytics. It enables flexibility, scalability, and student interaction in synchronous and asynchronous environments.

# Chapter 8
# Instilling Creative Confidence Through Experiential Challenge:
## The 21-Day Creativity Challenge

**Stacy Grau**
https://orcid.org/0000-0002-7150-3583
*Texas Christian University, USA*

## ABSTRACT

*Fostering creative confidence is essential for innovation and enables students to tackle problems with optimism and resilience. Organizations and businesses are increasingly interested in creativity and innovation in the workplace and are concerned that students are not developing that skill set in college. Many students express that they don't feel creative. However, creativity can be rejuvenated. In an era where employers rank creativity among the most critical skills for the future, nurturing creative confidence in students has become a priority. The 21-day creativity challenge is a structured approach that engages students regardless of their starting point. They are introduced to seven design mindsets (adapted from IDEO and Stanford's Hasso Plattner Institute of Design) and select from a menu of activities. This chapter outlines the premise for the activity, detailing the conceptual and theoretical foundations, considerations made during the assignment's creation, and a thematic analysis of reflection papers from 30 students in an entrepreneurship course taken in Spring 2023*

DOI: 10.4018/979-8-3373-7523-6.ch008

## INTRODUCTION

Fostering creativity and creative confidence is essential for innovation, enabling students to tackle problems with optimism and resilience. The World Economic Forum (2023) ranked creative thinking as one of the top five skills for the future. Organizations and businesses are increasingly interested in creativity and innovation in the workplace and are concerned that students are not developing this skill set in college. Moreover, many students express that they don't feel creative. Studies indicate that creative confidence declines from middle school through adulthood (Saggar et al., 2019), partly due to the influence of standardized testing, among other reasons. However, creativity can be rejuvenated.

Creativity cannot be taught through a lecture; instead, it must be experienced. Experiential education is crucial for increasing the engagement of Generation Z, which tends to value hands-on, real-world applications of knowledge. A study by the National Association of Colleges and Employers (NACE) found that 71% of experiential learners felt a stronger connection between their degrees and their jobs (Kahn & Patil 2025). There are several experience-based options to instill creativity, such as design-based learning, including design sprints or design thinking workshops, creative exercises, and opportunities for play. However, these are short in length and are rarely structured to scaffold experiences to connect to creative mindsets.

Creative confidence is the belief in one's ability to generate new ideas and bring them to life (Kelley & Kelley, 2013). Business leaders have identified creativity as a top leadership trait for handling complexity. Similarly, global skill forecasts rank creativity, originality, and initiative among the most essential skills by 2025 (Leopold, 2025). The AACSB has incorporated innovation and creativity into its updated accreditation standards (AACSB 2020).

The 21-day creativity challenge is a structured approach that engages students regardless of their starting point. Students are introduced to seven design mindsets (adapted from IDEO and Stanford's Hasso Plattner Institute of Design) and select from a menu of activities. Each student chooses two activities for each design mindset, leaving the remaining seven activities as free choice. Additionally, students are encouraged to step out of their comfort zones when selecting the seven activities that are unrelated to specific design abilities. They complete these activities and document their work and reflections in a design journal. At the end of the 30 days, students write an overall reflection paper. This chapter outlines the premise for the activity, detailing the conceptual and theoretical foundations, considerations made during the creation of the assignment, and a thematic analysis of reflection papers from 30 students enrolled in an entrepreneurship course taken in Spring 2023. The assignment can be found in Appendix A.

## CREATIVE CONFIDENCE

IDEO leaders Tom and David Kelley, who popularized the term, define creative confidence as the natural human ability to generate breakthrough ideas and the courage to act on them (Kelley & Kelley, 2013). This confidence is based on beliefs—that someone can achieve a goal as long as they have the right mindset and some guided mastery. As such, Bandura's theory of self-efficacy and Dweck's theory of the growth mindset play important foundational roles in creative confidence.

The theory of self-efficacy explains how belief in one's capability influences motivation and performance. High self-efficacy is linked to perseverance and resilience in the face of doubt and even failure, whereas low self-efficacy leads to avoidance of challenges (Bandura, 1997). Kelley & Kelley (2013) connect creative confidence to self-efficacy through "guided mastery," where small steps can help overcome fear of failure and self-doubt. The concept of guided mastery is crucial to developing creative confidence. Kelley recounts how people who experience a series of small creative successes gradually overcome their fear and doubt, gaining greater confidence in their creative abilities (Kelley & Kelley, 2013). Therefore, as individuals gather positive creative experiences, their confidence "muscle" becomes stronger.

In other words, creative confidence is the self-assurance necessary to generate creative ideas and bring them to life. It closely aligns with the construct of creative self-efficacy, defined by Tierney and Farmer (2002) as the belief one can produce creative outcomes. Creative confidence encompasses both the idea generation and execution aspects of creativity. It is not a fixed trait; rather, it can be developed and strengthened over time. There's been a connection with creativity and individuals and teams across several settings, including education, manufacturing, operations, financial, and insurance (Tierney & Farmer 2011). Bandura emphasized that self-efficacy develops through mastery experiences—repeated small successes that reinforce one's belief in their abilities. So, if creative self-efficacy is necessary for creative performance, it is important to understand the best way to foster it.

A second theoretical foundation for creative confidence is Dweck's concept of a growth mindset. Dweck's research distinguishes between a fixed mindset (believing abilities are innate and unchangeable) and a growth mindset (believing abilities can be developed through effort and learning) (Dweck, 2006). Applying this to creativity, a growth mindset means believing that one's creative ability is not static but can expand with practice. This belief is pivotal to creative confidence – students who think "I'm just not a creative person" are less likely to attempt creative tasks, whereas those who believe they can improve will persist and learn. Studies show that a growth creative mindset is positively linked to creative self-efficacy and creative performance (Royston & Reiter-Palmon, 2019). In a study of business students, those with malleable views of creativity showed higher creative self-efficacy and produced more original solutions to problems. In short, when students adopt the mindset that creativity is a skill to be developed, their confidence increases. This connects to Bandura's point that belief influences behavior – that believing in improvable creativity encourages students to engage in creative practice, further building competence and confidence.

Creative confidence (creative self-efficacy) is an important predictor of creative performance. And that makes sense for many majors – from fine arts to engineering to education to creative writing. It is also essential to a variety of people – from high school students and college students to graduate students and professionals. It is also essential as a set of skills for the future. But is it important to business majors? The answer, it seems, is yes.

## CREATIVE CONFIDENCE AND BUSINESS STUDENTS

Creative confidence has tangible importance for students, particularly for business students pursuing careers in entrepreneurship, innovation, and marketing. Research in organizational psychology and education shows a strong link between creative confidence and real-world creative performance (Haase et al., 2018). In other words, those who believe in their creative abilities tend to be more creative by objective measures. This is intuitive – confidence encourages individuals to attempt challenging creative tasks, persist through obstacles, and proactively put forth new ideas, all of which lead to more creative outcomes.

First, consider students in entrepreneurship and innovation (whether as a major, minor, or general interest). Entrepreneurs constantly encounter uncertain problems and must identify opportunities in the marketplace. Creative self-efficacy is a driver of opportunity recognition and innovative behavior. One study found that among college students, those who engaged in intrapreneurial activities were more effective at recognizing business opportunities when they had higher creative self-efficacy (Liao et al., 2022). In fact, creative self-efficacy mediated the relationship between intrapreneurial mindset and opportunity recognition, indicating that intrapreneurship led to opportunity identification largely by boosting students' confidence in their creative abilities. Creative self-belief serves as a "bridge" connecting individual initiative to entrepreneurial outcomes. Students with greater creative confidence are more likely to persevere through the ambiguity and risks inherent in launching new ventures. They view setbacks as learning rather than as proof of a lack of talent. This resilience is vital for innovation. Indeed, prior studies report that creative self-efficacy enhances individuals' motivation and persistence in the face of challenges, leading to greater success in innovation tasks. High creative confidence thus equips future entrepreneurs to handle the uncertainty of start-up life with optimism and grit.

Second, in fields like marketing and advertising, creativity is highly valued. Business students entering marketing roles will be expected to generate fresh campaign ideas, design creative content, and solve consumer problems in innovative ways. Creative confidence can significantly influence their performance in these tasks. In a recent study by Puente-Díaz and Cavazos-Arroyo (2022), students were given a divergent thinking challenge in a marketing context. Those who reported higher pre-task creative self-efficacy not only generated more creative ideas but also felt more creative confidence after completing the task. In short, believing "I can be creative in marketing" became a self-fulfilling prophecy – it led to objectively better creative performance and reinforced the students' confidence for future tasks. This finding highlights a cycle; for example, confidence enables performance, and successful performance reinforces greater confidence. For marketing students, such a cycle is crucial; it can mean the difference between sticking with a conventional, safe campaign or proposing an unconventional idea with the potential for high payoff.

Beyond specific roles, creative confidence broadly contributes to students' success. Students with higher creative self-efficacy tend to engage more in class projects that require creativity and display greater willingness to assume leadership in team innovation activities. Over the long term, creative confidence can significantly shape career trajectories. Employers consistently rank creativity and problem-solving as top competencies for new hires. In surveys by the World Economic Forum and others, creativity is listed alongside analytical thinking and problem-solving as essential for the modern workforce (Leopold 2025). For business students, this indicates that demonstrating creative confidence – the ability to propose innovative ideas and the initiative to implement them – can be a key differentiator in job applications and early career performance.

Finally, creative confidence contributes to personal growth and leadership. Leaders with creative confidence encourage a culture of innovation, as they are unafraid of experimentation and can inspire the same fearlessness in their teams. For today's business students—the CEOs of tomorrow—developing that creative confidence during their education is an investment in their leadership capacity. In summary, creative confidence is a catalyst for entrepreneurial activity, a driver of innovation, and a core professional skill in marketing and beyond. It empowers business students to not only envision novel solutions but also to confidently implement and advocate for them, bridging the knowing-doing gap that often hampers innovation.

## CRITERIA FOR BUILDING CREATIVE CONFIDENCE INTERVENTIONS

Given this foundation, there are important issues to consider when designing an assignment aimed at increasing creative confidence by fostering a growth mindset and enhancing confidence through elements of self-guided mastery. Whether using this one, adapting it, or designing a new one, there are important considerations. These include:

- Experiential and active. Creative confidence grows through action, not theory. Kolb's experiential learning theory (1984) posits that knowledge is created through the transformation of experience. The cycle of concrete experience, reflection, conceptualization, and experimentation is well suited for building creativity. Experiential learning supports risk-taking and active engagement in problem-solving (Kolb & Kolb, 2005). Assignments should require students to do or create something new regularly. In the 21-Day Challenge model, students engage in daily creativity exercises (e.g., improvising a solution to a random problem, drawing something, writing a short poem, trying a new technique to spark ideas). This consistent practice aligns with the idea that creative confidence is like a muscle – it strengthens with frequent use.
- Scaffold tasks. A crucial implication of Bandura's work is to sequence tasks from simple to more complex, allowing students to achieve early wins. By scaffolding in this way, students build confidence at each step. Each success, no matter how small, should be acknowledged – this could be via self-reflection ("What did I accomplish? How do I feel about it?").
- Encourage risk-taking in a safe environment. Building creative confidence requires addressing the fear that often hinders creativity. Classroom culture must therefore promote risk-taking and normalize failure as a part of learning. This can be achieved through in-class activities that enhance psychological safety, as well as by considering how challenges are graded. Grading schemes reflect this by rewarding reflection and effort, not just the "success" of the final product.
- Reflection and journaling. This consolidates learning and self-confidence. In a creativity challenge assignment, having students keep a design journal is highly effective. Each day, they document what they did, why they chose the activity, and most importantly, how it affected their creative confidence. Prompts like "How did this activity make you feel more (or less) creative? What surprised you?" can guide introspection. This practice serves two purposes: students become more mindful of their growth, and instructors gain insight into students' evolving mindsets. By writing about their small wins

and dissecting failures for lessons, students reframe setbacks as part of their growth. This reflective process ties into Bandura's notion of mastery experiences: even if an outcome wasn't a complete success, extracting learnings from it counts as a mastery experience that can build confidence.

- Choice and autonomy. Research suggests that giving students autonomy can enhance engagement. In building creative confidence, allowing students some choice in activities can be empowering. The 21-Day Challenge, for instance, lets students select from a menu of activities in each design ability category. This autonomy allows students to tailor the challenge to their interests or stretch areas. It likely increases buy-in – they feel ownership of their creative journey. Creative confidence is personal, so what challenges one student may be easy for another and vice versa. By offering options, you accommodate different starting points.
- Length and consistency. The duration of interventions can influence their effectiveness. A multi-week challenge has advantages over a one-off workshop because it reinforces habits and allows time for mindset changes. Consistency emphasizes that creativity is a practice, not a sporadic talent. At the same time, introducing variety during that period keeps students engaged, hence mixing the types of tasks as mentioned above.
- Assessment: focus on growth. When grading or evaluating creative confidence assignments, it's important to assess reflections, effort, and growth rather than merely the creative output. This communicates to students that the process and learning are what truly matter. By making growth explicit, students are more likely to recognize it within themselves, reinforcing their newfound confidence.

## THE 21-DAY CREATIVITY CHALLENGE

The purpose of the 21-Day Creativity Challenge is to provide a structured framework for students to enhance their creative confidence. The assignment consists of a set of practice activities designed to be completed almost every day. This challenge spans 21 days (and includes 21 activities). However, students are allowed 30 days to complete the course while balancing it with their other classes and activities. The challenge is rooted in seven core creative abilities (derived from information from IDEO and the Stanford D School). The activities within the challenge are based on the design mindset and serve as excellent ways to explore creativity. Students have the option to choose, but they must select at least two activities (14 in total) from each of the seven core areas. The remaining seven activities may be chosen from the creative abilities for which students desire additional practice or simply find interesting. Students document everything in a design journal and submit a reflection paper at the end of the challenge. The assignment is detailed in Appendix A.

Core creative abilities include:

- Navigate Ambiguity: This is the ability to recognize and endure the discomfort of uncertainty while developing strategies to address ambiguity when necessary.
- Learn from Others: This involves empathizing with and embracing diverse perspectives, testing new ideas collaboratively, and observing and learning from unfamiliar contexts.
- Synthesize Information: This is the ability to make sense of information and find insights and opportunities within.
- Experiment Quickly: This ability involves generating ideas swiftly – whether written, drawn, or built.
- Move between Concrete and Abstract: This skill involves understanding stakeholders and purposes to define the features of the product or service.
- Build & Craft Intentionally: This ability focuses on intentional construction, presenting work at the most suitable level of resolution for the audience and the feedback sought.
- Communicate Deliberately: The ability to create, capture, and share stories, ideas, concepts, reflections, and learnings with the appropriate audiences.

## METHODOLOGY

After completing the activities and recording the results in their design journals, students wrote a final reflection paper. The paper prompts included: (1) Describe your experience with the 21-day creativity challenge. What were your goals for this? Why? How well do you feel you moved the needle on your goals? What was your favorite activity and why? What is your least favorite activity and why? (2) Describe your creative confidence. How confident are you? Was it more or less than when you started this challenge? What areas do you excel in? Where do you wish to improve? In Spring 2023, 30 undergraduate students in an Entrepreneurship class completed the challenge. They were majors and minors in entrepreneurship. The papers were analyzed for key themes across the prompts, general themes, and themes specific to creative confidence/creative self-efficacy and growth mindset.

## ANALYSIS

Thirty students completed the overall reflection papers. Student information was deidentified, and quotes are identified as student 1, 2, and so on. The analysis includes more than 17,000 words of qualitative data. ChatGPT4 was used to analyze the first draft of the data. The author then refined the themes based on a manual analysis of the reflection comments. Braun and Clarke (2006) lay out a framework for thematic analysis that was utilized. Additionally, more recent studies (Soboleva et al., 2023) explore the use of AI tools to assist with coding themes. While these tools offer support, they did not replace human interpretation. The first analysis covers the general codes and overall themes of the papers, including respondent goals and their most and least favorite activities. The purpose was to identify patterns of meaning across the entire student experience. The second analysis focuses explicitly on the growth mindset and creative confidence. The analysis demonstrates that the 21-Day Creativity Challenge has achieved the goals of the assignment.

### Goals and Activities

The first analysis examined the key themes of the reflection without any additional structure or categories. This included student goals and their most and least favorite activities, as these were specific questions in the reflection. Student goals fell into five primary categories.

- Boosting Creative Confidence: Many students want to feel more confident in their creativity, especially in less familiar domains like visual arts, storytelling, or ideation. They used phrases like "I wanted to feel more confident," "believe in my ideas," and "take more creative risks."
- Trying New Things: Students aimed to expand their definition of "creative" and deliberately selected activities beyond their usual interests. They used phrases like "try things I never do," "step outside my comfort zone," and "use different parts of my brain."
- Reconnecting with Creativity: Some students had previously enjoyed creative expression but had lost touch with it. Their goal was to reconnect with these aspects of themselves. They talked about things like "getting back into creativity," "reigniting spark," and "remembering what I used to love."
- Mental Well-Being and Self-Reflection: A subset saw the challenge as a way to pause, reflect, de-stress, or introduce mindfulness into their routine. They used phrases like "slow down," "unplug," "use this for mental clarity," and "reflect on who I am."

- Developing a Creative Practice / Habit Formation: Some hoped to use the challenge to cultivate a daily habit or routine of intentional creativity. They used phrases like "do something creative every day," "develop a habit," and "establish structure."

*Table 1. Goals for the 21-Day Creativity Challenge*

| Type of Goal | % of Students | Example Indicators |
|---|---|---|
| Boost creative confidence | 80% | Confidence, voice, belief, fear of judgment |
| Try new things | 67% | Outside comfort zone, new activities |
| Reconnect with lost creativity | 50% | Rediscover, reignite, childhood creativity |
| Mental well-being / reflection | 40% | Pause, mindfulness, mental clarity |
| Build a creative habit | 30% | Daily practice, structure, routine |

## Themes in Favorite and Least Favorite Activities

Students were also asked about their favorite and least favorite activities. This insight helps refine the activities and understand what resonated with them. Students preferred activities that felt emotionally resonant, visually expressive, or playful. These created flow states and fostered intrinsic motivation. They tended to dislike tasks that felt like monitoring, either too tedious or overly abstract and ill-defined. Such tasks lacked emotional payoff or felt disconnected from creativity. Tactile activities like painting, collaging, and puzzles were widely enjoyed, likely due to the instant feedback and satisfaction from completing these tasks.

*Table 2. Most Favorite Activities*

| Theme | Activities | Quotes |
|---|---|---|
| Personal meaning & flow | Letter to future self<br>Wandering aimlessly<br>Recess / unstructured play<br>Daydreaming and drawing | "Writing a letter to myself helped me visualize my future in a way I never had."<br>"Recess reminded me what it felt like to just play — I needed that." |
| Activities that enabled tangible creative output | Mood boards<br>Watercolor painting<br>Designing logos<br>Sketching/doodling<br>Cooking something new | "I still look at my mood board every day. It keeps me going."<br>"Cooking alfredo from scratch was messy but made me feel proud." |
| Idea-heavy and playful challenges | 100 ideas challenge<br>Story dice<br>Ideation matrix<br>Cartoon self-portraits | "Drawing myself as a Jedi? That was the moment I started having fun." |

*Table 3. Least Favorite Activities*

| Theme | Activities | Quotes |
|---|---|---|
| Tasks perceived as tedious or unclear | Record your purchases<br>Track your social media use<br>Budget/time logs | "It felt like accounting homework, not creativity."<br>"Recording purchases didn't spark anything for me." |
| Conceptually Vague or difficult prompts | Think big to small<br>Design your own logo or crest<br>Create a coat of arms | "The logo took forever because I didn't know how to represent myself."<br>"Thinking from big to small was so tedious I almost quit that one." |
| Creative writing/storytelling (for some) | Create a story from a prompt or image<br>Write a bad poem | "Poetry isn't my thing. I dreaded that one."<br>"Storytelling feels forced and awkward for me." |

## Overall Themes

Several key themes emerged from the reflection papers, helping to identify the main issues across the entire experience.

### Self-Awareness and Identity Development

Students reflected deeply on who they are as learners, creators, and individuals. The challenge became a mirror for many, revealing long-forgotten passions, dormant interests, and internalized assumptions about their abilities. Some described reconnecting with their childhood selves, while others saw the experience as an awakening. Examples: "This was the first time since elementary school I was able to do fun and engaging exercises." — Student 6, "I realized I used to love being alone outside walking, running, reading… I had forgotten that." — Student 18, "I've started to think of myself as a creative person — in a more holistic sense." — Student 2.

## Rediscovery of Joy, Play, and Curiosity

Numerous students mentioned how the challenge rekindled joy, exploration, and play. These weren't just pleasant experiences; they were transformational. In contrast to traditional coursework, students valued the "permission" to experiment, play, and explore with no grades attached. Examples: "Recess reminded me of being a kid again… and made me rethink how I want my life to feel." — Student 22, "I liked pretending I was a detective putting a puzzle together without the box." — Student 8. The scavenger hunt made me really *see* my environment. It was like new eyes." — Student 29.

## Reflection on Time, Routine, and Presence

The challenge created disruptions in students' routines, and for many, this opened up space for reflection on time, structure, and mindfulness. Several students described how the activities shifted their perception of how they use their days, what they prioritize, and how often they operate on autopilot. Examples: "I learned how much time I waste scrolling on Instagram… now I go on walks." — Student 1, "These 21 days allowed me to discover parts of life I don't normally see." — Student 10, "I didn't build a habit of doing them daily… and I wish I had. I saw the power of small routines." — Student 11.

## Exploration of Discomfort and Ambiguity

Students often wrote about discomfort, frustration, or fear, and how these emotions became tools for growth. Challenges involving ambiguity, introspection, or new behaviors often triggered resistance but also led to some of the deepest insights. The emotional labor involved was real and significant. Examples: "I had to let go of my fear of being wrong and just start drawing." — Student 13, "Wandering aimlessly scared me… but I learned a lot from the discomfort." — Student 23, "I don't like poetry. Writing a terrible poem was my least favorite… but I did it anyway." — Student 7.

## Connection with Others and Social Creativity

While many challenges were completed solo, several students highlighted the social dimensions of creativity: interviewing people, observing human behavior, and collaborating with peers. Some students reflected on how shared experiences fostered deeper learning. Examples: "I did the daydreaming activity with a friend the next week to decompress." — Student 9, "Talking to Master Kim about South Korean culture blew my mind… I asked 30 questions." — Student 23.

## Discovery of New Tools and Practices for Well-Being

Students discovered strategies they could use to manage stress, find inspiration, or regulate emotions. These strategies ranged from journaling and sketching to social media detoxing and morning reflection. Several noted plans to maintain or adapt these activities after the assignment. Examples: "I learned how to integrate small creative practices into my corporate life after graduation." — Student 30, "My new habit is doing puzzles or going on walks to shift my mood." — Student 7, "I'm going to keep my mood board up — I love walking past it each day." — Student 10.

## Perspective-Taking and Cognitive Flexibility

Through challenges like cartoon self-portraits, interviews, and ideation exercises, students cultivated the ability to see from new vantage points. Several highlighted the value of looking at ordinary things differently — chairs, cards, logos, and even themselves. Examples: "Drawing myself as a Jedi cartoon taught me I can have fun and be creative in ways I never expected." — Student 6, "The chair observation — watching how people use such a simple thing — changed how I observe." —Student 19,

*Table 4. Overall Theme Frequencies (n = 30)*

| Theme | % of Students | Examples |
|---|---|---|
| Self-awareness & identity | 93% | Rediscovering passions, reflecting on creative self |
| Joy, play, curiosity | 80% | Recess, puzzles, cartooning, exploring |
| Time & routine reflection | 73% | Social media detox, new habits, slowing down |
| Ambiguity & emotional range | 77% | Tolerating fear, perfectionism, discomfort |
| Social & interpersonal learning | 60% | Interviews, group activities, observing others |
| Tools for well-being | 67% | Morning routines, sketching, journaling |
| Perspective-taking & flexibility | 70% | Unusual tasks, storytelling, rethinking "normal" |

While this was one of several assignments in the course, it seemed that most students did not approach it as a checklist but rather as something deeper. They viewed this as a way to disrupt thinking patterns and as a vehicle for play and purpose. Many students reignited their creativity and began to see themselves a little differently.

## Themes for Creative Self-Efficacy and Growth Mindset

Considering the theoretical implications of creative self-efficacy and growth mindset, it was important to explore these themes in greater detail.

### Letting Go of Perfection & Control

Many students began the challenge with perfectionist tendencies or fear of failure. Through repeated activities that required improvisation or ambiguity, many let go of rigid expectations. For example, students described an improved tolerance for messy drafts, initial failures, or less-polished results, and several cited this shift as the *most* important benefit of the challenge. Examples: "Even having the self-control to put the pencil down… avoiding perfection… was achievable." — Student 7, "I now feel more proud of my work… not every idea has to be perfect." — Student 11, "Art is like ideas—quantity can be just as important as quality." — Student 22.

### Purposeful Discomfort and New Experiences

A defining characteristic of a growth mindset is embracing challenges. Over 80% of students intentionally chose activities they didn't expect to excel at. Several overcame self-doubt regarding drawing, storytelling, or public expression, and some described choosing "the hardest looking activity" on purpose. Examples: "I pushed myself to do those activities I was avoiding… and saw a shift in perspective." — Student 20 "Storytelling was daunting... but I forced myself through it." — Student 10, "I did things I'd never have done without this. It changed me." — Student 29.

### Shifting Mindset on Creativity Itself

Students began to view creativity as a process rather than a product, and as accessible to everyone, not just those typically labeled as creative. Many expanded their personal definitions of creativity to include cooking, daydreaming, interviewing, and exploring, and some experienced a shift in mindset from seeing it as "creative talent" to understanding it as "creative practice." Examples: "I used to think creativity was drawing or art… now I know it's everywhere." — Student 1, "This challenge helped me see creativity as part of my daily life, not just projects."

— Student 5, "Creativity is more about being curious and willing than being good at something." — Student 30.

## Confidence Through Iteration and Action

All students reported increased creative confidence. Growth occurred not from mastery, but from repetition, risk-taking, and persistence. Confidence improved most in ideation, experimentation, and nonjudgmental self-expression. Some cited activities like the "100 ideas" or "story dice" as breakthrough moments. Examples: "I went from a 4 to an 8 on the confidence scale." — Student 2, "My creative confidence isn't through the roof… but it's undoubtedly higher than when I started." — Student 17, "Turns out I'm decent at watercoloring. That's exciting." — Student 20.

## From Fear to Flow: Navigating Ambiguity

Students acknowledged their discomfort with ambiguity, but many gained tools to navigate it with curiosity. Some initially dreaded unstructured tasks but later found enjoyment in them. Others learned to quiet their inner critic during the early stages of idea development. Examples: "Not knowing what's around the corner haunts me… but life is full of corners." — Student 11, "Once I stopped taking the challenges too seriously, my creativity went through the roof." — Student 18.

*Table 5. Growth Mindset and Creative Confidence Themes (n = 30 students)*

| Theme | % of Students | Indicators |
|---|---|---|
| Letting go of perfection/control | 87% | Released expectations, embraced messy drafts |
| Purposeful discomfort | 83% | Chose hard/unfamiliar tasks intentionally |
| Creative confidence increased | 100% | All students reported increased self-belief |
| Creativity redefined | 90% | Saw creativity in new domains (play, cooking, ideation) |
| Navigating ambiguity | 77% | Learned to start before knowing the outcome |
| Joy/play rediscovered | 65% | Activities brought back childhood-like fun |
| Idea generation improved | 70% | Reported growth in idea quantity |
| Fear of judgment reduced | 53% | Less reliant on validation, more self-trusting |

The 21-Day Creativity Challenge seemed to transform students' creative confidence. Across majors, personality types, and creative histories, students expanded their understanding of creativity, built resilience by engaging with discomfort, and developed lasting creative confidence rooted in experimentation, reflection, and risk-taking.

## CONCLUSION AND NEXT STEPS

There are several ways to increase students' levels of creative confidence—from design sprints to hackathons to creativity exercises. The 21-Day Creativity Challenge stands out as more longitudinal than others because it occurs over several weeks. This approach helps students adapt, iterate, and become comfortable outside their comfort zones.

Over four years, the instructor has added and removed various activities based on student feedback and new ideas. This indicates that the instructor is practicing the art of feedback and iteration, which is vital for creativity. Going forward, there may be a need to provide more intentionality around the "scaffolding" of the activities. Currently, students choose based on their own goals rather than any indication that one option is "more advanced" than others. This approach stems from the belief in meeting students where they are; what seems easy to one student may be difficult for another. However, as students progress, there may be a need for that structure. Additionally, it is important to consider how this assignment is assessed. Generally, the assignment is graded on "completeness," meaning that if students complete the work, create the design journal with reflections, and submit the reflection paper, the anchor grade is 88/100 (B+). If a student goes above and beyond in detail, the grade increases. Conversely, if a student misses elements of the challenge or does not put in any effort, the grade decreases. This way, the actual creativity and output are not judged; instead, the focus is on the effort put into building creative confidence.

In situations where active learning strategies are proving to be more effective for students, this challenge serves as a good example. It allows students to choose while also ensuring that they capitalize on each of the seven creative abilities. Moreover, it is quite different from their current work – noticeably, there is no technology needed to perform most of these activities, and the design journal is a key element of the practice.

## REFERENCES


AACSB. (2020). *2020 Guiding Principles and Standards for Business Accreditation*. Association to Advance Collegiate Schools of Business. https://www.aacsb.edu/accreditation/standards/business

Bandura, A. (1997). *Self-efficacy: The exercise of control*. W. H. Freeman.

Dweck, C. (2006). *Mindset: The new psychology of success*. Random House.

Haase, J., Hoff, E., Hanel, P., & Innes-Ker, Å. (2018). A meta-analysis of the relation between creative self-efficacy and creativity. *Creativity Research Journal*, *30*(1), 1–16. DOI: 10.1080/10400419.2018.1411436

Kahn, J., & Patil, S. (2025, April 18). Impacts of experiential learning on Gen Z early career experience. *National Association of Colleges and Employers (NACE)*. https://www.naceweb.org/talent-acquisition/trends-and-predictions/impacts-of-experiential-learning-on-the-gen-z-early-career-experience?utm_source=chatgpt.com

Kelley, T., & Kelley, D. (2013). *Creative confidence: Unleashing the creative potential within us all*. Crown Business.

Leopold, T. (2025, January 8). Future of jobs report 2025. *World Economic Forum*. https://www.weforum.org/stories/2025/01/future-of-jobs-report-2025-jobs-of-the-future-and-the-skills-you-need-to-get-them/

Liao, F., Zhang, Q., & Yang, J. (2022). Recognizing opportunities when engaged in intrapreneurship: The role of creative self-efficacy and support for innovation. *Frontiers in Psychology*, *13*, 937. Advance online publication. DOI: 10.3389/fpsyg.2022.937971

Puente-Díaz, R., & Cavazos-Arroyo, J. (2022). Creative self-efficacy and metacognitive feelings as sources of information when generating, evaluating, and selecting creative ideas: A metacognitive perspective. *The Journal of Creative Behavior*, *56*(4), 647–658. DOI: 10.1002/jocb.557

Royston, R., & Reiter-Palmon, R. (2019). Creative self-efficacy as mediator between creative mindsets and creative problem-solving. *The Journal of Creative Behavior*, *53*(4), 472–481. DOI: 10.1002/jocb.226

Saggar, M., Xie, H., Beaty, R., Stankov, A., Schrier, M., & Reiss, A. (2019). Creativity slumps and bumps: Expanding the neurobehavioral basis of creativity development during middle childhood. *NeuroImage*, *196*, 94–101. DOI: 10.1016/j.neuroimage.2019.03.080

Tierney, P., & Farmer, S. M. (2002). Creative self-efficacy: Potential antecedents and relationship to creative performance. *Academy of Management Journal*, *45*(6), 1137–1148. DOI: 10.2307/3069429

Tierney, P., & Farmer, S. M. (2011). Creative self-efficacy development and creative performance over time. *The Journal of Applied Psychology*, *96*(2), 277–293. DOI: 10.1037/a0020952

World Economic Forum. (2023). *Future of jobs report 2023*. https://www.weforum.org/reports/the-future-of-jobs-report-2023/

# APPENDIX A. 21-DAY CREATIVITY CHALLENGE

## Spring 2023

You have to start somewhere! The purpose of the class is to bring you from creative confidence to innovation stardom. The 21-Day ***Creativity Challenge*** is a set of practice activities meant to increase your creative confidence. Now, some of you may feel pretty confident in your creative ability. That is cool. Some, on the other hand, may need a boost. Also, cool.

This challenge is meant to "meet you where you are."

The goal is to do something almost every day. There are 21 days in this challenge and the idea is to do one each day or so. I am, however going to give you more than 30 days to this. Because, you know, life happens (and covid).

This is definitely one of the "get what you give" activities. Don't wait and do these all at once (well, you can't but don't even think about it). That is silly and a useless waste of time. This only works if you approach this with an open mind.

Below you will find **8 core creative abilities** (based on information from IDEO, the Stanford D School, and research). These are grounded in the design mindset and are great ways to think about creativity. You get a choice! But you must select at least 2 activities (14 total) from each of the 7 core areas. The other 7 can come from the abilities you may want extra work (or just find the activity interesting). Be strategic and don't be afraid. No double dipping. Try a few things that make you uncomfortable. That is the only way you will learn anything.

All of these will be documented in your design journal. So, go ahead and save 21 pages for that. I will conduct random checks … so that you can't wait until the end.

So, what do you do? Well, you need to select your activity and do it. The activity needs to be recorded – either by doing it in your design notebook and/or by taking photos of it and pasting into your notebook. Then you will need to answer the following (however you want to do that) in your design notebook:

- Describe the activity and what you did.
- Why did you choose this one? What was your goal for this one?
- How did this activity affect our creative confidence? Be specific here. (And be open and honest about this – even if things did not turn out how you expected).

Note: I need to be able to READ your reflection so if your handwriting is terrible, consider typing and pasting.

Plan to do 5 or so per week in order to get to your 21 activities in 30 days. Don't wait and do them all at once (this defeats the point completely) and don't wait and do them all on the weekend.

## Curiosity Is the Key

### 1. Navigate Ambiguity

This is the ability to recognize and persist in the discomfort of not knowing and develop tactics to overcome ambiguity when needed.

Creativity and design are loaded with uncertainty. As a result, it involves being present in the moment, re-framing problems, and finding patterns in information. Ambiguity can arise in many places – within a project, a process, or within oneself. It's important to put students in ambiguous situations and give them tactics to emerge from them.

*Table 6. Navigating Ambiguity*

| |
|---|
| Set your timer for 15 minutes, then dance. Wiggle your arms, do the twist, - even better – do a TIK TOK! Just get your body moving and don't worry about what this looks like. Add a friend if you wish. |
| Find something new you can do today. Pick up a guitar, or other instrument and learn to play a chord, trying playing a new sport, attend a local concert, or visit that restaurant you've been meaning to try. Do something different, big or small. |
| Immerse yourself in something different. Click on a wacky or odd-sounding link in your social media (or just google something that you have been curious about). Or watch a complete movie that looks like it will be terrible or has poor ratings. Or listen to music you wouldn't ordinarily listen to...you get the picture.... |
| Learn a completely new sport! Select it, watch it, and try to make sense of it. You are examining it from a beginner's mindset. |
| Create something terrible – Create something purposefully terrible. Write a horrible poem or take some truly bad photos or make a bad painting. Then show it. |
| Take a mini vacation – Set aside some time for a mini vacation. Your vacation could involve traveling to a nearby city, visiting a museum you have never been to or something similar. Get creative! |
| Cook something – Find a new recipe, online or in your favorite recipe book, that you can cook today. Think about how the process of preparing and cooking makes your mind feel. Serve the meal to your friends. |
| Explore other cultures – Spend today or tomorrow exploring another culture by reading about it, watching a presentation or movie about it, cooking food you would get from that part of the world, and otherwise imagining that you're living there for the day. |
| Write a letter to yourself describing what you hope to achieve in the future. Select the time frame that makes the most sense to you and be as specific as you would like. The goal is to get you into the mindset of thinking about charting a path towards your objectives. |
| Work on a puzzle without looking at the box. (Note – not a baby puzzle ☺) |
| Sit in a different part of your car as a passenger and write down all that you observe that is different from your normal experience |

continued on following page

*Table 6. Continued*

| |
|---|
| Take a social media break. Just allocate some time (say 1-2 days) and just say no to socials…no Instagram scrolling, no tiktoking, no tweets, or Snapchats and streaks (and I won't even mention Facebook b/c I know you are not likely there anymore). For those of you who are particularly bold, just say no to your whole phone for 1-2 days. Consider it a cleanse ☺ |
| Visit someplace new – it can be a new store, new church, new whatever. You are examining it from a beginner's mindset. |
| Consider a system (especially one that you are not familiar with). Now immerse yourself into it. Try to navigate this new system basically using information at your fingertips (meaning don't use your friends or family who may know). Think about things you are going to have to learn soon anyway. And limit your time too. |
| Wander aimlessly. Pick a day and time. Pack a bag. Start heading in any direction on instinct. Do the opposite of what you think you should do. If you start to think you are wasting time, then you are doing it right. Pay attention to all details. |

## 2. Learn From Others

This means empathizing with and embracing diverse viewpoints, testing new ideas with others, and observing and learning from unfamiliar contexts.

Throughout a design project, it's important to recognize and take the opportunity to learn from others–both end users and other stakeholders and team members. There is a sensitivity to others that develops with this ability.

*Table 7. Learn From Others*

| |
|---|
| People Watch - Go to a public place, like a shopping center or library or coffee shop (you decide), and quickly write a short story for some different people you see walking about. Combine the different traits and actions of your "characters" into one compelling story. |
| Do Something Completely Different – Find something new you can do today. Pick up a guitar, or other instrument and learn to play a chord, trying to play a new sport, attend a local concert, or visit that restaurant you've been meaning to try. Do something different, big or small. |
| Play. Choose a group of people and just play – play a game, go on an adventure. You name it. Best to do this with a new group (not your pals) and if you can do it with people very different from you, that is the best! |
| Create a mood board – Consider the different elements of inspiration in your life and think of how you might gather and combine them in a digital or physical way. Grab photos, quotes of inspiration, colors, even sound bites or videos, and anything else you can use to inspire your brain, then combine them into a board you can reference for future ideas. |
| Cook something – Find a new recipe, online or in your favorite recipe book, that you can cook today. Think about how the process of preparing and cooking makes your mind feel. Serve the meal to your friends or even better – get them involved in the cooking experience. |
| Explore other cultures – Spend today or tomorrow exploring another culture by reading about it, watching a presentation or movie about it, cooking food you would get from that part of the world, and otherwise imagining that you're living there for the day. |

continued on following page

*Table 7. Continued*

| |
|---|
| Volunteer – Find a way to volunteer (not virtually but in person). Be sure to take the time to listen to others and learn from them – especially those who you are helping. |
| Choose a new podcast series to listen to. |
| Find a weird, esoteric topic (but one that is interesting to you but you don't know much about). Now, find an "expert" and conduct an interview. |
| Take a photo of someone else's refrigerator, or bathroom cabinet or car trunk. Don't talk to them about it but review the photo. What do you notice? What might you infer about it? Why? Repeat until you get to a stopping point (and be sure to include the photo in your design journal). |
| A day in the life … your goal is to make a day in the life montage (video, photos) of someone. Spend a few days capturing photos and video interviews and then find a way to capture it in your design journal. |

## 3. Synthesize Information

This is the ability to make sense of information and find insight and opportunity within.

Data comes from multiple places and has many different forms, both qualitative and quantitative. This ability requires skills in developing frameworks, maps, and abductive thinking. Synthesis is hard for new students. It takes time and is interdependent with navigating ambiguity.

*Table 8. Synthesize Information*

| |
|---|
| People Watch - Go to a public place, like a shopping center or library or coffee shop (you decide), and quickly write a short story for some different people you see walking about. Combine the different traits and actions of your "characters" into one compelling story. |
| Know what a picture is worth – Find a picture you like – of a person, place or thing – and set a timer for 5 minutes. Make a list to see how many small details you can spot in the picture. |
| Take a mini vacation – Set aside some time for a mini vacation. Your vacation could involved traveling to a nearby city, visiting a museum you have never been to or something similar. Get creative! |
| Create a new ritual or habit. Keep up with it for at least one week. |
| Go Thrifting – Find a thrift store (or resale shop) and go shopping. Buy something! Do something with it! |
| Watch or listen to something you ordinarily would not listen to or watch. What are the patterns and how does this mesh with what you believe? |
| Design an experiment – try something you have never done before and see what happens. It can be social, physical or intellectual. Actively evaluate the results of the experiment to extract what you have learned. |
| Choose something in your everyday life that you don't enjoy and find a way to "reframe it" to make it enjoyable. Think of ways you could look at the situation differently and specific things you could do to change the experience. |
| Work on a puzzle without looking at the box. (Note – not a baby puzzle ☺) |

continued on following page

*Table 8. Continued*

| |
|---|
| Sit in a different part of your car as a passenger and write down all that you observe that is different from your normal experience |
| Consider a system (especially one that you are not familiar with). Now immerse yourself into it. Try to navigate this new system basically using information at your fingertips (meaning don't use your friends or family who may know). Think about things you are going to have to learn soon anyway. And limit your time too. |
| Take a photo of someone else's refrigerator, or bathroom cabinet or car trunk. Don't talk to them about it but review the photo. What do you notice? What might you infer about it? Why? Repeat until you get to a stopping point (and be sure to include the photo in your design journal). |
| Record everything that you purchase in one week. What patterns do you see? |
| Visit an open house. Tour 2-3 houses and look for design trends and insights. As well as unique or quirky expressions of the owners' personality. What did you see? |

## 4. Experiment Rapidly

This ability is about being able to quickly generate ideas – whether written, drawn, or built.

In order to rapidly experiment, you must be able to relax your mind and reach a mode of acceptance. This will eliminate the natural tendency to block ideas that seem off or unfeasible. Then, let your doing lead your thinking – and lead with your hands. This ability pairs naturally with 'Learn From Others'. In many instances, you are experimenting by both generating a flood of new concepts at low resolution (brainstorming) and testing some of those concepts with potential users.

*Table 9. Experiment Rapidly*

| |
|---|
| Make something. Look online (tik tok, Instagram) and find something you wish to make. Then do it. |
| Create a new design – Find an ad, packaging, book or other visually designed object that you can evaluate. Spend 10 to 15 minutes thinking about the decisions behind the design and drawing an alternative. |
| Create something terrible – Create something purposefully terrible. Write a horrible poem or take some truly bad photos or make a bad painting. Then show it. |
| Reinterpret something you make – Gather a few craft materials – paper, glue, scissors, sticks, markers, scraps of cardstock, anything – and spend just 10 minutes making something basic (a hat, a doll, a poster, anything). The goal isn't to create something specific at the outset, it's to figure out what your creative can become after the fact. What could it be used for? |
| Doodle something – Take the next 10 minutes to doodle how you feel right now. No matter how great (or terrible) of an artist you may be, try to create a doodle that captures exactly how you feel. |
| Design an experiment – try something you have never done before and see what happens. It can be social, physical or intellectual. Actively evaluate the results of the experiment to extract what you have learned. |

continued on following page

*Table 9. Continued*

| |
|---|
| 100 ideas – Choose a topic and practice coming up with ideas. Aim for 100. Write these down and see what patterns exist. |
| Take a social media break. Just allocate some time (say 1-2 days) and just say no to socials…no Instagram scrolling, no tiktoking, no tweets, or Snapchats and streaks (and I won't even mention Facebook b/c I know you are not likely there anymore). For those of you who are particularly bold, just say no to your whole phone for 1-2 days. Consider it a cleanse ☺ |
| Create a new ritual or habit. Keep up with it for at least one week. |

## 5. Move Between Concrete and Abstract

This ability involves understanding stakeholders and purpose in order to define the product or service's features.

Everything is connected. When students are building out a new concept –whether a product, service, or experience – they need to be able to nest the concept within the larger ecosystem that relates to it. It involves abstraction to define meaning, goals, and principles, as well as precision to define details and features.

*Table 10. Move Between Concrete and Abstract*

| |
|---|
| Think Big to Small - Pick something in your life that seems simple on its face. Make a list of everything that makes that thing what it is: list all of the smaller parts, then the smaller parts that make up those smaller parts. See how microscopic you can get with the details. |
| Find Invisible Gorillas - Take a minute to stop and think of all of the things going on around you that you haven't noticed. Spot ten things that you haven't noticed until this very moment. Challenge a friend to do the same and see who can reach 10 hard to notice things. |
| Start with the ending – Imagine how your ideal end of the day looks (as realistically as possible). Ask yourself what simple steps it would take to get from what you're imagining to wherever you are now. Work backwards within your imagination to outline each step it would take to get from there to hear, writing them down to ensure you don't miss a step. |
| Know what a picture is worth – Find a picture you like – of a person, place or thing – and set a timer for 5 minutes. Make a list to see how many small details you can spot in the picture |
| Explore other cultures – Spend today or tomorrow exploring another culture by reading about it, watching a presentation or movie about it, cooking food you would get from that part of the world, and otherwise imagining that you're living there for the day. |
| Design a detailed map of your house. |
| Take 10 minutes and just daydream (for some of you, this may take longer than 10 minutes). Now, draw your daydream. Where did you go and what did you experience? Does daydreaming have value? |
| Consider a system (especially one that you are not familiar with). Now immerse yourself into it. Try to navigate this new system basically using information at your fingertips (meaning don't use your friends or family who may know). Think about things you are going to have to learn soon anyway. And limit your time too. |

continued on following page

*Table 10. Continued*

| |
|---|
| Find a photograph. A documentary photo is best. Journalist photos are also good. Street scenes are great too. Record – what is going on in this photo? What do you see that makes you think that? What else do you see? What do you see that makes you think that? Repeat until you get to a stopping point. |
| Day in the life. Your goal is to make a day in the life video (3-4 min) or storyboard with images. Spend some time capturing routines with photos and then go back and video interviews based on 5 key images/photos. Find someone who will be the subject of your work – ideally, someone whose daily life has some challenges (think athletes, or health issues, or someone with something new to contend with). The goal is to find out what this person's life is like, what the challenges are and how he/she deals with it. |
| Find an object in your life that holds a special place in your heart. Place it on a table in front of you. When you see it, what does it make you think of? Be specific. How does this object affect your 5 senses? Then think about how you have connected the sensory clues you receive from the object to the way you think and feel about it. Identify those connections. |

## 6. Build & Craft Intentionally

This ability is about thoughtful construction: showing work at the most appropriate level of resolution for the audience and feedback desired.

There are many sub-disciplines of design, each with their own set of tools and techniques. This ability requires a sensitivity to the tools needed to create meaningful work in your domain. UX designers have a specific set of tools to create human-centered digital interfaces. Architects have an arsenal of particular techniques to bring new structures into the world. Every discipline – immunology, macroeconomics, K12 education, whatever it may be – has its own building methods, and in every case, the details matter.

*Table 11. Build and Craft Intentionally*

| |
|---|
| Think Big to Small - Pick something in your life that seems simple on its face. Make a list of everything that makes that thing what it is: list all of the smaller parts, then the smaller parts that make up those smaller parts. See how microscopic you can get with the details. |
| Do Something Completely Different – Find something new you can do today. Pick up a guitar, or other instrument and learn to play a chord, trying playing a new sport, attend a local concert, or visit that restaurant you've been meaning to try. Do something different, big or small. |
| Create a new design – Find an ad, packaging, book or other visually designed object that you can evaluate. Spend 10 to 15 minutes thinking about the decisions behind the design and drawing an alternative. |
| Storyboard – First draw a few squares or frames to create your storyboard. Then tell a story, or experience through your storyboard. |
| Reinterpret something you make – Gather a few craft materials – paper, glue, scissors, sticks, markers, scraps of cardstock, anything – and spend just 10 minutes making something basic (a hat, a doll, a poster, anything). The goal isn't to create something specific at the outset, it's to figure out what your creative can become after the fact. What could it be used for? |

continued on following page

*Table 11. Continued*

| |
|---|
| Create a mood board – Consider the different elements of inspiration in your life and think of how you might gather and combine them in a digital or physical way. Grab photos, quotes of inspiration, colors, even sound bites or videos, and anything else you can use to inspire your brain, then combine them into a board you can reference for future ideas. |
| Cook something – Find a new recipe, online or in your favorite recipe book, that you can cook today. Think about how the process of preparing and cooking makes your mind feel. Serve the meal to your friends. |
| I do not seek, I find – Randomly find something in your bag or a drawer. Make a Cubist drawing of it (see Pablo Picasso) |
| Throw a themed party – Design a prototype of a themed party. Include: vibe, decorations, dress, menu, activity, favors. |
| Draw yourself as a cartoon character. |
| Go Thrifting – Find a thrift store (or resale shop) and go shopping. Buy something! Do something with it! |
| Make something – Go to the craft store and find something to "make" – like jewelry or frames – you name it! Alternatively you can use random things around the house. Get creative! |
| Design a detailed map of your house. |
| Create a new game. You choose the goal and context of the game. Determine a way to "present" your game (visual is better) |
| A day in the life … your goal is to make a day in the life montage (video, photos) of someone. Spend a few days capturing photos and video interviews and then find a way to capture it in your design journal. |

## 7. Communicate Deliberately

This is the ability to form, capture, and relate stories, ideas, concepts, reflections, and learnings to the appropriate audiences.

Communication happens in a variety of contexts. It may include reflecting on your performance to a project team or crafting a video to show your product to a potential investor. Communication and storytelling are paramount.

*Table 12. Communicate Deliberately*

| |
|---|
| Think Big to Small - Pick something in your life that seems simple on its face. Make a list of everything that makes that thing what it is: list all of the smaller parts, then the smaller parts that make up those smaller parts. See how microscopic you can get with the details. |
| Storyboard – First draw a few squares or frames to create your storyboard. Then tell a story, or experience through your storyboard. |
| Write a 100-line poem – Write a 100 line poem using a pattern or other constraints, like starting with one word, then adding one additional word to each line, or by using a familiar pattern like haiku until you've written 33 haikus to form one 100 line poem. |

continued on following page

*Table 12. Continued*

| |
|---|
| Write it out in stages – Write one sentence explaining something you want to do within the next month. Then, write what the first step to pursing it might be (whether you've already started or not). Beneath that line write one thing you need to do before the first thing. Repeat the process util you are clear about what steps you need to take. |
| Create a mood board – Consider the different elements of inspiration in your life and think of how you might gather and combine them in a digital or physical way. Grab photos, quotes of inspiration, colors, even sound bites or videos, and anything else you can use to inspire your brain, then combine them into a board you can reference for future ideas. |
| Polish your Prose – Fill in this word scale for beauty from "exquisite" to "grotesque". Fill in this word scale for behavior from "unruffled" to "unhinged". |
| Design your own logo. |
| Write a story using the story spine. See appendix for the details. |
| Draw/design your own "coat of arms" |
| Develop your personal mission statement |
| Write your epitaph in 15 words or less |
| Learn how to create a bullet journal |
| Collect 3 objects that related to your childhood or inspire memories. Write a brief story to accompany each object. OR recreate objects from childhood from readily available materials (cardboard, glue, string, tape, leaves, wood or rocks) and write the stories to accompany it. |

## Challenge Sources


Arden, A. (2012). The book of Doing. Pedigree Books.

Christensen, T. (2015). The Creativity Challenge. Adams Media.

Greenberg, Sarah Stein (2021). Creative Acts for Curious People

Hasso Plattner School of Design at Stanford University - https://dschool.stanford.edu/about/#about-8-core-abilities

Seelig, T. (2015). Creativity Rules: Get ideas out of your head and into the world. Harper.

Smith, K. (2008). How to be an explorer of the world. Penguin Books.

# Chapter 9
# Enhancing Student Skill Development Through Behavioral Analytics in Business Simulations:
## A Mixpanel-Integrated Approach

**Hélder Fanha Martins**
https://orcid.org/0000-0003-3544-0703
*Polytechnic University of Lisbon, Portugal*

## ABSTRACT

*This chapter introduces a novel approach to enhancing business simulations by integrating Mixpanel-based behavioral analytics, aiming to improve students' decision-making, teamwork, leadership, and job preparedness. The system captures real-time interaction data, using machine learning to segment behaviors and outcomes. Personalized feedback and recommendations optimize learning experiences. Seamlessly integrated with educational modules, it dynamically informs simulations and teaching strategies through a feedback loop. Experiments with a business simulation platform involving 120 students validated the method, showing significant skill improvements and higher engagement through personalized feedback. The findings underscore the potential of behavioral analytics to enhance educational outcomes, prepare students for the job market, and enable future scalability in educational technology.*

DOI: 10.4018/979-8-3373-7523-6.ch009

## 1. INTRODUCTION

The rapid evolution of educational technology has profoundly reshaped pedagogical approaches, expanding traditional boundaries by introducing dynamic, interactive tools designed to bridge theoretical instruction and practical application. Among these tools, business simulations have emerged as a particularly powerful method for developing critical, real-world skills, such as decision-making, teamwork, leadership, and overall job preparedness (Hsu et al., 2023; Costin et al., 2019). Unlike traditional didactic methods, business simulations immerse students in realistic scenarios, enabling the practical application of theoretical knowledge in controlled yet dynamic environments. Such interactive approaches have increasingly gained recognition for their potential to significantly enhance student learning outcomes, student motivation, and professional readiness.

Historically, educational simulations have evolved markedly over the last few decades. Early iterations were primarily text-based, simplistic, and lacked significant interactivity. Technological advancements have since allowed for more sophisticated implementations involving real-time scenarios, rich multimedia environments, and collaborative interfaces. These advancements have substantially enhanced the realism and complexity of simulations, making them valuable pedagogical tools in business and management education.

Despite these significant technological advancements, contemporary business simulations continue to face critical limitations, particularly concerning personalized feedback and analytics-driven instructional support. Many existing simulations provide generalized feedback after scenario completion or rely on static performance metrics that do not effectively capture the nuance and complexity of real-time student behaviors and decisions. Consequently, students often lack timely insights into their performance and, more importantly, precise guidance on how to adjust behaviors to improve specific skill sets. This delayed or generalized feedback reduces the immediate pedagogical impact of simulations, potentially diminishing their educational effectiveness.

The rising demands of today's job market have increased expectations for higher education institutions to provide graduates with not only theoretical knowledge but practical competencies directly applicable to professional contexts. Employers consistently emphasize skills, such as strategic decision-making, effective teamwork, and leadership capabilities as critical determinants of workplace success (Suarta et al., 2017). Yet, traditional education often struggles to measure and enhance these skills in a meaningful and quantifiable manner. Consequently, institutions increasingly seek innovative technological solutions capable of delivering detailed, actionable insights to bridge the gap between educational outcomes and professional expectations (Meeks, 2017).

In this context, integrating behavioral analytics into educational technologies presents a promising path for addressing these challenges. Behavioral analytics, defined as the systematic collection, analysis, and interpretation of user interaction data, has showed substantial potential in digital learning environments. Through detailed behavioral tracking, educators and instructional designers gain deep insights into how learners engage with educational content, make decisions, and navigate complex tasks. These insights are invaluable for designing tailored educational experiences, providing real-time, personalized feedback, and ultimately enhancing learning outcomes (Wong et al., 2019; Viberg et al., 2018).

Mixpanel, a leading platform in behavioral analytics, provides advanced capabilities for tracking detailed user interactions and generating immediate, actionable insights. Its sophisticated infrastructure facilitates real-time event capturing, data analysis, and user segmentation. However, Mixpanel and similar analytics tools have primarily been used within contexts such as online learning management systems (LMS) or massive open online courses (MOOCs), where the learning environment is typically asynchronous and interaction patterns are relatively predictable (Hmedna et al., 2023). Limited research has explored the integration of such advanced behavioral analytics platforms within highly interactive, scenario-based educational environments like business simulations, which inherently require real-time, highly granular analytics for optimal effectiveness.

Addressing these identified gaps, this chapter proposes a novel methodological framework for integrating Mixpanel-based behavioral analytics into a comprehensive cloud-based business simulation environment. Our approach addresses two critical gaps in current educational practices: firstly, the absence of detailed real-time behavioral insights within dynamic simulations, and secondly, the lack of personalized, immediate feedback mechanisms aligned explicitly with instructional objectives and skill development goals.

The proposed system architecture combines the strengths of behavioral analytics, learning analytics methodologies, and educational data mining techniques into a unified, integrated educational technology platform. Specifically, it leverages Mixpanel to capture detailed real-time interaction data generated by students as they engage in complex business decision-making scenarios. Machine learning algorithms, particularly clustering techniques drawn from educational data mining, process and segment the collected behavioral data to identify distinct student profiles and performance patterns dynamically. These insights are then translated into actionable, personalized recommendations delivered instantaneously to students, significantly enhancing the immediacy and relevance of the learning experience.

An essential feature of the proposed system is its seamless integration with conventional educational modules and instructional frameworks. Simulation scenarios are explicitly designed to align with predefined learning objectives derived from curriculum content, ensuring relevance and contextual coherence. The real-time analytics-driven feedback not only helps students adjust their behaviors and strategies immediately but also informs educators about broader cohort trends, enabling dynamic adjustments to teaching strategies, scenario complexity, and overall instructional planning. This continuous feedback loop between behavioral analytics insights and instructional adjustments creates an adaptive educational environment responsive to the evolving needs of individual learners and cohorts alike.

To validate the effectiveness of our proposed approach, we conducted an experimental study involving 120 undergraduate business students. Using a comprehensive cloud-based business simulation platform enhanced with Mixpanel's analytics capabilities, we captured granular student interaction data and analyzed it using advanced clustering algorithms. Our findings revealed significant improvements across targeted skills, particularly in decision-making, teamwork, and leadership. The personalized feedback mechanism demonstrably increased student engagement, supporting the argument for adopting behavioral analytics in highly interactive educational contexts.

This study addresses several critical gaps identified in the current research. Firstly, it extends behavioral analytics into the dynamic, real-time context of business simulations, providing a level of detail and responsiveness rarely observed in existing educational systems. Secondly, it shows a clear methodological path for integrating advanced analytics technology into existing instructional frameworks, highlighting the pedagogical and practical implications of such integration. Finally, it underscores the potential for scalability and adaptation of this technology beyond business education contexts into broader areas, such as STEM education, healthcare training, and professional development programs.

The rest of this chapter is structured to provide a comprehensive understanding of our proposed approach. Section 2 reviews existing literature, highlighting contributions and gaps. Section 3 clarifies the technical foundations and concepts underpinning our research, outlining the technological infrastructure and analytical techniques employed. Section 4 describes our methodology, including the system architecture and algorithmic implementations. Section 5 presents the experimental results validating the effectiveness of our approach, while Section 6 discusses implications, limitations, and directions for future research. Finally, Section 7 concludes by summarizing our key findings, contributions, and potential future impacts on educational practices and policies.

By addressing fundamental gaps in educational technology implementation, particularly the integration of real-time behavioral analytics into interactive business simulations, our study aims to contribute substantially to the ongoing evolution of education technology methodologies. Through deeper engagement, enhanced skill development, and improved student outcomes, our approach aspires to bridge the critical divide between academic preparation and the professional competencies increasingly demanded by today's dynamic job market.

## 2. RELATED WORK

Integrating behavioral analytics in educational technologies has become an area of considerable research interest, driven by the potential to enhance educational outcomes through real-time, personalized learning experiences. This section synthesizes existing literature in four interconnected domains: behavioral analytics in educational settings, learning analytics methodologies, educational data mining (EDM) approaches, and the application of business simulations in education. It highlights significant contributions, identifies existing gaps, and underscores how the current research aims to address these gaps.

Behavioral analytics systematically collects and analyzes user interaction data to discover trends that inform instructional and learning strategies. Recent literature illustrates diverse applications, especially within online educational contexts. For example, clickstream analytics has provided insights into student engagement, interaction frequency, and content preferences within massive open online courses (MOOCs), enabling tailored interventions to improve student outcomes (Rizwan et al., 2025). Other studies have explored behavioral analytics within Learning Management Systems (LMS), tracking metrics like click rates, page views, and activity completion rates to enhance course design and student engagement (Elias, 2011).

However, despite proven effectiveness in digital learning contexts, behavioral analytics applications in more interactive, scenario-based environments, such as business simulations, are limited. Most existing literature has focused predominantly on asynchronous or minimally interactive digital learning environments, leaving a gap in real-time, behavior-driven feedback within interactive simulation contexts. This limitation presents an opportunity for the current study, which seeks to expand behavioral analytics capabilities into the dynamic context of business simulations, capturing granular interaction data for more precise and actionable student feedback.

Learning analytics encompasses the measurement, collection, analysis, and reporting of data about learners and their contexts to optimize learning outcomes. Existing literature extensively shows how analytics-driven interventions enhance self-regulated learning, improve academic achievement, and support instructional decision-making (Haynes et al., 2019). For instance, visual analytics dashboards providing real-time insights into student performance have shown measurable success in promoting learner reflection and improving overall academic achievement (Haynes et al., 2024; Ramaswami et al., 2023). Predictive analytics, another prominent sub-field, has successfully identified at-risk learners through early performance indicators, allowing timely interventions and improved retention rates (Jarke & Macgilchrist, 2021; Mikic-Fonte et al., 2019).

Despite these advances, existing learning analytics frameworks frequently lack the detailed granularity necessary to analyze complex, dynamic interactions typical of business simulations. Many current approaches rely heavily on historical performance data and static metrics, limiting real-time responsiveness (Chugh et al., 2023); Sottilare et al., 2023). The proposed system addresses this limitation by employing Mixpanel's analytical capabilities to deliver immediate, detailed, and personalized feedback. The system advances existing learning analytics practices by embedding real-time insights directly into the interactive simulation environment, creating a feedback loop that continuously refines student experiences and instructional strategies.

Educational Data Mining applies sophisticated data mining techniques, such as clustering, classification, and association rules, to educational data to uncover meaningful patterns and insights. Recent EDM studies have successfully implemented clustering methods to segment students based on online learning behaviors, enabling personalized educational experiences (Wu et al., 2024). Similarly, association rule mining techniques have identified significant correlations between specific learning behaviors and performance outcomes, guiding curriculum design and instructional strategies (Rizwan et al., 2025).

Although EDM techniques have proven valuable, their application in simulation-based learning environments remains under-explored (Dai et al., 2025; Dol & Jawandhiya, 2023; Sweta & Sweta, 2021; Charitopoulos et al., 2020). Existing studies primarily focus on either structured online platforms or traditional assessment methods, neglecting the more nuanced behaviors found in simulation-based environments. The current research fills this gap by employing clustering algorithms within interactive simulations, capturing intricate patterns of student decision-making and peer collaboration, enhancing the depth and relevance of personalized feedback.

Business simulations have become well-established educational tools, providing experiential learning environments that enable students to apply theoretical knowledge within practical contexts, enhancing their preparedness for professional settings (Adib, 2024; Kesse, 2023; Beranič & Heričko, 2022). Literature spanning several decades consistently highlights their educational value, emphasizing their effectiveness in bridging theoretical knowledge with applied practice, enhancing student engagement, and fostering essential business competencies such as strategic decision-making, leadership, and teamwork (Bell et al., 2016; Anderson & Lawton, 2009). Recently, increased attention has been given to business simulations because of their unique capability to simulate the complexities and dynamics of real-world business environments, offering educators practical paths to develop and assess critical business skills that are otherwise difficult to evaluate through traditional assessment methods (Ahuja, 2024; Wei et al., 2022; Samašonok et al., 2020; Farashahi & Tajeddin, 2018).

Empirical studies consistently show significant pedagogical benefits derived from incorporating simulations into the educational curriculum. For example, a comprehensive analysis by Anderson and Lawton (2009) found that business simulations considerably improved cognitive learning by enabling students to actively engage with complex, realistic scenarios, translating theoretical knowledge into actionable skills. Similar outcomes were observed by Vos and Brennan (2010), who reported significant enhancements in student motivation, engagement, and retention of business concepts following participation in simulations.

In a more recent comparative study conducted by Diachkova et al. (2020), business simulations were explicitly contrasted with traditional teaching methods (e.g., case studies, lectures), highlighting the superior effectiveness of simulations in fostering deeper conceptual understanding, higher-order thinking skills, and greater learner satisfaction. This study further noted that the immersive nature of business simulations substantially improved students' ability to apply complex theoretical frameworks to real-world problems, effectively bridging gaps between academic knowledge and practical business acumen.

However, despite these acknowledged benefits, traditional business simulations exhibit certain critical limitations that hinder their pedagogical effectiveness. A primary constraint identified in the literature relates to the absence of personalized, real-time feedback systems (Bell et al., 2016). Typical simulation platforms provide post-event feedback that is often generic, static, or minimally personalized. Such delayed feedback reduces the opportunities for learners to immediately adjust and improve their strategies, potentially diminishing the overall learning impact.

Several researchers have identified this limitation explicitly as a crucial barrier to maximizing the pedagogical value of business simulations (Rietsche et al., 2021; Boda & Ugrósdy, 2019; Nkhoma et al., 2014).

Despite this evidence, widespread adoption of integrated behavioral analytics in business simulations remains limited, largely due to technological and logistical barriers. Technological barriers include challenges related to real-time data processing, integration complexity, data security concerns, and the lack of accessible platforms specifically designed to merge advanced analytics with interactive pedagogical scenarios (Bell et al., 2016). Logistical barriers include limited technical expertise among instructional staff, concerns regarding data privacy and compliance with regulations (e.g., GDPR), and budgetary constraints that limit experimentation and adoption of advanced analytics-driven simulation platforms.

The current study addresses precisely these barriers by integrating Mixpanel's advanced behavioral analytics directly into cloud-based business simulations, providing both technological feasibility and pedagogical efficacy. Unlike previous approaches, the proposed integration leverages scalable cloud infrastructures capable of handling large volumes of real-time data efficiently and securely. Mixpanel's inherent capability for real-time event tracking and segmentation aligns well with educational objectives, offering significant improvements over traditional feedback mechanisms in terms of responsiveness, personalization, and actionable insights.

The practical significance of this innovation is substantial, offering educators and instructional designers powerful tools to enhance the quality and immediacy of student feedback, thereby substantially boosting the pedagogical effectiveness of simulation-based learning. Also, integrating advanced analytics into simulations aligns closely with the broader pedagogical shift toward personalized, adaptive educational methodologies that reflect contemporary demands from employers and industry stakeholders.

From an industry perspective, simulations enriched by behavioral analytics align closely with corporate training models that increasingly rely on real-time data analytics for employee development. Recent research by Gartner (2022) highlights that companies now prioritize training programs capable of delivering personalized, analytics-driven feedback to employees. These programs seek to enhance soft skills critical for workplace success, including leadership, collaborative problem-solving, and adaptive decision-making. The approach described in this chapter not only serves academic purposes but also offers direct relevance and applicability to professional training contexts, facilitating smoother transitions from academic environments to professional roles.

Finally, addressing the gap identified in the literature, this chapter contributes by demonstrating the practical application of behavioral analytics within business simulations. It provides empirical evidence supporting the claim that real-time, analytics-driven feedback significantly enhances student skill development, engagement, and learning outcomes. By achieving this integration, this study allows for further exploration into how educational institutions and professional training programs can leverage similar analytics-enabled environments to foster broader skill development across various educational and professional contexts.

Business simulations have shown substantial promise for enhancing student learning outcomes, yet their full pedagogical potential remains constrained by feedback limitations. The current research directly addresses these limitations by integrating advanced behavioral analytics, significantly expanding the educational and professional relevance of simulations. By leveraging these analytics methodologies, the proposed approach sets a foundation for future educational technology innovations, providing pathways for practical, personalized, and highly effective learning experiences in both academic and industry contexts.

While behavioral analytics, learning analytics, educational data mining, and business simulations each have established bodies of literature, their integration into a unified, interactive educational framework remains notably limited. Existing methodologies typically either neglect interactive, real-time feedback capabilities or lack the granularity needed for comprehensive behavioral analysis within dynamic simulation contexts.

This chapter addresses these gaps by integrating Mixpanel's advanced behavioral analytics with a cloud-based business simulation environment, applying clustering techniques to capture nuanced student behaviors and providing personalized, real-time feedback aligned with educational objectives. This integration presents a significant advancement in educational technology, fostering enhanced student skill development, engagement, and job market preparedness, ultimately contributing meaningfully to the ongoing evolution of business education methodologies.

## 2.1 Recent Developments and Critical Perspectives in AI-Driven Learning Analytics

A review by Zawacki-Richter et al. (2019) systematically mapped the landscape of learning analytics, highlighting both its rapid growth and the lack of integration between pedagogical theory and technological implementation. Luckin (2018) emphasized the importance of aligning AI systems in education with human-centered pedagogy, calling for greater educator involvement in system design and a shift away from purely data-driven approaches.

The landscape of AI-driven learning analytics has experienced significant evolution in recent years, with emerging research demonstrating both the promise and complexity of integrating artificial intelligence into educational contexts. Recent systematic reviews have identified AI-driven learning analytics as a rapidly developing field that combines artificial intelligence techniques with learning analytics approaches to provide real-time, adaptive, and personalized feedback in educational settings (Ouyang et al., 2023).

A notable development is the integration of AI performance prediction models with learning analytics feedback systems, which has shown competitive advantages in increasing student engagement, improving collaborative learning performances, and strengthening student satisfaction about learning experiences (Ouyang et al., 2023).

The emergence of human-centered learning analytics (HCLA) and human-centered AI (HCAI) in education has gained prominence, addressing the critical need for stakeholder involvement in the design and implementation of these systems (Topali et al., 2024).

Contemporary studies have also demonstrated the effectiveness of AI-driven learning analytics in collaborative learning contexts, with quasi-experimental research showing that integrated approaches can increase student engagement, improve collaborative learning performances, and strengthen student satisfaction (Ouyang et al.,

2023). However, systematic reviews indicate that while AI technologies can analyze and interpret multi-source and multi-modal data, the integration of educational and learning theories with tool design remains crucial for meaningful implementation.

Recent research has also emphasized the concept of "hybrid intelligence" in education, challenging narrow conceptions of AI's role and advocating for a multidimensional view that emphasizes the complex interplay among AI, analytics, and human learning processes (Cukurova, 2025). This perspective recognizes that effective AI-driven learning analytics must consider both technological capabilities and pedagogical contexts.

Despite the promising developments, contemporary research has raised significant concerns about the current trajectory of AI-driven learning analytics implementation. Critical analyses suggest that learning analytics has been developed without the active participation of students and teachers, as we previously mentioned, with central institutional units maintaining control over data gathering and analysis processes while relegating students and teachers to observational roles (Guzmán-Valenzuela et al., 2021).

Recent regulatory actions, including the FTC's 2023 order against education technology provider Edmodo for unlawfully using children's personal information for advertising purposes, highlight ongoing privacy violations in the EdTech sector (Federal Trade Commission, 2023). The proliferation of educational applications has created unprecedented data collection challenges that strain existing privacy protection frameworks. GDPR compliance issues in EdTech have become particularly pronounced, with research revealing inconsistencies in data privacy policies and insufficient transparency in how companies protect children's rights to privacy.

Researchers have criticized the field's tendency to underplay the complexity of teaching-learning processes, with research designs limited to quantifying impact rather than qualifying it and few studies actually testing whether analytically informed personalized learning environments causally improve student outcomes (Francis et al., 2019). This quantitative bias reflects broader concerns about learning analytics implementations that often present data and algorithms within an unproblematized "Big Data" discourse without adequately theorizing learning processes.

The critical question of measurement validity persists: not all important educational outcomes can be measured, and not everything measurable is necessarily important for learning (Guzmán-Valenzuela et al., 2021). This has led to calls for more sophisticated pedagogical frameworks and clearer theoretical reference points in learning analytics project design.

These critical perspectives have important implications for the development and implementation of analytics tools like Mixpanel in educational contexts. The research suggests that successful learning analytics implementation requires moving beyond purely technological considerations to embrace pedagogical sophistication and theoretical frameworks that account for the complexity of teaching-learning processes.

The emphasis on human-centered design approaches indicates that effective analytics tools must prioritize stakeholder involvement, transparency, and trustworthiness in their development and deployment (Topali et al., 2024). The need for qualitative assessment of impact, rather than purely quantitative metrics, suggests that analytics tools should be designed to support nuanced understanding of learning processes rather than simply providing numerical performance indicators.

While Mixpanel's specific advantages in educational analytics remain significant, these critical perspectives underscore the importance of implementing such tools within frameworks that prioritize privacy protection, pedagogical alignment, and stakeholder engagement to ensure meaningful educational impact.

## 2.2 Integration with Emerging Technologies

As the educational technology field continues to evolve rapidly, the integration of emerging technologies with established analytics platforms like Mixpanel presents unprecedented opportunities for enhanced learning experiences. This section explores how contemporary technological advances in machine learning, virtual and augmented reality, and artificial intelligence can be leveraged alongside traditional analytics frameworks to create more sophisticated, personalized, and immersive educational environments.

The integration of machine learning algorithms with Mixpanel's data collection capabilities represents a significant advancement in educational predictive analytics. Recent systematic reviews indicate that predictive learning analytics has witnessed substantial growth, with machine learning and deep learning models increasingly used to predict vital academic outcomes based on diverse student-related data sources (Sghir et al., 2023).

Mixpanel's comprehensive event tracking and user behavior data can serve as the foundation for sophisticated machine learning models that predict student performance, identify at-risk learners, and recommend personalized interventions. For instance, machine learning algorithms can analyze patterns in student engagement metrics collected through Mixpanel, such as time spent on specific learning modules, frequency of resource access, and interaction patterns, to create predictive models with accuracy rates exceeding 90-95% (Ahmed et al., 2024).

The implementation of such predictive models enables educational institutions to move from reactive to proactive approaches. By analyzing historical data patterns, machine learning algorithms can identify students who may struggle with upcoming coursework or are at risk of dropping out, allowing for timely interventions (Bird, 2024). This predictive capability extends beyond individual performance to encompass cohort-level insights, enabling administrators to optimize resource allocation and curriculum design based on predicted learning trends.

The integration supports the development of adaptive learning pathways that dynamically adjust based on real-time performance data. Machine learning models can continuously refine their predictions as new data flows from Mixpanel's tracking systems, creating increasingly personalized learning experiences that respond to individual student needs and learning styles.

The convergence of VR/AR technologies with analytics platforms like Mixpanel opens new frontiers for immersive educational experiences, particularly in business and management education.

Virtual reality environments can create sophisticated business simulations where students engage with realistic scenarios while their interactions are meticulously tracked through integrated analytics systems. For example, students might participate in virtual boardroom meetings, navigate complex negotiation scenarios, or manage simulated business operations, with every action, decision, and outcome captured and analyzed through Mixpanel's event tracking capabilities. This integration allows educators to gather unprecedented insights into student decision-making processes, collaboration patterns, and skill development trajectories.

The immersive nature of VR/AR experiences significantly enhances engagement and retention rates. Studies indicate that VR-trained learners demonstrate up to four times more focus compared to e-learning counterparts and achieve learning effectiveness rates 2.3 times higher than traditional methods (VirtualSpeech, 2024). When combined with Mixpanel's analytics capabilities, educators can quantify these improvements through detailed engagement metrics, completion rates, and performance assessments.

Augmented reality applications can overlay real-time analytics and performance feedback directly within the learning environment. Students working on AR-enabled business case studies might see their progress indicators, peer comparisons, and personalized recommendations appear contextually within their workspace, creating a seamless integration between immersive learning and data-driven insights.

While traditional analytics platforms rely heavily on rule-based recommendation systems, the integration of advanced AI technologies enables far more sophisticated personalization capabilities. Contemporary AI-powered personalization strategies leverage generative AI, predictive analytics, and continuous learning algorithms to create truly adaptive educational experiences (Ellikkal & Rajamohan, 2025).

Generative AI can work in conjunction with Mixpanel's user behavior data to create personalized learning content dynamically. Rather than simply recommending existing resources based on predefined rules, AI systems can generate customized explanations, practice problems, and assessment questions tailored to individual student needs and learning styles. This approach moves beyond traditional segmentation to enable true one-to-one personalization at scale.

The integration of continuous learning analytics with generative AI represents a transformational shift in educational technology. As students interact with learning materials, their behavioral patterns, performance metrics, and engagement levels are continuously analyzed through Mixpanel's tracking systems and fed into AI models that adapt content delivery, pacing, and complexity in real-time. This creates a feedback loop where the educational experience becomes increasingly personalized as more data is collected and analyzed.

The successful integration of these emerging technologies with established analytics platforms requires careful consideration of technical architecture, data privacy, and pedagogical alignment. Educational institutions must ensure that the integration preserves data integrity while enabling seamless flow between different technological systems.

Privacy and ethical considerations become particularly important when combining immersive technologies with comprehensive analytics tracking. Clear policies must be established regarding what data is collected in VR/AR environments, how AI systems use student data for personalization and what safeguards exist to protect student privacy and autonomy.

The convergence of these technologies points toward a future where educational analytics platforms serve as central nervous systems for complex, multi-modal learning environments. As AI, VR/AR, and machine learning technologies continue to advance, their integration with comprehensive analytics systems like Mixpanel will likely become essential for institutions seeking to provide competitive, effective, and engaging educational experiences.

## 2.3 Ethical Framework and Privacy Protections

The implementation of comprehensive analytics platforms like Mixpanel in educational contexts requires careful consideration of ethical principles and privacy protections to ensure that technological capabilities serve educational goals without compromising fundamental student rights or perpetuating systemic inequalities. This section outlines key ethical frameworks and practical considerations that institutions must address when deploying behavioral analytics in learning environments.

Educational technology implementations must align with established ethical frameworks that prioritize human welfare, dignity, and equity. The IEEE Code of Ethics emphasizes the paramount importance of safety, health, and welfare of the public, while mandating protection of privacy and fair treatment of all persons without discrimination (IEEE, 2023). Similarly, UNESCO's Recommendation on the Ethics of Artificial Intelligence establishes four core values that are directly applicable to educational analytics: human dignity and rights, environmental sustainability, diversity and inclusion, and social justice and fairness (UNESCO, 2021).

These foundational principles translate into specific obligations for educational institutions implementing analytics platforms. The principle of human dignity requires that students be treated as autonomous individuals rather than merely data sources, while the commitment to fairness demands that analytical insights do not perpetuate or amplify existing educational inequalities. Environmental sustainability, while less immediately obvious, encompasses the broader ecosystem impact of data-intensive technologies and the responsibility to use computational resources thoughtfully.

The educational context adds additional ethical dimensions that generic AI ethics frameworks may not fully address. Research has identified four unique ethical principles specific to educational AI applications: pedagogical appropriateness, children's rights, AI literacy, and teacher well-being (Holmes et al., 2022). These principles recognize that educational environments involve vulnerable populations, complex power dynamics, and learning objectives that extend beyond simple optimization metrics.

Student data privacy in analytics implementations requires multilayered protection strategies that go beyond simple compliance with regulations like FERPA or GDPR. Effective privacy protection must address data collection, storage, processing, sharing, and retention throughout the entire analytics lifecycle.

First, data minimization and purpose limitation emphasize that institutions should collect only the data strictly necessary for defined educational objectives, moving away from excessive or unjustified tracking. Each data point must serve a clear pedagogical purpose and be regularly reviewed to ensure ongoing relevance.

Transparency and informed consent require that students are fully informed about what data is collected, how it is used, and who has access to it. This goes beyond basic privacy notices to include meaningful explanations of how analytics influence decisions on curriculum, resources, and student support.

Data governance and access controls call for strong institutional policies that define roles, restrict data access to authorized personnel, and implement auditing mechanisms to ensure compliance.

Anonymization and de-identification recognize that while complete anonymization may be difficult in learning analytics, institutions should apply privacy-preserving techniques like pseudonymization to protect student identities while maintaining data utility. Together, these principles ensure that behavioral data is used ethically, transparently, and securely in education.

The clustering algorithms and predictive models that extract insights from Mixpanel data can inadvertently perpetuate or amplify biases that negatively impact certain student populations. Research demonstrates that algorithmic bias in educational settings can manifest through multiple pathways, including biased training data, inappropriate model assumptions, and discriminatory interpretation of results (Gardner et al., 2024).

Educational analytics implementations must balance institutional interests in improving educational outcomes with fundamental student rights to privacy, autonomy, and fair treatment. This balance requires clear policies and procedures that protect student agency while enabling beneficial uses of behavioral data.

The right to transparency ensures that students understand how their data is collected, analyzed, and used in institutional decision-making, including policies, resource allocation, and personalized interventions.

The right to accuracy and correction guarantees that students can review, challenge, and correct any inaccuracies in their data or flawed interpretations that may affect their academic experience. The right to opt-out and data portability acknowledges that while full opt-out may not always be possible, students should have meaningful control over non-essential data uses and the ability to access their own data to understand its role in broader analytics.

Finally, the principle of protection from discriminatory outcomes requires institutions to actively monitor analytics systems for biases and take corrective action if certain student groups are unfairly impacted. Together, these rights ensure that behavioral data is used responsibly, with respect for student agency, fairness, and accountability.

Successful ethical implementation of educational analytics requires ongoing institutional commitment rather than one-time policy development. Institutions should establish ethics review committees specifically focused on educational technology, implement regular auditing procedures for algorithmic bias, and create mechanisms for meaningful student participation in analytics governance.

Institutions must invest in training for faculty and staff who interpret and act on analytical insights, ensuring that decision-makers understand both the capabilities and limitations of behavioral analytics. This includes education about potential biases, appropriate use of predictive models, and the importance of maintaining human oversight in data-driven decision-making processes.

The goal is not to eliminate all risks associated with educational analytics but to implement thoughtful safeguards that maximize educational benefits while protecting student rights, promoting equity, and maintaining the trust necessary for effective educational relationships.

## 3. TECHNICAL FOUNDATIONS AND KEY CONCEPTS

This section provides the essential technical foundation necessary to grasp the methodologies, experimental approaches, and system integrations presented in subsequent sections of this study. Rather than revisiting previously addressed theoretical considerations, this section offers a comprehensive exploration of the underlying technological tools, analytical frameworks, computational processes, and data structures specifically implemented within the context of this research. Central components discussed include behavioral analytics through Mixpanel, analytical methods derived from Learning Analytics, Educational Data Mining (EDM) algorithms, particularly clustering methods, and the cloud-based technological infrastructure that supports the business simulation environment. Detailed explanations of how these elements cohesively integrate into a unified system for real-time interaction analysis, personalized feedback generation, and educational module adaptation are also provided.

Behavioral analytics involves systematically capturing and analyzing user interaction data to generate actionable insights (Martinez, 2022; Islam, 2021). The primary technology leveraged in this research is Mixpanel, an industry-standard, cloud-based analytics platform widely used for capturing detailed, real-time user interactions (Härdling & Bakhsh, 2022; Rafiq, 2022). Mixpanel is particularly adept at managing dynamic, interactive environments such as those found in business simulations, largely because of its infrastructure for tracking user-generated events instantaneously and its capability to efficiently process high volumes of streaming data.

From a technical standpoint, Mixpanel is integrated into the business simulation environment through the insertion of JavaScript-based Software Development Kits (SDKs) embedded directly into the front-end interface. These embedded snippets of JavaScript code actively capture student interactions as discrete, time stamped events, each tagged with unique identifiers and contextual properties. Typical captured interactions include navigational clicks, scenario selections, decision submissions, duration spent on specific tasks, and collaborative actions among participants. Each event is formatted in structured JavaScript Object Notation (JSON), allowing uniform data capture, seamless transmission, and structured querying.

Once captured, these events are asynchronously transmitted to Mixpanel's analytics servers via RESTful Application Programming Interfaces (APIs). Mixpanel's cloud infrastructure processes the incoming data streams, performing initial filtering, event grouping, and normalization. The data is subsequently stored in databases optimized for real-time queries and rapid retrieval, enabling instantaneous analysis of detailed user behavior patterns. Mixpanel's advanced querying interface supports dynamic segmentation of captured events based on customizable criteria, facilitating immediate identification of significant behavioral trends and informing subsequent stages of the analytics-driven feedback process.

Within the broader scope of learning analytics, this study strategically employs specific descriptive and prescriptive analytical methodologies tailored explicitly toward real-time application. Unlike retrospective analytics traditionally used for post-event assessments, real-time analytics approaches require the immediate interpretation and visualization of interaction data to guide educational interventions effectively.

Descriptive analytics, employed extensively in this research, use real-time dashboard interfaces that visually represent student interaction and engagement patterns instantly. Mixpanel's visualization modules power these dashboards, dynamically updating visual data representations such as heatmaps illustrating areas of highest student activity, scatter plots correlating interaction frequency with performance metrics, and histograms displaying comparative cohort versus individual engagement metrics. These real-time dashboards enable educators to monitor ongoing student activities actively, quickly identify at-risk learners, and track engagement levels across diverse simulation tasks.

Complementing descriptive analytics, prescriptive analytics methods form the foundation of the personalized recommendation engine integrated within the simulation. Technologically, this recommendation system generates immediate, contextually relevant guidance based on data-driven insights derived from clustering analyzes and performance tracking algorithms. These recommendations are constructed using predefined decision rules developed collaboratively by educational experts and algorithm designers. Implemented via programmatic logic involving conditional if-then rules and weighted decision matrices, the recommendation engine dynamically adjusts its outputs according to real-time analytics data streams, providing actionable, personalized feedback to individual students within the simulation interface itself. Technically supported by cloud-hosted APIs and webhook communications, this recommendation infrastructure ensures seamless interaction between Mixpanel's analytics capabilities and the simulation's front-end interface.

Central to the technical methodology employed in this research is the use of Educational Data Mining, specifically clustering algorithms that enable effective student segmentation based on behavioral data (Dol & Jawandhiya, 2024; Dutt et al., 2024; Sharma et al., 2023; Khare et al., 2018). Clustering algorithms systematically organize data points, in this context, student interactions, into distinct groupings characterized by shared behavioral traits. Such segmentation significantly aids in identifying instructional needs and personalizing feedback.

The K-means clustering algorithm represents the technical core of the segmentation methodology applied here. Technically, this algorithm partitions the behavioral dataset into clusters by minimizing intra-cluster variance, also known as Within-Cluster Sum of Squares (WCSS). This process begins with rigorous feature selection and normalization procedures, ensuring each interaction metric, such as click frequency, decision-making patterns, and task duration, receives equal weighting. Common normalization methods applied include min-max scaling and z-score normalization techniques.

Initialization of clusters within the K-means algorithm typically involves heuristic approaches or randomized centroid placement, selected to facilitate rapid convergence. Iteratively, each behavioral data point is assigned to the nearest cluster centroid using Euclidean distance calculations. Following each assignment, centroid positions are recalculated based on the arithmetic mean of all data points within each cluster. The iterative reassignment and centroid recalculations continue until cluster positions stabilize, showing convergence.

To assess the quality and meaningfulness of generated clusters, quantitative cluster validation metrics are employed. Specifically, the Silhouette score and Davies-Bouldin index are used. The Silhouette score assesses the cohesion within clusters and the separation between clusters, providing an intuitive metric wherein higher scores closer to +1 indicate clearly delineated, coherent clusters. Conversely, the Davies-Bouldin index evaluates cluster compactness and separation by computing the average similarity between clusters, where lower index values signify better clustering structures. Employing these validation measures ensures the generated clusters are pedagogically actionable and represent meaningful groupings based on genuine behavioral differences among students.

The business simulation platform central to this research operates within a comprehensive cloud-based environment specifically designed to emulate real-world business scenarios with high fidelity. Technologically, this environment is structured into three integrated subsystems working in cohesion: the front-end interface, the back-end computational engine, and the cloud infrastructure.

The front-end interface, crafted using web technologies, including HTML5, CSS3, and JavaScript frameworks such as React or Angular, provides an intuitive, responsive user experience. This interface enables students to interact seamlessly with the simulation's complex decision-making scenarios. Integrated within the front-end is Mixpanel's JavaScript SDK, enabling immediate capture and transmission of student interactions to analytics servers.

The back-end computational engine, typically developed using frameworks such as Python Flask and JavaScript's Node.js, manages the complex logic underpinning simulation scenarios, processes user-generated decisions, computes performance metrics, and coordinates interactions between front-end interfaces and analytics systems. It serves as the central hub managing data flow, ensuring real-time responsiveness, and handling complex computational simulations reflective of realistic business contexts.

Underlying both front-end and back-end operations is the scalable cloud infrastructure deployed on industry-standard platforms such as Microsoft Azure. Leveraging cloud capabilities ensures real-time data processing, instant scalability in response to varying user demands, and secure, reliable data storage using cloud-managed SQL and NoSQL database solutions optimized specifically for rapid data retrieval and analytical processing.

A distinctive technical contribution of this research is its integration of analytics capabilities, simulation environment functionalities, and educational module alignment within a coherent technical framework. Real-time student interaction data captured by Mixpanel's analytics infrastructure is instantaneously processed into actionable insights through clustering algorithms and descriptive analytical visualizations. These insights immediately feed into the simulation's recommendation engine, generating personalized, targeted instructional recommendations communicated directly within the simulation interface.

Simultaneously, insights derived from analytics are looped back into the educational framework, informing iterative adjustments to simulation difficulty levels, instructional design strategies, and curriculum alignment processes. This cyclical integration ensures continuous adaptation of instructional content based on real-time learner analytics, enhancing educational effectiveness and responsiveness to student needs.

Finally, the technical architecture and implementation procedures incorporate ethical considerations, especially concerning student data privacy and security. To this end, data encryption standards (AES-256 encryption), secure HTTPS/TLS protocols for data transmission, and strict access control mechanisms are systematically implemented. Compliance with international data privacy regulations, such as the General Data Protection Regulation (GDPR), is assured through data anonymization procedures and transparent communication of data usage practices to all participants.

While multiple analytics platforms are available for educational use, their effectiveness varies significantly depending on the instructional context, particularly when applied to real-time, simulation-based environments. Mixpanel stands out due to its advanced support for real-time event tracking, behavioral segmentation, and flexible integration via SDKs. These features make it particularly well-suited for interactive educational scenarios that demand immediate feedback and personalized insights. In contrast, Google Analytics, although widely adopted for monitoring general user engagement in web-based learning platforms, focuses primarily on aggregate metrics such as page views, session durations, and traffic sources. It lacks the fine-grained interaction tracking and real-time feedback capabilities necessary for adaptive learning within business simulations. Tableau, another commonly used tool, offers excellent data visualization capabilities and is effective for retrospective analysis of educational data. However, it does not natively support real-time data processing or behavioral tracking without substantial backend integration. Unlike Mixpanel, it is not designed to capture or respond to student interactions as they happen. For these reasons, Mixpanel is better aligned with the pedagogical goals of this study, which require granular, time-sensitive behavioral data to enable immediate, personalized feedback and dynamic instructional adaptation within active simulation environments.

## 4. METHODOLOGY

The proposed system integrates Mixpanel's behavioral analytics into a business simulation platform to capture and analyze student interactions in real-time. This section details the methodology, including the system architecture, the application of clustering algorithms for student segmentation, the development of the personalized feedback and recommendation system, the integration with educational modules, and the continuous monitoring and dynamic adjustment process.

To begin with, the integration of Mixpanel into the business simulation platform involves embedding Mixpanel's tracking code into the simulation environment. This allows for the collection of detailed interaction data, such as clicks, decision points, time spent on tasks, and collaboration activities. The data is then sent to Mixpanel's servers, where it is processed and stored for further analysis.

The overall system architecture, as shown in Figure 1, consists of three main components: the business simulation platform, the behavioral analytics engine, and the feedback and recommendation system. The business simulation platform provides the interactive environment where students engage in various activities. The behavioral analytics engine, powered by Mixpanel, captures and processes interaction data in real-time. Finally, the feedback and recommendation system uses the insights generated by the analytics engine to provide personalized feedback to students.

*Figure 1. Overall System Architecture*

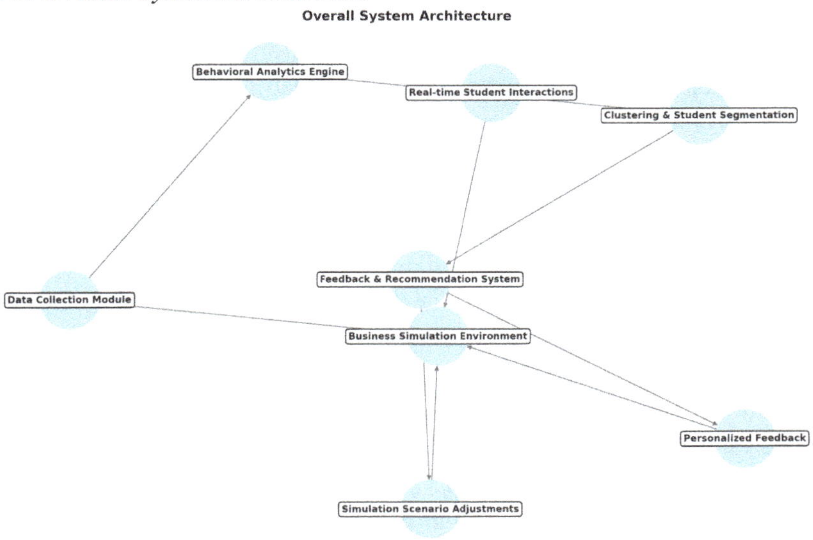


The overall system architecture depicted in Figure 1 illustrates the integrated workflow between the three core components: the business simulation platform, the behavioral analytics engine, and the personalized feedback and recommendation system. Each component plays a crucial role, functioning collaboratively to deliver a cohesive, responsive, and personalized educational experience.

The business simulation platform serves as the interactive environment where students engage actively in realistic business-related tasks and scenarios. Within this platform, students undertake roles that require making strategic decisions, managing resources, and interacting collaboratively with peers. These interactions generate diverse types of behavioral data points that are critical for subsequent analytical processing. Specifically, students engage with tasks such as formulating business strategies, making tactical and operational decisions, managing resources, and working collaboratively to achieve predefined simulation objectives. Every interaction within this simulation environment is systematically captured, ensuring comprehensive tracking of behaviors that reflect students' decision-making patterns and problem-solving approaches.

At the center of the architecture, the Behavioral Analytics Engine (Mixpanel) acts as the central processing unit responsible for real-time data acquisition, analysis, and generation of insights. When students interact with the simulation platform's interface, embedded Mixpanel JavaScript SDK snippets record these interactions as structured events. Each event is encoded with metadata, including student identifiers, interaction timestamps, decision contexts, task specifics, and outcomes achieved. Events are transmitted asynchronously to Mixpanel's cloud-based analytics infrastructure, where they undergo initial data preprocessing, removing redundancies, filtering irrelevant events, and ensuring uniform formatting for analytical consistency.

Mixpanel's cloud infrastructure supports immediate, high-throughput data processing, allowing instantaneous analysis even on scale. The processed event data is stored efficiently in databases specifically optimized for real-time querying and rapid data retrieval. Through Mixpanel's intuitive analytical dashboards, educators can quickly segment student interaction data based on customized parameters, enabling granular exploration and interpretation of student behavior. Educators and instructional designers use these insights to dynamically assess student progress, identify areas requiring targeted support, and adjust simulation scenarios accordingly.

The central innovation illustrated in Figure 1 lies in the seamless integration of Mixpanel's behavioral analytics engine with the recommendation and feedback system. Real-time insights generated by Mixpanel feed directly into the recommendation engine, allowing it to respond instantly to emerging student needs. Technically, this integration is achieved through aa Application Programming Interface (API) infrastructure, facilitating continuous two-way data communication. Analytical outputs, such as student segmentation results derived from clustering algorithms, are continuously transferred via APIs and used immediately to trigger personalized feedback. Consequently, students receive tailored recommendations directly within the simulation platform interface, providing immediate guidance precisely at the moment it is most beneficial, maximizing instructional impact.

Figure 1 highlights the presence of a continuous feedback loop, a critical aspect of the system's adaptability and responsiveness. The loop enables the system to iteratively enhance the educational environment by utilizing data-driven insights. As student interactions evolve during simulations, ongoing behavioral analytics inform the recommendation engine and subsequently update educational modules in near-real-time. Instructional content and scenario complexity can be continuously refined, adapting to students' changing skill development needs, ensuring the learning environment remains consistently relevant and appropriately challenging.

The integration architecture ensures scalability and flexibility, as depicted by the cloud-based nature of the components. Deploying the simulation and analytics components in the cloud guarantees strong performance regardless of user volume or interaction complexity. This scalability is essential for accommodating varying student cohorts, allowing the simulation to be effectively deployed across diverse educational settings without compromising performance quality or data integrity.

The architecture also addresses critical data privacy and security concerns inherent to educational analytics systems. Data security measures, including encryption of data in transit (HTTPS/TLS protocols) and at rest (AES-256), are fully embedded into the architecture. Strict access control mechanisms regulate the visibility of student data, limiting it exclusively to authorized personnel (educators and administrators). This emphasis on privacy aligns the proposed system with stringent data protection regulations, such as GDPR, underscoring the system's ethical integrity and compliance readiness.

Finally, this comprehensive system architecture sets a clear stage for the methodological processes described in subsequent subsections, including the specific clustering algorithms used for student segmentation, the algorithmic construction of personalized recommendations, the instructional design processes ensuring alignment with educational objectives, and the experimental validation strategies deployed to evaluate effectiveness rigorously.

Figure 1 not only illustrates the key technological components but also shows their dynamic interactions, reinforcing the innovative character and pedagogical effectiveness of the proposed Mixpanel-integrated approach. By capturing behavioral analytics data, processing it rapidly and accurately, generating actionable insights, and delivering timely, personalized feedback, this system establishes a strong foundation for enhanced student learning experiences within business simulation environments.

The next step involves the application of clustering algorithms to segment students based on their interaction patterns within the simulation. Specifically, the k-means clustering algorithm is used to group students into clusters that exhibit similar behaviors. The objective is to minimize the within-cluster sum of squares (WCSS), as shown in Equation 1.

$$\text{WCSS} = \sum_{j=1}^{k} \sum_{\mathbf{x}_i \in C_j} \| \mathbf{x}_i - \boldsymbol{\mu}_j \|^2 \tag{1}$$

Here, $\boldsymbol{\mu}_j$ represents the centroid of cluster $C_j$, and $\mathbf{x}_i$ denotes the interaction data point for student i. By minimizing WCSS, the algorithm ensures that students within the same cluster exhibit similar interaction patterns, making it easier to identify specific behaviors that lead to successful outcomes.

The clustering process involves several steps:

1. Data Preprocessing: Interaction data is preprocessed to remove noise and normalize the features.
2. Feature Selection: Relevant features, such as decision-making frequency, collaboration metrics, and time management, are selected for clustering.
3. Clustering: The k-means algorithm is applied to the preprocessed data to segment students into clusters.
4. Cluster Validation: The quality of the clusters is validated using metrics such as silhouette score and Davies-Bouldin index.

After successfully segmenting students into behaviorally distinct clusters through the clustering algorithms described earlier, the next methodological step was the development and implementation of a personalized feedback and recommendation system. The main objective of this system is to generate targeted, individualized recommendations based on detailed behavioral insights derived from analytics data, providing students with actionable guidance tailored precisely to their learning needs. This personalized feedback approach aims to enhance students' specific competencies in real-time, directly addressing their identified strengths and areas for improvement.

The workflow of the personalized feedback and recommendation system encompasses several interconnected stages that form a cyclical process, designed to continuously adapt to student behaviors and instructional objectives.

Initially, the workflow begins with behavioral analytics data collection, leveraging the integration of Mixpanel described previously. This first step involves real-time monitoring of student interactions within the simulation environment. Mixpanel's infrastructure captures comprehensive event data, which includes decision-making patterns, task durations, interaction frequency, collaborative activities, and scenario outcomes, all essential for assessing students' engagement and performance. These data points form the raw input material upon which the recommendation system subsequently operates.

The second stage of the workflow involves data preprocessing and clustering. Immediately after collection, the real-time data undergoes preprocessing routines within Mixpanel, including normalization and structuring, to maintain consistency and enable meaningful analyses. Subsequently, the clustering algorithm segments students into clearly defined groups based on behavioral characteristics. Each group represents a distinct pattern of student engagement, providing foundational insight for personalized instructional interventions.

In the following stage, labeled analytic interpretation and recommendation generation, cluster-specific insights are translated into personalized recommendations. This process involves applying predefined decision logic rules formulated collaboratively by instructional design experts and analytics specialists. These rules incorporate conditional logic, aligning specific behavioral patterns with pedagogical objectives and intervention strategies. For instance, students identified within clusters characterized by infrequent or hesitant decision-making behaviors are algorithmically assigned recommendations explicitly designed to enhance decision confidence, speed, and effectiveness. Conversely, students showing limited collaborative interactions receive recommendations prompting them toward increased peer engagement, team communication, and active participation in shared tasks.

The underlying algorithmic process that generates these personalized recommendations employs weighted scoring functions. Each type of captured interaction is associated with predefined weights based on expert knowledge and empirical insights. A composite feedback vector is algorithmically calculated for each student, dynamically synthesizing the relevance and priority of various interaction metrics. This weighted scoring approach ensures personalized feedback aligns with each student's most immediate learning needs. Mathematically, the recommendation vector for a specific student is generated as shown in Equation 2.

$$\mathbf{f}_s = \sum_{i=1}^{n} w_i \cdot \mathbf{r}_i \qquad (2)$$

In this equation, $\mathbf{r}_i$ represents the recommendation vector for interaction i, and $w_i$ is the weight assigned based on the relevance of the interaction to the student's skill development needs. The weights are determined using a combination of expert knowledge and data-driven approaches, ensuring that the feedback is both relevant and effective.

Fs denotes the overall feedback vector for student s, Wi represents the weighting factor assigned to each interaction or decision type based on its educational importance, and Ri signifies the specific recommendation vector associated with each interaction type i. These weights are dynamically adjusted based on the evolving analysis of real-time behavioral data and pedagogical priorities identified by educators.

Following the generation of personalized recommendations, the system proceeds to the feedback delivery stage. Recommendations are transmitted directly to students through real-time notifications and embedded interface prompts within the simulation platform. The immediacy of this communication significantly enhances the pedagogical effectiveness of the recommendations. Students receive guidance precisely at the moment of interaction, enabling immediate implementation of suggested improvements, reinforcing adaptive learning behaviors effectively.

After delivering feedback, the system moves to the stage of student response tracking, continuously monitoring subsequent interactions to evaluate the effectiveness of recommendations. The analytics system captures new interactions post-feedback delivery, evaluating whether students successfully incorporate the suggested behavioral adjustments. This real-time assessment process facilitates rapid recalibration of recommendations, maintaining relevance to evolving student needs and ensuring continuous instructional alignment.

The final stage of the feedback workflow, continuous adaptive refinement, leverages insights obtained through monitoring student responses to recommendations. These insights inform iterative adjustments to recommendation logic, simulation difficulty levels, and instructional support strategies. For example, if behavioral analytics show that a group of students consistently struggles with a specific task despite targeted recommendations, instructional designers dynamically refine scenario content or intervention strategies to better support these students. Conversely, insights revealing rapid mastery or high engagement prompt gradual increases in scenario complexity to maintain student motivation and challenge.

The feedback and recommendation workflow forms a continuous adaptive cycle: real-time data collection informs analytics-driven clustering, clustering outputs inform targeted recommendations, and subsequent student responses further inform future adjustments. This iterative cycle maintains the system's responsiveness, enabling it to dynamically adapt to students' continuously evolving learning trajectories.

Beyond technical implementation, this methodology's strength lies in its alignment with educational best practices, particularly formative assessment principles. By providing timely, specific, actionable feedback, students remain consistently informed about their performance relative to clearly defined learning objectives. Educators simultaneously benefit from real-time, granular insights into individual and collective student behaviors, enabling continuous adaptation of instructional strategies to maximize educational effectiveness. This alignment between technical capability and instructional best practices significantly strengthens the pedagogical impact of the overall approach.

To ensure that the simulation scenarios are relevant and aligned with the learning objectives, the proposed system integrates behavioral analytics with conventional educational modules. This integration involves several steps:

1. Curriculum Mapping: The learning objectives and curriculum content are mapped to the simulation scenarios, ensuring that the activities within the simulation are aligned with the educational goals.
2. Scenario Design: Simulation scenarios are designed based on the mapped curriculum, incorporating elements that target specific skills, such as decision-making, teamwork, and leadership.
3. Feedback Loop: The insights generated by the behavioral analytics engine are fed back into the educational framework, informing teaching strategies and student evaluations.

This dynamic feedback loop ensures that the simulation remains adaptive and responsive to the evolving needs of students, providing a more personalized and effective learning experience.

Finally, the system continuously monitors student progress and dynamically adjusts the feedback to ensure optimal learning outcomes. This involves:

1. Real-Time Monitoring: The behavioral analytics engine continuously captures and processes interaction data, providing real-time insights into student behaviors.

2. Dynamic Adjustment: The feedback and recommendation system dynamically adjusts the feedback based on the latest interaction data, ensuring that the suggestions remain relevant and effective.
3. Performance Tracking: Student performance is tracked over time, allowing educators to identify trends and make data-driven decisions to enhance the learning experience.

By continuously monitoring and dynamically adjusting the feedback, the proposed system aims to provide a more personalized and effective learning experience, ultimately enhancing student skill development and job market preparedness.

## 5. EXPERIMENTAL SETUP AND RESULTS

To evaluate the effectiveness of the proposed system, a series of experiments were conducted using a business simulation platform integrated with Mixpanel. This section details the experimental setup, including the simulation environment, participant demographics, data collection methods, and the metrics used for evaluation. The results of the experiments are then presented, demonstrating the impact of the proposed system on student skill development and job market preparedness.

The business simulation platform used in this study is a cloud-based system specifically designed to replicate real-world business scenarios, enabling students to apply theoretical knowledge practically. Within this environment, students actively engage in making strategic decisions, collaborating closely with peers, and showing leadership capabilities to successfully accomplish predefined objectives. The simulation encompasses multiple interconnected modules, including marketing, finance, operations, and human resources, ensuring a comprehensive and realistic learning experience aligned closely with professional settings.

The study involved 120 undergraduate business students enrolled at a major higher education institution in Lisbon. These students were systematically divided into four equally sized groups of 30 participants each, with each group participating actively in the business simulation activities for a period of four weeks. Careful attention was given to ensuring balanced representation among these groups, considering key demographic and academic variables, such as gender distribution, academic performance levels, and prior exposure to business simulation environments. This balance ensured comparability and reliability across the experimental groups, minimizing biases and enhancing the generalizability of the study's outcomes.

Throughout the simulation, detailed interaction data was systematically collected utilizing Mixpanel's event-tracking capabilities. Specifically, the collected metrics encompassed comprehensive data points reflecting various dimensions of student engagement and performance, such as the number and quality of decisions made during simulation scenarios, the amount of time students allocated to specific tasks, frequency of collaborative activities, and instances of demonstrated leadership behaviors. This granular interaction data subsequently served as input for the clustering analysis, enabling precise behavioral segmentation and facilitating the provision of tailored, real-time feedback to enhance student learning outcomes.

To rigorously evaluate the effectiveness and educational impact of the proposed behavioral analytics-driven feedback system, the study incorporated multiple well-defined evaluation metrics. Skill improvement was quantitatively assessed through structured pre- and post-simulation assessments, explicitly targeting improvements in decision-making, teamwork, and leadership competencies. Student engagement levels were objectively measured by analyzing both the quantity of interactions (interaction frequency) and the duration students spent actively participating in simulation tasks. Lastly, the effectiveness and acceptability of the personalized feedback provided by the system were qualitatively evaluated through comprehensive student satisfaction surveys and direct qualitative feedback, offering deeper insights into the students' perceptions and overall experience with the simulation and analytics-based educational interventions.

The results showed a significant improvement in student skills across all three areas: decision-making, teamwork, and leadership. The average improvement scores for each skill are presented in Table 1.

*Table 1. Average improvement scores*

| Skill | Pre-Simulation Score | Post-Simulation Score | Improvement |
|---|---|---|---|
| Decision-Making | 65.2 | 78.4 | *13.2* |
| Teamwork | 70.1 | 82.3 | *12.2* |
| Leadership | 68.5 | 80.7 | *12.2* |

The integration of Mixpanel's behavioral analytics significantly increased student engagement. The average number of interactions per student and the average time spent on the simulation are shown in Table 2.

*Table 2. Average number of interactions per student and the average time spent*

| Metric | Control Group | Experimental Group | Increase |
|---|---|---|---|
| Interactions per Student | 45 | 68 | *23* |
| Time Spent (hours) | 12.5 | 18.3 | *5.8* |

Student satisfaction surveys conducted as part of this study revealed a notably high level of satisfaction with the personalized feedback delivered through the analytics-driven system. In particular, qualitative feedback obtained from participants emphasized the relevance, clarity, and practical usefulness of the recommendations provided. Students frequently commented that receiving targeted, actionable feedback enabled them to clearly identify and address specific areas needing improvement, significantly enhancing their decision-making abilities, teamwork dynamics, and leadership skills.

The clustering algorithm successfully segmented students into distinct behavioral groups based on their interaction patterns within the simulation environment. An analysis of these clusters, depicted in Figure 2, highlights the distribution and relative frequency of three primary types of interactions, decision points, collaboration instances, and leadership actions, across four identified student clusters resulting from the K-means clustering procedure. This behavioral segmentation enabled a detailed understanding of student engagement and provided educators with valuable insights to deliver precisely tailored feedback and instructional interventions aligned with the specific needs and behaviors of each student group.

As illustrated in Figure 2, Cluster 3 exhibits the highest overall frequency of interactions, showing highly active and engaged students across all measured interaction types. Within this cluster, there is notably high intensity in collaboration instances, reflecting peer engagement and teamwork behaviors. This pattern suggests students in Cluster 3 are highly collaborative, often starting teamwork interactions and frequently assuming leadership roles. Their frequent engagement at decision points indicates proactive decision-making behaviors, reflecting strong confidence and skill in navigating complex scenarios.

In contrast, Cluster 4 demonstrates significantly lower frequencies across all interaction categories. Students in this cluster exhibit limited collaborative and leadership actions, showing a tendency toward individual work or lower overall engagement with simulation scenarios. Their frequency of interaction at decision points is relatively consistent with the other clusters proportionally, suggesting that these students are still participating in essential simulation activities, albeit less actively engaging in collaborative or leadership roles.

Cluster 1 and Cluster 2 provide intermediate interaction profiles. Cluster 1 shows balanced frequencies across the three types of interactions but with notable emphasis on leadership actions, suggesting that these students are inclined to take initiative and frequently assume leadership roles during the simulation activities. Cluster 2, on the other hand, demonstrates moderate levels of collaboration and decision-point interactions, paired with comparatively lower leadership activity. This profile may indicate students who effectively engage with the simulation tasks collaboratively but are less likely to step forward into leadership roles voluntarily.

Overall, Figure 2 effectively visualizes behavioral distinctions among student clusters, enabling educators to precisely understand engagement patterns and tailor instructional interventions accordingly. Such segmentation is instrumental for personalized educational strategies, as it provides insights into which specific behaviors and skills, decision-making, teamwork, and leadership, should be reinforced or further developed within each student group.

*Figure 2. Distribution of interaction types across student clusters*

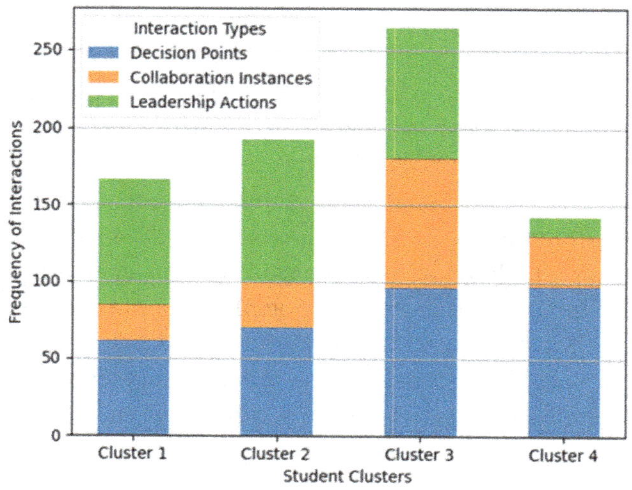


The cumulative skill development of students throughout the four-week simulation period is clearly represented in Figure 3, which employs an area chart to illustrate progress across three key skill domains: Decision-Making, Teamwork, and Leadership. The vertical axis reflects the cumulative skill scores, while the horizontal axis denotes the progression over the four-week duration of the study, allowing an intuitive visualization of students' skill acquisition trajectories.

The chart distinctly shows a continuous, incremental improvement across all three competencies throughout the simulation. Notably, Leadership emerges as the most significantly developed skill over the simulation period, occupying the largest portion of the cumulative skill score at each weekly interval. This suggests that repeated, real-time feedback provided by the behavioral analytics integration effectively encouraged students to progressively take initiative, engage in leadership behaviors, and display increased confidence within team contexts as the simulation advanced.

Steady and consistent growth can be observed in the teamwork dimension. The teamwork area steadily broadens each week, reflecting that collaborative skills were systematically developed as students engaged more actively with their peers. The steady expansion of this segment shows students became increasingly adept at communicating effectively, coordinating actions, and collaboratively solving problems as the simulation scenarios increased in complexity.

The Decision-Making skill area, although smaller relative to Leadership and Teamwork, shows a consistent incremental increase over the four-week period, clearly showing sustained and progressive improvement. This growth aligns with the expectation that repeated decision-point interactions combined with personalized real-time feedback substantially improve students' abilities to analyze complex information, evaluate alternatives, and make effective strategic decisions within business contexts.

Overall, Figure 3 emphasizes the effectiveness of the simulation platform enhanced by behavioral analytics in fostering a continuous and balanced skill acquisition process. The visualization strongly supports the argument that personalized, analytics-driven feedback promotes sustained growth in essential professional skills, preparing students comprehensively for future professional challenges.

*Figure 3. Cumulative skill development of students over time*

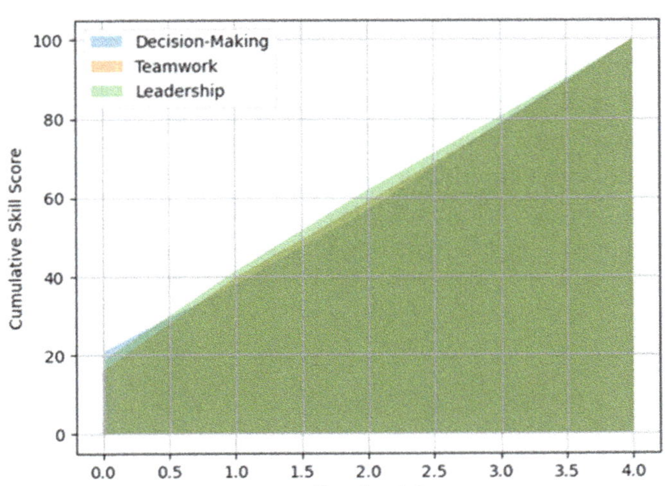

Figure 4 presents a scatter plot illustrating the relationship between the number of interactions students had within the simulation environment and the corresponding improvement in their skills, measured as percentage points. Each data point on the plot represents an individual student, with the horizontal axis indicating the total number of recorded interactions and the vertical axis displaying the observed percentage point improvement in skill scores from baseline to the end of the simulation period.

The positive trend line clearly depicted in red demonstrates a strong positive correlation, highlighting a clear relationship between increased frequency of interactions and higher levels of skill improvement. Students who engaged more frequently, evidenced by higher interaction counts, consistently achieved larger skill gains. For instance, students with fewer than 20 interactions generally exhibited modest skill improvement, typically less than 10 percentage points. Conversely, those students who surpassed approximately 60 interactions commonly displayed significantly higher skill gains, often ranging between 15 and 25 percentage points.

Importantly, while most data points closely follow the positive trend line, some variability is observed, suggesting individual differences in learning trajectories and responsiveness to feedback. Several students, despite relatively moderate interaction frequencies, still achieved notable skill improvements, indicating that interaction quality or responsiveness to personalized feedback could also play critical roles in learning outcomes. Similarly, a small subset of students with relatively high interaction frequencies showed slightly lower skill gains, hinting at possible saturation effects or diminishing returns after extensive interaction, which could be further explored in future studies.

Overall, Figure 4 compellingly supports the study's central premise that regular engagement with personalized, analytics-driven feedback within simulations directly fosters meaningful skill development. It underscores the pedagogical importance of consistent and sustained student interactions, suggesting that active, frequent participation significantly amplifies learning effectiveness and skill mastery. This positive correlation highlights the practical value of incorporating real-time analytics and feedback mechanisms to stimulate ongoing student engagement and maximize educational outcomes.

*Figure 4. Relationship between interaction frequency and skill improvement*

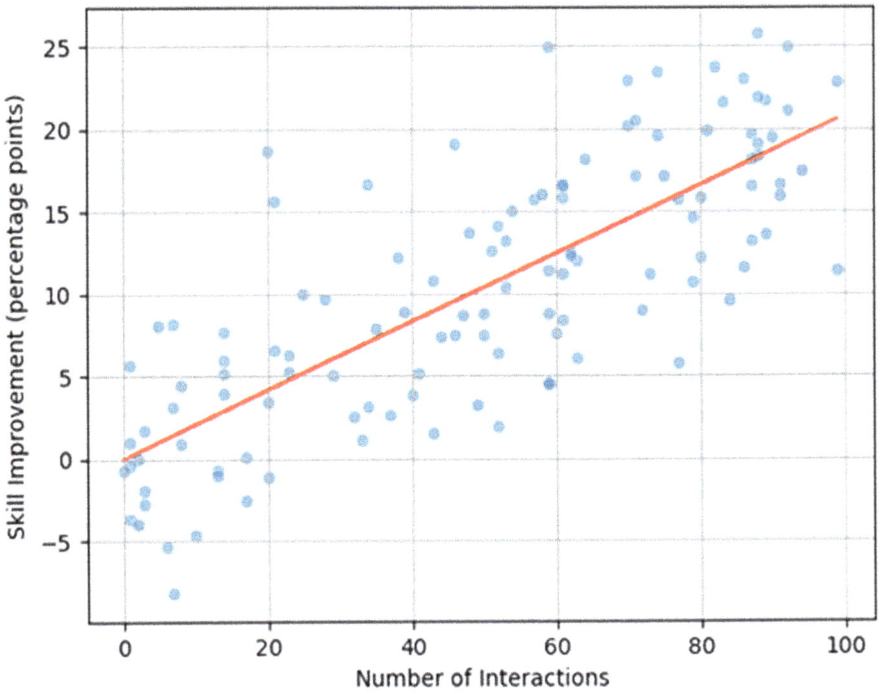


## 6. DISCUSSION AND FUTURE WORK

The results of the experiments show the effectiveness of integrating Mixpanel's behavioral analytics into business simulations for enhancing student skill development. This section discusses the implications of these findings for educational practice, explores broader considerations related to scalability and adaptability, examines potential limitations and ethical considerations of the approach, and identifies directions for future research to further develop and optimize behavioral analytics-driven educational frameworks.

The significant improvement observed in critical competencies such as decision-making, teamwork, and leadership confirms the pedagogical value of incorporating behavioral analytics into simulation-based learning. By capturing detailed, real-time interaction data through Mixpanel and leveraging sophisticated clustering algorithms to segment student behavior, educators gain an unprecedented ability to deliver immediate, actionable, and personalized feedback. This approach directly addresses a longstanding challenge in educational simulations, where feedback has traditionally been either generic or delayed, limiting its immediate instructional value. The successful results underline the pedagogical necessity of timely and personalized feedback systems, reaffirming findings from the broader literature that advocate tailored educational experiences for enhancing learner engagement and achievement.

One major implication for educational practice is the heightened precision with which educators can now identify students' individual learning needs. Through clearly defined behavioral profiles, instructors can more accurately tailor their instructional interventions, facilitating focused, effective skill development. This granular understanding of student behavior enhances educators' ability to manage the classroom dynamically, adapt instructional strategies swiftly, and reinforce specific competencies that students find challenging.

Another important implication is the notable increase in student engagement observed through the integration of personalized feedback mechanisms. The real-time nature of this system aligns closely with contemporary pedagogical theories emphasizing continuous formative assessment and immediate corrective feedback. Personalization creates a more interactive, motivating, and empowering learning environment, fostering student autonomy and engagement. Students who receive direct feedback closely matched to their immediate actions demonstrate higher levels of motivation and satisfaction, validating existing literature advocating for adaptive learning technologies that prioritize personalization.

The integration of analytics into simulations closely aligns education with the skill requirements increasingly emphasized by industry stakeholders. Employers consistently highlight teamwork, leadership, adaptability, and decision-making as critical determinants of professional success. By directly addressing these competencies through targeted feedback, the proposed system effectively bridges theoretical academic learning and practical skill application, increasing graduates' workplace readiness and employability.

Also, from an institutional perspective, this approach supports continuous quality improvement of instructional materials and scenario design. The analytics insights generated by the system enable educators and instructional designers to rapidly identify curricular gaps, adapt scenario complexity, and refine instructional approaches. Over time, this iterative process promotes curricular optimization aligned directly with evolving student needs and broader educational objectives, ultimately enhancing overall instructional effectiveness.

A critical strength of the proposed system is its inherent scalability and adaptability. Integrating Mixpanel's analytics capabilities into the cloud-based business simulation platform ensures support for large-scale deployments. Cloud-based infrastructure inherently provides scalability, accommodating high volumes of concurrent interactions and dynamically adjusting to fluctuating demands without compromising performance or data integrity. As educational institutions increasingly move toward digital and hybrid learning models, this scalable approach allows for seamless expansion from small classroom environments to institution-wide or even cross-institutional deployments.

Adaptability further enhances the system's appeal, as its data-driven feedback and clustering mechanisms can be easily customized and integrated into diverse educational contexts beyond business and management. This adaptability offers significant opportunities for implementation in STEM fields, healthcare education, humanities programs, and vocational training, where scenario-based learning combined with real-time behavioral analytics could similarly enhance learner outcomes. The underlying analytics framework, reliant on universally applicable interaction tracking and clustering algorithms, allows straightforward customization of simulation scenarios to match distinct curricular objectives across disciplines, making the proposed system versatile and broadly applicable.

Despite demonstrated effectiveness, several limitations and potential challenges must be considered. First, the quality and reliability of analytics-driven feedback depend heavily on the accuracy and granularity of captured data. Any disruptions or inconsistencies in data capture, such as missing interaction events or latency in data transmission, can adversely affect the feedback system's accuracy and effectiveness. Ensuring uninterrupted data flow requires maintaining a strong technological infrastructure, continuous system monitoring, and adequate technical expertise among educators, presenting a practical limitation for institutions with limited technical resources.

Second, the reliance on algorithmically generated feedback raises potential concerns regarding interpretability and transparency. Students might struggle to fully understand or accept automated recommendations without sufficient context or clear rationale. Consequently, there is a need to ensure transparency in the recommendation logic, possibly incorporating explanatory mechanisms or human-in-the-loop oversight, especially during initial implementation phases.

Another challenge relates to educators' technical proficiency. Successful deployment of analytics-integrated simulation platforms requires educators to develop a certain level of competency in interpreting analytics data, effectively using dashboards, and managing technology-driven feedback processes. Addressing these challenges necessitates comprehensive professional development initiatives, ensuring educators become comfortable interpreting analytics data, interpreting cluster profiles, and effectively translating insights into instructional strategies.

Additionally, the issue of data privacy and ethical management presents a persistent challenge. Even though technical measures (e.g., AES-256 encryption and GDPR compliance) are integrated, concerns remain around data privacy, informed consent, and the ethical handling of student data. Educators and institutions must proactively address these ethical issues through transparent data usage policies, clear communication with students, and explicit consent processes.

The promising findings and recognized limitations open several compelling avenues for future research. First, future research could explore integrating more sophisticated analytical methodologies, including advanced machine learning and artificial intelligence techniques, such as predictive analytics or deep learning algorithms, to further refine personalized recommendations and predictive capabilities.

Investigating the longitudinal impact of analytics-enhanced simulations represents an important future direction. Longitudinal studies could track student performance over extended periods, assessing long-term retention of skills and sustained engagement improvements. Such studies could provide further empirical validation of the lasting educational benefits of integrating behavioral analytics in simulations.

Future research could also expand the technical integration model explored in this study into other disciplines or professional training contexts. Applying the developed methodology in healthcare simulations, STEM lab-based learning scenarios, or continuous professional development settings would significantly broaden the scope and validate its effectiveness across diverse professional education contexts.

Finally, future studies should consider integrating advanced analytics techniques beyond clustering. For example, the incorporation of predictive analytics, natural language processing, or deep learning algorithms could enhance the system's ability to interpret nuanced behavioral patterns or qualitative student interactions (e.g., textual or verbal responses during simulations). Such advanced analytic integrations could further enrich feedback mechanisms, facilitating even more precise, personalized educational experiences.

Integrating Mixpanel's behavioral analytics into business simulations substantially enhances skill development, student engagement, and pedagogical effectiveness. Despite identified limitations, the demonstrated scalability, adaptability, and potential for broader applicability highlight the significant future potential of this innovative approach. Continued methodological refinement, addressing identified challenges, and exploring advanced analytic integrations will further reinforce the educational impact and practical value of behavioral analytics-enabled simulations.

## 6.1 Limitations and Challenges

While the implementation of Mixpanel in educational contexts demonstrates significant potential for improving learning outcomes and institutional decision-making, a balanced assessment must acknowledge several other important limitations and challenges that can impact successful adoption and effectiveness. These challenges range from practical implementation barriers to fundamental concerns about privacy, equity, and pedagogical authenticity.

One of the most significant barriers to widespread Mixpanel adoption in educational institutions is the substantial cost associated with scaling beyond basic usage. Mixpanel's pricing structure, while offering a generous free tier supporting up to 20 million monthly events, can become expensive as institutions expand their analytics capabilities (Userpilot, 2024).

For educational institutions operating under constrained budgets, these costs present particular challenges. Unlike commercial enterprises that can directly monetize user data insights, educational institutions must justify analytics expenses against competing priorities such as faculty hiring, infrastructure improvements, and student support services. The pricing model's event-based structure can create unpredictable costs as student engagement increases, making budget planning difficult for institutional administrators.

The hidden costs associated with successful implementation extend beyond software licensing to include staff training, system integration, and ongoing maintenance. Educational institutions often lack the technical expertise internally to maximize Mixpanel's capabilities, necessitating additional investments in training or external consulting services that can significantly increase the total cost of ownership.

The sophisticated nature of Mixpanel's analytics platform presents substantial technical barriers for educators who lack extensive data analytics background. Research indicates that learning analytics adoption faces significant challenges related to technical expertise requirements, with institutions struggling to bridge the gap between available data and educators' analytical capabilities (Alzahrani et al., 2023).

Many educators report feeling overwhelmed by the complexity of setting up meaningful tracking events, interpreting dashboard data, and translating analytical insights into actionable pedagogical interventions.

This technical complexity barrier is particularly problematic in higher education, where faculty members are expected to integrate analytics into their teaching practices without comprehensive training or dedicated technical support. The learning curve associated with mastering event tracking, cohort analysis, and retention metrics can discourage adoption, particularly among faculty members who are already managing heavy teaching and research loads.

The comprehensive behavioral tracking capabilities that make Mixpanel valuable for educational insights simultaneously raise significant privacy concerns that can undermine student trust and institutional relationships. Research demonstrates that students express considerable privacy concerns regarding learning analytics implementations, particularly regarding the granular level of behavioral data collection and its potential uses (Mutimukwe et al., 2022).

Mixpanel's ability to track detailed user interactions, including time spent on specific content, click patterns, navigation sequences, and engagement timing, creates comprehensive behavioral profiles that may feel invasive to students. As we discussed in section 2, unlike commercial applications where users voluntarily engage with tracking in exchange for personalized services, educational analytics involve mandatory data collection that students cannot easily opt out of without compromising their academic participation.

The persistence of this data across multiple academic terms and its potential accessibility to various institutional stakeholders raises additional concerns about long-term implications for student privacy and autonomy. Students may alter their authentic learning behaviors when aware of comprehensive tracking, potentially undermining the very metrics that institutions seek to measure and improve.

The visibility of engagement metrics and performance dashboards can inadvertently incentivize students to game the system rather than pursue authentic learning. When students become aware that their time-on-task, click-through rates, and interaction frequencies are being monitored, they may engage in superficial behaviors designed to improve their analytics profiles rather than meaningful learning activities.

This phenomenon, documented in gamification research, demonstrates how the measurement of behavior can fundamentally alter the behavior being measured (Koivisto & Hamari, 2019). Students may learn to manipulate engagement metrics by leaving course pages open, clicking through content without reading, or participating in discussion forums with low-quality contributions designed primarily to register activity rather than contribute meaningfully to learning discourse.

These limitations do not negate the value of Mixpanel's capabilities in educational contexts, but they underscore the importance of thoughtful, evidence-based implementation strategies that acknowledge both technical and ethical complexities. Successful adoption requires substantial institutional investment in training, transparent communication with students about data use, and careful attention to balancing analytical insights with pedagogical judgment and student autonomy.

Educational institutions must also develop sustainable financial models for analytics adoption that account for long-term costs and demonstrate clear return on investment through improved learning outcomes rather than merely increased data collection capabilities. Most critically, implementations must maintain focus on educational goals rather than analytical sophistication, ensuring that data collection serves learning rather than surveillance.

## 7. CONCLUSION

This research proposed and rigorously validated an innovative integration of Mixpanel's behavioral analytics within a cloud-based business simulation environment, significantly enhancing student skill development and professional readiness. By systematically capturing real-time behavioral interaction data, analyzing it using advanced clustering algorithms, and leveraging these insights to provide personalized, actionable feedback, the proposed methodology has demonstrated interesting improvements in key competencies critical to students' professional success, specifically, decision-making efficiency, teamwork, leadership capability, and overall job preparedness.

One of the primary contributions of this research is its successful demonstration of integrating sophisticated behavioral analytics technology, specifically Mixpanel, into the educational context of business simulations. By effectively capturing comprehensive student interaction data in real-time, educators are now equipped with a granular, nuanced understanding of how students navigate, engage, and make decisions within complex simulated environments. This ability addresses a notable limitation of conventional educational simulation platforms, which traditionally rely on retrospective, generalized, or delayed feedback that significantly reduces opportunities for immediate learning adjustments.

The significant improvements observed in student performance, coupled with measurable increases in student engagement and motivation, validate the underlying hypothesis driving this research that personalized, real-time, analytics-driven feedback substantially enhances educational outcomes. This study's empirical results confirm that delivering tailored instructional guidance precisely at critical interaction moments empowers students to reflect on, adjust, and improve their behaviors proactively. This finding aligns clearly with existing literature emphasizing the pedagogical advantages of personalized learning and formative assessment methods, further reinforcing the growing consensus on the effectiveness of adaptive educational technologies.

Another critical contribution of the study is the seamless technical integration architecture, which effectively bridges analytics insights with conventional instructional methods and curricular content. By explicitly aligning simulation scenarios with predefined learning objectives and dynamically adjusting instructional design based on real-time behavioral analytics, the system ensures educational relevance and coherence. This cyclical integration mechanism provides educators with continuous, granular insights into student learning behaviors, allowing prompt pedagogical interventions and agile scenario adjustments that continuously refine educational effectiveness. Such iterative adaptability significantly enhances educational responsiveness to students' evolving learning trajectories, ensuring curricular content remains relevant and optimally challenging.

The comprehensive technological infrastructure described and validated through this research, combining cloud-based platforms, advanced clustering algorithms, and sophisticated visualization capabilities, highlights another significant strength of the proposed approach: scalability and adaptability. The system's inherent flexibility allows institutions to implement it across various educational contexts beyond business education, such as healthcare education, engineering training, STEM disciplines, and other professional development scenarios. The scalable cloud-based architecture also facilitates deployment across diverse institutional settings, including larger student cohorts or multi-institutional partnerships, without compromising performance, responsiveness, or data security.

Despite the clear strengths and positive outcomes demonstrated through this study, several limitations and challenges warrant consideration. The system's effectiveness critically depends on accurate and consistent data capture. Potential technical issues, such as incomplete data collection or data loss due to connectivity disruptions, could limit feedback accuracy or timeliness. Student acceptance of automated feedback requires ongoing consideration, particularly regarding transparency and trust in recommendation algorithms. Addressing these concerns through clear communication, transparency of analytic processes, and incorporating human oversight, especially in early adoption stages, will be crucial to maintaining student trust and maximizing feedback effectiveness.

Also, while the current research provides promising empirical evidence of the effectiveness of behavioral analytics integration, it also highlights several other opportunities for future research. Longitudinal studies examining long-term impacts on skill retention and career performance outcomes would further strengthen the system's validity and practical applicability. Future research should focus explicitly on quantifying long-term skill retention, exploring how continued exposure to analytics-driven feedback influences sustained skill development, employability, and professional success.

Another essential area for future exploration involves extending the technical framework by incorporating advanced analytical methodologies. Integrating techniques such as predictive analytics, deep learning algorithms, or natural language processing could enrich the understanding of nuanced behavioral and qualitative interaction patterns within simulation environments. Such enhancements could significantly broaden the depth, accuracy, and pedagogical precision of personalized feedback, further elevating the learning experience's sophistication.

The inclusion of objective, standardized measures for evaluating feedback effectiveness represents an additional meaningful future direction. While the present study used a combination of performance metrics, student engagement measures, and clustering-based behavioral analytics, incorporating standardized assessment instruments or external validation measures could further substantiate the robustness and generalizability of the findings.

From a practical perspective, the system presented in this chapter not only addresses pedagogical limitations but also aligns closely with the skills increasingly prioritized by industry stakeholders. Modern employers consistently highlight the value of adaptive decision-making, collaborative teamwork, effective leadership, and strategic thinking, competencies explicitly targeted and demonstrably enhanced by the proposed approach. Consequently, adopting such analytics-integrated simulation environments may enable educational institutions to produce graduates better prepared to meet real-world professional challenges. This industry alignment further emphasizes the significance of this research's contributions and underscores its broader relevance to workforce development and professional training.

In conclusion, this study makes substantial contributions to both educational theory and practice by successfully integrating behavioral analytics within business simulation environments. Through technical integration, methodological implementation, and experimental validation, the research demonstrates clear improvements in critical student competencies and engagement levels, providing a compelling argument for broader adoption of similar technologies in educational contexts. By overcoming historical feedback limitations inherent in traditional simulation-based educational methods, this approach opens many areas for future research and practical innovation, ensuring educators can deliver personalized learning experiences that effectively prepare students for evolving professional demands.

## REFERENCES


Adib, H. (2024). Experiential learning in higher education: Assessing the role of business simulations in shaping student attitudes towards sustainability. *International Journal of Management Education, 22*(2), 100968. DOI: 10.1016/j.ijme.2024.100968

Ahmed, S., Kumar, R., & Hassan, M. (2024). Student performance prediction using machine learning algorithms. *Applied Computational Intelligence and Soft Computing, 2024*(1), 4067721. Advance online publication. DOI: 10.1155/2024/4067721

Ahuja, V. (2024). Simulations in business education: Unlocking experiential learning. Practices and implementation of gamification in higher education, 1-21. DOI: 10.4018/979-8-3693-0716-8.ch001

Alzahrani, A. S., Tsai, Y.-S., Iqbal, S., Marcos, P. M. M., Scheffel, M., Drachsler, H., Kloos, C. D., Aljohani, N., & Gasevic, D. (2023). Untangling connections between challenges in the adoption of learning analytics in higher education. *Education and Information Technologies, 28*(4), 4563–4595. DOI: 10.1007/s10639-022-11323-x

Anderson, P. H., & Lawton, L. (2009). Business simulations and cognitive learning: Developments, desires, and future directions. *Simulation & Gaming, 40*(2), 193–216. DOI: 10.1177/1046878108321624

Bell, B. S., Tannenbaum, S. I., Ford, J. K., Noe, R. A., & Kraiger, K. (2016). 100 years of training and development research: What we know and where we should go. *The Journal of Applied Psychology, 101*(3), 305–323. DOI: 10.1037/apl0000142

Beranič, T., & Heričko, M. (2022). The impact of serious games in economic and business education: A case of ERP business simulation. *Sustainability (Basel), 14*(2), 683. DOI: 10.3390/su14020683

Bird, K. (2024). Predictive analytics in higher education: The promises and challenges of using machine learning to improve student success. Association for Institutional Research. https://www.airweb.org/publication/article-161

Boda, M. A., & Ugrósdy, G. (2019). Enhancing Learning Outcome of Business Simulation Games via Process Feedback. *Vadyba*, (1), 67.

Charitopoulos, A., Rangoussi, M., & Koulouriotis, D. (2020). On the use of soft computing methods in educational data mining and learning analytics research: A review of years 2010–2018. *International Journal of Artificial Intelligence in Education, 30*(3), 371–430. DOI: 10.1007/s40593-020-00200-8

Chugh, R., Turnbull, D., Cowling, M. A., Vanderburg, R., & Vanderburg, M. A. (2023). Implementing educational technology in Higher Education Institutions: A review of technologies, stakeholder perceptions, frameworks and metrics. *Education and Information Technologies*, *28*(12), 16403–16429. DOI: 10.1007/s10639-023-11846-x

Costin, Y., O'Brien, M. P., & Hynes, B. (2019). Developing cognitive and non-cognitive entrepreneurial competences through business simulation games. *Journal of Enterprising Culture*, *27*(04), 471–498. DOI: 10.1142/S0218495819500171

Cukurova, M. (2025). The interplay of learning, analytics and artificial intelligence in education: A vision for hybrid intelligence. *British Journal of Educational Technology*, *56*(2), 387–404. DOI: 10.1111/bjet.13514

Dai, X., Fu, X., Zuo, J., & Shi, L. (2025). Application of Virtual Simulation in Education: Current Status, Hot Spots and Trends. *Advances in Computer and Materials Scienc Research*, *1*(1), 384–392. DOI: 10.70114/acmsr.2024.1.1.P384

Diachkova, A. V., Sandler, D. G., & Avramenko, E. S. (2020). Case of using simulation in education for business analysts. Economic consultant, (3), 104-114. DOI: 10.46224/ecoc.2020.3.7

Dol, S. M., & Jawandhiya, P. M. (2023). A review of data mining in education sector. *Journal of Engineering Education Transformations*, *36*(Special Issue), 13–22. DOI: 10.16920/jeet/2023/v36is2/23003

Dol, S. M., & Jawandhiya, P. M. (2024). Systematic review and analysis of EDM for predicting the academic performance of students. Journal of The Institution of Engineers (India): Series B, 105(4), 1021-1071. DOI: 10.1007/s40031-024-00998-0

Dutt, A., Ismail, M. A., Herawan, T., & Targio, I. A. (2024). *Partition-Based Clustering Algorithms Applied to Mixed Data for Educational Data Mining: A Survey From 1971 to 2024*. IEEE., DOI: 10.1109/ACCESS.2024.3496929

Elias, T. (2011). Learning Analytics: Definitions, Processes and Potential. *Learning*, *1*, 22.

Ellikkal, A., & Rajamohan, S. (2025). AI-enabled personalized learning: Empowering management students for improving engagement and academic performance. Vilakshan - XIMB. *Journal of Management*, *22*(1), 28–44. DOI: 10.1108/XJM-02-2024-0023

Farashahi, M., & Tajeddin, M. (2018). Effectiveness of teaching methods in business education: A comparison study on the learning outcomes of lectures, case studies and simulations. *International Journal of Management Education, 16*(1), 131–142. DOI: 10.1016/j.ijme.2018.01.003

Federal Trade Commission. (2023, May 24). FTC says ed tech provider Edmodo unlawfully used children's personal information for advertising and outsourced compliance to school districts. FTC News Release. Retrieved from https://www.ftc.gov/news-events/news/press-releases/2023/05/ftc-says-ed-tech-provider-edmodo-unlawfully-used-childrens-personal-information-advertising

Francis, P., Broughan, C., Foster, C., & Wilson, C. (2019). Thinking critically about learning analytics, student outcomes, and equity of attainment. *Assessment & Evaluation in Higher Education, 45*(6), 811–821. DOI: 10.1080/02602938.2019.1691975

Gardner, J., Brooks, C., & Baker, R. (2024). Investigating algorithmic bias in student progress monitoring. Computers & Education. *Artificial Intelligence, 6*, 100205. Advance online publication. DOI: 10.1016/j.caeai.2024.100205

Gartner, Inc. (2022). *Market guide for web, product and digital experience analytics* (Davis, M., Norrie, D., Markkanen, A., & Lee, A., Eds.). Gartner, Inc.

Guzmán-Valenzuela, C., Gómez-González, C., Rojas-Murphy Tagle, A., & Lorca-Vyhmeister, A. (2021). Learning analytics in higher education: A preponderance of analytics but very little learning? *International Journal of Educational Technology in Higher Education, 18*(1), 23. DOI: 10.1186/s41239-021-00258-x

Härdling, E., & Bakhsh, H. (2022). Deciding the most optimal data analytics tool for startups (Dissertation). Retrieved from https://urn.kb.se/resolve?urn=urn:nbn:se:kth:diva-320116

Haynes, D., Ahmadkhani, M., & Numainville, J. (2024). The next generation of dashboards: A spatial online analytical processing (SOLAP) platform for COVID-19. *Journal of Maps, 20*(1), 2276763. DOI: 10.1080/17445647.2023.2276763

Haynes, M., Groen, J., Sturzinger, E., Zhu, D., Shafer, J., & McGee, T. (2019, September). Integrating data science into a general education information technology course: An approach to developing data savvy undergraduates. In *Proceedings of the 20th Annual SIG Conference on Information Technology Education* (pp. 183-188). DOI: 10.1145/3349266.3351417

Hmedna, B., Bakki, A., Mezouary, A. E., & Baz, O. (2023). Unlocking teachers' potential: MOOCLS, a visualization tool for enhancing MOOC teaching. *Smart Learning Environments, 10*(1), 58. DOI: 10.1186/s40561-023-00277-3

Holmes, W., Persson, J., Chounta, I.-A., Wasson, B., & Dimitrova, V. (with Europarat). (2022). Artificial intelligence and education: a critical view through the lens of human rights, democracy and the rule of law. Council of Europe.

Hsu, C. Y., & Wu, T. T. (2023). Application of business simulation games in flipped classrooms to facilitate student engagement and higher-order thinking skills for sustainable learning practices. *Sustainability (Basel)*, *15*(24), 16867. DOI: 10.3390/su152416867

IEEE. (2023). IEEE code of ethics. Institute of Electrical and Electronics Engineers. https://www.ieee.org/about/corporate/governance/p7-8.html

Islam, M. R. (2021). *Customer Behavior Analytics and Visualization*. University of Technology Sydney., http://hdl.handle.net/10453/162385

Jarke, J., & Macgilchrist, F. (2021). Dashboard stories: How narratives told by predictive analytics reconfigure roles, risk and sociality in education. *Big Data & Society*, *8*(1), 20539517211025561. Advance online publication. DOI: 10.1177/20539517211025561

Kesse, M. (2023). The Efficacy of an Interactive Business Simulation Game Compared to Static Games to Teach Strategic Decisions in Entrepreneurship and Economics Education (Doctoral dissertation, University of Georgia).

Khare, K., Lam, H., & Khare, A. (2018). Educational data mining (EDM): Researching impact on online business education. On the line: Business education in the digital age, 37-53. DOI: 10.1007/978-3-319-62776-2_3

Koivisto, J., & Hamari, J. (2019). The rise of motivational information systems: A review of gamification research. *International Journal of Information Management*, *45*, 191–210. DOI: 10.1016/j.ijinfomgt.2018.10.013

Luckin, R. (2018). *Machine learning and human intelligence: The future of education for the 21st century*. UCL Institute of Education Press.

Martinez, L. S. (2022). Behavioral Analytics. In Schintler, L. A., & McNeely, C. L. (Eds.), *Encyclopedia of Big Data*. Springer., DOI: 10.1007/978-3-319-32010-6_18

Meeks, G. A. (2017). Critical soft skills to achieve success in the workplace (Doctoral dissertation, Walden University).

Mikic-Fonte, F., Haynes, C. C., Caeiro-Rodríguez, M., & Nistor, N. (2019). Systematic literature review of predictive analysis tools in higher education. *Applied Sciences (Basel, Switzerland)*, *9*(24), 5569. DOI: 10.3390/app9245569

Mutimukwe, C., Kolkowska, E., & Grönlund, Å. (2022). Students' privacy concerns in learning analytics: Model development. *British Journal of Educational Technology, 53*(4), 924–944. DOI: 10.1111/bjet.13234

Nkhoma, M., Calbeto, J., Sriratanaviriyakul, N., Muang, T., Ha Tran, Q., & Kim Cao, T. (2014). Towards an understanding of real-time continuous feedback from simulation games. *Interactive Technology and Smart Education, 11*(1), 45–62. DOI: 10.1108/ITSE-03-2013-0005

Ouyang, F., Wu, M., Zheng, L., Xu, W., & Chen, J. (2023). Integration of artificial intelligence performance prediction and learning analytics to improve student learning in online engineering course. *International Journal of Educational Technology in Higher Education, 20*(1), 4. DOI: 10.1186/s41239-022-00372-4

Ramaswami, G., Susnjak, T., Mathrani, A., & Umer, R. (2023). Use of predictive analytics within learning analytics dashboards: A review of case studies. Technology. *Knowledge and Learning, 28*(3), 959–980. DOI: 10.1007/s10758-022-09613-x

Rietsche, R., Aier, S., & Rivera, M. (2021). How does real-time feedback effect organizational performance does real-time feedback matter? A simulation study to link individual and organizational performance. (November 18, 2021). Fox School of Business Research Paper.

Rizwan, S., Nee, C. K., & Garfan, S. (2025). Identifying the factors affecting student academic performance and engagement prediction in MOOCs using deep learning: A systematic literature review. *IEEE Access : Practical Innovations, Open Solutions, 13*, 18952–18982. DOI: 10.1109/ACCESS.2025.3533915

Samašonok, K., Išoraitė, M., & Žirnelė, L. (2020). Education of entrepreneurship by participation in a business simulation enterprise activities: Conditions of effectiveness and opportunities for improvement. *Entrepreneurship and Sustainability Issues, 7*(4), 3122–3144. DOI: 10.9770/jesi.2020.7.4(36)

Sghir, N., Adadi, A., & Lahmer, M. (2023). Recent advances in predictive learning analytics: A decade systematic review (2012–2022). *Education and Information Technologies, 28*(7), 8299–8333. DOI: 10.1007/s10639-022-11536-0

Sharma, R., Shrivastava, S. S., & Sharma, A. (2023). Predicting Student Performance Using Educational Data Mining and Learning Analytics Technique. *Journal of Intelligent Systems and Internet of Things, 10*(2), 24–37. DOI: 10.54216/JISIoT.100203

Sottilare, R., McGroarty, C., Ballinger, C., & Aris, T. (2023, July). Investigating the effect of realistic agents on team learning in adaptive simulation-based training environments using GIFT. In Proceedings of the 11th Annual Generalized Intelligent Framework for Tutoring (GIFT) Users Symposium (GIFTSym11) (p. 31). US Army Combat Capabilities Development Command–Soldier Center.

Suarta, I. M., Suwintana, I. K., Sudhana, I. F. P., & Hariyanti, N. K. D. (2017, September). Employability skills required by the 21st century workplace: A literature review of labor market demand. In *International Conference on Technology and Vocational Teachers (ICTVT 2017)* (pp. 337-342). Atlantis Press. DOI: 10.2991/ictvt-17.2017.58

Sweta, S., & Sweta, S. (2021). Educational data mining in e-learning system. Modern Approach to Educational Data Mining and Its Applications, 1-12. DOI: 10.1007/978-981-33-4681-9_1

Topali, P., Ortega-Arranz, A., Rodríguez-Triana, M. J., Er, E., Khalil, M., & Akçapınar, G. (2024). Designing human-centered learning analytics and artificial intelligence in education solutions: A systematic literature review. *Behaviour & Information Technology*, *44*(5), 1071–1098. DOI: 10.1080/0144929X.2024.2345295

UNESCO. (2021). Recommendation on the ethics of artificial intelligence. United Nations Educational, Scientific and Cultural Organization. https://www.unesco.org/en/artificial-intelligence/recommendation-ethics

Userpilot. (2024, March 11). Mixpanel for user analytics: Features, pricing, and review. Userpilot Blog. https://userpilot.com/blog/mixpanel-user-analytics/

Viberg, O., Hatakka, M., Bälter, O., & Mavroudi, A. (2018). The current landscape of learning analytics in higher education. *Computers in Human Behavior*, *89*, 98–110. DOI: 10.1016/j.chb.2018.07.027

VirtualSpeech. (2024). VR stats for the training & education industry in 2025. https://virtualspeech.com/blog/vr-stats-training-education

Vos, L., & Brennan, R. (2010). Marketing simulation games: Student and lecturer perspectives. *Marketing Intelligence & Planning*, *28*(7), 882–897. DOI: 10.1108/02634501011086472

Wei, C. L., Wang, Y. M., Lin, H. H., Wang, Y. S., & Huang, J. L. (2022). Developing and validating a business simulation systems success model in the context of management education. *International Journal of Management Education*, *20*(2), 100634. DOI: 10.1016/j.ijme.2022.100634

Wong, J., Baars, M., Davis, D., Van Der Zee, T., Houben, G. J., & Paas, F. (2019). Supporting self-regulated learning in online learning environments and MOOCs: A systematic review. *International Journal of Human-Computer Interaction, 35*(4-5), 356–373. DOI: 10.1080/10447318.2018.1543084

Wu, R., Luo, X., Ma, Y., & Nie, Y. (2024). Research on online learning behavior of college students based on learning analytics technology. *Journal of Educational Technology Development, 12*(1), 45–62. DOI: 10.1109/CSTE62025.2024.00048

Zawacki-Richter, O., Marín, V. I., Bond, M., & Gouverneur, F. (2019). Systematic review of research on artificial intelligence applications in higher education – where are the educators? *International Journal of Educational Technology in Higher Education, 16*(1), 1–27. DOI: 10.1186/s41239-019-0171-0

## KEY TERMS AND DEFINITIONS

**Behavioral Analytics:** The systematic collection, analysis, and interpretation of user interaction data to identify patterns, trends, and insights that inform decision-making and improve processes.

**Business Simulations:** Interactive, scenario-based learning environments that replicate real-world business challenges, enabling students to apply theoretical knowledge to practical decision-making.

**Educational Data Mining (EDM):** The application of data mining techniques, such as clustering and classification, to educational data to uncover patterns, predict student performance, and enhance personalized learning.

**Learning Analytics:** The measurement, collection, analysis, and reporting of data about learners and their contexts to optimize learning experiences and improve educational outcomes.

**Mixpanel:** A cloud-based behavioral analytics platform used to track real-time user interactions, segment data, and generate actionable insights for improving digital experiences, including educational simulations.

**Personalized Feedback:** Real-time, data-driven recommendations tailored to individual learners based on their interaction patterns, aimed at improving skill development and engagement.

**Skill Development:** The process of acquiring and refining abilities such as decision-making, teamwork, and leadership, particularly within an educational setting through experiential learning tools like simulations.

# Chapter 10
# Skill Development Exercises in International Business Venturing and "Glocal" Socio-Economic Development

**Anatoly Zhuplev**
https://orcid.org/0009-0008-5124-5063
*Loyola Marymount University, USA*

## ABSTRACT

*This chapter explores active learning's role in developing applied competencies for international business venturing (IBV) and socio-economic development (SED). As global dynamics evolve, traditional passive instruction falls short in preparing students for real-world challenges. Integrating IBV and SED through case studies, project-based work, and both problem-solving and skill development exercises helps bridge theory and practice. Problem-solving exercises emphasize decision-making in complex scenarios, while skill development exercises build core business competencies for global engagement. The chapter presents a structured approach to export-related analysis and outlines a five-stage export development model. Emphasizing the triple bottom line—profit, people, planet—these exercises promote multidisciplinary learning aligned with student interests in societal impact. Active learning emerges as essential for advancing student readiness, enhancing U.S. competitiveness, and addressing the underrepresentation of U.S. SMEs in global trade.*

DOI: 10.4018/979-8-3373-7523-6.ch010

## INTRODUCTION

This chapter explores the role of active learning in applied skill development and their broader implications for international business venturing (IBV) and socio-economic development (SED). By bridging the gap between theoretical knowledge and balancing this knowledge with applied business practice, skill development exercises equip students with the necessary tools and core competencies to thrive in a globalized, competitive job market.

The rapidly evolving global and national socio-political-economic landscape presents challenges and opportunities for higher education, particularly in business education (Zhuplev et al., 2025). The integration of IBV and SED into the curriculum is increasingly critical as businesses and societies experience varying and often conflicting trends in globalization and localization (Ricks et al., 2022), economic liberalism and political protectionism culminating in the national autarky, technological advancements, shifting job market patterns and requirements, and political-economic paradigms. These trends in the U.S. have been sharpened and amplified by new political winds, directions, and regulatory initiatives under the Trump administration since January 2025. In the technological age of artificial intelligence (AI) and digital transformation, traditional learning approaches that emphasize rote memorization and passive knowledge acquisition in an instructor-centered teaching format become obsolete and inadequate. Instead, higher education must prepare students for career advancement in the increasingly fluid and competitive marketplace by prioritizing skill development that facilitates students' abilities to apply knowledge in practical, real-world contexts.

Being a major country by its demographic and economic size, U.S. accounts for about 5% of the world population and 26% of the global GDP. This points out to significant potential of global market outreach. Despite this potential, participation of U.S. businesses in global trade remains limited. In 2023, exports of goods and services from the U.S. accounted for just about 11% of its GDP in contrast to 18% in Japan, 50% in Germany, 30% in the UK, 22% in China, and 46% average across the world (The Global Economy, 2025). According to the U.S. Department of Commerce (2021), less than 1% of America's 30 million companies engage in exports, and of those that do, the majority export to only one country. This limited engagement constitutes stark contrast with other advanced economies where small and medium-sized enterprises (SMEs) are significantly more active in international markets (OECD, 2020). Apart from America's geography and sheer size of domestic market, the reasons for this lag include insufficient global business skills, lack of international market knowledge, and risk aversion among U.S. firms (Ricks et al., 2022). Addressing these gaps through business education is critical, as research indicates that firms with leaders possessing international business expertise are more likely to successfully enter and sustain operations in foreign markets (Knight & Cavusgil, 2015). B-education has an important long-term role to play in bridging this gap and contributing to the U.S. global competitiveness.

Lecturing in classic business disciplines such as Management, Marketing, or Human Resource Management was once the cornerstone of academic instruction in B-schools. However, with the advent and wide proliferation of easy accessibility of conventional knowledge through online platforms and AI-driven tools, often at minimal cost, effort, and time, the value proposition of business education must evolve if it is to command demand and sustain relevance. Empirical studies suggest that students who engage in experiential and active learning methods demonstrate significantly higher retention rates and problem-solving abilities compared to those relying on passive instruction (Freeman et al., 2014; Li at al., 2007). Brink and Costigan (2021) examined the alignment between skills taught in business programs and employer expectations, particularly emphasizing critical thinking as a core career readiness skill. Research indicates that skill-based learning enhances employability, with 87% of employers emphasizing the importance of critical thinking and problem-solving abilities in hiring decisions (Hart Research Associates, 2018). This finding is supported by the Clark et al. (2020) study presenting evidence-based insights into how entrepreneurship education contributes to employability and the development of transferable competencies. It is further nuanced by Lee & Beattie (2022) research that offered practical applications for integrating AI and digital tools into business curricula to foster future-proof skills.

The evolving competitive global landscape necessitates that students develop competencies and - most importantly – applied skills in strategic decision-making, cross-cultural negotiation, and entrepreneurial agility—essential for successful IBV. Furthermore, effective linkages between IBV, SED, and comparative analysis and application of best global practices require a multidisciplinary approach. This approach integrates economic, social, and technological considerations in contrast to the traditionally siloed instruction relying on the "transmission model" organized around specialized academic subjects that views education as a specialized body of knowledge to be transmitted from the teacher to the student. The "transmission model" emphasizes teacher - centric learning where students act as passive absorbers of information and implies the purpose of learning as memorization of facts. Meanwhile, case-based learning, project-based engagements, and other forms of active learning have been shown to improve students' ability to analyze complex international market dynamics and contribute to local and regional economic initiatives (Kolb, 2015; Kolb & Kolb, 2005; Paul & Mukhopadhyay, 2005).

However, according to some studies, students regularly report that they learn more from well-delivered lectures than from active learning, even though we know from many studies that the opposite is true. One recent paper was evocatively titled

"Measuring Active Learning Versus the Feeling of Learning." Another concludes that instructor fluency increases perceptions of learning without increasing actual learning (Shirky, 2025).

The chapter begins by discussing international business venturing (IBV) or international entrepreneurship in the broader context of socio-economic development (SED) and problem solving. This approach is stemming from societal expectations of business mission progressively shifting from the narrowly defined money making proposition, the "bottom line," to the "triple bottom line." The triple bottom line is a business framework that measures an organization's performance based on three key areas: profit, people, and planet (also known as the three P's), rather than solely focusing on financial gains. This is also amplified by the young generation of students being more and more interested in balancing monetary business interests and goals with societal priorities.

Further, the chapter discusses arguments supporting the strategic logic/process of internationalization of the company. This discussion covering the rationale, pros, cons, risks, approaches, analytical tools, practical applications, sources of information and assistance related to international expansion is organized around three key units of strategic analysis related to international business expansion: company analysis, industry analysis, and country analysis. More specifically, the chapter examines the step-by-step approach for export-related market research and the five-stage export development framework.

The chapter includes a set of skill development exercises related to main areas of B-school learning/skill development. They range from comparative cross-country analysis of strategic benefits, costs and risks of doing business to background market research for export-related international expansion by a SME or comparative analysis of investment climate across the states in the U.S. and major global cities. In essence, the set of skill development exercises represent a "knowhow" that can be applied in a classroom after situational adjustments and modifications.

## Linkages between International Business Venturing, Socio-Economic Development and Best Practices in the "Glocal" Context of B-Education

Nations, provinces, municipalities, communities, social groups, and individuals around the world vary in their dynamics and socio-economic development (SED)/problem solving priorities. Many of them face similar SED problems but often diverge in their solutions and search for solutions. Western democracies operate as interdependent units, as outlined above, with each unit having autonomous political-economic, SED, and strategic interests. Despite commonalities in shared interests across those units, there is widespread duplication of efforts on national, provincial, and local levels due to a lack of awareness, integration, and collaboration. This causes inefficiencies, waste, and multiplication of effort in addressing issues of common societal interest and concerns like public transportation, energy, housing, or unemployment.

In the pre-internet era, cross-country collaboration has often been hindered by geographic distances, global logistics, transportation, national, and information barriers. Proliferation of IT, AI, technological innovations, improvements in logistics management, and other advances in transportation, communications, and political-economic landscape call for integration and collaboration grounded in comparative analysis, adaptation, and application of best global practices toward local problem-solving and SED.

Universities and colleges possess significant intellectual potential and information resources such as academic talent, expansive libraries, or electronic databases. However, by and large, except for generating employment, they have limited impact of local SED and problem solving, while enjoying various forms of local support from government agencies, NGOs, and other sources, including a non-profit organization tax exemption status.

In the increasingly competitive higher education landscape, universities and B-schools should be seeking to reimagine and reposition themselves by striving to serve as catalysts for positive transformation. This involves channeling creative energy of the younger generation away from passivity, dependency, let alone even destructive activities, toward positive values and meaningful community engagement in regional SED and problem solving in the "glocal"[1] context.

Of paramount importance is bridging an existing gap between the real world and academia that has been long known as the "ivory tower." In bridging this gap, universities and B-schools can facilitate the SED of mutual interest across countries and position themselves as agents of progress. The mutual benefits of global engagement and collaboration through IBV/SED extend beyond business, offering valuable lessons for America nationally, across the regions, local municipalities, and private entities in critical areas of SED and problem solving such as homelessness, healthcare, transportation, governance, and sustainable urban development (Heartland Forward, 2022).

For instance, European cities like Helsinki and Vienna have been successful in implementing innovative housing-first strategies to address homelessness, significantly reducing chronic homelessness rates compared to major U.S. cities (OECD, 2021). Similarly, countries with universal healthcare models, such as Germany and the Netherlands, demonstrate cost-effective and equitable healthcare best practices and solutions that could inform U.S. policy making discussions and applications (WHO, 2020).

In transportation, Japan's well developed high-speed rail infrastructure offers insights into sustainable and efficient public transit models that could alleviate congestion and environmental concerns in urban U.S. centers (International Transport Forum, 2019). In China, as of December 2024, the operational length of the high-speed rail (HSR) amounted to around 48,000 kilometers (300,000 miles). It accounts for almost 30 percent of China's railroad network, which is about 162,000 kilometers (100,662 miles) long (Statista, 2025). In contrast, the U.S. as of today does not have a nationwide high-speed bullet train network although some high-speed rail projects are under development. For instance, California High-Speed Rail, the major infrastructural development project, has been fraught with significant project delays and budget overruns. With the planned 800 miles (1,287 km) when fully completed (the completing date uncertain), the first segment under construction is 171 miles (275 km) between Bakersfield and Merced. The full project was initially estimated to cost around $40 billion but has now jumped to $128 billion.

In another example, with a view of the upcoming 2028 Olympics in Los Angeles, U.S.A., Barcelona's preparation for the 1992 Olympics serves a vivid illustration of successful socio-economic development grounded in application of best global practices. Barcelona has strategically leveraged international expertise in urban planning, transportation, and governance to execute large-scale infrastructure projects, including modernizing its port, expanding its airport, and constructing new highways and public transport systems. These investments significantly improved mobility and connectivity, enhancing Barcelona's quality of life, business environment, and global accessibility (Brunet, 2005). The Olympic Games also catalyzed the transformation of industrial waterfronts into vibrant, mixed-use districts, attracting businesses and tourism while revitalizing neglected urban areas (Preuss, 2004). Economically, Barcelona's GDP grew by an average of 4.4% annually in the years leading up to the Olympics, creating over 20,000 permanent jobs in hospitality, construction, and services (Brunet, 2012). This example underscores the importance of strategic planning, public-private partnerships, and international collaboration in driving sustainable urban and economic development grounded in best global practices. The Olympics apart, U.S. municipalities could adopt similar approaches to address its perpetual challenges such as housing shortages, transportation inefficiencies, crime, and economic stagnation, fostering long-term prosperity and global competitiveness.

By studying, refining, and adapting best global practices, U.S. businesses, policymakers, and government offices can develop more effective, cost-efficient, data-driven strategies to address socio-economic challenges at home while fostering a more globally integrated economic presence (Porter, 2012).

## THE INSTRUCTIONAL ROLE AND APPLICATIONS OF SKILL DEVELOPMENT EXERCISES IN ACTIVE LEARNING

Skill development exercises support and facilitate active learning in international business and entrepreneurship education. They serve as experiential learning tools that engage students in practical applications of theoretical concepts, thus enhancing comprehension, critical thinking, and decision-making skills. By simulating real-world scenarios, these exercises bridge the gap between academic knowledge and professional practice, preparing students to navigate the competitive global business and political-economic landscape.

Active learning through skill development exercises encourages student-centered engagement, where learners actively participate in problem-solving, comparative data analysis, and strategic decision-making (Dole at al., 2016). Exercises covering diverse topics such as foreign direct investment (FDI), comparative country attractiveness for exporting, and cross-cultural business dynamics help students develop analytical capabilities and adaptability to international markets. These exercises often incorporate case studies, data-driven research, state of the art databases, sources of assistance/support, and role-playing activities, allowing students to apply frameworks, assess strategic benefits, costs, risks, and formulate actionable strategies.

Moreover, the integration of these exercises into international business curricula enhances interdisciplinary learning by combining elements of economics, political science, marketing, entrepreneurship, culture, and management. For example, an exercise evaluating the attractiveness of different countries for export expansion not only improves students' understanding of trade regulations and market potential but also strengthens their ability to assess economic and socio-political costs and risks.

Additionally, technology-enhanced exercises utilizing AI, data visualization, and digital collaboration tools further enhance active learning. These methodologies simulate complex business environments where students can test different strategies and receive real-time feedback. Such an approach fosters a better understanding of dynamic global challenges and equips students with the problem-solving skills necessary for success in their international business venturing and socio-economic development endeavors.

Skill-development exercises can play essential roles in teaching/learning International Business Venturing/International Entrepreneurship. Rather than being mutually exclusive, these approaches reinforce one another: Skill-development exercises ensure students have the practical tools needed to implement those solutions effectively. Problem-solving exercises train students to think strategically and address uncertainties in global business.

## Skill-Development Exercises

These exercises focus on practicing and refining specific skills essential for entrepreneurial success, ensuring students build competencies required in global business. Their essential characteristics include: Hands-on Training with the focus on practical, actionable skills such as international market research, AI-supported export analysis; Repetition and mastery facilitating continuous improvement through practice and feedback; Competency-based approach emphasizing skill acquisition over solving a specific business challenge; and Transferable learning involving skill application across multiple scenarios beyond a single problem-solving context. Example in International Entrepreneurship includes a business pitch development exercise where students prepare and present a funding proposal for a startup targeting a foreign market.

Faculty striving to implement skill development exercises rooted in active learning and experiential approaches may also face barriers and challenges. These include institutional constraints, resource availability, faculty readiness and training, and student preparedness and engagement. Institutional constraints is one of the most common barriers. These can include lack of logistical infrastructure, limited classroom time, rigid curricula, or insufficient administrative support. These constraints can hinder faculty's ability to introduce innovative instructional methods that require more time, flexibility, management skills and coordination than traditional lectures. Another significant challenge is resource availability. Some exercises may necessitate access to equipment, digital tools, AI platforms, or specialized software that not all institutions can afford or maintain. In particular, schools serving underserved populations may struggle with technological infrastructure or face issues related to digital inclusion and equity. Faculty readiness and training also present obstacles. Not all educators are motivated or familiar with experiential learning design, assessment, or facilitation techniques. Without professional development or peer collaboration opportunities and support, faculty may feel unequipped to effectively implement and adapt such exercises to different student populations or course contexts. Finally, student preparedness, motivation, and engagement can be a stumbling block. Not all students are comfortable with non-traditional learning formats, especially those requiring self-direction, collaboration, or public presentation. Faculty must be prepared to scaffold instruction and support students in facilitating the confidence and competencies needed for these exercises to be successful.

Some of the institutional barriers - technological, financial, and administrative - and adaptation of experiential learning are discussed in detail by Peterson & Nguyen in their multi-campus study of barriers to experiential learning (2024). A contemporary look at how active learning approaches vary by culture and institutional setting, with empirical evidence on student skill acquisition and engagement is analyzed and explored by Zhou & Su (2023).

## Problem-Solving Exercises

These exercises focus on addressing real-world challenges and developing analytical and decision-making skills by engaging students in critical thinking and strategic problem-solving. Their key characteristics include: Scenario-based format where students are presented with a specific business challenge (e.g., navigating trade barriers, managing global supply chain disruptions); Decision-oriented emphasis including evaluating options and making strategic decisions; Application of knowledge that requires students to apply theories, frameworks, and case analysis to solve problems, and Outcome-driven: Success is measured by how well students can devise and justify solutions. Example in International Business Venturing/International Entrepreneurship may be a case study of market entry challenges for a real life startup expanding to India: Students must analyze regulatory risks, cultural barriers, and competitive dynamics to recommend and justify an entry strategy.

*Table 1.* ***Problem-Solving Exercises vs. Skill-Development Exercises***

| Feature | Skill-Development Exercises | Problem-Solving Exercises |
|---|---|---|
| Purpose | Focus on practicing, refining, and mastering specific skills necessary for global entrepreneurial success. | Focus on identifying, analyzing, and solving real-world business challenges in international markets. |
| Format | Hands-on, practice-based – students engage in structured exercises to build and strengthen key competencies. | Scenario-driven, decision-oriented – students work through a specific challenge and find viable solutions. |
| Focus | Practical competency building – developing technical, communication, and research skills. | Strategic and analytical thinking – applying theories, frameworks, and problem-solving methodologies. |
| Scope | Generalizable – develops skills that can be applied in various entrepreneurial settings. | Case-specific – deals with a unique challenge in a particular context (e.g., a company entering a new market). |
| End Goal | Achieve mastery and fluency in a specific entrepreneurial skill. | Arrive at a well-reasoned, justifiable solution to a complex business problem. |
| Learning Outcome | Equips students with functional capabilities to perform specific tasks (e.g., financial modeling, AI-assisted research, pitching). | Develops students' ability to analyze problems, assess risks, and make strategic decisions in global markets. |

continued on following page

*Table 1. Continued*

| Feature | Skill-Development Exercises | Problem-Solving Exercises |
|---|---|---|
| Examples in International Business Venturing/ International Entrepreneurship | - Investor Pitch Training: Practicing and refining an elevator pitch for international investors.<br>- AI-Supported Export Market Research: Using AI tools to analyze export opportunities.<br>- Negotiation Simulations: Practicing cross-cultural negotiation techniques. | - Market Entry Decision: Choosing the best foreign market and mode of entry for a startup.<br>- Supply Chain Challenge: Solving logistics and cost issues in an international supply chain.<br>- Regulatory Barrier Analysis: Developing a strategy to navigate foreign legal restrictions. |
| Assessment | Demonstration of proficiency, clarity, and effectiveness in executing the skill. | Quality of reasoning, feasibility of solution, depth of analysis – how well students apply knowledge to solve the problem. |
| Typical Classroom Application | Typically found in workshops, role-playing exercises, and technical skill-building labs where students get hands-on practice. | Often used in case studies, simulations, and business strategy projects where students must analyze and resolve real-world issues. |
| Timeframe | Often shorter-term – structured as practice sessions or incremental skill-building exercises. | Usually longer-term – requires research, analysis, and iterative decision-making. |
| Level of Guidance | More structured and guided, with step-by-step instruction and feedback loops to refine skills. | Involves open-ended exploration, requiring students to use creative problem-solving and independent thinking. |
| Real-World Application | Provides practical competencies that students can immediately use in entrepreneurial ventures, consulting, or business operations. | Prepares students for strategic leadership roles, enabling them to tackle complex, high-level challenges in global markets. |

In essence, the set of skill development exercises offered below, some of them supported and amplified by AI, is a "knowhow" that can be applied in a classroom with necessary situational adjustments and modifications. Incorporating skill development exercises into business education facilitates applied learning, cultivates analytical and strategic thinking, and better prepares students for leadership roles in the global marketplace.

## INTERNATIONALIZATION OF THE COMPANY

This section discusses an essential framework and provides arguments for the internationalization of a company, outlines the rationale, pros, cons, risks, approaches, analytical tools, practical applications, and sources of information and assistance related to international expansion.

## Rationale for Going International

The primary economic mission of a corporation is to maximize financial performance and profits, although in a broader context, as mentioned earlier, corporations tend or compelled by societal forces to balance this economic mission – profitability - with two other Ps, "people" and "planet" under the triple bottom line framework.

In the contemporary political-economic era defined by global interdependence, the pursuit of international expansion, with all privileges and responsibilities, has become a fundamental consideration for companies striving for sustained growth and competitive advantage. Driven by their primary economic mission, corporations increasingly realize that their horizons extend beyond domestic borders. Globalization, particularly the rapid advancements witnessed in the latter half of the 20th century, has dramatically reshaped the socio-economic landscape, creating a web of interconnectedness that presents both opportunities and competitive pressures for businesses of all sizes.

The impetus for a company to venture into international markets typically stems from either the allure of opportunity or the pressure of necessity. Internationalization driven by opportunity is characterized by the strategic attraction of overseas markets. These "pull" factors might include the potential for accessing new customer bases, expanding market share, tapping into faster-growing economies, leveraging unique resources or capabilities available abroad, or extending the lifecycle of existing products and services. In contrast, internationalization driven by necessity arises from "push" factors, such as intensifying domestic competition that puts pressures and squeezes profit margins, saturated and stagnant local markets limiting growth potential, or restrictive domestic government regulations that hinder operational efficiency or innovation and compel for alternative locations overseas. Regardless of the initial trigger, the decision to go international is rarely arbitrary; unless driven by personal aspirations or political motivations, it is a strategic response to the evolving global business environment.

From a strategic perspective, internationalization should not be viewed as an isolated event but rather exercised as an organic and integral component of a company's overall development and growth trajectory. In today's fiercely competitive global arena, maintaining the inward oriented status quo is no longer a viable long-term strategy. Companies that fail to embrace internationalization risk missing out on significant business opportunities and may experience strategic erosion as competitors expand their global footprint. Engaging in international rivalry, forming strategic alliances with foreign entities, and actively seeking out international ventures are increasingly becoming essential elements of a robust competitive strategy.

The decision to embark on international expansion necessitates a thorough understanding of the multifaceted environment a company will encounter. This new landscape can be broadly analyzed through frameworks like the PEST/PESTEL/PESTLE model, which considers the interplay of political, economic, social, technological, environmental, and legal factors in the context of their impacts on business. The nature of the host country's political-economic system significantly influences the business environment. State-controlled or mixed economies often exhibit greater regulatory oversight and protectionist tendencies favoring domestic entities, while free market economies tend to foster more open competition. Navigating these diverse environments requires careful consideration and adaptation of business strategies.

Before committing to international expansion, a company must do its homework, business research, encompassing three key aspects: company analysis, industry analysis, and country analysis.[2]

## Company analysis

In international strategic assessment, company analysis serves as the crucial starting point, focusing on identifying the company's internal capabilities, available resources, and overall readiness for internationalization. Tools like the SWOT framework can be invaluable in assessing internal strengths and weaknesses in relation to external opportunities and threats in a competitive context where the company contrasts itself with the competition. Furthermore, specialized tools such as the Export Readiness Assessment Tool and the CORE Diagnostic Tool[3] can provide focused insights into a company's preparedness for exporting activities. Key questions a company must address during this phase include the strategic fit of international expansion with its existing mission, its potential to enhance strengths and mitigate weaknesses, the availability of adequate resources, and a preliminary assessment of potential benefits, costs, and risks. Figure 1 provides an organizational framework for a company contemplating international expansion.

*Figure 1. International entry modes*

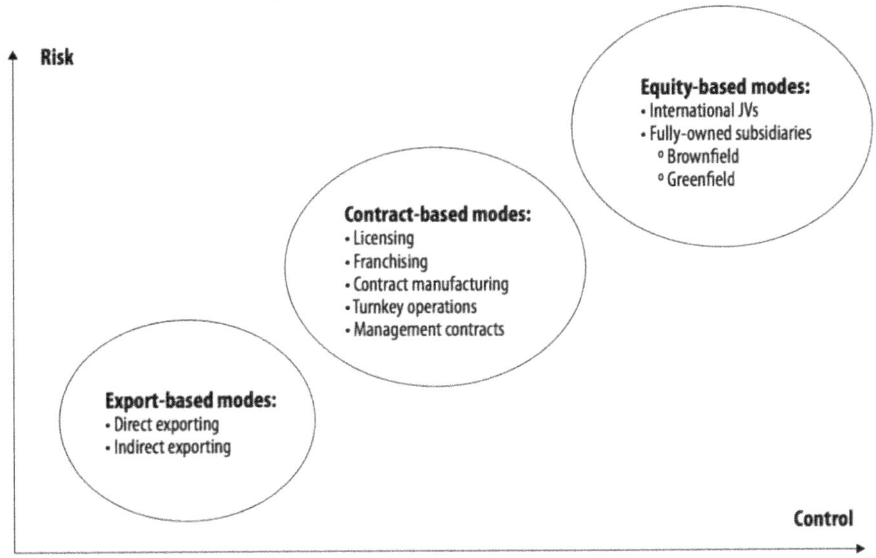


## Industry analysis

In general, industry-specific analysis involves assessment of the following parameters: Industry size (output, supply, demand), industry leaders, their output shares, and strategic positions in the market. Industry structure (concentrated versus fragmented). Developmental drivers and constraints, patterns and trends in performance and output over a period of time (upward, downward, or stagnant; stable or erratic; cyclical or random). Growth rates and patterns over a period of time. Future trends, development, and opportunities (products, technologies, processes, markets). Economic dynamics (profitability, return on investment) over a period of time. Cost structure (main cost components and their dynamics over a period of time). Marketing mix (the 4Ps—products, pricing, place/distribution, promotion—and their trends and dynamics over a period of time). Critical success factors (innovation, cost efficiency, global outreach). Social, environmental, sustainable performance (external environmental factors: regulations, policies and politics, social responsibility norms; internal environmental factors: prevalent corporate internal attitudes toward employees, customer, and shareholders). Competitive analysis (industry's competitive environment along the SWOT, Porter's 5-force competitive framework, or 4Ps marketing mix framework (global, geo-regional, national, or regional levels).

## Country analysis

Large and small companies in their international expansion decisions identify attractive markets, conduct comparative analysis of the competitive landscape within those markets, and select their target market from more than 200 national markets across the world in a pursuit of strategic benefits, and minimizing/optimizing costs and risks on the balance. Companies in their strategic decisions are driven by maximization of economic gains (profitability, return on investment). Apart from numerous commercial subscription databases (multiple examples can be accessed here https://libguides.lmu.edu/IB) analytical tools like the Market Potential Index (MPI - https://globaledge.msu.edu/mpi) provide a comparative overview of the country attractiveness based on various economic indicators. The World Bank's Business Ready (B-Ready) brand new database (https://www.worldbank.org/en/businessready) assesses regulatory framework and public services directed at firms and the cost-efficiency with which regulatory framework and public services are combined in practice. The World Competitiveness Center by the International Institute for Management Development (IMD) based in Switzerland offers access to a comprehensive database (https://www.imd.org/centers/wcc/world-competitiveness-center/) on how nations and enterprises compete, their strengths and weaknesses in the global competitive landscape. Major global insurance companies like Coface (https://www.coface.com/news-economy-and-insights/business-risk-dashboard, headquartered in France) or AM Best (https://www3.ambest.com/ratings/cr/crisk.aspx, headquartered in the U.S.) maintain extensive databases regarding country and industry/sectorial risks.

Table 2 and Figures 1-2 present analytical frameworks reflective of export development stages and steps, international entry modes, and their advantages and disadvantages.

*Table 2. Five-stage export development framework*

| Stage 1 | State 2 | Stage 3 | Stage 4 | Stage 5 |
|---|---|---|---|---|
| **Build Export Capacity** | **Develop Export Markets** | **Make Sales/Get Paid** | **Comply with Trade Regulations** | **Deliver the Goods** |
| **Improve Export Competitiveness** | **Identify Best Markets** | **Close the Deal** | **U.S. Regulations** | **Prepare Goods for Delivery** |
| Situation analysis/SWOT | Market research/analysis | Respond to inquiries | National security controls | Package goods for export |

continued on following page

*Table 2. Continued*

| Stage 1 | State 2 | Stage 3 | Stage 4 | Stage 5 |
|---|---|---|---|---|
| Solidify fundamentals | Select target markets | Quote prices (Incoterms) | Other export controls | Mark/label goods for export |
| Production processes | Assess target markets | Negotiate sales/ delivery terms | | |
| Business practices | Competition | | | |
| Operating capital | Market channels/ end users | | | |
| | Market conditions/ barriers | | | |
| **Develop Export Readiness** | **Develop Entry Strategies** | **Finance Sales/ Get Paid** | **Foreign Country Regulations** | **Transport Goods per Incoterms** |
| Assess export potential | Develop market entry plan | Payment methods/ services | Import duties | Book/track cargo |
| Enhance company readiness | Distribution/pricing plan | Advance or installment payment | Non-tariff barriers | |
| Export counseling | Promotion plan | LCs, documentary collections | | |
| Export training | Adaptation/localization plan | Open account | | |
| Develop global tools | Resource/budget | Pre-export financing | | |
| Website globalization | | Transaction financing | | |
| Ecommerce functions | | Export credit insurance | | |
| Digital/social media platforms | | | | |
| **Get/Use Export Help** | **Implementation Strategy** | | **Prepare Shipping Documents** | |
| Trade assistance network | Find foreign buyers/ distributors | | U.S.-required documents | |
| USDOC/USEACs &Embassies | Trade leads | | Foreign-required documents | |
| State/county/city export centers | International partner searches | | | |
| Chambers/associations | Screen/select/support partners | | | |

continued on following page

*Table 2. Continued*

| Stage 1 | State 2 | Stage 3 | Stage 4 | Stage 5 |
|---|---|---|---|---|
| Export management companies | Promote export sales | | | |
| Freight forwarding services | Broadcast promotion | | | |
| Export banking/ financing services | Targeted promotion | | | |
| Export legal services | Market promotion financing | | | |
| Trade assistance resources | | | | |
| Partner programs/ services | | | | |
| Internet trade sites | | | | |

Source: International Trade Compliance Institute (2025).

*Figure 2. Advantages and disadvantages of international modes of entry*

| MODE OF ENTRY | ADVANTAGES | DISADVANTAGES |
|---|---|---|
| Exporting | Low risk<br>Easy market entry or exit<br>Gain local market knowledge<br>Bypass FDI restrictions | Tariffs and quotas<br>Transportation costs<br>Possible distributor relationship issues |
| Licensing | Low risk<br>Fast market access<br>Bypass regulations and tariffs<br>Gain local market knowledge | Less control over market and revenues<br>Intellectual property concerns<br>Potential problems with licensees/future competitors |
| Franchising | Low financial risk<br>Bypass regulations and tariffs<br>Keep more control<br>Gain local market knowledge | Less control over market and revenues<br>Some loss of control over operations<br>Potential franchisee relationship issues |
| Contract manufacturing | Low financial risk<br>Save on manufacturing costs<br>Flexibility of short term commitment<br>Emphasis on marketing/sales | Less control over operations<br>Less knowledge about local market<br>Potential damage to brand/finances if human rights issues arise |
| Management contracts | Insider access to market<br>Emphasis on firm's expertise<br>Low financial risk | Limited profits and market access<br>Potential copyright and intellectual property issues |
| Turnkey operations | Access to FDI-unfriendly markets<br>No long term operational risks<br>Emphasis on firm's expertise | Some financial risks<br>Potential issues with partners/ infrastructure/ labor / profit repatriation |
| Joint ventures | Insider access to market<br>High profit potential<br>More control over operations<br>Shared risks<br>Gain knowled ge from partner(s) | High investment of resources<br>Potential issues between partners over control/contributions/goals, etc.<br>More management levels<br>Potential intellectual property issues |
| Fully owned subsidiaries | Full market access/acceptance<br>Full control over operations/profits<br>Bypass tariffs<br>Diversify operations | High financial/resources investment<br>High political and environmental risks<br>Potential profits repatriation issues<br>More management levels |

Ultimately, the decision to internationalize and the subsequent choices regarding target markets, entry strategies, and other parameters of this strategic move hinge on balancing potential strategic benefits, associated costs, and inherent risks. Strategic benefits can range from increased market share and profitability to access to cheaper factors of production and enhanced competitive advantage. However, these benefits must be weighed against the costs of establishing and operating in foreign markets, which can vary significantly depending on the chosen entry mode and the specific conditions in the target country. Furthermore, international business inherently involves a higher degree of complexity and potential risks compared to domestic operations, stemming from factors such as lack of understanding, uncertainty and predictability, political-economic volatility, legal and regulatory challenges, cultural differences, and logistical roadblocks. Thorough due diligence, intelligence gathering, and the utilization of risk assessment resources are crucial for mitigating these potential downsides.

## Skill Development Exercises

### Exercise: "American Factory": strategic, cross-cultural, and political-economic issues associated with inward Chinese acquisition of the U.S. automotive factory

**To**: <Name of the class>
**From**: <Name of the instructor>
**Date**: 10/14/2025
**Re**: Video case "American Factory"
**Goal:** skill development in strategic assessment of inward oriented (going into the U.S.) Chinese foreign direct investment (FDI)

## Background

Typically, international business-related discussions in American B-schools focus on outward-oriented expansion projects (exporting, FDI outflows, etc.). The global business landscape is changing, however: America's global economic power (as a share of global GDP) is gradually shrinking while some other nations rise in their global clout. This 2019 documentary represents an emerging global trend where a foreign business entity, a Chinese entrepreneur/tycoon, aspires to succeed in his FDI-based expansion to the U.S. Hopes soar when a Chinese company reopens a shuttered factory in Ohio, but a culture clash threatens to shatter an American dream.

## Assignment

Assuming you have a NETFLIX account (if not, create one - can be cancelled later at any time if you wish), please watch on your own the AMERICAN FACTORY documentary https://www.netflix.com/title/81090071. This educational and timely documentary requires 1 h 50 min time commitment to watch and about 15 min to compile your thoughts.

In watching this documentary, please prioritize the following international strategic expansion issues in your critical thinking:

1. Root problems causing a decline in the U.S. manufacturing and, in a grand scope of things, its global competitiveness.
2. Possible motivations by the Chinese foreign investor/business tycoon to invest in the automotive plant in the U.S.
3. Attitudes among American stakeholders in this int'l acquisition (local workers, general population, unions, government).

4. Cross-cultural differences between the U.S. and China (work attitudes, business communications, leadership, negotiation, management, style, mannerisms, etc.).

Upload your ≤1 page report in Word (bullet point format is acceptable) via Brightspace. Your findings and opinions will be discussed in class.

## Exercise: Best practices in socio-economic development: Comparative analysis of best global practices and their application in regional contexts.

**To**: <Name of the class>
**From**: <Name of the instructor>
**Date**: 10/14/2025
**Re**: Identification and regional application of best global practices in socio-economic development and problem solving

**Goal:** skill development in "glocal" socio-economic development (SED) and problem solving.

You are part of the IBV/SED Consult, U.S.-based international consulting firm. XYZ, your client, is a regional government office (L.A. Mayor's Office, San Francisco Mayor's Office, Taipei Mayor's Office, or any other government office representing a city/region/municipality).

**Assignment:** estimated completion time – 1 hour.

1. Work individually or in groups of 2.
2. Based on your client assignment, identify and prioritize 5 top socio-economic problems/ development priorities specific to this region/municipality. You are encouraged to use AI in completing this task. Select 1 of these SED priorities (a target priority) for further exploration.
3. Go to the UN Sustainable Development Goals (SDGs) https://sdgs.un.org/goals. Identify one of the 17 SDGs closely associated to your target priority from step 2.
    - Explore the state of the SDG and analytical resources pertaining to your target priority.
4. Identify and explore 2-3 global industry/market/subject reports specific to your target priority.
5. Identify and explore 2-3 top global cities/regions characterized by best practices pertaining to your target priority. You are encouraged to apply AI and/or global indices of best practices.

6. Explore and refine best practices suitable for a regional/municipal application (L.A. Mayor's Office, San Francisco Mayor's Office, Taipei Mayor's Office or another government office representing a city/region/province/municipality).
7. Give your critical assessment of applying these crystallized/modified best global practices on a regional/municipal level.

Report your findings to the class.

## Exercise: Investment climate attractiveness in the U.S.A. on the state level: evaluating investment climate for inward-bound FDI: California vs. Texas.

**To**: <Name of the class>
**From**: <Name of the instructor>
**Date**: 10/14/2025
**Re**: Exploring comparative business attractiveness: California vs. Texas
**Goal**: skill development in international market research and strategic business positioning in the U.S.A.

You are part of IBV/SED Consult, an international consulting firm advising XYZ Inc. on its contemplated international expansion to U.S.A. Specifically, XYZ is deciding between establishing its operation/headquarter in California vs. Texas as a small business entity (why is it important to position as a small business?).

XYZ, your client, is a manufacturer of solar panels (industry background: https://globaledge.msu.edu/industries/energy/background) based in China.

XYZ asked IBV/SED Consult to make a recommendation on selecting California vs. Texas for XYZ's expansion of its manufacturing operation (green-field investment). Country recommendation should include comparative analysis based on the following criteria presented in order of descending priority: Economy, Infrastructure, Quality of life, Education, and Government incentives offered to investors.

**Assignment:** estimated completion time – 1 hour.

1. Work in groups of two or individually.
2. Compare and contrast California and Texas by analyzing these sources:
   a. US News & World Report. Best States Rankings. https://www.usnews.com/news/best-states/rankings.
   b. Small Business Profiles for the States and Territories https://www.sba.gov/advocacy/2018-small-business-profiles-states-and-territories. –Small business profiles for California and Texas.

c. Government incentives for businesses and investors https://businessportal.ca.gov/Incentives/ - California; https://gov.texas.gov/business/page/incentives - Texas.

3. After completing your comparative research and providing justification in support of your recommended selection (CA or TX?) conduct a comparative microanalysis via SizeUp https://www.sizeup.com/. For the purpose of this exercise, input fictitious parameters into your analysis.
4. Report your findings and state recommendation to the class.

## Exercise: Investment climate in global cities: A comparative study of Berlin and Los Angeles' attractiveness in inward foreign direct investment (FDI).

**To**: <Name of the class>
**From**: <Name of the instructor>
**Date**: 10/14/2025
**Re**: Comparing investment climate in a global city: Berlin vs. Los Angeles
**Goal**: skill development in global strategic positioning

You are part of the IBV/SED Consult, U.S.-based international consulting firm. In preparation for the 2028 Olympics, the L.A. Mayor's Office contracted IBV Consult to conduct a comparative analysis of investment climate L.A. v. Berlin with the purpose of preparing for the 2028 Olympics. You are encouraged to use AI applications as a tool in conducting your multipronged background research in this exercise along with conventional sources and tools.

**Assignment**: estimated completion time – 1 hour.

1. Work individually or in groups of 2.
2. Identify critical parameters (critical factors) that constitute an attractive investment climate in a big global metropolitan city. Prioritize 5 critical factors to be included in your comparative analysis of L.A. vs. Berlin.
3. Based on the critical parameters from step 2, conduct a comparative analysis of investment climate in L.A. and Berlin.
4. Compile a summary of comparative strengths and weaknesses reflective of the investment climate in L.A. and Berlin.
5. Compile a list of key agencies and resources (NGOs, think tanks, databases, etc.) in L.A. and Berlin that might be instrumental in the analysis and implementation of investment climate.
6. Recommend 5 takeaways/lessons that L.A. can learn from Berlin in improving its investment climate (and branding/promotion) in preparation for the 2028 Olympics.

7. Present your findings and recommendations in a ≤5 min PP presentation.

## Suggested AI Prompts

- Identify critical parameters (critical factors) that constitute an attractive investment climate in a big global metropolitan city. Prioritize 5 critical factors in a comparative table: L.A. v. Berlin.
- Based on the critical parameters identified in the earlier step, conduct a comparative assessment of investment climate in L.A. and Berlin.
- Compile a summary of relative strengths and weaknesses reflective of the investment climate in L.A. and Berlin.
- Compile a list of key agencies (NGOs, thinktanks, databases, etc.) in L.A. and Berlin that might be instrumental in the analysis and improvements of investment climate.
- Compile a list of promotional materials (largely the video clips) offered by the cities of L.A. and Berlin designated to attract business and investment to the respective region demonstrating attractiveness of its business climate to potential investors.

## Exercise: Country attractiveness in global manufacturing: Comparing China, Mexico, and Vietnam as alternative destinations for foreign manufacturing.

**To**: <Name of the class>
**From**: <Name of the instructor>
**Date**: 10/14/2025
**Re**: Selecting a country for foreign manufacturing: China vs. Mexico vs. Vietnam
**Goal**: skill development in global strategic positioning

You are part of the IBV/SED Consult, U.S.-based international consulting firm. XYZ, your client, is an international manufacturing company (a conglomerate) contemplating the next step for international expansion in manufacturing. XYZ's business units (divisions) operate in 20 industries (https://globaledge.msu.edu/global-insights/by/industry). XYZ considers three country alternatives for this expansion: China, Mexico, and Vietnam.

**Assignment**: estimated completion time – 1 hour.

1. Work in individually or in groups of 2.
2. Click on this link https://globaledge.msu.edu/global-insights/by/industry and select one of the 20 industries representative of XYZ's business unit.

3. Identify 3-5 top drivers/strategic factors critical for your selected industry (You are suggested to focus on top cost components). Identify and prioritize relative importance (the share of this factor in the overall costs) by using AI. These may include availability/cost of qualified labor/talent, land, energy, demand drivers, profitability drivers, access to investment capital, general cost of doing business, strategic risks, government regulations and incentives, etc.).
4. Compare and contrast these drivers/factors for three country alternatives: China, Mexico, and Vietnam.
    a. Use the globalEDGE platform https://globaledge.msu.edu/global-insights/by/country and other sources https://libguides.lmu.edu/c.php?g=1050003&p=7621506 for your comparative analysis.
5. Make and justify your country recommendation in a short ~5 min PP presentation.

Report your findings to the class

## Exercise: The dollarization of Argentina and Venezuela

**To**: <Name of the class>
**From**: <Name of the instructor>
**Date**: 10/14/2025
**Re**: The dollarization of Argentina and Venezuela
**Goal**: skill development in the international monetary system

You have been recently appointed as the IMF Director for Western Hemisphere Department tasked with the evaluation and development of recommendations for the dollarization of Argentina and Venezuela.

**Assignment**: estimated completion time – 2 hours 30 min.

1. Work in small groups (2-4 students).
2. Watch the video lecture "International Monetary Systems" (1 hour 44 min) at https://www.youtube.com/watch?v=vKYCXasTbOw.
3. Review the "Argentina" Risk Assessment" sites:
    a. https://www.coface.com/news-economy-and-insights/business-risk-dashboard/country-risk-files/argentina
    b. https://www3.ambest.com/ratings/cr/crisk.aspx?_gl=1*1b7c5kv*_ga*MTUzNjc5NDY5My4xNzQxNDg2Nzgy*_ga_VNWYD5N5NL*MTc0MTgzNzEwNC4yLjEuMTc0MTgzNzE1NS4wLjAuMA..
4. Review the "Venezuela Risk Assessment" sites:
    a. https://www.coface.com/news-economy-and-insights/business-risk-dashboard/country-risk-files/venezuela-bolivarian-republic-of and

b. https://www3.ambest.com/ratings/cr/crisk.aspx?_gl=1*1b7c5kv*_ga*MTUzNjc5NDY5My4xNzQxNDg2Nzgy*_ga_VNWYD5N5NL*MTc0MTgzNzEwNC4yLjEuMTc0MTgzNzE1NS4wLjAuMA..https://www3.ambest.com/ratings/cr/reports/Venezuela.pdfhttps://globaledge.msu.edu/countries/venezuela/risk.

5. Based on ##3 and 4, outline the political-economic pros, cons, and constraints associated with the dollarization of Argentina and Venezuela.
   a. Use this prompt in your exploratory AI application: Outline 5 IMF geo-political priorities for the Latin American region centered around Argentina and Venezuela, two large countries with significant geo-regional political-economic impacts.
6. Based on your research of the geo-political interests and dynamics in Latin America, justify your recommendation for dollarization of Argentina vs. Venezuela on a priority basis.
   a. Use these prompts in your exploratory AI applications:
      - Outline the possibility and process of the dollarization of Argentina.
      - Outline the possibility and process of the dollarization of Venezuela.
7. Submit your ≤½ -1 page written group summary in the bullet format via Brightspace. Present your findings to the class.

## Exercise: Intellectual property protection (IPP): Strategies for safeguarding IPP in international business venturing.

**To**: <Name of the class>
**From**: <Name of the instructor>
**Date**: 10/14/2025
**Re**: IPP-Related issues for the case Foreign Proposal
**Goal**: skill development in strategic applications related to intellectual property protection (IPP) issues.

John Smith, of XYZ Computer, a small US-based international firm, is contemplating a joint venture proposal from a Taiwanese firm (please refer to the case Foreign Proposal (below). John asked you for your assessment and recommendations regarding the Taiwanese JV proposal.

**Assignment**: estimated completion time – 1 hour.

1. Work in groups of 2.
2. Evaluate the following IPP issues in Taiwan:
   a. The overall IPP climate

- Country Commercial Guide (CCG) Taiwan à Section: Investment Climate à Protection of Property Rights https://www.state.gov/reports/2024-investment-climate-statements/taiwan/

b. Key IPP registration issues and procedures for a new entrant
    - CCG Taiwan à Investment Climate à Protection of Property Rights.

c. Potential IPP-related strategic concerns for Bruning Computer

The latest National Trade Estimate Report on Foreign Trade Taiwan report by the U.S. Trade Representative (USTR) Office, Section "Intellectual Property Rights Protection."

## FOREIGN TRADE BARRIERS

The U.S. International Trade Administration: assistance in IPP

https://www.stopfakes.gov/welcome
https://2016.export.gov/taiwan/servicesforu.s.companies/index.asp.

3. Formulate and present your strategic and operational recommendations on XYZ Computer's entrance into the proposed JV.
4. Examine the above issues for Thailand and Mexico as alternatives to Taiwan.

Report your findings to the class.

## Case: A Foreign Proposal

John Smith left his job at a major computer-manufacturing firm and started his own business five years ago, naming it XYZ Computer. Since then, John has secured five patents for computer-related equipment. His latest is a computer chip that can increase the speed of most personal computers by 35%. The cost of one of these computer chips is only $50, and the unit wholesales for $850. As a result, John's profits have mushroomed.

Realizing that everything he developed is time-sensitive and can be copied by foreign competitors, John entered into contractual arrangements with three European firms to market his product. These three firms have predetermined sales areas that cover all of Europe and the Middle East. John Smith ships 50% of its production output to these three films, while the rest is sold to companies in the U.S. John recently has been thinking about expanding his production facilities. He is certain he could sell 40% more chips if he were able to make them.

Last week John had a visit from the chief executive of a Taiwanese firm. The company has proposed a joint venture between itself and XYZ Computer. The venture would work this way: John would ship the company as many chips as are currently sent to the three firms in Europe. These chips would be paid for on a 90-day basis. The Taiwanese firm would act as XYZ Computer's Far East sales representative during this part of the agreement. Then within 90 days the Taiwanese firm would purchase manufacturing equipment that would allow it to make the chips in Taiwan. "This will save us both labor and shipping costs," the Taiwanese executive pointed out. "And all profits will be divided on a 50/50 basis. Your only expenses will be your share of the manufacturing equipment, and we will apply your profits against those expenses. So, you will have no out-of-pocket expenses."

The idea sounds very profitable to John, but he is not sure he wants to give someone else the right to produce his product. "Technological secrecy is important in this business. It's the key to success," he noted to a colleague. On the other hand, John realizes that without having someone to sell his product in the Far East, he is giving up a large lucrative market. Over the next ten days John intends to make a decision about what to do.

## Activating questions in this case

1. Critically evaluate XYZ Computer's business venture proposal from Taiwan.
2. Complete strategic/market research/analysis.
3. Offer recommendations in feasibility strategic marketing/expansion, based on the Taiwanese proposal.

## Exercise: International strategic expansion in photovoltaics (solar panels): Strategic opportunities in international markets.

**To**: <Name of the class>
**From**: <Name of the instructor>
**Date**: 10/14/2025
**Re**: Comprehensive international comparative strategic market research
**Goal**: skill development in international strategic market research.

Solar Panels Plus (SPP), LLC https://www.solarpanelsplus.com/, U.S.-based SME, has developed proprietary solar photovoltaic (solar panel) energy technology. At this stage of their business development, SPP is not making money on its innovative product in the U.S. However, with the "green" movement gaining momentum worldwide. In particular, SPP learned about market opportunities for photovoltaic solar panels in the EU where "green" is widespread and government financial support for environmentally friendly technologies is generous. There also seems to be business potential in emerging markets in Asia, Latin America, and other regions.

**Assignment**: Groups of students are assigned to complete background analysis and offer recommendations in a 5-min PP presentation each.

Sources for background research

- https://www.eia.gov/ - U.S. Energy Information Administration.
- https://www.iea.org/ - International Energy Agency.
- https://globaledge.msu.edu/industries/energy - Energy Sector/Industry.
- https://energy.ec.europa.eu/index_en - European Commission: Energy.
- https://my-ibisworld-com.electra.lmu.edu/us/en/industry/22111e/at-a-glance - Solar Panel Power in the U.S. (IBISWorld – access via the library).
- https://my-ibisworld-com.electra.lmu.edu/home - Solar Panels; statewide reports on CA, FL, and TX. (IBISWorld – access via the library).
- AI applications in business research (ChatGPT, Gemini, or others as appropriate).

*Table 3. Team assignments for background research and recommendations (include the names of the students assigned to research themes)*

| Team | Assignment |
|---|---|
| Solar panel industry dynamics | Comparative analysis of the general (internal, regardless of geography) industry/market dynamics: solar panel energy vs. traditional fossil energy and other alternatives in renewable energy. |
| Entry strategies in SPP'S contemplated int'l expansion | Assuming a positive outcome of the contemplated int'l expansion decision by SPP, compile the company SWOT, assess its domestic strategic competitiveness against 1-2 major competitors and potential/readiness for international expansion, justify the best entry strategy (exporting vs. FDI vs. int'l joint venture. |
| International | Comparative analysis of the global market trends (supply/demand; current, future) and dynamics: solar panel energy vs. traditional fossil energy and other alternatives in renewable energy. |
| EU | Comparative analysis of the national (EU) market trends (supply/demand; current, future) and dynamics: solar panel energy vs. traditional fossil energy and other alternatives in renewable energy. |
| China/Asia | Comparative analysis of the national (China, selected Asian countries (e.g., Indonesia, Thailand, or Vietnam) market trends (supply/demand; current, future) and dynamics: solar panel energy vs. traditional fossil energy and other alternatives in renewable energy. |
| National | Comparative analysis of the national (U.S.A.) market trends (supply/demand; current, future) and dynamics: solar panel energy vs. traditional fossil energy and other alternatives in renewable energy. |
| Cross-state (CA, FL, TX) | Comparative analysis of the state-level (CA, FL, TX) market trends (supply/demand; current, future) and dynamics: solar panel energy vs. traditional fossil energy and other alternatives in renewable energy. |

## Exercise: Political-economic differences and country attractiveness in IBV: Strategic benefits, costs, and risks across countries and country attractiveness.

**To**: <Name of the class>
**From**: <Name of the instructor>
**Date**: 10/14/2025
**Re**: Strategic benefits, costs, and risks in international business venturing
**Goal**: developing conceptual and comparative analytical skills in international business venturing (IBV)) via exposure to state-of the art technologies and sources of information.

Assignment

1. Go to the globalEDGE http://globaledge.msu.edu/Knowledge-Tools/mpi and review the table of the Market Potential Indicators (MPI) for 97 countries. From the countries included in the list, select one country with the best MPI index rating from Asia, one from Europe, and one from Central/South America - please use one of the 8 indicators or the overall score as a criterion for country selection. Compare, contrast, and rank these 3 target countries in terms of their comparative IB appeal.
2. Go to the World Factbook https://www.cia.gov/the-world-factbook/https://www.cia.gov/the-world-factbook/https://www.cia.gov/library/publications/the-world-factbook/. Click on the COUNTRIES heading. Find, compare and contrast the GDP PPP per capita numbers for your three target countries (click on the ECONOMY on the left-hand side. How do your target countries rank in terms of their comparative IBV appeal on this specific dimension?
3. Go to the Index of Economic Freedom https://www.heritage.org/index/. Identify the economic freedom ranks and scores for your 3 target countries. Click on your target countries one by one and review the summaries characterizing these countries' political-economic profiles. Compare and contrast your target countries. How do they rank in terms of their IB appeal?
4. Go to globalEDGE by country https://globaledge.msu.edu/global-insights/by/country. On this site, find your target countries identified in step 1. Click on the INDICES button on the left-hand side of your target country site. Click on the Ease of Doing Business Rank index button. Low numbers mean easy/low cost of doing business; high numbers mean high cost of doing business. Repeat for each of your three target countries. Compare and contrast your target countries on the ease/cost of doing business.
5. Go to globalEDGE by country https://globaledge.msu.edu/global-insights/by/country. On this site, find your target countries identified in step 1. Click on the

RISK button on the left-hand side of your target country site. Evaluate, compare and contrast your target countries on the risk of doing business.

6. Report your findings to the class

## Exercise: Setting up a company overseas: Steps and considerations for establishing operations abroad.

**To**: <Name of the class>
**From**: <Name of the instructor>
**Date**: 10/14/2025
**Re**: Strategic assessment and administrative-organizational logistics in overseas start-ups

**Goal**: skill development in strategic assessment and administrative-organizational logistics in overseas start-ups.

XYZ, your U.S.-based corporate client, is a small/medium size enterprise (SME) with its business model placing top priority on intellectual property protection (IPP). XYZ (please select a real company of your choice from this database https://www.thomasnet.com/browse/) aspires to expand internationally. XYZ asked you as an IBVSED consultant to explore possibilities and key procedures for setting up a 100% subsidiary or a joint venture internationally for one of its divisions specialized.

**Assignment**: estimated completion time – 1 hour.

1. Work individually or in groups of 2.
2. Choose one of the following as your target country: Brazil, Czech Republic, China, Germany, India, Kuwait, Japan, Saudi Arabia, Vietnam, or Ukraine.
3. Choose one of the following as your target industry in manufacturing: agrifood, automotive, chemicals, electronics, medical devices, pharmaceuticals, and telecommunications https://globaledge.msu.edu/global-insights/by/industry.
4. Go to the GlobalEDGE and select your target country in the scroll-down menu or the interactive map https://globaledge.msu.edu/global-insights/by/country. Glance at the target country memo (lower-left corner of your screen. Make a judgment about the country's suitability for setting up a manufacturing operation in your industry (pros, cons).
5. Find a Country Commercial Guide (CCG) for your target country https://www.trade.gov/ccg-landing-page. Click on the SELLING U.S. PRODUCTS AND SERVICES button à DISTRIBUTION CHANNELS.
6. Under the time constraints, review the DISTRIBUTION CHANNELS section to get understanding on establishing a company in the target country as XYZ requested.
7. Report your most important findings to the class.

8. After a demonstration by instructor:
   a. Identify 3 potential partners for your client company's international joint venture (IJV) in the target country by using AI.
   b. Compare and contrast their strengths and weaknesses as an IJV partner your client company.
   c. Complete a due diligence research/background check by using AI.
   d. Recommend your client a program for conducting due diligence on foreign parties offered by the U.S. Commercial Service https://www.trade.gov/virtual-services. Include program description and information on fees https://www.trade.gov/us-commercial-service-user-fees.

## Exercise: SME's business expansion into Germany: exploring strategic entry modes and operational dynamics in real life scenario.

**To**: <Name of the class>
**From**: <Name of the instructor>
**Date**: 10/14/2025
**Re**: Business expansion into Germany
**Goal**: skill development in international strategic expansion.
**Background**: You act as an IBV/SED consultant for U.S.-based SME (please select your client company from the THOMAS database https://www.thomasnet.com/browse/; this company must belong to one of the sectors listed in the GERMANY COUNTRY COMMERCIAL GUIDE
[REMOVED HYPERLINK FIELD] https://www.trade.gov/germany-country-commercial-guide.
**Assignment**: estimated completion time – 1 hour.

1. Review the GERMANY COUNTRY COMMERCIAL GUIDE, sections Leading Sectors for US Exports & Investments https://www.trade.gov/country-commercial-guides/germany-agricultural-sector?navcard=1859 and https://www.trade.gov/country-commercial-guides/germany-distribution-sales-channels?navcard=1951.
2. Develop an action plan (compile a list of 5-10 strategically important items) associated with your client's expansion into Germany.
3. Review the GERMANY - CULTURE, ETIQUETTE AND BUSINESS PRACTICES country guide by Commisceo Global Consulting at https://www.commisceo-global.com/resources/country-guides/germany-guide.

4. Offer 5-10 cross-cultural recommendations in preparation for your client's negotiations with a potential German partner, particularly focusing on building relationships and trust.
5. Report your findings to the class.

## Exercise: SME's Business expansion into Mexico: Exploring strategic entry modes and operational dynamics in a real-life scenario.

**To**: <Name of the class>
**From**: <Name of the instructor>
**Date**: 10/14/2025
**Re**: Business Expansion into Mexico
**Goal**: Skill development in international strategic expansion.

**Background**: You act as an international business consultant for U.S.-based SME (please select your client company from the THOMAS database at https://www.thomasnet.com/browse/; this company must belong to one of the sectors listed in the MEXICO COUNTRY COMMERCIAL GUIDE at https://www.trade.gov/country-commercial-guides/mexico-leading-sectors-us-exports-investments-overview?navcard=9429.

**Assignment**: estimated completion time – 1 hour.

1. Review the MEXICO COUNTRY COMMERCIAL GUIDE, sections Leading Sectors for Exports & Investments https://www.trade.gov/country-commercial-guides/germany-agricultural-sector?navcard=1859 and Selling U.S. Products & Services https://www.trade.gov/country-commercial-guides/germany-distribution-sales-channels?navcard=1951.
2. Develop an action plan (compile a list of 5-10 strategically important items) associated with your client's expansion into Mexico.
3. Review the MEXICO - CULTURE, ETIQUETTE AND BUSINESS PRACTICES country guide by Commisceo Global Consulting at https://www.commisceo-global.com/resources/country-guides/mexico-guide
4. Offer 5-10 cross-cultural recommendations in preparation for your client's negotiations with a potential Mexican partner, particularly focusing on building relationships and trust.

Report your findings to the class.

## REFERENCES


Brink, C. H., & Costigan, R. D. (2021). Business school graduates and career readiness: The role of critical thinking and problem-solving skills. *Journal of Education for Business*, *96*(6), 341–349. DOI: 10.1080/08832323.2021.1886724

Brunet, F. (2005). *The economic impact of the Barcelona Olympic Games, 1986–2004*. Centre d'Estudis Olímpics UAB.

Brunet, F. (2012). Analysis of the economic impact of the Barcelona Olympic Games: Success factors and post-event legacy. *The International Journal of the History of Sport*, *29*(12), 1755–1770. DOI: 10.1080/09523367.2012.708307

Clark, G., Marsden, R., & Whyatt, J. D. (2020). *Enhancing graduate employability through enterprise and entrepreneurship education: A longitudinal study of pedagogical impact.*

Dole, S., Bloom, L., & Kowalske, K. (2016). Transforming pedagogy: Changing perspectives from teacher-centered to learner-centered. *The Interdisciplinary Journal of Problem-Based Learning*, *10*(1). Advance online publication. DOI: 10.7771/1541-5015.1538

Hart Research Associates. (2018). *Fulfilling the American dream: Liberal education and the future of work*. Association of American Colleges and Universities. https://www.aacu.org/research/2018-employer-research

Knight, G. A., & Cavusgil, S. T. (2015). The born global firm: Evolution of a research paradigm. *Journal of Business Research*, *69*(6), 1482–1492. DOI: 10.1016/j.jbusres.2015.10.013

Kolb, A. Y., & Kolb, D. A. (2005). Learning styles and learning spaces: Enhancing experiential learning in higher education. *Academy of Management Learning & Education*, *4*(2), 193–212. DOI: 10.5465/amle.2005.17268566

Kolb, D. A. (2015). *Experiential learning: Experience as the source of learning and development* (2nd ed.). Pearson Education.

Lee, A., & Beattie, S. (2022). Designing AI-integrated learning environments to enhance employability in business education. *International Journal of Management Education*, *20*(1), 100603. DOI: 10.1016/j.ijme.2021.100603

The Global Economy. (2025). *The global economy rankings: Exports as a percentage of GDP*. The Global Economy. Retrieved from https://www.theglobaleconomy.com/rankings/exports

Li, T., Greenberg, B. A., & Nicholls, J. A. F. (2007). Teaching experiential learning: Adoption of an innovative course in an MBA marketing curriculum. *Journal of Marketing Education*, *29*(1), 25–33. DOI: 10.1177/0273475306297380

OECD. (2020). *SME and entrepreneurship outlook 2020*. OECD Publishing., DOI: 10.1787/34907e9c-

OECD. (2021). *Local employment and economic development.* Organisation for Economic Co-operation and Development. https://www.oecd.org/en/topics/local-employment-and-economic-development.html

Paul, P., & Mukhopadhyay, K. (2005). Experiential learning in international business education. *Journal of Teaching in International Business*, *16*(2), 7–25. DOI: 10.1300/J066v16n02_02

Peterson, L., & Nguyen, T. (2024). *Institutional constraints and pedagogical innovation in business schools: A multi-campus study of barriers to experiential learning.*

Porter, M. E. (2012). *The role of business in social and economic development: Creating shared value.* Harvard Business School. https://www.hbs.edu/ris/download.aspx?name=20120802+-+Michael+E.+Porter+-+World+Bank+CSV+Presentation+-+For+Distribution.pdf

Preuss, H. (2004). *The economics of staging the Olympics: A comparison of the Games 1972-2008*. Edward Elgar Publishing. DOI: 10.4337/9781781008690

Ricks, D. A., Toyne, B., & Martinez, Z. (2022). *International business research: Global and local perspectives*. Routledge.

Shirky, C. (2025, April 29). Is AI enhancing education or replacing it? The Chronicle of Higher Education. https://www-chronicle-com.lmu.idm.oclc.org/article/is-ai-enhancing-education-or-replacing-it

U.S. Department of Commerce. (2021). *A new era for U.S. exporters: Expanding global markets for small businesses.* https://www.trade.gov/export-strategy

World Bank. (2006). *Local economic development: A primer.* World Bank. https://documents1.worldbank.org/curated/en/763491468313739403/pdf/337690REVISED0ENGLISH0led1primer.pdf

Zhou, M., & Su, Q. (2023). Embedding active learning in business education: A cross-cultural study of experiential pedagogies and student engagement. *Entrepreneurship Education and Pedagogy*, *6*(1), 3–22. DOI: 10.1177/25151274221142945

Zhuplev, A., Valle, F. J., Rincón, J. J., & Plithides, M. (2025). Challenges and future strategies for B-schools. In *Insights into international higher education leadership and the skills gap* (p. 48). IGI Global., DOI: 10.4018/979-8-3693-3443-0.ch015

## ENDNOTES

1. Glocal is a blend of global and local, referring to the adaptation of global ideas, products, or practices to fit local cultures, markets, or conditions. It emphasizes the balance between global reach and local relevance in business, marketing, and social contexts. This conceptual definition is generated by ChatGPT.
2. These and numerous other business models and analytical frameworks are accessible at 12Manage, a knowledge network about management and business administration (https://www.12manage.com/).
3. The Export Readiness Assessment developed by Maurice Kogon determines a company's export readiness by its answers to 23 questions about its present operations, attitudes and products.

# Chapter 11
# From Classroom to Community:
## Optimizing Public Relations Education in Vietnam

**Tuong-Minh Ly-Le**
https://orcid.org/0000-0001-8203-7357
*School of Media and Applied Arts, University of Management and Technology, Ho Chi Minh City, Vietnam*

**Kim Chi Dang**
*Faculty of Social Sciences and Humanities, Van Lang University, Vietnam*

## ABSTRACT

*This chapter investigates how combining outcome-based education (OBE) and experience-based education (EBE) can enhance public relations education in Vietnam. It seeks to identify the essential skills needed for successful public relations work and assess how experiential learning experiences can better equip students for success in the field. The research reveals that both professional and personal competencies are crucial for public relations practitioners. Professional competencies include research skills, statistical and data proficiency, content development, audio-visual design, and communication plan execution. Personal competencies encompass effective communication, professional ethics, and lifelong learning. Moreover, integrating experiential learning from the classroom to the workplace and community locations offers students valuable opportunities to apply theoretical knowledge, develop practical skills, and understand the societal impact of public relations..*

DOI: 10.4018/979-8-3373-7523-6.ch011

## 1. INTRODUCTION

Public relations, as a professional field, has witnessed significant growth and development over the past century. In this process, attention has been drawn to the role of education and training, which is one of the substantial components of the professionalization of public relations activities (Erzikova & Berger, 2012; Adams & Lee, 2021; Kim et al., 2021b). Understanding the historical context of public relations education is essential for realizing the pathway education has taken and constantly improving instructional design and curricula. The historical perspective of public relations education has recently begun to attract more attention from researchers (Wright & Flynn, 2017; Fitch & L'Etang, 2020; Luttrell et al., 2021). However, there still is scanty information that reflects how enhancement of education is a regional concept, such as in Vietnam. This study, therefore, aimed at exploring public relations education in Vietnam and suggesting ways to integrate outcome-based and experience-based approaches to optimize instructional design and curricula.

Public relations education has a well-documented start within North America, where pioneering initiatives began in the early 20th century. A college-level public relations course called "Publicity Techniques" was first taught at the University of Illinois in 1920, and the subject was first taught at New York University in 1923 and 1924 by Edward Bernays (Wright, 2011). Bernays lobbied for public relations education to be offered as a separate discipline from journalism or business studies. It was only in the 1970s that public relations undergraduate degree programs started to flourish in the United States (Wright, 2011).

The expansion of public relations education was not region-specific, and educational institutions throughout the globe expressed a similar aim in terms of specialized education. In Vietnam, the development of public relations education has been influenced by global trends but still faces unique challenges. While there is recognition of the importance of public relations as a strategic discipline in Vietnam's rapidly growing economy, there is a need to align instructional design and curricula with current international standards. Therefore, the landscape of public relations education in Vietnam needs to be studied to incorporate the required changes to prepare the students to provide the requisite knowledge and skills to serve the public relations profession.

To achieve these objectives, the research studies the importance of outcome-based and experience-based education in public relations. Outcome-based education focuses on defining specific learning outcomes and aligning teaching methods and assessments to achieve those outcomes (Biggs, 1996). Since outcome-based education sets the expectations accordingly, the students under this education can acquire skills that are easily implementable in practical situations. Experience-based education further strengthens this approach of practical learning through internships, industry collaborations, and immersive experiences (Kim et al., 2021a).

This would mean evaluate the quality of the current instructional design of public relations in Vietnam and assess whether these approaches are suitable for public relations education, and if they have been implemented correctly. By conducting a comprehensive study that includes input from public relations graduates and employers, valuable insights can be obtained to inform future improvements in curriculum development and enhance graduates' readiness for professional practice.

To address the above objectives, the following research questions were proposed to guide this research:

RQ1: What are the expectations and requirements of employers regarding the skills and competencies of public relations graduates?

RQ2: How can outcome-based and experience-based approaches be integrated into public relations education in Vietnam to enhance graduates' readiness for professional practice?

## 2. LITERATURE REVIEW

### 2.1. Outcome-Based Education

Outcome-based education (OBE) is a widely recognized educational framework that emphasizes defining clear learning outcomes and designing curricula and instructional practices to achieve those outcomes. One of the key principles of OBE is the establishment of clear and measurable learning outcomes. Ho et al. (2020) point out that learning outcomes, although intended to create comparable standards and improve education quality, can be subject to varying interpretations and may not be generalized across different programs, disciplines, or subject areas. However, advocates of OBE claim that clearly defined learning outcomes specify to the students what they are expected to do and allow teachers to come up with appropriate teaching and assessment methods. (Mauleon-Palay et al., 2022). OBE helps the teachers to set the assessment standards and the approach to set curricular and teaching activities.

The implementation of OBE has been associated with several reported successes. According to Brown (1988), OBE increases the level of self-esteem among students, provides improved attendance records, and ensures higher achievement of the learning objectives along with better grades. Li et al. (2024) investigated the impact of OBE on graduate competencies in China's higher vocational education system, revealing notable improvements in student outcomes. Further, OBE provides potential feedback for the teachers to understand the success of their teaching and learning strategies. The feedback obtained helps the teachers restructure and modify more flexible and responsive teaching techniques to support the students toward achievement of the desired education outcomes (Mauleon-Palay et al., 2022). OBE also promotes the reshaping of the outcome and rethinking of the task of teaching, learning, and assessment that at the end prepares students for life more than academic success (Macayan, 2017).

However, OBE also faces certain challenges. Critics argue that defining and assessing abstract conceptualizations such as humanism, altruism, and commitment can be difficult within an outcome-based framework (Ho et al., 2020). There may be concerns about how to promote excellence when "good enough" performance is deemed competent (Morcke et al., 2014). Another challenge, according to Sin (2014), is that the learning outcomes are of little relevance to the students. These challenges suggest the need for careful consideration and thoughtful implementation of OBE to ensure its effectiveness.

OBE is characterized by several important concepts and principles. Hoang et al. (2023) identify four key principles of OBE: a focus on skills or learning outcomes, backward program design, constructive alignment, and the creation of learning opportunities. The focus on skills or learning outcomes emphasizes the importance of clearly defining the knowledge, skills, and competencies that students need to attain. Backward design involves starting with what is to be achieved in the future, and thereafter planning how the students will achieve it. Constructive alignment, on the other hand, ensures the activities of learning, the assessment, and the methodology of teaching are in line with the intended learning outcomes.

The principles of OBE highlight a shift toward student-centered learning, where students' knowledge and abilities are central. Understanding the definition and principles of OBE works as a basis for integrating outcome-based approaches into public relations education and contributes to the improvement of instructional design in Vietnam.

## 2.2. Experienced-Based Education

Experience-based education (EBE) is an instructional approach that emphasizes learning through direct engagement with real-world experiences. EBE gained popularity in the 1970s as a response to criticism of traditional teaching methodologies. Kolb and Kolb (2005) developed the Experiential Learning Theory (ELT), which provided a framework for different types of learning based on individuals' encounters and reflections on experiences. ELT consists of two main components: the experience itself and the subsequent reflective activity (Boud & Keogh, 1985).

While there has been extensive discussion on the experience portion of experiential learning, reflection has received relatively less attention (Ziek, 2022).

In various educational institutions worldwide, EBE has become a widely used model, particularly in fields where theoretical and practical skills are essential, such as media and communication (Austin & Rust, 2015). Experiential learning is particularly valuable in engaging students in the practices involved in media creation, performance, evaluation, and reflection. Internships, case studies, and service-learning are common forms of experiential learning, but they often overlook important aspects of media content creation (Ziek & Fink, 2018). Traditional approaches tend to focus on industry-specific tasks, neglecting important soft skills such as communication, negotiation, conflict resolution, and interdisciplinary collaboration, which are crucial for success in the workplace (Ziek, 2022). To address these gaps, the concept of Class Collab has emerged, which integrates multiple classes to focus on applied competencies and understanding in a specific field or industry (Ziek, 2021).

EBE is closely associated with the idea of learning by doing, emphasizing the connection between teaching, learning, and real-life experiences. EBE promotes skills acquisition and development through practical experiences and collaborations with industry partners. University-industry collaborations, such as internships and industrial attachments, provide students with opportunities for experiential learning and bridge the gap between theory and practice (Pacho, 2022). This relates to the general belief that experience is a powerful teacher, and learning by doing in real-life situations enhances the immediate relevance of education to students' lives (Dewey, 2011). EBE has gained wide acceptance as an instructional method at the higher education levels, stressing the importance of lifelong experiential learning for personal growth and career accomplishment (Kim et al., 2021a).

## 2.3. Applying OBE and EBE to Public Relations Education

Integrating EBE with OBE can create a comprehensive educational framework that combines the achievement of specific learning outcomes with practical application. Traditional classroom-based teaching often focuses on theoretical knowledge, but OBE shifts the emphasis to measurable learning outcomes (Grunig, 1989). OBE provides a structured approach to define desired learning outcomes and assess students' achievement of those outcomes. By integrating EBE into the OBE framework, students have opportunities to apply their knowledge and skills in real-world contexts, ensuring that the learning outcomes are not only theoretical but also practical and relevant to public relations practice. The integration of OBE and EBE can enhance the quality of public relations education by fostering a deeper understanding of the field and promoting active learning. Grunig (1989) highlights the importance of teaching students the theoretical foundations of public relations and how these theories are applied in practice.

A comprehensive study of public relations education globally revealed that most educators define public relations as the "strategic management of relational communications" and position it within a social science framework (Berger, 2010). Undergraduate education programs predominantly focus on practical orientation, preparing students with the technical skills and critical- and strategic-thinking capabilities necessary for future practitioners. The study also highlighted the need for greater interaction between students, educators, and seasoned professionals to improve public relations education. Practitioners can make a substantial difference by engaging with education programs, offering insights, mentoring students, providing internships, funding scholarships, and serving on education advisory boards. By promoting collaboration between professionals and educators, students can benefit from the expertise and experiences of industry practitioners, thereby enriching their learning experience. The study's findings reinforce the importance of integrating OBE and EBE in public relations education. By offering practical experiences and emphasizing measurable learning outcomes, this approach aligns with the global trends in public relations education and ensures that Vietnamese graduates are equipped with the necessary competencies to excel in the profession.

In the Vietnamese context, the integration of OBE and EBE in public relations education can have significant advantages (Nguyen et al., 2020). Vietnam's rapidly growing economy and evolving communication landscape require public relations professionals with diverse skill sets and practical experience. The Class Collab model of EBE, which integrates multiple classes and promotes interdisciplinary collaboration, aligns well with the needs of the industry (Ziek, 2021). This model enables students to develop applied competencies and understandings relevant to the field of public relations. The integration of OBE and EBE creates a comprehensive educational framework that combines specific learning outcomes with practical applications. By merging these approaches, public relations education can better equip students with the knowledge, skills, and experiences necessary for successful careers in the field.

## 3. RESEARCH DESIGN

The research methodology consists of two parts: investigating the outcome-based approach through a focus group, and studying the experience-based approach through case studies of Canadian universities known for their effective use of experiential learning.

The focus group consisted of 20 participants. Ten participants were representatives from industry employers who have previously recruited and worked with public relations graduates. The other ten participants were public relations practitioners with a minimum of five years of experience in the field, providing insights into the competencies required for successful performance in the industry.

Before the focus group session, the researchers developed a list of competencies that public relations practitioners should possess. These competencies include both professional competencies (industry knowledge and skills) and personal competencies (soft skills). During the focus group session, participants engaged in a discussion regarding the competencies required for public relations practitioners, their alignment with job tasks, and achieving them through university-level education.

To study the experience-based approach, the research focused on case studies of Canadian universities known for effectively incorporating experiential learning into their public relations and communication programs. Canadian universities were chosen due to their reputation for integrating skills-based complements with theory-based coursework over the past decade (Edwards, 2022). These universities serve as exemplars for experiential learning practices.

Fifteen Canadian universities that offered public relations and/or communication programs were selected as study samples. Data collection involved reviewing program materials, curricula and the school's experiential learning policy. The data collected from the case studies were analyzed qualitatively to identify the various experiential learning activities and approaches employed by these Canadian universities.

## 4. FINDINGS

### 4.1. Industry Competencies are as Important as Personal Competencies

The focus group discussion involved experienced public relations practitioners and industry employers, aiming to identify and discuss the public relations program learning outcomes and define competencies required for effective public relations practice. Different sets of competencies were identified into two thematic groups: professional, and personal competencies, as presented in Table 1.

*Table 1.Key Competencies for Public Relations Graduates*

| Professional Competencies | Personal Competencies |
|---|---|
| **Research skills** | Effective communication |
| **Data/statistical proficiency** | Ethical behavior and professionalism |
| **Content development and storytelling** | Self-awareness and emotional intelligence |
| **Audio-visual design** | Empathy and cultural sensitivity |
| **Communication planning and execution** | Lifelong learning and adaptability |

For professional competencies, the participants emphasized the importance of *research skills* in public relations. They highlighted the need to collect and select information from various sources, stay updated on current affairs and relevant industry issues, and transform research results into their own knowledge and understanding. The public relations curriculum could introduce courses or modules that focus on research methodologies, data collection, and analysis techniques. The curriculum should also seek to provide hands-on training on conducting comprehensive research and surveys, and how to transform the findings into valuable industry knowledge.

A skillset related to research skills is *statistical and data proficiency*. The focus group participants recognized the need for public relations practitioners to possess competencies in statistical analysis and data management. They emphasized the importance of utilizing modern data analysis software and synthesizing analyzed information to draw accurate and scientific judgments and conclusions. To meet this industry demand, public relations programs could offer courses that develop students' skills in data analysis and interpretation, and provide training on modern software and tools used in data analysis for public relations purposes.

Other job-related skills that the participants are concerned about include *content development*, *audio-visual design*, and *communication plan execution*. The participants discussed the competencies related to content development, which involved adjusting communication objectives, strategies, and plans. They emphasized the need for public relations practitioners to convey content accurately and appropriately in different public relations and media contexts. Selecting the right language system to achieve maximum effect for specific communication purposes was also highlighted as a crucial competency.

The participants also discussed the importance of design thinking and creative thinking in image design and audio-visual media production for effective audience engagement. They emphasized the need to evaluate the effectiveness of visual and audio-visual media in conveying media messages accurately and engagingly.

Further, managing the implementation of communication plans, including resource management, scheduling, and performance evaluation, emerged as key competencies discussed by the focus group participants. Timely improvement and evaluation of the effectiveness of communication activities were emphasized.

On the other hand, it was noted that personal competencies should be equally focused. The participants discussed that public relations students should also pay attention to *effective communication*, *professional ethics*, and *lifetime learning*.

Participants highlighted the importance of extracting insights, sympathy, and understanding from media audience interactions, information exchange, and research. They emphasized the need to ensure effective communication through personal branding, including style, clothing, and image projection. Building empathy and understanding, along with effective communication skills, were considered essential.

Maintaining professional ethics, implementing social responsibility, managing emotions, and building personal credibility and trust were emphasized as important qualities, attitudes, and behaviors for public relations practitioners. Respecting others and preserving the humanity and cultural spirit of Vietnamese people in communication work were also highlighted.

Finally, the focus group participants emphasized the significance of continuous learning and professional development. They highlighted the importance of exchanging experiences, participating in career networks, attending specialized training seminars, and learning from experienced professionals to improve professional capacity. Curiosity, self-study, and the continuous update of knowledge and experiences were also seen as essential qualities for public relations practitioners.

## 4.2. Alignment of Learning Activities with Learning Outcomes

The focus group discussed the alignment of learning activities and assessments with learning outcomes to ensure that the entire educational process is purposeful, coherent, and focused on achieving the desired competencies and skills in students. The participants provided recommendations on how public relations education in Vietnam can effectively align learning activities and assessments with the identified learning outcomes.

*Incorporating practical projects*: To align learning activities with the desired competencies, public relations programs can integrate practical projects into the curriculum. These projects should reflect real-world scenarios that students are likely to encounter in their professional careers. By engaging in hands-on projects, students can apply their research, communication, and content-creation skills, allowing them to bridge the gap between theory and practice. This approach also fosters problem-solving abilities and critical thinking, as students navigate complex situations that require strategic decision-making.

*Case studies and simulations*: Case studies and simulations are powerful tools for facilitating active learning and enhancing students' analytical skills. By presenting students with real or hypothetical public relations challenges, they can analyze the situation, identify potential solutions, and evaluate their outcomes. This approach encourages students to think critically, collaborate, and make informed decisions. Moreover, case studies and simulations enable instructors to assess students' understanding of the subject matter and their ability to apply theoretical knowledge to practical situations.

*Diverse learning opportunities*: Public relations is a multidisciplinary field that requires students to develop a wide range of skills. To provide students with a comprehensive learning experience, public relations programs should offer diverse learning opportunities. This may include internships with reputable organizations, partnerships with industry professionals, guest lectures by experts, and participation in relevant workshops and conferences. Exposing students to various perspectives and experiences enriches their learning journey, fosters professional development, and enables them to build valuable networks within the industry.

*Group work and collaboration*: In the field of public relations, teamwork and collaboration are essential skills. To align learning activities with these competencies, instructors can encourage group work and collaboration within the classroom setting. By working together on projects or assignments, students learn how to communicate effectively, manage conflicts, and leverage diverse perspectives to achieve common goals. Instructors can observe and assess students' ability to function as part of a team, as well as their contributions to the group's success.

*Formative and summative assessments*: Assessment is an integral part of the educational process. In OBE, both formative and summative assessments play key roles. Formative assessments occur throughout the learning process, providing feedback to students and instructors about progress and areas for improvement. Suggestions for formative assessments in public relations education include quizzes, class discussions, or peer evaluations. Summative assessments are used to evaluate students' overall performance at the end of a course or module. These assessments can take the form of final projects, presentations, or comprehensive exams. By aligning assessments with specific learning outcomes, instructors can ensure that student's knowledge and skills are accurately measured against the intended objectives.

## 4.3. Experiential Learning Starts from the Classroom, to the Workplace, to Community Locations

Fifteen Canadian universities that offer public relations and communications programs were included in this research. They are the University of Guelph-Humber, Toronto Metropolitan University, Mohawk College, University of Calgary, Sheridan College, University of Ottawa, Cape Breton University, Mount Saint Vincent University, Thompson Rivers University, Concordia University, Ontario Tech University,

Carleton University, St. Lawrence College, Conestoga College, and the University of Windsor. From the case studies, these universities demonstrate a commitment to experiential learning that starts from the classroom, extends to the workplace, and encompasses community locations.

*Table 2. Experiential Learning Activities Across Canadian Universities*

| Activity Type | Number of Universities Implementing | Examples |
|---|---|---|
| **In-class experiential learning** | 11 | Labs, workshops, case-based learning |
| **Workplace engagement** | 8 | Internships, co-op placements |
| **Community-based projects** | 4 | NGO internships, service learning |
| **Reflective practices** | 4 | Journals, feedback sessions |
| **Collaboration & networking** | 10 | Mentorships, student-run agencies |

As presented in Table 2, eleven out of the 15 examined universities emphasize the importance of *experiential learning within the classroom setting*. This involves activities such as internships, client and community-based projects, field placements, practical labs, and workshops. By integrating experiential learning directly into the curriculum, these universities provide students with opportunities to apply theoretical knowledge, develop practical skills, and gain hands-on experience in simulated professional environments.

Besides classroom activities, *workplace engagement* is also a focus. Eight universities recognize the value of bridging the gap between the classroom and the workplace. They offer internships, cooperative education programs, and work experience placements. These initiatives provide students with the opportunity to work in real-world public relations positions, collaborate with professionals, and gain valuable industry insights. By immersing themselves in workplace settings, students acquire practical skills, build professional networks, and develop a deeper understanding of the field.

The case studies also see the importance of *community engagement* in public relations education. Four universities promote community-based projects, cultural and heritage internships, volunteering opportunities, and involvement with non-profit organizations. These experiences enable students to contribute to their communities, develop a sense of social responsibility, and understand the broader societal impact of public relations. By working with community partners, students gain exposure to diverse perspectives and learn to navigate complex communication challenges in real-world contexts.

Besides, four universities emphasize the importance of reflection and skill development in experiential learning. Students are encouraged to engage in self-reflection, receive feedback from supervisors, and actively participate in the learning process. Through this *reflective practice*, students enhance their critical thinking abilities, improve their communication skills, and develop a greater sense of self-awareness. These universities provide a supportive environment that fosters personal and professional growth.

Another activity to encourage experiential learning is *collaboration and networking*. Several universities emphasize collaborative and networking opportunities. Through projects, mentorship programs, student-run agencies, and industry partnerships, students are encouraged to work in teams, build effective relationships, and develop essential interpersonal and teamwork skills. These collaborative experiences mirror the dynamics of the public relations industry and prepare students for successful professional careers.

By incorporating experiential learning from the classroom to the workplace and community locations, these universities provide students with valuable opportunities to apply their knowledge, develop practical skills, and engage with real-world public relations contexts.

## 5. DISCUSSION

### 5.1. Matching Public Relations Education to Industry Demands

The research findings from the focus group discussions emphasize the importance of industry and personal competencies for public relations practitioners. Some of the industry competencies that the study has identified as important include research skills and data, content development, audio-visual design, and the ability to execute a communication plan. Industry competencies help public relations practitioners meet the changing trends in communication in Vietnam's communication landscape. For this to be possible, the public relations professional should have broad research skills, including data analysis and content development, to effectively help in effective communication to the target audience to meet communication objectives.

This supports some previous studies which showed that industry research skills are a significant emphasis in public relations education (Berger, 2010). Public relations is all about effective research to execute a successful campaign. For one to set sound communication objectives, they must have data on the target audience, which reveals the strength of the relationship and communication challenges. Strengthening public relations educational programs requires incorporating research-based courses and hands-on training on data analysis software.

Furthermore, the focus group participants highlighted the significance of personal competencies, including effective communication, professional ethics, and continuous learning. Effective communication is a fundamental skill for public relations practitioners, enabling them to convey messages clearly and persuasively to diverse audiences. Professional ethics are crucial for building trust and credibility with stakeholders, while continuous learning ensures that public relations practitioners stay abreast of industry trends and best practices.

The emphasis on personal competencies aligns with previous research on experiential learning (Ziek & Fink, 2018). Experiential learning promotes the development of soft skills, such as effective communication, self-awareness, and emotional intelligence, which are essential for building successful relationships with clients, colleagues, and the public. Through experiential learning opportunities that encourage reflection and skill development, public relations programs can foster the personal growth of students and prepare them for the challenges and complexities of the profession.

The focus group's emphasis on incorporating practical projects and case studies is in line with the experiential learning approach advocated by EBE. By engaging students in hands-on projects and real-world scenarios, they can apply their theoretical knowledge in practical contexts, fostering critical thinking and problem-solving skills. This aligns with previous studies that highlight the value of experiential learning in the media and communication fields (Ziek & Fink, 2018).

Moreover, the focus group's recommendation to provide diverse learning opportunities, such as internships and guest lectures, aligns with the idea of bridging the gap between theory and practice through university-industry collaborations (Pacho, 2022). These experiences can enhance students' understanding of the field and provide them with valuable insights from industry professionals, as suggested in the literature review (Berger, 2010).

The focus group's proposal to use formative and summative assessments to measure student's progress aligns with OBE's emphasis on defining clear and measurable learning outcomes (Hoang et al., 2023). This approach allows instructors to evaluate students' achievement of specific competencies and provides valuable feedback to enhance teaching and learning practices. The focus group's findings resonate with previous research that indicates outcome-based assessment supports students' academic achievement and self-esteem (Brown, 1988).

In terms of challenges, the focus group did not explicitly address the potential difficulties of defining and assessing abstract concepts within an outcome-based framework, as mentioned in the literature review (Ho et al., 2020). However, their emphasis on aligning learning activities with specific competencies may implicitly address this challenge. By focusing on practical and measurable outcomes, the implementation of OBE in public relations education can potentially mitigate some of these challenges.

Another significant finding from the research is the recognition of the importance of collaboration and networking in public relations practice. The focus group participants emphasized the value of teamwork, relationship-building, and interdisciplinary collaboration for successful communication campaigns. These findings align with the literature on experiential learning, which highlights the benefits of collaborative learning experiences in preparing students for real-world work environments (Ziek, 2022). By engaging in collaborative projects, students can develop essential interpersonal and teamwork skills that are highly valued in the public relations industry.

Moreover, the research findings emphasize the importance of community engagement and social responsibility in public relations practice. Public relations professionals play a crucial role in shaping public opinion and facilitating positive social change. Engaging in community-based projects and cultural internships allows students to understand the broader societal impact of public relations and develop a sense of social responsibility. This aligns with the principles of experiential learning, which emphasizes learning through direct engagement with real-world experiences and fostering a sense of social awareness and responsibility (Austin & Rust, 2015).

The relevance of experiential learning in public relations education is further underscored by the case studies of Canadian universities. These universities demonstrate a commitment to experiential learning that starts from the classroom, extends to the workplace, and encompasses community locations. By incorporating internships, client projects, field placements, and community-based initiatives, these universities provide students with valuable opportunities to apply their knowledge, develop practical skills, and engage with real-world public relations contexts.

Overall, the findings in this research present that by integrating OBE and EBE, public relations programs can ensure that students are well-prepared for successful careers in the dynamic and evolving field of public relations. The focus on research skills, effective communication, professional ethics, and continuous learning aligns with the demands of the industry, while experiential learning opportunities foster personal and professional growth, collaboration, and social responsibility. As the communication landscape continues to evolve, OBE and EBE integration is a crucial step in enhancing public relations education and producing competent professionals who can thrive in the fast-paced world of communication.

## 5.2. Considerations for Vietnamese Public Relations Programs

As highlighted in the research findings, a key principle of OBE is the establishment of clear and measurable learning outcomes. However, it can be challenging to define and assess abstract conceptualizations, such as humanism, altruism, and commitment, within an outcome-based framework (Ho et al., 2020). To address this challenge, public relations educators must collaborate with industry professionals to identify and prioritize specific, measurable, and relevant learning outcomes that align with the demands of the evolving communication landscape in Vietnam. The research findings on industry competencies can serve as a valuable resource in guiding the development of precise learning outcomes that reflect the skills and knowledge required by employers.

On the other hand, critics of OBE raise concerns about promoting excellence when "good enough" performance is deemed competent (Morcke et al., 2014). To ensure that public relations education encourages students to strive for excellence, the integration of EBE becomes crucial. Experiential learning, as demonstrated by the case studies of Canadian universities, provides students with opportunities to go beyond theoretical knowledge and engage in real-world public relations practices. By including practical experiences and reflective activities, educators can inspire students to set higher standards for their professional development, leading to a workforce of proactive and competent PR practitioners.

Another challenge highlighted by Sin (2014) is the limited relevance of learning outcomes to students. To address this concern, public relations programs should focus on aligning learning outcomes with industry competencies and current market demands. By integrating EBE through workplace engagement and community-based projects, students gain exposure to authentic communication challenges, making the learning outcomes more meaningful and applicable to their future careers. The research findings on industry competencies can serve as a basis for refining and adapting learning outcomes to meet the practical needs of the public relations profession in Vietnam.

The research findings also emphasize the significance of both professional and personal competencies in public relations education. While developing industry-specific skills is crucial, fostering personal qualities such as effective communication, professional ethics, and continuous learning is equally important for producing well-rounded and ethical PR practitioners. By integrating EBE into the curriculum, students can develop soft skills such as empathy, teamwork, and adaptability, which are essential for building strong relationships and navigating diverse communication contexts. Balancing the development of professional and personal competencies ensures that public relations graduates possess not only technical expertise but also the interpersonal skills necessary for successful careers in the field. Successfully integrating OBE and EBE requires faculty members to adopt innovative teaching methods and create diverse learning opportunities. Faculty development programs and ongoing support are essential to equip educators with the necessary skills to implement experiential learning approaches effectively. By investing in faculty development, institutions can ensure that educators are well-prepared to facilitate experiential learning, engage students in reflective practices, and provide constructive feedback, ultimately enhancing the quality of public relations education.

To align public relations education with industry demands, close collaboration with industry partners is vital. The case studies of Canadian universities demonstrate the value of engaging with professionals, offering internships, and involving students in community-based projects. In the context of Vietnam, public relations programs should establish strong ties with industry stakeholders, allowing students to gain exposure to real-world scenarios and receive valuable feedback from practitioners. This collaboration not only enhances the relevance of learning outcomes but also fosters a dynamic learning environment where students can learn from the experiences and expertise of industry professionals.

## 5.3. Limitations and Next Steps

Despite the valuable insights gained from the research on enhancing public relations education in Vietnam through the integration of OBE and EBE, certain limitations need to be acknowledged. Firstly, the research focused primarily on the perspectives of public relations practitioners and industry employers in identifying the required competencies. While their insights provided valuable information, the views of students and educators were not fully explored. Including the perspectives of students and educators could have provided a more comprehensive understanding of the challenges and opportunities in implementing OBE and EBE in the Vietnamese context.

Additionally, the research findings were based on case studies of Canadian universities known for effectively incorporating experiential learning into their public relations programs. While these case studies offer valuable insights, they may not fully represent the diverse educational landscape and cultural context in Vietnam. Thus, generalizing the findings to all public relations education in Vietnam should be done with caution, as the local context, resources, and institutional practices may vary significantly. While these insights are relevant, it would have been beneficial to delve deeper into the specific needs and challenges faced by the Vietnamese public relations industry to ensure the relevance and applicability of the proposed integration.

To address the limitations and enhance the relevance and effectiveness of the research, future research could consider the perspectives of students and educators in public relations programs in Vietnam. Conducting surveys, focus groups, or interviews with these stakeholders can provide valuable insights into their experiences, needs, and challenges in integrating OBE and EBE.

To expand the scope and ensure a more comprehensive understanding, research could include a broader sample of public relations programs in Vietnam. This would involve collaborating with multiple universities and institutions to capture the diverse approaches to public relations education in the country.

Future research could explore successful models of experiential learning and OBE implementation in different cultural contexts and educational systems. By drawing insights from various countries, educators can identify adaptable best practices and strategies that align with the unique context of Vietnam.

By fostering collaboration between stakeholders, considering local needs, and incorporating diverse perspectives, the research can help develop a robust and responsive educational framework that equips public relations graduates with the skills, knowledge, and experiences necessary for success in their careers.

## 6. CONCLUSIONS

The findings from this research highlighted the importance of both professional and personal competencies in public relations practice. Professional competencies such as research skills, statistical and data proficiency, content development, audio-visual design, and communication plan execution were identified as essential for effective public relations practitioners. Personal competencies encompassing effective communication, professional ethics, and lifelong learning were also emphasized as crucial for successful careers in the field.

The study demonstrated that experiential learning in public relations education should start from the classroom and extend to the workplace and community locations. By providing opportunities for hands-on experiences, internships, community-based projects, and collaborative initiatives, students can gain practical skills, build industry networks, and develop a deeper understanding of the societal impact of public relations.

The integration of OBE and EBE in public relations education holds significant implications for educators and researchers in Vietnam. By incorporating well-defined learning outcomes and practical experiences into the curriculum, educators can create a more comprehensive and effective learning framework for students. Implementing OBE allows for the establishment of clear and measurable learning outcomes, guiding educators in designing instructional strategies and assessments to assess students' achievements effectively.

Experiential learning through EBE offers students valuable opportunities to apply theoretical knowledge in real-world contexts, fostering active learning and bridging the gap between academia and industry. As educators continue to refine public relations curricula, the insights gained from this research can inform the development of competency-based courses and experiential learning activities that align with industry demands and prepare students for successful careers in the field.

For researchers, the study serves as a foundation for further investigations into the challenges and opportunities of integrating OBE and EBE in public relations education. Future research could explore the perspectives of students and educators to gain a more comprehensive understanding of the benefits and barriers to the implementation of experiential learning in Vietnamese public relations programs. Additionally, researchers can delve into specific industry needs and evolving communication trends to ensure that public relations curricula remain relevant and responsive to industry demands.

As educators and researchers continue to refine public relations curricula and pedagogies, it is essential to remain adaptive and responsive to industry demands, ensuring that graduates are well-prepared to excel in the dynamic and fast-paced world of public relations. Through collaboration, innovation, and a commitment to excellence, public relations education in Vietnam can reach new heights and produce competent and skilled professionals who contribute significantly to the growth and development of the communication industry.

## ACKNOWLEDGMENT

The authors would like to thank University of Management and Technology Ho Chi Minh City and Van Lang University for their continued support.

## REFERENCES

Adams, M. B., & Lee, N. M. (2021). Analytics in PR education: Desired skills for digital communicators. *Journal of Public Relations Education*, *7*(2), 203–212.

Austin, M. J., & Rust, D. Z. (2015). Developing an experiential learning program: Milestones and challenges. *International Journal on Teaching and Learning in Higher Education*, *27*(1), 143–153.

Berger, B. K. (2010). *The globalization of PR education?* IPRA. https://www.ipra.org/news/itle/the-globalization-of-pr-education/

Biggs, J. B. (1996). Enhancing teaching through constructive alignment. *Higher Education*, *32*(3), 1–18. DOI: 10.1007/BF00138871

Boud, D. K., & Keogh, R. (1985). Promoting reflection in learning: A model. In Boud, D., Keogh, R., & Walker, D. (Eds.), *Reflection: Turning experience into learning* (pp. 18–40). Routledge.

Brown, A. S. (1988, October). Outcome-based education: A success story. *Educational Leadership*, 12.

Dewey, J. (2011). *Democracy and education*. Simon & Brown.

Edwards, N. (2022, November 16). Canadian universities future-proof students with experiential learning. *The Globe and Mail*. https://www.theglobeandmail.com/business/article-canadian-universities-future-proof-students-with-experiential-learning/

Erzikova, E., & Berger, B. K. (2012). Leadership education in the public relations curriculum: Reality, opportunities, and benefits. *The Public Relations Journal*, *6*(3), 1–24.

Fitch, K., & L'Etang, J. (2020). Problematising history in the public relations curriculum. *Corporate Communications*, *25*(4), 703–716. DOI: 10.1108/CCIJ-11-2019-0122

Grunig, J. E. (1989). Teaching public relations in the future. *Public Relations Review*, *15*(1), 12–24. DOI: 10.1016/S0363-8111(89)80029-3

Ho, T. T. N., Sivapalan, S., & Nguyen, T. M. L. (2020). Implementing an outcome-based education framework: Case studies of FPT Education. *ICMET '20: Proceedings of the 2020 2nd International Conference on Modern Educational Technology*, 15-20.

Hoang, N. H., Nguyen, T. T. H., Pham, T. P. H., Ngo, T. P., & Nguyen, T. T. (2023). The development of curricular and training programs in Vietnam. *Problems of Education in the 21st Century, 81*(1), 90-116.

Kim, C., Quesenberry, K., Sutherland, K., & Freberg, K. (2021b). Digital learning: Standards and best practices for public relations education in undergraduate programs. *Journal of Public Relations Education*, *7*(2), 77–105.

Kim, Y., Meganck, S., Kristiansen, L., & Woo, C. W. (2021a). Taking experiential learning to the next level with student-run agencies. *Journal of Public Relations Education*, *7*(1), 80–121.

Kolb, A. Y., & Kolb, D. A. (2005). Learning styles and learning spaces: Enhancing experiential learning in higher education. *Academy of Management Learning & Education*, *4*(2), 193–212. DOI: 10.5465/amle.2005.17268566

Li, X., Zhang, Y., & Wang, Q. (2024). The relationship between learning outcomes and graduate competence: An outcome-based education perspective. *Sustainability*, *16*(14), 6080. DOI: 10.3390/su16146080

Luttrell, R., Wallace, A., McCollough, C., & Lee, J. (2021). Public relations curriculum: A systematic examination of curricular offerings in social media, digital media, and analytics in accredited programs. *Journal of Public Relations Education*, *7*(2), 1–43.

Macayan, J. (2017). Implementing outcome-based education (OBE) framework: Implications for assessment of students' performance. *Educational Measurement and Evaluation Review*, *8*(1), 1–10.

Mauleon-Palay, M. M., Villena, A. C. D., & Caiga, B. T. (2022). Assessment of OBE implementation and the level of attainment of students outcomes of the communication programs: AY 2017-2018. *Asia Pacific Journal of Academic Research in Social Studies*, *7*(2), 49–58.

Morcke, A., Dornan, T., & Eika, B. (2014). Outcome-based education in undergraduate medical education. *Proceedings of the International Consortium for Educational Development 2014*.

Nguyen, H. T., Sivapalan, S., & Linh, N. T. (2020, May). Implementing an outcome-based education framework: Case studies of FPT Education. *Proceedings of the 2020 2nd International Conference on Modern Educational Technology*. DOI: 10.1145/3401861.3401863

Pacho, T. O. (2022). Transforming higher education in Africa through university-industry collaboration. *Proceedings of the 20th International Conference on Private Higher Education in Africa*, 57-71.

Sin, C. (2014). Lost in translation: The meaning of learning outcomes across national and institutional policy contexts. *Studies in Higher Education*, *39*(10), 1823–1837. DOI: 10.1080/03075079.2013.806463

Wright, D. K. (2011). History and development of public relations education in North America: A critical analysis. *Journal of Communication Management (London)*, *15*(3), 236–255. DOI: 10.1108/13632541111151005

Wright, D. K., & Flynn, T. (2017). Public relations education and the development of professionalization in Canada and the USA. In T. Watson (Ed.), *North American Perspectives on the Development of Public Relations: Other Voices* (pp. 51-64). Springer. DOI: 10.1057/978-1-349-95044-7_5

Ziek, P. (2021). *The media production loop and class collabs* [Conference presentation]. Humanities Education and Research Association Virtual Conference 2021. Virtual Presentation.

Ziek, P. (2022). Class collabs: Assessing inter-disciplinary relationship building in media education. *Media Education Research Journal*, *11*(2), 1–13.

Ziek, P., & Fink, K. (2018). Networks within the competitive media environment. *Review of Journalism and Mass Communication*, *6*(1/2), 1–11.

# Compilation of References


AACSB. (2020). *2020 Guiding Principles and Standards for Business Accreditation*. Association to Advance Collegiate Schools of Business. https://www.aacsb.edu/accreditation/standards/business

Aboderin, O. S., & Havenga, M. (2024). Essential skills and strategies in higher education for the Fourth Industrial Revolution: A systematic literature review. *South African Journal of Higher Education*, *38*(2), 24–43. https://www.researchgate.net/publication/379843842_Essential_skills_and_strategies_in_higher_education_for_the_Fourth_Industrial_Revolution_A_systematic_literature_review. DOI: 10.20853/38-2-5430

Adams, M. B., & Lee, N. M. (2021). Analytics in PR education: Desired skills for digital communicators. *Journal of Public Relations Education*, *7*(2), 203–212.

Adebiyi, D. R. (2019). The role of social interaction in learning: A Vygotskian perspective.

Adedoyin, O. B., & Soykan, E. (2023). Covid-19 pandemic and online learning: The challenges and opportunities. *Interactive Learning Environments*, *31*(2), 863–875. DOI: 10.1080/10494820.2020.1813180

Adib, H. (2024). Experiential learning in higher education: Assessing the role of business simulations in shaping student attitudes towards sustainability. *International Journal of Management Education*, *22*(2), 100968. DOI: 10.1016/j.ijme.2024.100968

Agarwal, S., & Kaushik, J. S. (2020). Student's perception of online learning during COVID pandemic. *Indian Journal of Pediatrics*, *87*(7), 554–554. DOI: 10.1007/s12098-020-03327-7 PMID: 32385779

Ahmed, S., Kumar, R., & Hassan, M. (2024). Student performance prediction using machine learning algorithms. *Applied Computational Intelligence and Soft Computing*, *2024*(1), 4067721. Advance online publication. DOI: 10.1155/2024/4067721

Ahuja, V. (2024). Simulations in business education: Unlocking experiential learning. Practices and implementation of gamification in higher education, 1-21. DOI: 10.4018/979-8-3693-0716-8.ch001

Aisma, N. H. (2024). *The influence of using cooperative learning (think pair share technique) towards students writing ability at the first semester of the eighth grade at SMP Negeri 19 Bandar Lampung in academic year of 2023/2024* (Doctoral dissertation). https://repository.radenintan.ac.id/32749/1/PERPUS%20PUSAT%20BAB%201%20DAN%202.pdf

Alarifi, I. M. (2023). *Learning Limitless Knowledge: Transformative Learning Pathway to Unlocking and Harnessing the Endless Power of Knowledge*. Balboa Press.

Al-Fraihat, D., Joy, M., & Sinclair, J. (2020). Evaluating E-learning systems success: An empirical study. *Computers in Human Behavior, 102*, 67–86. DOI: 10.1016/j.chb.2019.08.004

Al-Freih, M., & Alkhalaf, S. (2021). Challenges of digital transformation in higher education: A case study in Saudi Arabia. *Education and Information Technologies, 26*, 7607–7626.

Allen, I. E., & Seaman, J. (2017). Digital learning compass: Distance education enrollment report 2017. Babson Survey Research Group. https://onlinelearningsurvey.com/reports/digtiallearningcompassenrollment2017.pdf

Almaiah, M. A., Al-Khasawneh, A., & Althunibat, A. (2020). Exploring the critical challenges and factors influencing the E-learning system usage during COVID-19 pandemic. *Education and Information Technologies, 25*(6), 5261–5280. DOI: 10.1007/s10639-020-10219-y PMID: 32837229

Alshater, M. M. (2022). Exploring the Role of Artificial Intelligence in Enhancing Academic Performance: A Case Study of ChatGPT. *SSRN*. https://papers.ssrn.com/sol3/papers.cfm?abstract_id=4312358 DOI: 10.2139/ssrn.4312358

Al-Zahrani, A. M., & Alasmari, T. M. (2024). Exploring the impact of artificial intelligence on higher education: The dynamics of ethical, social, and educational implications. *Humanities & Social Sciences Communications, 11*(1), 1–12. DOI: 10.1057/s41599-024-03432-4

Alzahrani, A. S., Tsai, Y.-S., Iqbal, S., Marcos, P. M. M., Scheffel, M., Drachsler, H., Kloos, C. D., Aljohani, N., & Gasevic, D. (2023). Untangling connections between challenges in the adoption of learning analytics in higher education. *Education and Information Technologies, 28*(4), 4563–4595. DOI: 10.1007/s10639-022-11323-x

Amri, M., Prasetyo, J., Halim, C., & Adhimas, Y. B. (2024). Assessing the influence of peer collaboration, classroom management, and assessment practices on student motivation in secondary education. *International Journal of Business, Law, and Education, 5*(2). Advance online publication. DOI: 10.56442/ijble.v5i2.660

Anderson, P. H., & Lawton, L. (2009). Business simulations and cognitive learning: Developments, desires, and future directions. *Simulation & Gaming, 40*(2), 193–216. DOI: 10.1177/1046878108321624

An, F., Xi, L., & Yu, J. (2024). The relationship between technology acceptance and self-regulated learning: The mediation roles of intrinsic motivation and learning engagement. *Education and Information Technologies, 29*(3), 2605–2623. DOI: 10.1007/s10639-023-11959-3 PMID: 37361728

Ansari, J. A. N., & Khan, N. A. (2020). Exploring the role of social media in collaborative learning the new domain of learning. *Smart Learning Environments, 7*(1), 9. DOI: 10.1186/s40561-020-00118-7

Anthonysamy, L., Koo, A. C., & Hew, S. H. (2020). Self-regulated learning strategies and non-academic outcomes in higher education blended learning environments: A one decade review. *Education and Information Technologies, 25*(5), 3677–3704. DOI: 10.1007/s10639-020-10134-2

Anthony, W. L., Zhu, Y., & Nower, L. (2021). The relationship of interactive technology use for entertainment and school performance and engagement: Evidence from a longitudinal study in a nationally representative sample of middle school students in China. *Computers in Human Behavior, 122*, 106846. Advance online publication. DOI: 10.1016/j.chb.2021.106846

Aparicio, M., Bacao, F., & Oliveira, T. (2017). Grit in the path to e-learning success. *Computers in Human Behavior, 66*, 388–399. DOI: 10.1016/j.chb.2016.10.009

Aporbo, R. J. (2023). Impact of cooperative learning strategy on students' academic productivity. *Journal of Student and Education, 1*(1), 16–26.

Austin, M. J., & Rust, D. Z. (2015). Developing an experiential learning program: Milestones and challenges. *International Journal on Teaching and Learning in Higher Education, 27*(1), 143–153.

Baber, H. (2021). Modelling the acceptance of e-learning during the pandemic of COVID-19-A study of South Korea. *International Journal of Management Education, 19*(2), 100503. DOI: 10.1016/j.ijme.2021.100503

Bailenson, J. (2018). *Experience on Demand: What Virtual Reality Is, How It Works, and What It Can Do*. HarperCollins.

Bandura, A. (1986). *Social foundations of thought and action: A social cognitive theory*. Prentice-Hall.

Bandura, A. (1997). *Self-efficacy: The exercise of control*. W. H. Freeman.

Barnett, R. (2000). *Realizing the University in an Age of Supercomplexity*. Open University Press.

Barrett, H. C. (2007). *Digital Portfolios: Powerful Tools for Promoting Professional Growth and Reflection*. Corwin Press.

Barron, B., & Darling-Hammond, L. (2008). Teaching for Meaningful Learning: A Review of Research on Inquiry-Based and Cooperative Learning. In Darling-Hammond, L., & Barron, B. (Eds.), *Powerful Learning: What We Know About Teaching for Understanding* (pp. 11–70). Jossey-Bass.

Barua, L., & Lockee, B. B. (2024). A review of strategies to incorporate flexibility in higher education course designs. *Discover Education*, *3*(1), 127. DOI: 10.1007/s44217-024-00213-8

Basilaia, G., & Kvavadze, D. (2020). Transition to online education in schools during a SARS-CoV-2 coronavirus (COVID-19) pandemic in Georgia. *Pedagogical Research, 5*(4).

Bates, T., Cobo, C., Mariño, O., & Wheeler, S. (2020). Can artificial intelligence transform higher education? *International Journal of Educational Technology in Higher Education, 17*(1), 42. Advance online publication. DOI: 10.1186/s41239-020-00218-x

Bayaga, A. (2024). Leveraging AI-enhanced and emerging technologies for pedagogical innovations in higher education. *Education and Information Technologies*, •••, 1–28.

Beane, J. A. (1997). *Curriculum Integration: Designing the Core of Democratic Education*. Teachers College Press.

Beatson, N., Gabriel, C.-A., Howell, A., Scott, S., van der Meer, J., & Wood, L. C. (2020). Just opt in: How choosing to engage with technology impacts business students' academic performance. *Journal of Accounting Education, 50*, 100641. Advance online publication. DOI: 10.1016/j.jaccedu.2019.100641

Beatty, B. (2019). *Hybrid-flexible course design*. EdTech Books. DOI: 10.59668/33

Becker, J. M., Cheah, J. H., Gholamzade, R., Ringle, C. M., & Sarstedt, M. (2023). PLS-SEM's most wanted guidance. *International Journal of Contemporary Hospitality Management*, *35*(1), 321–346. DOI: 10.1108/IJCHM-04-2022-0474

Bedenlier, S., Bond, M., Buntins, K., Zawacki-Richter, O., & Kerres, M. (2020). Facilitating student engagement through educational technology in higher education: A systematic review in the field of arts and humanities. *Australasian Journal of Educational Technology*, *36*(4), 126–150. DOI: 10.14742/ajet.5477

Bell, B. S., Tannenbaum, S. I., Ford, J. K., Noe, R. A., & Kraiger, K. (2016). 100 years of training and development research: What we know and where we should go. *The Journal of Applied Psychology*, *101*(3), 305–323. DOI: 10.1037/apl0000142

Beranič, T., & Heričko, M. (2022). The impact of serious games in economic and business education: A case of ERP business simulation. *Sustainability (Basel)*, *14*(2), 683. DOI: 10.3390/su14020683

Berger, B. K. (2010). *The globalization of PR education?* IPRA. https://www.ipra.org/news/itle/the-globalization-of-pr-education/

Bergmann, J., & Sams, A. (2012). *Flip Your Classroom: Reach Every Student in Every Class Every Day*. International Society for Technology in Education.

Bernardo, N., & Duarte, E. (2022). Immersive virtual reality in an industrial design education context: What the future looks like according to its educators. *Computer-Aided Design and Applications*, *19*(2), 238–255. DOI: 10.14733/cadaps.2022.238-255

Bernard, R. M., Abrami, P. C., Borokhovski, E., Wade, A., Tamim, R., Surkes, M., & Bethel, E. (2009). A meta-analysis of three types of interaction treatments in distance education. *Review of Educational Research*, *79*(3), 1243–1289. DOI: 10.3102/0034654309333844

Bhat, S., Raju, R., Bikramjit, A., & D'Souza, R. (2018). Leveraging e-learning through google classroom: A usability study. *Journal of Engineering Education Transformations*, 129-135.

Bicen, H., & Kocakoyun, S. (2018). Perceptions of students for gamification approach: Kahoot as a case study. *International Journal of Emerging Technologies in Learning*, *13*(2), 72–93. DOI: 10.3991/ijet.v13i02.7467

Biggs, J. B. (1996). Enhancing teaching through constructive alignment. *Higher Education*, *32*(3), 1–18. DOI: 10.1007/BF00138871

Bird, K. (2024). Predictive analytics in higher education: The promises and challenges of using machine learning to improve student success. Association for Institutional Research. https://www.airweb.org/publication/article-161

Bishop, J. L., & Verleger, M. A. (2013). The flipped classroom: A survey of the research. 2013 ASEE Annual Conference & Exposition, 1–18. https://peer.asee.org/22585

Bishop, J. L., & Verleger, M. A. (2013). The Flipped Classroom: A Survey of the Research. *ASEE National Conference Proceedings, 30*(9), 1–18. DOI: 10.18260/1-2--22585

Black, P., & Wiliam, D. (1998). Assessment and Classroom Learning. *Assessment in Education: Principles, Policy & Practice*, *5*(1), 7–74. DOI: 10.1080/0969595980050102

Boda, M. A., & Ugrósdy, G. (2019). Enhancing Learning Outcome of Business Simulation Games via Process Feedback. *Vadyba*, (1), 67.

Boelens, R., De Wever, B., & Voet, M. (2017). Four key challenges to the design of blended learning: A systematic literature review. *Educational Research Review*, *22*, 1–18. DOI: 10.1016/j.edurev.2017.06.001

Bolliger, D. U., & Halupa, C. (2012). Student perceptions of satisfaction and anxiety in an online doctoral program. *Distance Education*, *33*(1), 81–98. DOI: 10.1080/01587919.2012.667961

Bond, M., Bedenlier, S., Marín, V. I., & Händel, M. (2021). Emergency remote teaching in higher education: Mapping the first global online semester. *International Journal of Educational Technology in Higher Education*, *18*(1), 50. DOI: 10.1186/s41239-021-00282-x PMID: 34778537

Bond, M., Buntins, K., Bedenlier, S., Zawacki-Richter, O., & Kerres, M. (2020). Mapping research in student engagement and educational technology in higher education: A systematic evidence map. *International Journal of Educational Technology in Higher Education*, *17*(1), 2. DOI: 10.1186/s41239-019-0176-8

Bonk, C. J., & Graham, C. R. (2005). *The Handbook of blended learning: Global perspectives, local designs*. Pfeiffer., https://www.wiley.com/en-us/The+Handbook+of+Blended+Learning%3A+Global+Perspectives%2C+Local+Designs-p-9780787977580

Bonwell, C. C., & Eison, J. A. (1991). Active learning: Creating excitement in the classroom (ASHE-ERIC Higher Education Report No. 1). The George Washington University, School of Education and Human Development. https://files.eric.ed.gov/fulltext/ED336049.pdf

Bonwell, C. C., & Eison, J. A. (1991). *Active Learning: Creating Excitement in the Classroom* (ASHE-ERIC Higher Education Report No. 1). Washington, DC: The George Washington University, School of Education and Human Development. Available from ERIC ED336049: https://eric.ed.gov/?id=ED336049

Bosch, C. (2017). Promoting self-directed learning through the implementation of cooperative learning in higher education blended learning environment. (Doctoral thesis). http://dx.doi.org/DOI: 10.13140/RG.2.2.22135.11687

Bosch, C., & Laubscher, D. (2022). Cooperative learning in blended environments: Challenges and prospects in South African TVET colleges. *South African Journal of Education*, *42*(2), 1–12.

Boss, S., & Krauss, J. (2022). *Reinventing project-based learning: Your field guide to real-world projects in the digital age*. International Society for Technology in Education.

Boud, D. K., & Keogh, R. (1985). Promoting reflection in learning: A model. In Boud, D., Keogh, R., & Walker, D. (Eds.), *Reflection: Turning experience into learning* (pp. 18–40). Routledge.

Bourrie, D. M., Jones-Farmer, L. A., & Sankar, C. S. (2016). Learning technologies: Bridging the gap between intention, adoption and routine use. *Technology*, *26*, 27.

Bozkurt, A., & Sharma, R. C. (2020). Emergency remote teaching in a time of global crisis due to CoronaVirus pandemic. *Asian journal of distance education, 15*(1), i-vi.

Bradley, V. M. (2021). Learning Management System (LMS) use with online instruction. *International Journal of Technology in Education*, *4*(1), 68–92. DOI: 10.46328/ijte.36

Brame, C. J., & Biel, R. (2015). Test-enhanced learning: The potential for testing to promote greater learning in undergraduate science courses. *CBE Life Sciences Education*, *14*(2), es4. DOI: 10.1187/cbe.14-11-0208 PMID: 25999314

Brindley, J. E., Blaschke, L. M., & Walti, C. (2009). Creating effective collaborative learning groups in an online environment. *International Review of Research in Open and Distance Learning*, *10*(3). Advance online publication. DOI: 10.19173/irrodl.v10i3.675

Brink, C. H., & Costigan, R. D. (2021). Business school graduates and career readiness: The role of critical thinking and problem-solving skills. *Journal of Education for Business*, *96*(6), 341–349. DOI: 10.1080/08832323.2021.1886724

Brode, E. C., Bernal, J. M., Cornes, S. B., Santhosh, L., Rivera, J. A., Kulkarni, S. A., Mandal, J. R., Henry, D. M., Bartz, K. S., & Van Schaik, S. M. (2025). Faculty Development for the People: Workplace-Based Solutions for Busy Clinicians. *The Clinical Teacher*, *22*(3), e70073. DOI: 10.1111/tct.70073 PMID: 40159456

Brown, M., McCormack, M., Reeves, J., Brooks, D. C., & Grajek, S. with Alexander, B., Bali, M., Bulger, S., Dark, S., Engelbert, N., Gannon, K., Gauthier, A., Gibson, D., Gibson, R., Lundin, B., Veletsianos, G., & Weber, N. (2020). *2020 EDUCAUSE Horizon Report: Teaching and learning edition*. EDUCAUSE. https://library.educause.edu/-/media/files/library/2020/3/2020_horizon_report_pdf.pdf

Brown, A. S. (1988, October). Outcome-based education: A success story. *Educational Leadership*, 12.

Bruner, J. S. (1966). *Toward a theory of instruction*. Harvard University Press.

Brunet, F. (2005). *The economic impact of the Barcelona Olympic Games, 1986–2004*. Centre d'Estudis Olímpics UAB.

Brunet, F. (2012). Analysis of the economic impact of the Barcelona Olympic Games: Success factors and post-event legacy. *The International Journal of the History of Sport*, *29*(12), 1755–1770. DOI: 10.1080/09523367.2012.708307

Burton-Jones, A., & Grange, C. (2013). From Use to Effective Use: A Representation Theory Perspective. *Information Systems Research*, *24*(3), 632–658. DOI: 10.1287/isre.1120.0444

Cabau, B. (2014). Higher Education Ambitions and Societal Expectations. *Athens Journal of Education*, *1*(2), 143–154. DOI: 10.30958/aje.1-2-4

Çakıroğlu, Ü., Başıbüyük, B., Güler, M., Atabay, M., & Yılmaz Memiş, B. (2017). Gamifying an ICT course: Influences on engagement and academic performance. *Computers in Human Behavior*, *69*, 98–107. DOI: 10.1016/j.chb.2016.12.018

CAST. (2024). Universal Design for Learning guidelines version 3.0. http://udlguidelines.cast.org

Catthoor, L. (2023). THE FUTURE OF HYBRID AND BLENDED LEARNING (Doctoral dissertation, Ghent University).

Charitopoulos, A., Rangoussi, M., & Koulouriotis, D. (2020). On the use of soft computing methods in educational data mining and learning analytics research: A review of years 2010–2018. *International Journal of Artificial Intelligence in Education*, *30*(3), 371–430. DOI: 10.1007/s40593-020-00200-8

Cheah, J.-H., Roldán, J. L., Ciavolino, E., Ting, H., & Ramayah, T. (2021). Sampling weight adjustments in partial least squares structural equation modeling: Guidelines and illustrations. *Total Quality Management & Business Excellence*, *32*(13-14), 1594–1613. DOI: 10.1080/14783363.2020.1754125

Chi, M. T. H., Bassok, M., Lewis, M. W., Reimann, P., & Glaser, R. (1989). Self-explanations: How students study and use examples in learning to solve problems. *Cognitive Science*, *13*(2), 145–182. DOI: 10.1207/s15516709cog1302_1

Chim, H. Q., Dolmans, D. H., Oude Egbrink, M. G., & Savelberg, H. H. (2024). Experiences of face-to-face and online collaborative learning tutorials: A qualitative community of inquiry approach. *Education and Information Technologies*, *29*(14), 1–29. DOI: 10.1007/s10639-024-12533-1

Chiu, T. K. (2021). Digital support for student engagement in blended learning based on self-determination theory. *Computers in Human Behavior*, *124*, e106909. DOI: 10.1016/j.chb.2021.106909

Chugh, R., Turnbull, D., Cowling, M. A., Vanderburg, R., & Vanderburg, M. A. (2023). Implementing educational technology in Higher Education Institutions: A review of technologies, stakeholder perceptions, frameworks and metrics. *Education and Information Technologies*, *28*(12), 16403–16429. DOI: 10.1007/s10639-023-11846-x

Clark, G., Marsden, R., & Whyatt, J. D. (2020). *Enhancing graduate employability through enterprise and entrepreneurship education: A longitudinal study of pedagogical impact.*

Coburn, C. E. (2003). Rethinking scale: Moving beyond numbers to deep and lasting change. *Educational Researcher*, *32*(6), 3–12. DOI: 10.3102/0013189X032006003

Collaborative for Academic, Social, and Emotional Learning (CASEL). (2021). *SEL Framework.* https://casel.org

Cook-Sather, A. (2006). Sound, Presence, and Power: "Student Voice" in Educational Research and Reform. *Curriculum Inquiry*, *36*(4), 359–390. DOI: 10.1111/j.1467-873X.2006.00363.x

Cornell University. (2025). *Engaging students in discussions.* Cornell University. https://teaching.cornell.edu/teaching-resources/engaging-students/engaging-students-discussions

Costin, Y., O'Brien, M. P., & Hynes, B. (2019). Developing cognitive and non-cognitive entrepreneurial competences through business simulation games. *Journal of Enterprising Culture*, *27*(04), 471–498. DOI: 10.1142/S0218495819500171

Crawford, J., Butler-Henderson, K., Rudolph, J., Malkawi, B., Glowatz, M., Burton, R., ... & Lam, S. (2020). COVID-19: 20 countries' higher education intra-period digital pedagogy responses. *Journal of applied learning & teaching, 3*(1), 1-20.

Crawford, J., Butler-Henderson, K., Rudolph, J., Malkawi, B., Glowatz, M., Burton, R., & Lam, S. (2020). COVID-19: 20 countries' higher education intra-period digital pedagogy responses. *Journal of Applied Learning & Teaching*, *3*(1), 1–20. DOI: 10.37074/jalt.2020.3.1.7

Crompton, H., & Burke, D. (2023). Artificial intelligence in higher education: The state of the field. *International Journal of Educational Technology in Higher Education*, *20*(1), 1–22. DOI: 10.1186/s41239-023-00392-8

Crouch, C. H., & Mazur, E. (2001). Peer instruction: Ten years of experience and results. *American Journal of Physics*, *69*(9), 970–977. DOI: 10.1119/1.1374249

Cukurova, M. (2025). The interplay of learning, analytics and artificial intelligence in education: A vision for hybrid intelligence. *British Journal of Educational Technology*, *56*(2), 387–404. DOI: 10.1111/bjet.13514

Dai, X., Fu, X., Zuo, J., & Shi, L. (2025). Application of Virtual Simulation in Education: Current Status, Hot Spots and Trends. *Advances in Computer and Materials Scienc Research*, *1*(1), 384–392. DOI: 10.70114/acmsr.2024.1.1.P384

Darling-Hammond, L., Hyler, M. E., & Gardner, M. (2017). *Effective Teacher Professional Development*. Learning Policy Institute. DOI: 10.54300/122.311

Day, D. V., Fleenor, J. W., Atwater, L. E., Sturm, R. E., & McKee, R. A. (2014). Advances in leader and leadership development: A review of 25 years of research and theory. *The Leadership Quarterly*, *25*(1), 63–82. DOI: 10.1016/j.leaqua.2013.11.004

De Bruijn-Smolders, M., & Prinsen, F. R. (2024). Effective Student Engagement with Blended Learning A systematic review. *Heliyon*, *10*(23), e39439. DOI: 10.1016/j.heliyon.2024.e39439 PMID: 39687123

De Guinea, A. O., & Markus, M. L. (2009). Why Break the Habit of a Lifetime? Rethinking the Roles of Intention, Habit, and Emotion in Continuing Information Technology Use. *Management Information Systems Quarterly*, *33*(3), 433–444. DOI: 10.2307/20650303

Deci, E. L., & Ryan, R. M. (1985). *Intrinsic Motivation and Self-Determination in Human Behavior*. Springer. DOI: 10.1007/978-1-4899-2271-7

Deci, E. L., & Ryan, R. M. (1985). The general causality orientations scale: Self-determination in personality. *Journal of Research in Personality, 19*(2), 109–134. DOI: 10.1016/0092-6566(85)90023-6

Deci, E. L., & Ryan, R. M. (2000). The" what" and" why" of goal pursuits: Human needs and the self-determination of behavior. *Psychological Inquiry, 11*(4), 227–268. DOI: 10.1207/S15327965PLI1104_01

Dede, C. (2009a). Comparing frameworks for 21st century skills. In J. Bellanca & R. Brandt (Eds.), *21st century skills: Rethinking how students learn* (pp. 51–76). Solution Tree Press.

Dede, C. (2009b). Comparing Frameworks for 21st Century Skills. *21st century skills: Rethinking how students learn, 20*, 51–76.

Deng, R., Benckendorff, P., & Gannaway, D. (2019). Progress and new directions for teaching and learning in MOOCs. *Computers & Education, 129*, 48–60. DOI: 10.1016/j.compedu.2018.10.019

Department of Higher Education and Training (DHET). (2013). White Paper for Post-School Education and Training: Building an expanded, effective and integrated post-school system. Pretoria: Department of Higher Education and Training.

Deterding, S., Dixon, D., Khaled, R., & Nacke, L. (2011). From Game Design Elements to Gamefulness: Defining "Gamification." *Proceedings of the 15th International Academic MindTrek Conference: Envisioning Future Media Environments*, 9–15. DOI: 10.1145/2181037.2181040

Dewey, J. (1938). Experience and education. *Macmillan.* https://www.schoolofeducators.com/wp-content/uploads/2011/12/EXPERIENCE-EDUCATION-JOHN-DEWEY.pdf

Dewey, J. (1938). *Experience and Education*. Macmillan.

Dewey, J. (2011). *Democracy and education*. Simon & Brown.

Dhawan, S. (2020). Online learning: A panacea in the time of COVID-19 crisis. *Journal of Educational Technology Systems, 49*(1), 5–22. DOI: 10.1177/0047239520934018

Diachkova, A. V., Sandler, D. G., & Avramenko, E. S. (2020). Case of using simulation in education for business analysts. Economic consultant, (3), 104-114. DOI: 10.46224/ecoc.2020.3.7

Diamantopoulos, A., & Siguaw, J. A. (2006). Formative versus reflective indicators in organizational measure development: A comparison and empirical illustration. *British Journal of Management, 17*(4), 263–282. DOI: 10.1111/j.1467-8551.2006.00500.x

Dol, S. M., & Jawandhiya, P. M. (2024). Systematic review and analysis of EDM for predicting the academic performance of students. Journal of The Institution of Engineers (India): Series B, 105(4), 1021-1071. DOI: 10.1007/s40031-024-00998-0

Dole, S., Bloom, L., & Kowalske, K. (2016). Transforming pedagogy: Changing perspectives from teacher-centered to learner-centered. *The Interdisciplinary Journal of Problem-Based Learning*, *10*(1). Advance online publication. DOI: 10.7771/1541-5015.1538

Doll, W. E. (2012). The Four R's—An Alternative to the Tyler Rationale. In *Curriculum: Toward New Identities* (pp. 267–287). Routledge.

Dol, S. M., & Jawandhiya, P. M. (2023). A review of data mining in education sector. *Journal of Engineering Education Transformations*, *36*(Special Issue), 13–22. DOI: 10.16920/jeet/2023/v36is2/23003

Domínguez, A., Saenz-de-Navarrete, J., de-Marcos, L., Fernández-Sanz, L., Pagés, C., & Martínez-Herráiz, J. J. (2013). Gamifying Learning Experiences: Practical Implications and Outcomes. *Computers & Education*, *63*, 380–392. DOI: 10.1016/j.compedu.2012.12.020

Du Plessis, A. E., Küng, E., & du Plessis, E. (2024). Challenges for Pedagogical Effectiveness in an Ever-Changing Education Landscape: Conceptualisation of Pedagogical Mobility and Flexibility as a Context-Consciousness. *Education Sciences*, *14*(4), 349. DOI: 10.3390/educsci14040349

Du Toit-Brits, C. (2017). Towards a transformative and holistic continuing professional teacher development (CPTD) through self-directed learning. *South African Journal of Higher Education*, *31*(2), 54–72.

Du Toit-Brits, C. (2018). Towards a transformative and holistic continuing self-directed learning theory. *South African Journal of Higher Education*, *32*(4), 1753–5913. DOI: 10.20853/32-4-2434

Du Toit-Brits, C. (2019). A focus on self-directed learning: The role that educators' expectations play in enhancing student motivation. *South African Journal of Education*, *39*(2), 1–11. DOI: 10.15700/saje.v39n2a1645

Duan, H., Fernández, G., Van Dongen, E., & Kohn, N. (2020). The effect of intrinsic and extrinsic motivation on memory formation: Insight from behavioral and imaging study. *Brain Structure & Function*, *225*(5), 1561–1574. https://link.springer.com/article/10.1007/s00429-020-02074-x. DOI: 10.1007/s00429-020-02074-x PMID: 32350643

DuFour, R., & Eaker, R. (1998). *Professional Learning Communities at Work: Best Practices for Enhancing Student Achievement.* Solution Tree Press.

Dumford, A. D., & Miller, A. L. (2018). Online learning in higher education: Exploring advantages and disadvantages for engagement. *Journal of Computing in Higher Education*, *30*(3), 452–465. DOI: 10.1007/s12528-018-9179-z

Durlak, J. A., Weissberg, R. P., Dymnicki, A. B., Taylor, R. D., & Schellinger, K. B. (2011). The impact of enhancing students' social and emotional learning: A meta-analysis of school-based universal interventions. *Child Development*, *82*(1), 405–432. DOI: 10.1111/j.1467-8624.2010.01564.x

Dutt, A., Ismail, M. A., Herawan, T., & Targio, I. A. (2024). *Partition-Based Clustering Algorithms Applied to Mixed Data for Educational Data Mining: A Survey From 1971 to 2024.* IEEE., DOI: 10.1109/ACCESS.2024.3496929

Dweck, C. (2006). *Mindset: The new psychology of success.* Random House.

Dziuban, C., Graham, C. R., Moskal, P. D., Norberg, A., & Sicilia, N. (2018). Blended learning: The new normal and emerging technologies. *International Journal of Educational Technology in Higher Education*, *15*(1), 3. DOI: 10.1186/s41239-017-0087-5

Earley, P. C., & Mosakowski, E. (2004). Cultural intelligence. *Harvard Business Review*, *82*(10), 139–146. https://hbr.org/2004/10/cultural-intelligence PMID: 15559582

Edwards, N. (2022, November 16). Canadian universities future-proof students with experiential learning. *The Globe and Mail.* https://www.theglobeandmail.com/business/article-canadian-universities-future-proof-students-with-experiential-learning/

Eisner, E. W. (2002). *The Arts and the Creation of Mind.* Yale University Press.

Elias, T. (2011). Learning Analytics: Definitions, Processes and Potential. *Learning*, *1*, 22.

Ellikkal, A., & Rajamohan, S. (2024). AI-enabled personalized learning: Empowering management students for improving engagement and academic performance. *Vilakshan – XIMB. Journal of Management.* Advance online publication. DOI: 10.1108/xjm-02-2024

Ellikkal, A., & Rajamohan, S. (2025). AI-enabled personalized learning: Empowering management students for improving engagement and academic performance. Vilakshan - XIMB. *Journal of Management*, *22*(1), 28–44. DOI: 10.1108/XJM-02-2024-0023

Elmaadaway, M. A. N., & Abouelenein, Y. A. M. (2023). In-service teachers' TPACK development through an adaptive e-learning environment (ALE). *Education and Information Technologies*, *28*(7), 8273–8298. DOI: 10.1007/s10639-022-11477-8 PMID: 36571083

Eltahir, M. E., & Babiker, F. M. E. (2024). The influence of artificial intelligence tools on student performance in e-learning environments: Case study. *Electronic Journal of e-Learning*, *22*(9), 91–110. DOI: 10.34190/ejel.22.9.3639

Erzikova, E., & Berger, B. K. (2012). Leadership education in the public relations curriculum: Reality, opportunities, and benefits. *The Public Relations Journal*, *6*(3), 1–24.

Esposito, M., & Virili, F. (2014). Improving student success with the goal setting theory: A literature review. In *XI conference of the Italian chapter of AIS, Genova* (pp. 1-14). http://www.itais.org/proceedings/itais2014/pdf/17.pdf

Exter, M., & Ashby, I. (2022). Lifelong learning of instructional design and educational technology professionals: A heutagogical approach. *TechTrends*, *66*(2), 254–264. DOI: 10.1007/s11528-021-00657-x

Farashahi, M., & Tajeddin, M. (2018). Effectiveness of teaching methods in business education: A comparison study on the learning outcomes of lectures, case studies and simulations. *International Journal of Management Education*, *16*(1), 131–142. DOI: 10.1016/j.ijme.2018.01.003

Federal Trade Commission. (2023, May 24). FTC says ed tech provider Edmodo unlawfully used children's personal information for advertising and outsourced compliance to school districts. FTC News Release. Retrieved from https://www.ftc.gov/news-events/news/press-releases/2023/05/ftc-says-ed-tech-provider-edmodo-unlawfully-used-childrens-personal-information-advertising

Feng, M., Heffernan, N. T., & Koedinger, K. R. (2021). Using Learning Analytics to Improve the Adaptive Learning Environment. *Journal of Educational Data Mining*, *13*(1), 1–20.

Ferguson-Patrick, K. (2018). The importance of teacher role in cooperative learning: The effects of high stakes testing on pedagogical approaches of early career teachers in primary schools. *Education 3-13, 46*(1), 89-101.

Finn, J. D., & Zimmer, K. S. (2012). Student Engagement: What Is It? Why Does It Matter? In Christenson, S. L., Reschly, A. L., & Wylie, C. (Eds.), *Handbook of Research on Student Engagement* (pp. 97–131). Springer. DOI: 10.1007/978-1-4614-2018-7_5

Fisher, D., Frey, N., Almarode, J., & Henderson-Rosser, A. (2021). *The quick guide to simultaneous, hybrid, and blended learning*. Corwin Press. DOI: 10.4135/9781071852644

Fitch, K., & L'Etang, J. (2020). Problematising history in the public relations curriculum. *Corporate Communications, 25*(4), 703–716. DOI: 10.1108/CCIJ-11-2019-0122

Francis, P., Broughan, C., Foster, C., & Wilson, C. (2019). Thinking critically about learning analytics, student outcomes, and equity of attainment. *Assessment & Evaluation in Higher Education, 45*(6), 811–821. DOI: 10.1080/02602938.2019.1691975

Fredricks, J. A., Blumenfeld, P. C., & Paris, A. H. (2004). School engagement: Potential of the concept, state of the evidence. *Review of Educational Research, 74*(1), 59–109. DOI: 10.3102/00346543074001059

Fredricks, J. A., Filsecker, M., & Lawson, M. A. (2016). Student Engagement, Context, and Adjustment: Addressing Definitional, Measurement, and Methodological Issues. *Learning and Instruction, 43*, 1–4. DOI: 10.1016/j.learninstruc.2016.02.002

Freeman, S., Eddy, S. L., McDonough, M., Smith, M. K., Okoroafor, N., Jordt, H., & Wenderoth, M. P. (2014). Active learning increases student performance in science, engineering, and mathematics. *Proceedings of the National Academy of Sciences of the United States of America, 111*(23), 8410–8415. DOI: 10.1073/pnas.1319030111 PMID: 24821756

Fullan, M. (2007). *The New Meaning of Educational Change* (4th ed.). Teachers College Press.

Fullan, M. (2011). *Change Leader: Learning to Do What Matters Most*. Jossey-Bass.

Fullan, M. (2016). *The new meaning of educational change*. Teachers College Press.

Gaffoor, A., & Van der Bijl, A. (2019). Factors influencing the intention of students at a selected TVET college in the Western Cape to complete their National Certificate (Vocational) Business Studies programme. Journal of Vocational. *Adult and Continuing Education and Training, 2*(2), 23–42. DOI: 10.14426/jovacet.v2i2.70

Gardner, J., Brooks, C., & Baker, R. (2024). Investigating algorithmic bias in student progress monitoring. Computers & Education. *Artificial Intelligence, 6*, 100205. Advance online publication. DOI: 10.1016/j.caeai.2024.100205

Garrison, D. R. (1997). Self-directed learning: Toward a comprehensive model. *Adult Education Quarterly, 48*(1), 18–33. DOI: 10.1177/074171369704800103

Garrison, D. R., Anderson, T., & Archer, W. (2000). Critical inquiry in a text-based environment: Computer conferencing in higher education. *The Internet and Higher Education*, *2*(2–3), 87–105.

Garrison, D. R., & Vaughan, N. D. (2008). *Blended learning in higher education: Framework, principles, and guidelines*. Jossey-Bass.

Gartner, Inc. (2022). *Market guide for web, product and digital experience analytics* (Davis, M., Norrie, D., Markkanen, A., & Lee, A., Eds.). Gartner, Inc.

Gay, G. (2010). *Culturally Responsive Teaching: Theory, Research, and Practice* (2nd ed.). Teachers College Press.

Gay, G. (2010). *Culturally responsive teaching: Theory, research, and practice*. Teachers College Press.

Gee, J. P. (2003). *What Video Games Have to Teach Us About Learning and Literacy*. Palgrave Macmillan. DOI: 10.1145/950566.950595

Gelles, L. A., Lord, S. M., Hoople, G. D., Chen, D. A., & Mejia, J. A. (2020). Compassionate flexibility and self-discipline: Student adaptation to emergency remote teaching in an integrated engineering energy course during COVID-19. *Education Sciences*, *10*(11), 304. DOI: 10.3390/educsci10110304

Gillies, R. M. (2004). The effects of cooperative learning on junior high school students during small group learning. *Learning and Instruction*, *14*(2), 197–213. DOI: 10.1016/S0959-4752(03)00068-9

Gillies, R. M. (2016). Cooperative learning: Review of research and practice. *The Australian Journal of Teacher Education*, *41*(3), 39–54. DOI: 10.14221/ajte.2016v41n3.3

Glazer, F. S. (Ed.). (2023). *Blended learning: Across the disciplines, across the academy*. Taylor & Francis.

Gold, A. H., Malhotra, A., & Segars, A. H. (2001). Knowledge management: An organizational capabilities perspective. *Journal of Management Information Systems*, *18*(1), 185–214. DOI: 10.1080/07421222.2001.11045669

Gorski, P. C. (2013). *Reaching and teaching students in poverty: Strategies for erasing the opportunity gap*. Teachers College Press.

Gresham, F. M. (1986). Conceptual and definitional issues in the assessment of children's social skills: Implications for classifications and training. [REMOVED HYPERLINK FIELD]. *Journal of Clinical Child Psychology*, *15*(1), 3–15. DOI: 10.1207/s15374424jccp1501_1

Grier, D., Lindt, S. F., & Miller, S. C. (2021). Formative assessment with game-based technology. *International Journal of Technology in Education and Science, 5*(2), 173–187. DOI: 10.46328/ijtes.97

Grunig, J. E. (1989). Teaching public relations in the future. *Public Relations Review, 15*(1), 12–24. DOI: 10.1016/S0363-8111(89)80029-3

Guskey, T. R. (2002). Professional Development and Teacher Change. *Teachers and Teaching, 8*(3), 381–391. DOI: 10.1080/135406002100000512

Guzmán-Valenzuela, C., Gómez-González, C., Rojas-Murphy Tagle, A., & Lorca-Vyhmeister, A. (2021). Learning analytics in higher education: A preponderance of analytics but very little learning? *International Journal of Educational Technology in Higher Education, 18*(1), 23. DOI: 10.1186/s41239-021-00258-x

Haase, J., Hoff, E., Hanel, P., & Innes-Ker, Å. (2018). A meta-analysis of the relation between creative self-efficacy and creativity. *Creativity Research Journal, 30*(1), 1–16. DOI: 10.1080/10400419.2018.1411436

Hair, J. F., Sarstedt, M., & Ringle, C. M. (2019). Rethinking some of the rethinking of partial least squares. *European Journal of Marketing, 53*(4), 566–584. DOI: 10.1108/EJM-10-2018-0665

Halili, S. H. (2019). Technological advancements in education 4.0. *The Online Journal of Distance Education and e-Learning : TOJDEL, 7*(1), 63–69.

Hall, G. E., & Hord, S. M. (2011). *Implementing Change: Patterns, Principles, and Potholes*. Allyn & Bacon.

Halverson, L. R., Graham, C. R., Spring, K. J., Drysdale, J. S., & Henrie, C. R. (2014). A thematic analysis of the most highly cited scholarship in the first decade of blended learning research. *The Internet and Higher Education, 20*, 20–34. DOI: 10.1016/j.iheduc.2013.09.004

Hamari, J., Koivisto, J., & Sarsa, H. (2014). Does Gamification Work? A Literature Review of Empirical Studies on Gamification. *Proceedings of the 47th Hawaii International Conference on System Sciences (HICSS)*, 3025–3034. DOI: 10.1109/HICSS.2014.377

Hamilton, E. R., Rosenberg, J. M., & Akcaoglu, M. (2016). The Substitution Augmentation Modification Redefinition (SAMR) Model: A critical review and suggestions for its use. *TechTrends, 60*(5), 433–441. DOI: 10.1007/s11528-016-0091-y

Hanafi, A. G., Ahmad, H. H., Mansor, M. F., & Mustafa, W. A. (2023). An integrated approach in empowering technical and vocational education and training (TVET) for Malaysian Asnaf in the IR4.0 era. *Journal of Advanced Research in Applied Sciences and Engineering*

Hanus, M. D., & Fox, J. (2015). Assessing the effects of gamification in the classroom: A longitudinal study on intrinsic motivation, social comparison, satisfaction, effort, and academic performance. *Computers & Education*, *80*, 152–161. DOI: 10.1016/j.compedu.2014.08.019

Harasim, L. (2017). *Learning theory and online technologies* (2nd ed.). Routledge., DOI: 10.4324/9781315716831

Härdling, E., & Bakhsh, H. (2022). Deciding the most optimal data analytics tool for startups (Dissertation). Retrieved from https://urn.kb.se/resolve?urn=urn:nbn:se:kth:diva-320116

Hargreaves, A., & Fullan, M. (2012). *Professional Capital: Transforming Teaching in Every School*. Teachers College Press.

Harini, E., Islamia, A. N., Kusumaningrum, B., & Kuncoro, K. S. (2023). Effectiveness of e-worksheets on problem-solving skills: A study of students' self-directed learning in the topic of ratios. *International Journal of Mathematics and Mathematics Education*, *1*(2), 150–162. DOI: 10.56855/ijmme.v1i02.333

Harlen, W. (2007a). *Assessment of Learning*. Sage Publications. DOI: 10.4135/9781446214695

Harlen, W. (2007b). *The Quality of Learning: Assessment Alternatives for Primary Education*. Routledge.

Harris, A., & Jones, M. (2018). Why leadership matters: The role of leaders in engaging and supporting student learning. *Asia Pacific Journal of Education*, *38*(2), 194–206.

Hart Research Associates. (2018). *Fulfilling the American dream: Liberal education and the future of work*. Association of American Colleges and Universities. https://www.aacu.org/research/2018-employer-research

Harvard Business School. (2025). *Harvard Business School Online*. https://online.hbs.edu/

Harvard Business School. (2025a). *Executive education*. https://www.exed.hbs.edu/

Hattie, J. (2009). *Visible Learning: A Synthesis of Over 800 Meta-Analyses Relating to Achievement*. Routledge.

Haynes, D., Ahmadkhani, M., & Numainville, J. (2024). The next generation of dashboards: A spatial online analytical processing (SOLAP) platform for COVID-19. *Journal of Maps*, *20*(1), 2276763. DOI: 10.1080/17445647.2023.2276763

Haynes, M., Groen, J., Sturzinger, E., Zhu, D., Shafer, J., & McGee, T. (2019, September). Integrating data science into a general education information technology course: An approach to developing data savvy undergraduates. In *Proceedings of the 20th Annual SIG Conference on Information Technology Education* (pp. 183-188). DOI: 10.1145/3349266.3351417

Hazrat, M. A., Hassan, N. M. S., Chowdhury, A. A., Rasul, M. G., & Taylor, B. A. (2023). Developing a skilled workforce for future industry demand: The potential of digital twin-based teaching and learning practices in engineering education. *Sustainability (Basel)*, *15*(23), 16433. DOI: 10.3390/su152316433

Henseler, J., Ringle, C. M., & Sarstedt, M. (2015). A new criterion for assessing discriminant validity in variance-based structural equation modeling. *Journal of the Academy of Marketing Science*, *43*(1), 115–135. DOI: 10.1007/s11747-014-0403-8

Hermita, N., Alim, J. A., Putra, Z. H., Mahartika, I., & Sulistiyo, U. (2024). Hybrid learning, blended learning or face-to-face learning: Which one is more effective in remediating misconception? *Quality Assurance in Education*, *32*(1), 64–78. DOI: 10.1108/QAE-02-2023-0019

Herreid, C. F., & Schiller, N. A. (2013). Case studies and the flipped classroom. *Journal of College Science Teaching*, *42*(5), 62–67. https://eric.ed.gov/?id=EJ1011743

Hew, K. F., Jia, C., Gonda, D. E., & Bai, S. (2020). Transitioning to the "new normal" of learning in unpredictable times: Pedagogical practices and learning performance in fully online flipped classrooms. *International Journal of Educational Technology in Higher Education*, *17*(1), 57. DOI: 10.1186/s41239-020-00234-x PMID: 34778516

Hmedna, B., Bakki, A., Mezouary, A. E., & Baz, O. (2023). Unlocking teachers' potential: MOOCLS, a visualization tool for enhancing MOOC teaching. *Smart Learning Environments*, *10*(1), 58. DOI: 10.1186/s40561-023-00277-3

Hoang, N. H., Nguyen, T. T. H., Pham, T. P. H., Ngo, T. P., & Nguyen, T. T. (2023). The development of curricular and training programs in Vietnam. *Problems of Education in the 21st Century, 81*(1), 90-116.

Hochuli, K., & Jud, J. (2024). No Place for Remote Students? Navigating Transitions of Hybrid Co-Presence in Seminar Rooms and Lecture Halls. In Navigating Transitions of Hybrid Co-Presence in Seminar Rooms and Lecture Halls. DOI: 10.2139/ssrn.4733524

Hodges, C., Moore, S., Lockee, B., Trust, T., & Bond, A. (2020). The difference between emergency remote teaching and online learning. *EDUCAUSE Review, 27*(1), 1–9.

Holmes, W., Bialik, M., & Fadel, C. (2019). Artificial intelligence in education: Promises and implications for teaching and learning. Center for Curriculum Redesign. https://curriculumredesign.org/wp-content/uploads/AI-in-Education.pdf

Holmes, W., Persson, J., Chounta, I.-A., Wasson, B., & Dimitrova, V. (with Europarat). (2022). Artificial intelligence and education: a critical view through the lens of human rights, democracy and the rule of law. Council of Europe.

Holmes, W., Bialik, M., & Fadel, C. (2021). *Artificial Intelligence in Education: Promises and Implications for Teaching and Learning*. Center for Curriculum Redesign.

Ho, T. T. N., Sivapalan, S., & Nguyen, T. M. L. (2020). Implementing an outcome-based education framework: Case studies of FPT Education. *ICMET '20: Proceedings of the 2020 2nd International Conference on Modern Educational Technology*, 15-20.

Hrastinski, S. (2008). Asynchronous and synchronous e-learning. *EDUCAUSE Quarterly, 31*(4), 51–55. https://er.educause.edu/articles/2008/11/asynchronous-and-synchronous-elearning

Hrastinski, S. (2009). A theory of online learning as online participation. *Computers & Education, 52*(1), 78–82. DOI: 10.1016/j.compedu.2008.06.009

Hsu, C. Y., & Wu, T. T. (2023). Application of business simulation games in flipped classrooms to facilitate student engagement and higher-order thinking skills for sustainable learning practices. *Sustainability (Basel), 15*(24), 16867. DOI: 10.3390/su152416867

Huang, R. H., Liu, D. J., Tlili, A., Yang, J., Wang, H., & Zhang, M. (2020). Handbook on facilitating flexible learning during educational disruption: The Chinese experience in maintaining undisrupted learning in COVID-19 outbreak. *Beijing: Smart Learning Institute of Beijing Normal University, 46*.

Hultquist, B. L. (2024). Using Lecture in Active Classrooms. Innovative Teaching Strategies in Nursing and Related Health Professions, 115.

Hu, Q., & Pan, Z. (2023). Can AI benefit individual resilience? The mediation roles of AI routinization and infusion. *Journal of Retailing and Consumer Services, 73*, 103339. Advance online publication. DOI: 10.1016/j.jretconser.2023.103339

Ibrahim, M. M., & Nat, M. (2019). Blended learning motivation model for instructors in higher education institutions. *International Journal of Educational Technology in Higher Education*, *16*(1), 12. DOI: 10.1186/s41239-019-0145-2

IEEE. (2023). IEEE code of ethics. Institute of Electrical and Electronics Engineers. https://www.ieee.org/about/corporate/governance/p7-8.html

Ifenthaler, D., & Yau, J. Y. K. (2020). Utilizing learning analytics to support study success in higher education: A systematic review. *Educational Technology Research and Development*, *68*(4), 1961–1990. DOI: 10.1007/s11423-020-09788-z

Imran, M. K., Iqbal, S. M. J., Aslam, U., & Fatima, T. (2019). Does social media promote knowledge exchange? A qualitative insight. *Management Decision*, *57*(3), 688–702. DOI: 10.1108/MD-05-2017-0477

Indian Institute of Management Bangalore. (2025). *IIMBx*. https://iimbx.iimb.ac.in/

Ishaq, K., Mat Zin, N. A., Rosdi, F., Abid, A., & Ijaz, M. (2020). The Impact of ICT on Students' Academic Performance in Public Private Sector Universities of Pakistan. *International Journal of Innovative Technology and Exploring Engineering*, *9*(3), 1117–1121. DOI: 10.35940/ijitee.C8093.019320

Islam, M. R. (2021). *Customer Behavior Analytics and Visualization*. University of Technology Sydney., http://hdl.handle.net/10453/162385

Ismail, F. A., Bungsu, J., & Shahrill, M. (2023). Improving students' participation and performance in building quantities through think-pair-share cooperative learning. *Indonesian Journal of Educational Research and Technology*, *3*(3), 203–216. DOI: 10.17509/ijert.v3i3.50348

Januszyk, R., Miller, E. C., & Lee, O. (2016). Addressing student diversity and equity. *Science and Children*, *53*(8), 28–31. DOI: 10.2505/4/sc16_053_08_28

Jarke, J., & Macgilchrist, F. (2021). Dashboard stories: How narratives told by predictive analytics reconfigure roles, risk and sociality in education. *Big Data & Society*, *8*(1), 20539517211025561. Advance online publication. DOI: 10.1177/20539517211025561

Jayanti, K. (Deemed to be University). (2025). *KJLMS*. https://www.kristujaya ntiexamlms.com/login/index.php

Jensen, K. (2024). *The Ethics of Entrepreneurship Education*. MIT Press. DOI: 10.7551/mitpress/15073.001.0001

Johnson, D. W., & Johnson, R.T. (2018). Cooperative learning: The foundation for active learning. DOI: 10.5772/intechopen.81086

Johnson, D. W., & Johnson, R. T. (1989). *Cooperation and competition: Theory and research*. Interaction Book Company.

Johnson, D. W., & Johnson, R. T. (2009). An educational psychology success story: Social interdependence theory and cooperative learning. *Educational Researcher, 38*(5), 365–379. DOI: 10.3102/0013189X09339057

Johnson, D. W., & Johnson, R. T. (2018). The impact of cooperative learning on achievement and engagement. In Slavin, R. E. (Ed.), *Cooperative learning: Theory, research, and practice* (pp. 23–37). Allyn and Bacon.

Johnson, D. W., Johnson, R. T., & Smith, K. A. (2007). The state of cooperative learning in postsecondary postsecondary and professional settings. *Educational Psychology Review*, *19*(1), 15–29. DOI: 10.1007/s10648-006-9038-8

Johnson, D., & Johnson, R. (2017). The use of cooperative procedures in teacher education and professional development. *Journal of Education for Teaching*, *43*(3), 284–295. DOI: 10.1080/02607476.2017.1328023

Jokhan, A., Sharma, B., & Singh, S. (2018). Early warning system as a predictor for student performance in higher education blended courses. *Studies in Higher Education*, *44*(11), 1900–1911. DOI: 10.1080/03075079.2018.1466872

Juniar, D. T., Suherman, A., Tarigan, B., & Mahendra, A. (2023). Effects of project-based learning model and cooperative learning model in improving student social skills in physical education. *Jurnal Pendidikan Jasmani dan Olahraga, 8*(1), 49-57.

Kahn, J., & Patil, S. (2025, April 18). Impacts of experiential learning on Gen Z early career experience. *National Association of Colleges and Employers (NACE)*. https://www.naceweb.org/talent-acquisition/trends-and-predictions/impacts-of-experiential-learning-on-the-gen-z-early-career-experience?utm_source=chatgpt.com

Kahu, E. R. (2013). Framing student engagement in higher education. *Studies in Higher Education*, *38*(5), 758–773. DOI: 10.1080/03075079.2011.598505

Kalenskyi, A., Gerliand, T., Kravets, S., Homeniuk, D., & Nagayev, V. (2023). Dual educational system of professional training of future skilled workers. In Ivanov, V., Trojanowska, J., Pavlenko, I., Rauch, E., & Piteľ, J. (Eds.), *Advances in Design, Simulation and Manufacturing VI. DSMIE 2023. Lecture Notes in Mechanical Engineering* (pp. 369–378). Springer Nature. DOI: 10.1007/978-3-031-32767-4_35

Kanellopoulou, C., & Giannakoulopoulos, A. (2020). Engage and conquer: An online empirical approach into whether intrinsic or extrinsic motivation leads to more enhanced students' engagement. *Creative Education*, *11*(02), 143–165. DOI: 10.4236/ce.2020.112011

Kapp, K. M. (2012). *The Gamification of Learning and Instruction: Game-Based Methods and Strategies for Training and Education*. Pfeiffer.

Katsaris, I., & Vidakis, N. (2021). Adaptive e-learning systems through learning styles: A review of the literature. *Advances in Mobile Learning Educational Research*, *1*(2), 124–145. DOI: 10.25082/AMLER.2021.02.007

Kaufman, D. B., Felder, R. M., & Fuller, H. (2000). Peer ratings in cooperative learning teams: What do they tell us? Proceedings of the 2000 Annual ASEE Meeting, St. Louis, MO. https://www.researchgate.net/publication/2450650_Peer_Ratings_in_Cooperative_Learning_Teams

Kayyali, M. (2025). E-Learning Platforms and Their Influence on Lifelong Learning. In Impact of Digitalization on Education and Social Sustainability (pp. 155-176). IGI Global.

Kayyali, M. (2026). Online and Blended Learning in Doctoral Studies: Opportunities and Challenges. Improving Doctoral Education and Research Development for Sustainability, 103-138.

Kayyali, M. (2022). The Importance of Faculty Development in Higher Education. *International Journal of Higher Education Policies and Leadership*, *1*(1), 1–9.

Kayyali, M. (2024). Quality Assurance in Online and Blended Learning Environments. In *Quality Assurance and Accreditation in Higher Education: Issues, Models, and Best Practices* (pp. 227–292). Springer Nature Switzerland. DOI: 10.1007/978-3-031-66623-0_5

Kelley, T., & Kelley, D. (2013). *Creative confidence: Unleashing the creative potential within us all*. Crown Business.

Kelly, A. V. (2009). *The Curriculum: Theory and Practice* (6th ed.). SAGE Publications.

Keržič, D., Tomaževič, N., Aristovnik, A., & Umek, L. (2019). Exploring critical factors of the perceived usefulness of blended learning for higher education students. *PLoS One*, *14*(11), e0223767. DOI: 10.1371/journal.pone.0223767 PMID: 31751345

Kesse, M. (2023). The Efficacy of an Interactive Business Simulation Game Compared to Static Games to Teach Strategic Decisions in Entrepreneurship and Economics Education (Doctoral dissertation, University of Georgia).

Khalid, M. S.. (2020). Measuring self-directed learning skills: Development and validation of the SDL instrument. *Education + Training*, *62*(2), 1–15.

Khalid, M., Bashir, S., & Amin, H. (2020). Relationship between self-directed learning (SDL) and academic achievement of university students: A case of online distance learning and traditional universities. *Bulletin of Education and Research, 42*(2), 131–148. https://files.eric.ed.gov/fulltext/EJ1281053.pdf

Khare, K., Lam, H., & Khare, A. (2018). Educational data mining (EDM): Researching impact on online business education. On the line: Business education in the digital age, 37-53. DOI: 10.1007/978-3-319-62776-2_3

Kim, C., Quesenberry, K., Sutherland, K., & Freberg, K. (2021b). Digital learning: Standards and best practices for public relations education in undergraduate programs. *Journal of Public Relations Education*, *7*(2), 77–105.

Kim, J. M., & Park, J. H. (2024). When is digital transformation beneficial for coupled open innovation? The contingent role of the adoption of industry 4.0 technologies. *Technovation*, *136*, 103087. DOI: 10.1016/j.technovation.2024.103087

Kim, Y., Meganck, S., Kristiansen, L., & Woo, C. W. (2021a). Taking experiential learning to the next level with student-run agencies. *Journal of Public Relations Education*, *7*(1), 80–121.

Knight, G. A., & Cavusgil, S. T. (2015). The born global firm: Evolution of a research paradigm. *Journal of Business Research*, *69*(6), 1482–1492. DOI: 10.1016/j.jbusres.2015.10.013

Knowles, M. S. (1975). *Self-directed learning: A guide for learners and teachers.* Association Press.

Kocdar, S., Karadeniz, A., Bozkurt, A., & Buyuk, K. (2018). Measuring self-regulation in self-paced open and distance learning environments. *International Review of Research in Open and Distance Learning*, *19*(1). Advance online publication. DOI: 10.19173/irrodl.v19i1.3255

Koehler, M. J., & Mishra, P. (2009a). What Is Technological Pedagogical Content Knowledge (TPACK)? *Contemporary Issues in Technology & Teacher Education*, *9*(1), 60–70.

Koehler, M., & Mishra, P. (2009b). What is technological pedagogical content knowledge (TPACK)? *Contemporary Issues in Technology & Teacher Education*, *9*(1), 60–70.

Koivisto, J., & Hamari, J. (2019). The rise of motivational information systems: A review of gamification research. *International Journal of Information Management*, *45*, 191–210. DOI: 10.1016/j.ijinfomgt.2018.10.013

Kolb, D. A. (1984). Experiential learning: Experience as the source of learning and development. *Prentice-Hall.* https://www.learningfromexperience.com/images/uploads/process-of-experiential-learning.pdf

Kolb, D. A. (1984). Experiential learning: Experience as the source of learning and development. Prentice-Hall. https://www.researchgate.net/publication/235701029_Experiential_Learning_Experience_As_The_Source_Of_Learning_And_Development

Kolb, A. Y., & Kolb, D. A. (2005). Learning styles and learning spaces: Enhancing experiential learning in higher education. *Academy of Management Learning & Education*, *4*(2), 193–212. DOI: 10.5465/amle.2005.17268566

Kolb, D. A. (2015). *Experiential learning: Experience as the source of learning and development* (2nd ed.). Pearson Education.

Kryukov, V., & Gorin, A. (2017). Digital technologies as education innovation at universities. *Australian Educational Computing*, *32*(1), 1–16.

Kuh, G. D. (2009). What Student Engagement Data Tell Us About College Readiness. *Peer Review : Emerging Trends and Key Debates in Undergraduate Education*, *11*(1), 4–8.

Kuleto, V., Ilić, M., Dumangiu, M., Ranković, M., Martins, O. M. D., Păun, D., & Mihoreanu, L. (2021). Exploring Opportunities and Challenges of Artificial Intelligence and Machine Learning in Higher Education Institutions. *Sustainability (Basel)*, *13*(18), 10424. DOI: 10.3390/su131810424

Kumar, R., & Sharma, A. (2021). Adaptive Learning Systems: A Review and Future Directions. *Journal of Educational Technology & Society*, *24*(1), 1–15.

Kumar, V., & Nanda, P. (2019). Social media in higher education: A framework for continuous engagement. [IJICTE]. *International Journal of Information and Communication Technology Education*, *15*(1), 97–108. DOI: 10.4018/IJICTE.2019010107

Laal, M., & Ghodsi, S. M. (2012). Benefits of collaborative learning. *Procedia: Social and Behavioral Sciences*, *31*, 486–490. DOI: 10.1016/j.sbspro.2011.12.091

Laubscher, D. J., & Bosch, C. (2025). Promoting Student Engagement and Self-Directed Learning in a Blended Learning Environment Using Cooperative Learning. In *Case Studies on Blended Learning in Higher Education: Design, Development, and Delivery* (pp. 157–174). Springer Nature Singapore. DOI: 10.1007/978-981-96-0722-8_9

Laurillard, D. (2016). *Teaching as a design science: Building pedagogical patterns for learning and technology*. Routledge.

Leal Filho, W., Lange Salvia, A., Beynaghi, A., Fritzen, B., Ulisses, A., Avila, L. V., Shulla, K., Vasconcelos, C. R., Moggi, S., Mifsud, M., Anholon, R., Rampasso, I. S., Kozlova, V., Iliško, D., Skouloudis, A., & Nikolaou, I. (2024). Digital transformation and sustainable development in higher education in a post-pandemic world. *International Journal of Sustainable Development and World Ecology*, *31*(1), 108–123. DOI: 10.1080/13504509.2023.2237933

Leask, B. (2015). *Internationalizing the curriculum*. Routledge. DOI: 10.4324/9781315716954

Lee, A., & Beattie, S. (2022). Designing AI-integrated learning environments to enhance employability in business education. *International Journal of Management Education*, *20*(1), 100603. DOI: 10.1016/j.ijme.2021.100603

Leopold, T. (2025, January 8). Future of jobs report 2025. *World Economic Forum*. https://www.weforum.org/stories/2025/01/future-of-jobs-report-2025-jobs-of-the-future-and-the-skills-you-need-to-get-them/

Liao, F., Zhang, Q., & Yang, J. (2022). Recognizing opportunities when engaged in intrapreneurship: The role of creative self-efficacy and support for innovation. *Frontiers in Psychology*, *13*, 937. Advance online publication. DOI: 10.3389/fpsyg.2022.937971

Librenjak, S., Kocijan, K., & Janjic, M. (2016). Improving Students' Language Performance Through Consistent Use of E-Learning: An Empirical Study in Japanese, Korean, Hindi and Sanskrit. *Acta Linguistica Asiatica*, *6*(2), 79–94. DOI: 10.4312/ala.6.2.79-94

Li, J., Luo, H., Zhao, L., Zhu, M., Ma, L., & Liao, X. (2022). Promoting STEAM education in primary school through cooperative teaching: A design-based research study. *Sustainability (Basel)*, *14*(16), 10333. DOI: 10.3390/su141610333

Limayem, M., Hirt, S. G., & Cheung, C. M. K. (2007). How habit limits the predictive power of intention: The case of information systems continuance. *Management Information Systems Quarterly*, *31*(4), 705–737. DOI: 10.2307/25148817

Lin, S. R. (2021). Understanding university-industry collaboration on project-based learning in business education.

Lindeman, B. M., & Lipsett, P. A. (2016). Evaluation and feedback. In *Curriculum development for medical education* (pp. 121–167). Radcliffe Publishing.

Li, T., Greenberg, B. A., & Nicholls, J. A. F. (2007). Teaching experiential learning: Adoption of an innovative course in an MBA marketing curriculum. *Journal of Marketing Education*, *29*(1), 25–33. DOI: 10.1177/0273475306297380

Liu, Q., Geertshuis, S., & Grainger, R. (2020). Understanding academics' adoption of learning technologies: A systematic review. *Computers & Education*, *151*, 103857. DOI: 10.1016/j.compedu.2020.103857

Li, X., Zhang, Y., & Wang, Q. (2024). The relationship between learning outcomes and graduate competence: An outcome-based education perspective. *Sustainability*, *16*(14), 6080. DOI: 10.3390/su16146080

Loh, R. C. Y., & Ang, C. S. (2020). Unravelling cooperative learning in higher education: A review of research. *Research in Social Sciences and Technology*, *5*(2), e2395–e6518. DOI: 10.46303/ressat.05.02.2

Lowes, D. (2024). The effect of cooperative self-directed blended learning on intrinsic motivation in a Technical Vocational Education and Training college. [Unpublished doctoral dissertation]. North-West University.

Low, M. P., Cham, T. H., Chang, Y. S., & Lim, X. J. (2021). Advancing on weighted PLS-SEM in examining the trust-based recommendation system in pioneering product promotion effectiveness. *Quality & Quantity*, •••, 1–30. DOI: 10.1007/s11135-021-01147-1 PMID: 33879929

Luckin, R. (2018). *Machine learning and human intelligence: The future of education for the 21st century*. UCL Institute of Education Press.

Luckin, R., Holmes, W., Griffiths, M., & Forcier, L. B. (2016). *Intelligence Unleashed: An Argument for AI in Education*. Pearson.

Luttrell, R., Wallace, A., McCollough, C., & Lee, J. (2021). Public relations curriculum: A systematic examination of curricular offerings in social media, digital media, and analytics in accredited programs. *Journal of Public Relations Education*, *7*(2), 1–43.

Lyman, F. T., Tredway, L., & Purser, M. (2023). Think-pair-share and Thinktrix: Standard bearers of student dialogue. In R. M. Gillies, M. Millis, & N. Davidson (Eds.), *Contemporary Global Perspectives on Cooperative Learning: Applications across educational contexts* (pp. 124-143). Routledge.

Lyman, F. T. (1985). *Think-Pair-Share (Mimeograph)*. University of Maryland.

Macayan, J. (2017). Implementing outcome-based education (OBE) framework: Implications for assessment of students' performance. *Educational Measurement and Evaluation Review*, *8*(1), 1–10.

Magagula, M. M., & Awodiji, O. A. (2024). The implications of the fourth industrial revolution on technical and vocational education and training in South Africa. *Social Sciences & Humanities Open*, *10*(100896), 1–11. DOI: 10.1016/j.ssaho.2024.100896

Magni, M., Susan Taylor, M., & Venkatesh, V. (2010). "To play or not to play": A cross-temporal investigation using hedonic and instrumental perspectives to explain user intentions to explore a technology. *International Journal of Human-Computer Studies*, *68*(9), 572–588. DOI: 10.1016/j.ijhcs.2010.03.004

Magut, C. K., & Kihara, A. (2019). Influence of student retention strategies on performance of TVETs in Nairobi County, Kenya. *Journal of Business and Strategic Management*, *4*(1), 1–24. DOI: 10.47941/jbsm.279

Marsh, J. A., Pane, J. F., & Hamilton, L. S. (2006). *Making Sense of Data-Driven Decision Making in Education: Evidence from Recent Research*. RAND Corporation.

Martinez, L. S. (2022). Behavioral Analytics. In Schintler, L. A., & McNeely, C. L. (Eds.), *Encyclopedia of Big Data*. Springer., DOI: 10.1007/978-3-319-32010-6_18

Maruping, L. M., & Magni, M. (2015). Motivating Employees to Explore Collaboration Technology in Team Contexts. *Management Information Systems Quarterly*, *39*(1), 1–16. https://www.jstor.org/stable/26628338. DOI: 10.25300/MISQ/2015/39.1.01

Mastrogiacomi, F. (2021, November). A hybrid teaching and learning toolkit for a creative and curious mindset. In Innovate Learning Summit (pp. 263-271). Association for the Advancement of Computing in Education (AACE).

Matongo, M., & Goronga, P. (2025). Embracing collaborative learning: Innovative teaching methods at tertiary level. In Burris-Melville, T. S., & Burris, S. T. (Eds.), *Developing effective and high-performing teams in higher education* (pp. 187–216). IGI Global., DOI: 10.4018/979-8-3693-3852-0.ch007

Mauleon-Palay, M. M., Villena, A. C. D., & Caiga, B. T. (2022). Assessment of OBE implementation and the level of attainment of students outcomes of the communication programs: AY 2017-2018. *Asia Pacific Journal of Academic Research in Social Studies*, *7*(2), 49–58.

Mayisela, T., & Govender, S. (2024). *Open learning as a means of advancing social justice: Cases in post-school education and training in South Africa*. African Books Collective.

Mazur, E. (1997). *Peer instruction: A user's manual*. Prentice Hall., https://www.pearson.com/en-us/subject-catalog/p/Mazur-Peer-Instruction-A-User-s-Manual/P200000006892?view=educator

Means, B., Toyama, Y., Murphy, R., Bakia, M., & Jones, K. (2013). The effectiveness of online and blended learning: A meta-analysis of the empirical literature. *Teachers College Record*. https://eric.ed.gov/?id=EJ1018090

Means, B., Toyama, Y., Murphy, R., Bakia, M., & Jones, K. (2014). *The effectiveness of online and blended learning: A meta-analysis of the empirical literature*. U.S. Department of Education. https://tech.ed.gov/files/2013/10/impacts-of-online-learning.pdf

Meeks, G. A. (2017). Critical soft skills to achieve success in the workplace (Doctoral dissertation, Walden University).

Mentz, E., & Van Zyl, S. (2018). The impact of cooperative learning on self-directed learning abilities in the computer applications technology class. *International Journal of Lifelong Education*, *37*(4), 482–494. DOI: 10.1080/02601370.2018.1513426

Meyer, A., Rose, D. H., & Gordon, D. (2014). *Universal Design for Learning: Theory and Practice*. CAST Professional Publishing.

Michaelsen, L. K., & Sweet, M. (2008). The essential elements of team-based learning. *New Directions for Teaching and Learning*, *2008*(116), 7–27. DOI: 10.1002/tl.330

Mikic-Fonte, F., Haynes, C. C., Caeiro-Rodríguez, M., & Nistor, N. (2019). Systematic literature review of predictive analysis tools in higher education. *Applied Sciences (Basel, Switzerland)*, *9*(24), 5569. DOI: 10.3390/app9245569

Mnasri, S., & Papakonstantinidis, S. (2023). The teaching-learning dynamic from behaviourism to social constructionism: A communication-centred narrative. *International Journal of Learning and Change*, *15*(3), 312–327. DOI: 10.1504/IJLC.2023.130629

Moore, M. G. (Ed.). (2013). *Handbook of distance education* (3rd ed.). Routledge., DOI: 10.4324/9780203803738

Moore, S., & Kuol, N. (2005). Students evaluating teachers: Exploring the importance of faculty reaction to feedback on teaching. *Teaching in Higher Education*, *10*(1), 57–73. DOI: 10.1080/1356251052000305534

Morcke, A., Dornan, T., & Eika, B. (2014). Outcome-based education in undergraduate medical education. *Proceedings of the International Consortium for Educational Development 2014*.

Muhria, L., Supriatna, N., & Nurfirdaus, N. (2023). Students' challenges of blended learning model in higher education. *Journal Corner of Education, Linguistics, and Literature*, *2*(3), 223–233. DOI: 10.54012/jcell.v2i3.123

Mulenga, R., & Shilongo, H. (2025). Hybrid and blended learning models: Innovations, challenges, and future directions in education. *Acta Pedagogia Asiana*, *4*(1), 1–13. DOI: 10.53623/apga.v4i1.495

Mutimukwe, C., Kolkowska, E., & Grönlund, Å. (2022). Students' privacy concerns in learning analytics: Model development. *British Journal of Educational Technology*, *53*(4), 924–944. DOI: 10.1111/bjet.13234

Mwale, B. J., & Ntsobi, M. (2023). Trends in access and success at Gert Sibande Technical and Vocational Education and Training (TVET) College. *Journal of Education and Practice*, *14*(19), 34–55. DOI: 10.7176/JEP/14-19-05

Nafis, S. A. B. M., & Nasri, N. B. M. (2024). The effectiveness of cooperative learning towards low-achieving students in class: A concept paper. *International Journal of Academic Research in Progressive Education and Development*, *13*(1).

Nah, F. F.-H., Zeng, Q., Telaprolu, V. R., Ayyappa, A. P., & Eschenbrenner, B. (2014). Gamification of Education: A Review of Literature. *Proceedings of the International Conference on HCI in Business*, 401–409. DOI: 10.1007/978-3-319-07293-7_39

Naik, G., Chitre, C., Bhalla, M., & Rajan, J. (2020). Impact of use of technology on student learning outcomes: Evidence from a large-scale experiment in India. *World Development*, *127*, 104736. DOI: 10.1016/j.worlddev.2019.104736

Namyssova, G., Tussupbekova, G., Helmer, J., Malone, K., Mir, A., & Jonbekova, D. (2019). Challenges and benefits of blended learning in higher education. *International Journal of Technology in Education*, *2*(1), 22–31. http://nur.nu.edu.kz/handle/123456789/4494

National Association of Colleges and Employers. (2023). Job Outlook 2023. https://www.naceweb.org

Navarro-Martinez, O., & Peña-Acuña, B. (2022). Technology Usage and Academic Performance in the PISA 2018 Report. *Journal of New Approaches in Educational Research*, *11*(1), 130–145. https://eric.ed.gov/?id=EJ1325570. DOI: 10.7821/naer.2022.1.735

Nayak, J. K. (2018). Relationship among smartphone usage, addiction, academic performance and the moderating role of gender: A study of higher education students in India. *Computers & Education*, *123*, 164–173. DOI: 10.1016/j.compedu.2018.05.007

Nguyen, H. T., Sivapalan, S., & Linh, N. T. (2020, May). Implementing an outcome-based education framework: Case studies of FPT Education. *Proceedings of the 2020 2nd International Conference on Modern Educational Technology*. DOI: 10.1145/3401861.3401863

Nhlongo, A. H. (2020). *University lecturers' perspectives of Moodle usage in teaching postgraduate modules: a case study of the School of Education* (Doctoral dissertation). https://researchspace.ukzn.ac.za/items/e9092741-b45e-4ac5-8b1f-137ef0d6f866

Niemiec, C. P., & Ryan, R. M. (2009). Autonomy, competence, and relatedness in the classroom: Applying self-determination theory to educational practice. *Theory and Research in Education*, *7*(2), 133–144. DOI: 10.1177/1477878509104318

Niess, M. L. (2011). Investigating TPACK: Knowledge growth in teaching with technology. *Journal of Educational Computing Research*, *44*(3), 299–317. DOI: 10.2190/EC.44.3.c

Nkhoma, M., Calbeto, J., Sriratanaviriyakul, N., Muang, T., Ha Tran, Q., & Kim Cao, T. (2014). Towards an understanding of real-time continuous feedback from simulation games. *Interactive Technology and Smart Education*, *11*(1), 45–62. DOI: 10.1108/ITSE-03-2013-0005

Oakley, B., Felder, R. M., Brent, R., & Elhajj, I. (2004). Turning student groups into effective teams. *Journal of Student-Centered Learning*, *2*(1), 9–34.

OECD. (2020). *Education responses to COVID-19: Embracing digital learning and online collaboration*. OECD Publishing.

OECD. (2020). *SME and entrepreneurship outlook 2020*. OECD Publishing., DOI: 10.1787/34907e9c-

OECD. (2021). *Local employment and economic development*. Organisation for Economic Co-operation and Development. https://www.oecd.org/en/topics/local-employment-and-economic-development.html

Olelewe, C. J., Agomuo, E. E., & Obichukwu, P. U. (2019). Effects of B-Learning and F2F on College Students' Engagement and Retention in QBASIC Programming. *Education and Information Technologies*, *24*(5), 2701–2726. DOI: 10.1007/s10639-019-09882-7

Ouyang, F., Wu, M., Zheng, L., Xu, W., & Chen, J. (2023). Integration of artificial intelligence performance prediction and learning analytics to improve student learning in online engineering course. *International Journal of Educational Technology in Higher Education*, *20*(1), 4. DOI: 10.1186/s41239-022-00372-4

Ouyang, F., Zheng, L., & Jiao, P. (2022). Artificial Intelligence in Online Higher education: A Systematic Review of Empirical Research from 2011 to 2020. *Education and Information Technologies*, *27*(6), 7893–7925. DOI: 10.1007/s10639-022-10925-9

Pacho, T. O. (2022). Transforming higher education in Africa through university-industry collaboration. *Proceedings of the 20th International Conference on Private Higher Education in Africa*, 57-71.

Pan, Z., Lu, Y., Wang, B., & Chau, P. Y. K. (2017). Who Do You Think You Are? Common and Differential Effects of Social Self-Identity on Social Media Usage. *Journal of Management Information Systems*, *34*(1), 71–101. DOI: 10.1080/07421222.2017.1296747

Pardo-Cueva, M., Chamba-Rueda, L. M., Rios-Zaruma, J., & Gómez, A. H. (2019, June). Information and communication technologies and their relationship with academic performance in higher education. In *2019 14th Iberian Conference on Information Systems and Technologies (CISTI)* (pp. 1-6). IEEE. DOI: 10.23919/CISTI.2019.8760718

Paris, D., & Alim, H. S. (2017). *Culturally sustaining pedagogies: Teaching and learning for justice in a changing world.* Teachers College Press.

Paul, P., & Mukhopadhyay, K. (2005). Experiential learning in international business education. *Journal of Teaching in International Business*, *16*(2), 7–25. DOI: 10.1300/J066v16n02_02

Peterson, L., & Nguyen, T. (2024). *Institutional constraints and pedagogical innovation in business schools: A multi-campus study of barriers to experiential learning.*

Piaget, J. (1952). *The origins of intelligence in children.* W. W. Norton & Company., DOI: 10.1037/11494-000

Piaget, J. (1954). *The construction of reality in the child.* Basic Books. DOI: 10.1037/11168-000

Picciano, A. G. (2021). Theories and frameworks for online education. *A guide to administering distance learning, 21*(3), 166-190.Rasheed, R. A., Kamsin, A., & Abdullah, N. A. (2020). Challenges in the online component of blended learning: A systematic review. *Computers & Education, 144*, 103701.

Pinar, W. F. (2012). *What Is Curriculum Theory?* (2nd ed.). Routledge.

Polly, D., & Brantley-Dias, L. (2009). TPACK: Where do we go now? *TechTrends*, *53*(5).

Polymeropoulou, P., Potsis, K., & Kameas, A. (2024). A MODEL FOR ASSESSING THE EFFECTIVE INTEGRATION OF TECHNOLOGY INTO EDUCATIONAL PRACTICE FROM A PEDAGOGICAL PERSPECTIVE. In INTED2024 Proceedings (pp. 3651-3658). IATED.

Porter, M. E. (2012). *The role of business in social and economic development: Creating shared value.* Harvard Business School. https://www.hbs.edu/ris/download.aspx?name=20120802+-+Michael+E.+Porter+-+World+Bank+CSV+Presentation+-+For+Distribution.pdf

Porter, L., Bailey Lee, C., Simon, B., & Zingaro, D. (2011). Peer instruction: Do students really learn from peer discussion in computing? *Proceedings of the Seventh International Workshop on Computing Education Research,* 45–52. DOI: 10.1145/2016911.2016923

Porter, W. W., Graham, C. R., Spring, K. A., & Welch, K. R. (2014). Blended learning in higher education: Institutional adoption and implementation. *Computers & Education, 75,* 185–195. DOI: 10.1016/j.compedu.2014.02.011

Prensky, M. (2010). *Teaching Digital Natives: Partnering for Real Learning.* Corwin Press.

Preuss, H. (2004). *The economics of staging the Olympics: A comparison of the Games 1972-2008.* Edward Elgar Publishing. DOI: 10.4337/9781781008690

Prince, M. (2004). Does Active Learning Work? A Review of the Research. *Journal of Engineering Education, 93*(3), 223–231. DOI: 10.1002/j.2168-9830.2004.tb00809.x

Puente-Díaz, R., & Cavazos-Arroyo, J. (2022). Creative self-efficacy and metacognitive feelings as sources of information when generating, evaluating, and selecting creative ideas: A metacognitive perspective. *The Journal of Creative Behavior, 56*(4), 647–658. DOI: 10.1002/jocb.557

Puentedura, R. R. (2013). *SAMR and TPCK: Intro to advanced practice.*

Qawasmeh, E. F., Alnafisi, S. Y., Almajali, R., Alromaih, B. S., & Helali, M. M., & Ismail al-lawama, H. (2024). The impact of human resources management practices on employee performance: A comparative study between Jordanian and Saudi Arabian Universities. *Migration Letters : An International Journal of Migration Studies, 21*(2), 243–257.

Raes, A., Detienne, L., Windey, I., & Depaepe, F. (2020). A systematic literature review on synchronous hybrid learning: Gaps identified. *Learning Environments Research, 23*(3), 269–290. DOI: 10.1007/s10984-019-09303-z

Ramaswami, G., Susnjak, T., Mathrani, A., & Umer, R. (2023). Use of predictive analytics within learning analytics dashboards: A review of case studies. Technology. *Knowledge and Learning*, *28*(3), 959–980. DOI: 10.1007/s10758-022-09613-x

Ranjan, S., & Kumar, A. (2020). Artificial Intelligence in Education: A Review of the Current State and Future Directions. *International Journal of Educational Technology in Higher Education*, *17*(1), 1–19.

Rao, S. S. P., Sekhar, S. C., Yadav, T. C. S., Kumar, V. P., & Haran, H. B. M. (2024). Implementing experiential learning strategies for enhanced business education in India: Challenges and opportunities. Journal of Innovations in Educational Research, 4(3). https://jier.org/index.php/journal/article/view/1301

Rashid, T., & Asghar, H. M. (2016). Technology use, self-directed learning, student engagement and academic performance: Examining the interrelations. *Computers in Human Behavior*, *63*, 604–612. DOI: 10.1016/j.chb.2016.05.084

Redecker, C. (2017). *European framework for the digital competence of educators: DigCompEdu*. Publications Office of the European Union.

Reeve, J. (2016). Autonomy-supportive teaching: What it is, how to do it. In Liu, W. C., Wang, J., & Ryan, R. M. (Eds.), *Building autonomous learners* (pp. 129–152). Springer. DOI: 10.1007/978-981-287-630-0_7

Reuter, J., Dias, M. F., & Sousa, M. J. (2022). Collaborative learning: Increasing work motivation through game-based learning. In Bernardes, O., Amorim, V., & Moreira, A. C. (Eds.), *Handbook of research on cross-disciplinary uses of gamification in organizations* (pp. 277–292). IGI Global., DOI: 10.4018/978-1-7998-9223-6.ch013

Ricks, D. A., Toyne, B., & Martinez, Z. (2022). *International business research: Global and local perspectives*. Routledge.

Rietsche, R., Aier, S., & Rivera, M. (2021). How does real-time feedback effect organizational performance does real-time feedback matter? A simulation study to link individual and organizational performance. (November 18, 2021). Fox School of Business Research Paper.

Rizwan, S., Nee, C. K., & Garfan, S. (2025). Identifying the factors affecting student academic performance and engagement prediction in MOOCs using deep learning: A systematic literature review. *IEEE Access : Practical Innovations, Open Solutions*, *13*, 18952–18982. DOI: 10.1109/ACCESS.2025.3533915

Robey, D., Ross, J. W., & Boudreau, M.-C. (2002). Learning to Implement Enterprise Systems: An Exploratory Study of the Dialectics of Change. *Journal of Management Information Systems*, *19*(1), 17–46. https://www.jstor.org/stable/40398565. DOI: 10.1080/07421222.2002.11045713

Royston, R., & Reiter-Palmon, R. (2019). Creative self-efficacy as mediator between creative mindsets and creative problem-solving. *The Journal of Creative Behavior*, *53*(4), 472–481. DOI: 10.1002/jocb.226

Ryan, L. (2023). *Visual Analytics Fundamentals: Creating Compelling Data Narratives with Tableau*. Addison-Wesley Professional.

Ryan, R. M., & Deci, E. L. (2000). Intrinsic and extrinsic motivations: Classic definitions and new directions. *Contemporary Educational Psychology*, *25*(1), 54–67. DOI: 10.1006/ceps.1999.1020 PMID: 10620381

Ryan, R. M., & Deci, E. L. (2017). *Self-Determination Theory: Basic Psychological Needs in Motivation, Development, and Wellness*. Guilford Press., DOI: 10.1521/978.14625/28806

Ryan, R. M., & Deci, E. L. (2020). Intrinsic and extrinsic motivation from a self-determination theory perspective: Definitions, theory, practices, and future directions. *Contemporary Educational Psychology*, *61*, e101860. https://psycnet.apa.org/doi/10.1016/j.cedpsych.2020.101860. DOI: 10.1016/j.cedpsych.2020.101860

Sadler, D. R. (1989). Formative Assessment and the Design of Instructional Systems. *Instructional Science*, *18*(2), 119–144. DOI: 10.1007/BF00117714

Saggar, M., Xie, H., Beaty, R., Stankov, A., Schrier, M., & Reiss, A. (2019). Creativity slumps and bumps: Expanding the neurobehavioral basis of creativity development during middle childhood. *NeuroImage*, *196*, 94–101. DOI: 10.1016/j.neuroimage.2019.03.080

Sailer, M., Hense, J., Mayr, S. K., & Mandl, H. (2017). How Gamification Motivates: An Experimental Study of the Effects of Specific Game Design Elements on Psychological Need Satisfaction. *Computers in Human Behavior*, *69*, 371–380. DOI: 10.1016/j.chb.2016.12.033

Salas, E., Rosen, M. A., Held, J. D., & Weissmuller, J. J. (2009). Performance measurement in simulation-based training: A review and best practices. *Simulation & Gaming*, *40*(3), 328–376. DOI: 10.1177/1046878108326734

Samašonok, K., Išoraitė, M., & Žirnelė, L. (2020). Education of entrepreneurship by participation in a business simulation enterprise activities: Conditions of effectiveness and opportunities for improvement. *Entrepreneurship and Sustainability Issues*, *7*(4), 3122–3144. DOI: 10.9770/jesi.2020.7.4(36)

Sari, I. P., & Susiani, S. (2021). The effects of Jigsaw, Student Teams Achievement Divisions (STAD), and Think-Pair-Share (TPS) techniques in writing narrative text. *Journal of Educational Sciences*, *5*(1), e2581–e2203. DOI: 10.31258/jes.5.1.p.66-79

Schippers, M. C., Morisano, D., Locke, E. A., Scheepers, A. W., Latham, G. P., & De Jong, E. M. (2020). Writing about personal goals and plans regardless of goal type boosts academic performance. *Contemporary Educational Psychology*, *60*, e101823. https://www.sciencedirect.com/science/article/pii/S0361476X1930428X. DOI: 10.1016/j.cedpsych.2019.101823

Schwarz, A., & Chin, W. W. (2007). Looking forward: Toward an understanding of the nature and definition of IT acceptance. *Journal of the Association for Information Systems*, *8*(6), 1–14. DOI: 10.17705/1jais.00123

Scott, C. L., & Ivala, E. N. (2019). Moving from apartheid to a post-apartheid state of being and its Impact on transforming higher education institutions in South Africa. In Scott, C. L., & Ivala, E. N. (Eds.), *Transformation of higher education institutions in post-apartheid South Africa*. Routledge. DOI: 10.4324/9781351014236-1

Selwyn, N. (2020). Should robots replace teachers? AI and the future of education. Polity Press. https://www.wiley.com/en-se/Should+Robots+Replace+Teachers%3F%3A+AI+and+the+Future+of+Education-p-9781509528967

Selwyn, N. (2016). *Education and Technology: Key Issues and Debates*. Bloomsbury Academic.

Selwyn, N. (2022). *Should robots replace teachers? AI and the future of education*. Polity Press.

Sergis, S., Sampson, D. G., & Pelliccione, L. (2018). Investigating the impact of Flipped Classroom on students' learning experiences: A Self-Determination Theory approach. *Computers in Human Behavior*, *78*, 368–378. DOI: 10.1016/j.chb.2017.08.011

Sghir, N., Adadi, A., & Lahmer, M. (2023). Recent advances in predictive learning analytics: A decade systematic review (2012–2022). *Education and Information Technologies*, *28*(7), 8299–8333. DOI: 10.1007/s10639-022-11536-0

Sharma, R., Shrivastava, S. S., & Sharma, A. (2023). Predicting Student Performance Using Educational Data Mining and Learning Analytics Technique. *Journal of Intelligent Systems and Internet of Things, 10*(2), 24–37. DOI: 10.54216/JISIoT.100203

Shepard, L. A. (2000). The Role of Assessment in a Learning Culture. *Educational Researcher, 29*(7), 4–14. DOI: 10.3102/0013189X029007004

Shi, H. (2021). Examining college-level ELLs' self-efficacy beliefs and goal orientation. *Journal of Comparative and International Higher Education, 13*(2), 2380–9205. https://www.ojed.org/index.php/jcihe/article/view/2978. DOI: 10.32674/jcihe.v13i2.2978

Shimizu, I., Matsuyama, Y., Duvivier, R., & Van der Vleuten, C. (2022). Perceived positive social interdependence in online versus face-to-face team-based learning styles of collaborative learning: A randomized, controlled, mixed-methods study. *BMC Medical Education, 22*(1), 567. DOI: 10.1186/s12909-022-03633-y PMID: 35869477

Shin, T., Koehler, M., Mishra, P., Schmidt, D., Baran, E., & Thompson, A. (2009, March). *Changing technological pedagogical content knowledge (TPACK) through course experiences.* Society for Information Technology & Teacher Education International Conference, 4152–4159. Association for the Advancement of Computing in Education (AACE).

Shirky, C. (2025, April 29). Is AI enhancing education or replacing it? The Chronicle of Higher Education. https://www-chronicle-com.lmu.idm.oclc.org/article/is-ai-enhancing-education-or-replacing-it

Shmueli, G., Sarstedt, M., Hair, J. F., Cheah, J. H., Ting, H., Vaithilingam, S., & Ringle, C. M. (2019). Predictive model assessment in PLS-SEM: Guidelines for using PLSpredict. *European Journal of Marketing, 53*(11), 2322–2347. DOI: 10.1108/EJM-02-2019-0189

Sin, C. (2014). Lost in translation: The meaning of learning outcomes across national and institutional policy contexts. *Studies in Higher Education, 39*(10), 1823–1837. DOI: 10.1080/03075079.2013.806463

Singha, R. (2024). Cultivating holistic learning environments in higher education: Mindfulness, compassion, and Ubuntu philosophies. In Omona, K., & Kayi O'dama, M. (Eds.), *Global perspectives on micro-learning and micro-credentials in higher education* (pp. 174–194). IGI Global., DOI: 10.4018/979-8-3693-0343-6.ch011

Singha, R. (2025). Empowering students through mindfulness and meditation practices. In Gonçalves, S. P. (Ed.), *Nurturing student well-being in the modern world* (pp. 141–170). IGI Global., DOI: 10.4018/979-8-3693-1455-5.ch006

Singha, R., & Kanna, Y. S. (2025). Supporting educators with addiction: Intentional learning communities in higher education. In Velliaris, D. M. (Ed.), *Academic support services and strategies in higher education* (pp. 171–192). IGI Global., DOI: 10.4018/979-8-3693-4175-9.ch007

Slavin, R. E. (1996). Research on cooperative learning and achievement: What we know, what we need to know. *Contemporary Educational Psychology*, *21*(1), 43–69. DOI: 10.1006/ceps.1996.0004

Sottilare, R., McGroarty, C., Ballinger, C., & Aris, T. (2023, July). Investigating the effect of realistic agents on team learning in adaptive simulation-based training environments using GIFT. In Proceedings of the 11th Annual Generalized Intelligent Framework for Tutoring (GIFT) Users Symposium (GIFTSym11) (p. 31). US Army Combat Capabilities Development Command–Soldier Center.

Spady, W. G. (1994). *Outcomes-Based Education: Critical Issues and Answers*. American Association of School Administrators.

Strelan, P., Osborn, A., & Palmer, E. (2020). Student satisfaction with courses and instructors in a flipped classroom: A meta-analysis. *Journal of Computer Assisted Learning*, *36*(3), 295–314. DOI: 10.1111/jcal.12421

Strom, K. J., & Martin, A. D. (2022). Toward a critical posthuman understanding of teacher development and practice: A multi-case study of beginning teachers. *Teaching and Teacher Education*, *114*, 103688. DOI: 10.1016/j.tate.2022.103688

Suarta, I. M., Suwintana, I. K., Sudhana, I. F. P., & Hariyanti, N. K. D. (2017, September). Employability skills required by the 21st century workplace: A literature review of labor market demand. In *International Conference on Technology and Vocational Teachers (ICTVT 2017)* (pp. 337-342). Atlantis Press. DOI: 10.2991/ictvt-17.2017.58

Sukkamart, A., Pimdee, P., Leekitchwatana, P., Kongpiboon, W., & Kantathanawat, T. (2023). Predicting student-teacher self-directed learning using intrinsic and extrinsic factors: A theory of planned behavior adoption. *Frontiers in Psychology*, *14*, 1211594. DOI: 10.3389/fpsyg.2023.1211594 PMID: 37780149

Sundaram, S., Schwarz, A., Jones, E., & Chin, W. W. (2007). Technology use on the front line: How information technology enhances individual performance. *Journal of the Academy of Marketing Science*, *35*(1), 101–112. DOI: 10.1007/s11747-006-0010-4

Sun, H. (2012). Understanding User Revisions When Using Information System Features: Adaptive System Use and Triggers. *Management Information Systems Quarterly*, *36*(2), 453–478. DOI: 10.2307/41703463

Sun, H., Wright, R. T., & Thatcher, J. B. (2019). Revisiting the Impact of System Use on Task Performance: *An Exploitative-Explorative System Use Framework. Journal of the Association for Information Systems*, *20*(4), 398–433. Advance online publication. DOI: 10.17705/1jais.00539

Sutarman, S., Sunendar, D., & Mulyati, Y. (2019). Investigating cooperative learning model based on interpersonal intelligence on language learners skill to write article. *International Journal of Instruction*, *12*(4), e201–e218. DOI: 10.29333/iji.2019.12413a

Sweller, J. (1988). Cognitive load during problem-solving: Effects on learning. *Cognitive Science*, *12*(2), 257–285. DOI: 10.1207/s15516709cog1202_4

Swerzenski, J. D. (2021). Why teaching technology must adapt to our teaching. *Communication Education*, *70*(2), 211–213. DOI: 10.1080/03634523.2020.1857414

Sweta, S., & Sweta, S. (2021). Educational data mining in e-learning system. Modern Approach to Educational Data Mining and Its Applications, 1-12. DOI: 10.1007/978-981-33-4681-9_1

Tang, T. L.-P., & Austin, M. J. (2009). Students' perceptions of teaching technologies, application of technologies, and academic performance. *Computers & Education*, *53*(4), 1241–1255. DOI: 10.1016/j.compedu.2009.06.007

Taylor, R. D., Oberle, E., Durlak, J. A., & Weissberg, R. P. (2017). Promoting positive youth development through school-based social and emotional learning interventions: A meta-analysis of follow-up effects. *Child Development*, *88*(4), 1156–1171. DOI: 10.1111/cdev.12864

Thaibah, H. (2023, December). Cooperative learning to improve social skills in acceleration students. In *Proceedings of the 6th International Conference on Learning Innovation and Quality Education (ICLIQE 2022)* (pp. 1151-1164). Atlantis Press. DOI: 10.2991/978-2-38476-114-2_106

The Global Economy. (2025). *The global economy rankings: Exports as a percentage of GDP*. The Global Economy. Retrieved from https://www.theglobaleconomy.com/rankings/exports

The Wharton School. (2025). *Wharton Interactive*. The University of Pennsylvania. https://interactive.wharton.upenn.edu/

Thomas, J. W. (2000). *A Review of Research on Project-Based Learning*. Autodesk Foundation.

Tierney, P., & Farmer, S. M. (2002). Creative self-efficacy: Potential antecedents and relationship to creative performance. *Academy of Management Journal*, *45*(6), 1137–1148. DOI: 10.2307/3069429

Tierney, P., & Farmer, S. M. (2011). Creative self-efficacy development and creative performance over time. *The Journal of Applied Psychology*, *96*(2), 277–293. DOI: 10.1037/a0020952

Tiwari, R., Arya, R. K., Bansal, M., & Bansal, A. (2014). Application of collaborative learning in business education. *International Journal of Advanced Research in Management and Social Sciences*, *3*(11), 134–145.

Toda, A. M., Valle, P. H. M., & Isotani, S. (2019). The dark side of gamification: An overview of negative effects of gamification in education. *Communications in Computer and Information Science*, *1005*, 143–156.

Topali, P., Ortega-Arranz, A., Rodríguez-Triana, M. J., Er, E., Khalil, M., & Akçapınar, G. (2024). Designing human-centered learning analytics and artificial intelligence in education solutions: A systematic literature review. *Behaviour & Information Technology*, *44*(5), 1071–1098. DOI: 10.1080/0144929X.2024.2345295

Tran, V. D., Nguyen, T. M. L., Van De, N., Soryaly, C., & Doan, M. N. (2019). Does cooperative learning may enhance the use of students' learning strategies? International Journal of Higher Education, 8(4), Article e.

Tyler, R. W. (1949). *Basic Principles of Curriculum and Instruction*. University of Chicago Press.

U.S. Department of Commerce. (2021). *A new era for U.S. exporters: Expanding global markets for small businesses.* https://www.trade.gov/export-strategy

UNESCO. (2021). Recommendation on the ethics of artificial intelligence. United Nations Educational, Scientific and Cultural Organization. https://www.unesco.org/en/artificial-intelligence/recommendation-ethics

UNESCO. (2022). *Global Education Monitoring Report: Technology in Education – A Tool on Whose Terms?* UNESCO.

UNESCO. (2023). *Global education monitoring report: Technology in education—A tool on whose terms?* https://www.unesco.org/gem-report/en/publication/technology-education

University, I. E. (2025). *Liquid learning*. https://www.ie.edu/liquid-learning/

Userpilot. (2024, March 11). Mixpanel for user analytics: Features, pricing, and review. Userpilot Blog. https://userpilot.com/blog/mixpanel-user-analytics/

Van Dijk, J. (2019). The digital divide. Polity. https://www.politybooks.com/bookdetail?book_slug=the-digital-divide--9781509534449

Viberg, O., Hatakka, M., Bälter, O., & Mavroudi, A. (2018). The current landscape of learning analytics in higher education. *Computers in Human Behavior*, *89*, 98–110. DOI: 10.1016/j.chb.2018.07.027

VirtualSpeech. (2024). VR stats for the training & education industry in 2025. https://virtualspeech.com/blog/vr-stats-training-education

Vos, L., & Brennan, R. (2010). Marketing simulation games: Student and lecturer perspectives. *Marketing Intelligence & Planning*, *28*(7), 882–897. DOI: 10.1108/02634501011086472

Vygotsky, L. S. (1980). Mind in society: The development of higher psychological processes. Harvard University Press. https://www.hup.harvard.edu/books/9780674576292

Vygotsky, L. S. (1978). *Mind in society: The development of higher psychological processes* (Cole, M., John-Steiner, V., Scribner, S., & Souberman, E., Eds.). Harvard University Press.

Wang, W., & Hsieh, J. J. P.-A. (2006). Beyond Routine: Symbolic Adoption, Extended Use, and Emergent Use of Complex Information Systems in the Mandatory Organizational Context. *Computer Information Systems Faculty Publications*. https://scholarworks.gsu.edu/cis_facpub/8/

Wang, C., Wang, H., Li, Y., Dai, J., Gu, X., & Yu, T. (2024). Factors influencing university students' behavioral intention to use generative artificial intelligence: Integrating the theory of planned behavior and AI literacy. *International Journal of Human-Computer Interaction*, •••, 1–23.

Wang, F., Wang, Y., & Zhang, Y. (2020). Personalized Learning in the Era of Artificial Intelligence: A Review of the Literature. *Journal of Educational Technology Systems*, *48*(3), 309–331.

Wang, L., Qu, G., & Chen, J. (2022). Towards a meaningful innovation paradigm: Conceptual framework and practice of leading world-class enterprise. *Chinese Management Studies*, *16*(4), 942–964. DOI: 10.1108/CMS-12-2020-0536

Wang, W., Schmidt-Crawford, D., & Jin, Y. (2018). Preservice teachers' TPACK development: A review of literature. *Journal of Digital Learning in Teacher Education, 34*(4), 234–258. DOI: 10.1080/21532974.2018.1498039

Wecks, J. O., Voshaar, J., Plate, B. J., & Zimmermann, J. (2024). Generative AI Usage and Academic Performance. *ArXiv*. https://doi.org//arXiv.2404.19699DOI: 10.48550

Wei, C. L., Wang, Y. M., Lin, H. H., Wang, Y. S., & Huang, J. L. (2022). Developing and validating a business simulation systems success model in the context of management education. *International Journal of Management Education, 20*(2), 100634. DOI: 10.1016/j.ijme.2022.100634

Wentworth, D. K., & Middleton, J. H. (2014). Technology use and academic performance. *Computers & Education, 78*, 306–311. DOI: 10.1016/j.compedu.2014.06.012

West, B. K., & Witt, A. (2020). Challenge, fantasy, and curiosity: Activating students' intrinsic motivation within information literacy sessions. The Journal of Creative Library Practice. https://knightscholar.geneseo.edu/library-research/6?utm_source=knightscholar.geneseo.edu%2Flibrary-research%2F6&utm_medium=PDF&utm_campaign=PDFCoverPages

Westerhout, E., Drijvers, P., & Bakker, A. (2019). The impact of a mathematics game programming project on student motivation in grade 8. In Eleventh Congress of the European Society for Research in Mathematics Education,25, Freudenthal Group; Freudenthal Institute; ERME. https://hal.archives-ouvertes.fr/hal-02410276

West, H., Hill, J., Abzhaparova, A., Cox, W., & Alexander, A. (2024). Pandemic pedagogies: Reflecting on online learning using the community of inquiry framework. *Journal of Geography in Higher Education, 48*(2), 157–176. DOI: 10.1080/03098265.2023.2190962

Wijnia, L., Noordzij, G., Arends, L. R., Rikers, R. M., & Loyens, S. M. (2024). The effects of problem-based, project-based, and case-based learning on students' motivation: A meta-analysis. *Educational Psychology Review, 36*(1), 29. DOI: 10.1007/s10648-024-09864-3

Williams, D., & Bower, M. (2025). The impact of technology-mediated dialogue on critical thinking in the secondary English classroom. *Education and Information Technologies*. Advance online publication. DOI: 10.1007/s10639-025-13680-9

Williamson, B., & Hogan, A. (2020). *Commercialisation and privatisation in/of education in the context of COVID-19*. Education International Research.

Wong, J., Baars, M., Davis, D., Van Der Zee, T., Houben, G. J., & Paas, F. (2019). Supporting self-regulated learning in online learning environments and MOOCs: A systematic review. *International Journal of Human-Computer Interaction, 35*(4-5), 356–373. DOI: 10.1080/10447318.2018.1543084

Woodward, R., & Pattinson, N. (2023). Informal peer learning of diverse undergraduate students: Some learners make meaning through collaborative activity. *Practitioner Research in Higher Education, 15*(1), 72–85. https://files.eric.ed.gov/fulltext/EJ1409406.pdf

World Bank. (2006). *Local economic development: A primer.* World Bank. https://documents1.worldbank.org/curated/en/763491468313739403/pdf/337690REVISED0ENGLISH0led1primer.pdf

World Economic Forum. (2020). *The future of jobs report 2020.* https://www.weforum.org/reports/the-future-of-jobs-report-2020

World Economic Forum. (2023). *Future of jobs report 2023.* https://www.weforum.org/reports/the-future-of-jobs-report-2023/

Wormeli, R. (2023). *Fair isn't always equal: Assessment & Grading in the Differentiated Classroom.* Routledge. DOI: 10.4324/9781032681122

Wright, D. K., & Flynn, T. (2017). Public relations education and the development of professionalization in Canada and the USA. In T. Watson (Ed.), *North American Perspectives on the Development of Public Relations: Other Voices* (pp. 51-64). Springer. DOI: 10.1057/978-1-349-95044-7_5

Wright, D. K. (2011). History and development of public relations education in North America: A critical analysis. *Journal of Communication Management (London), 15*(3), 236–255. DOI: 10.1108/13632541111151005

Wu, J., & Yu, X. (2025). The influence of formative assessment on academic performance: Exploring the role of teachers' emotional support. *Frontiers in Psychology, 16*, 1567615. DOI: 10.3389/fpsyg.2025.1567615 PMID: 40271370

Wu, R., Luo, X., Ma, Y., & Nie, Y. (2024). Research on online learning behavior of college students based on learning analytics technology. *Journal of Educational Technology Development, 12*(1), 45–62. DOI: 10.1109/CSTE62025.2024.00048

Yeung, K. L., Carpenter, S. K., & Corral, D. (2021). A Comprehensive Review of Educational Technology on Objective Learning Outcomes in Academic Contexts. *Educational Psychology Review, 33*(4), 1583–1630. DOI: 10.1007/s10648-020-09592-4

Youssef, A. B., Dahmani, M., & Ragni, L. (2022). ICT Use, Digital Skills and Students' Academic Performance: Exploring the Digital Divide. *Information (Basel), 13*(3), 129. DOI: 10.3390/info13030129

Yu, C., Walsh, J., & Boone, J. (2023). Optimizing online collaborative learning: Challenges and strategies in online teaching and learning. In Keengwe, J. (Ed.), *Handbook of research on facilitating collaborative learning through digital content and learning technologies* (pp. 20–43). IGI Global., DOI: 10.4018/978-1-6684-5709-2.ch002

Zawacki-Richter, O., Marín, V. I., Bond, M., & Gouverneur, F. (2019). Systematic review of research on artificial intelligence applications in higher education – where are the educators? *International Journal of Educational Technology in Higher Education, 16*(1), 39. Advance online publication. DOI: 10.1186/s41239-019-0171-0

Zhai, C., Wibowo, S., & Li, L. D. (2024). The effects of over-reliance on AI dialogue systems on students' cognitive abilities: A systematic review. *Smart Learning Environments, 11*(1), 28. Advance online publication. DOI: 10.1186/s40561-024-00316-7

Zhao, Y., & Liu, G. (2019). How Do Teachers Face Educational Changes in Artificial Intelligence Era. *Proceedings of the 2018 International Workshop on Education Reform and Social Sciences (ERSS 2018)*. https://doi.org/DOI: 10.2991/erss-18.2019.9

Zhao, Y., Pugh, K., Sheldon, S., & Byers, J. L. (2002). Conditions for Classroom Technology Innovations. *Teachers College Record, 104*(3), 482–515. DOI: 10.1111/1467-9620.00170

Zhou, M., & Su, Q. (2023). Embedding active learning in business education: A cross-cultural study of experiential pedagogies and student engagement. *Entrepreneurship Education and Pedagogy, 6*(1), 3–22. DOI: 10.1177/25151274221142945

Zhuplev, A., Valle, F. J., Rincón, J. J., & Plithides, M. (2025). Challenges and future strategies for B-schools. In *Insights into international higher education leadership and the skills gap* (p. 48). IGI Global., DOI: 10.4018/979-8-3693-3443-0.ch015

Ziek, P. (2021). *The media production loop and class collabs* [Conference presentation]. Humanities Education and Research Association Virtual Conference 2021. Virtual Presentation.

Ziek, P. (2022). Class collabs: Assessing inter-disciplinary relationship building in media education. *Media Education Research Journal, 11*(2), 1–13.

Ziek, P., & Fink, K. (2018). Networks within the competitive media environment. *Review of Journalism and Mass Communication, 6*(1/2), 1–11.

Zyngier, D. (2008). (Re)conceptualising Student Engagement: Doing Education Not Doing Time. *Teaching and Teacher Education*, *24*(7), 1765–1776. DOI: 10.1016/j.tate.2007.09.004

# About the Contributors

**Anatoly Zhuplev** is a professor of international business and entrepreneurship at Loyola Marymount University (Los Angeles, California) and former editor-in-chief at the Journal of East West Business (2011-2013). He taught for ten years at the Moscow Management Institute, and subsequently at the Advanced Training Institute of the State Committee for Printing and Publishing in Moscow; in Bonn, Germany in 1994, 1998, 2009; in Warsaw, Poland (as a Fulbright scholar) in 2005; in Paris, France in 2004-2007, and at Northeastern University in Boston, Massachusetts in 1989-1990. His books, book chapters, and articles on International Management, International Entrepreneurship, International Business, European Energy Security and Corporate Governance (around 100 overall) have been published in the U.S., Canada, Western Europe, Russia, and the former USSR. He received his PhD from the Moscow Management Institute, Russia, in 1981, and his BS from the Moscow Engineer-Economics Institute in 1974.

**Bryan Christiansen** is the Chief Executive Officer at Soluvex, LLC, which is a global technology consulting firm in the USA. A former adjunct professor at Southern New Hampshire University, Christiansen earned his MBA at Capella University and his BS in Marketing degree at the University of the State of New York. To date he has published 45 Reference books on various topics of which over 60 percent are Scopus- and/or Web of Science-indexed. Christiansen is a Book Series Editor-in-Chief of "Advances in Psychology, Mental Health, and Behavioral Studies" and "Advances in Digital Crime, Forensics, and Cyber Terrorism". His works have been cited in articles, books, doctoral dissertations, and master's theses in Chinese, Czech, English, French, Greek, Russian, Spanish, and Turkish.

***

**Xuereb Archer** has delivered lectures for the University of Chester, Global College Malta, the University of Buckingham and the University of Malta for different Masters and Bachelor Degree Level programmes. He also provides corporate training and workshops with public and private organisations. Previously, Mr. Xuereb Archer also held roles in business development management within digital marketing, IT and aviation companies. He has an MBA, NLP Practitioner Certificate and is reading for a Masters In Gestalt Psychotherapy.

**Akhilesh D. Bacchoo** is a globally minded business professional and active researcher, whose academic and professional journey spans Mauritius, Singapore, the United Arab Emirates, and Malta. With a Bachelor's degree in Economics, he brings a strong analytical foundation to his work in business strategy and financial analysis. His international experiences have equipped him with the agility to operate across diverse cultural and commercial environments, making him particularly adept at navigating complex, dynamic settings. Akhilesh's academic interests lie at the intersection of financial markets, entrepreneurship, and strategic management. He is especially passionate about leveraging data-driven insights to support innovation and drive sustainable business growth. His professional focus is informed by a strong fascination with the structure and behaviour of global financial markets, and he continuously builds on his expertise through the mastery of industry-recognised tools and ongoing study of market trends.

**Chantelle Bosch** is an NRF-rated researcher and Associate Professor in the School of Mathematics, Science and Technology. She leads the Computer Science Education subject group and focuses her research on blended learning environments that promote self-directed and cooperative learning. She is an executive member of the UNESCO Chair on Multimodal Learning and leads the blended learning sub-area in the Self-Directed Learning research unit.

**Wie Jane Chin** is a Bachelor of International Business student at Universiti Tunku Abdul Rahman (UTAR), Malaysia. Her academic interests include artificial intelligence and its impact on academic performance. She has fundamental experience in research and data analysis and aims to further explore these fields through continuous learning.

**Kim Chi Dang** holds a Bachelor's degree in journalism and has over 15 years of experience in the journalism and communication industry, working as both a practitioner and lecturer. She is currently a Ph.D. student in Cultural Studies and a faculty member at Van Lang University, Faculty of Social Sciences and Humanities. Her research interests focus on public relations, internal communication, and creative industries.

**Stacy Grau** With more than 20 years teaching marketing, entrepreneurship and innovation, Stacy currently serves as the Associate Dean in the John V Roach Honors College at TCU. She teaches courses on human centered design and social innovation. Her current research centers on human centered AI, design for social impact and human centered design in education and healthcare

**Pravin Kumar** is an experienced academic with over a decade of teaching Marketing Management and related subjects at reputed institutions across India. He currently serves as Assistant Professor at Brainware University, Kolkata, and has previously taught at different Management Institutions. He holds a Ph.D. in Management from T.M. Bhagalpur University, focusing on visual merchandising on consumer behavior in branded apparel. He also holds an MBA in Marketing and an M.A. in English, reflecting his interdisciplinary background. Dr. Kumar has published widely in Scopus, UGC-CARE, and peer-reviewed journals on topics including consumer behavior, brand personality, and AI in sales. He has presented at numerous national and international seminars and FDPs on subjects like cross-cultural marketing and leadership. His industry experience in the automobile and pharmaceutical sectors adds practical value to his teaching. Known for his engaging teaching style and commitment to Universal Design for Learning.

**Low Mei Peng** is an Associate Professor at the Faculty of Accountancy and Management, Universiti Tunku Abdul Rahman (UTAR). She holds a PhD in Organizational Behavior, with core research interests in employee-centered corporate social responsibility (CSR), organizational behavior, and digital transformation. Her work on employee-centered CSR has been published in several reputable journals, including Business Ethics, Environmental Responsibility Journal, Social Responsibility Journal, and Quality and Quantity. In addition to her research, she serves as a reviewer for several high-impact journals and has been invited as a keynote speaker at numerous academic and professional conferences. She has made valuable contributions to the realm of research and education, serving as a source of inspiration for both students and fellow scholars. Dr. Low has also collaborated with various government agencies on research grants and consultancy projects,

**Dorothea Lowes** is an Education Specialist at Western TVET College with over 25 years' experience in vocational education. She holds a master's in education (UJ, 2008) and is completing a PhD in Curriculum Studies, focused on blended learning in TVET. A former national examiner, moderator, and registered assessor, she remains committed to improving teaching and learning through curriculum innovation.

**Tuong-Minh Ly-Le** is dean of the School of Applied Arts and Media Production at the University of Management and Technology Ho Chi Minh City, Vietnam.

She is also a professional communications consultant and managing director of EloQ Communications, a leading PR and marketing agency based in Vietnam. Graduated from Bond University with a Master of Communication and a Doctoral degrees, Dr. Ly-Le has been involved in many successful public relations and integrated marketing projects at both national and regional scales. She has put her professional knowledge and extensive connections with business media and influencers to serve clients from a diversified clientele, including hospitality, education, technology, finance, healthcare, etc. Along with her professional career, Dr. Ly-Le is also interested in academic research activities. Her research foci include public relations, crisis communication, and social media. She strongly believes in the complementary power between practical experience and academic knowledge.

**Hélder Fanha Martins** currently holds the position of Full Professor at the Lisbon Accounting and Business School, part of the Polytechnic University of Lisbon (LABS-ISCAL). Furthermore, he is an Integrated Researcher affiliated with CETAPS at NOVA University of Lisbon. With a doctoral degree conferred by Nova University (UNL), Professor Martins has dedicated his research endeavours to the fields of Business Simulation Studies, Languages for Specific Purposes, and Computer-Assisted Language Learning. He serves on the editorial boards of multiple academic journals. Within LABS-ISCAL, he is responsible for overseeing the Department of Information and Communication Sciences and spearheads the International Business Simulation course.

**Prashant K Mishra** has been the Chief Operating Officer of Study World Global College Malta since April 2022. With PhD in marketing and double Master's (MBA & MA in English), Dr. Prashant also did one year of PGC in HR & Marketing from IIT Bombay. Dr. Mishra has occupied various managerial positions in Education Institutions in Dubai & India. He started his career in Marketing and moved on to higher leadership positions, thanks to his academic qualifications, work experience, and charismatic approach. Akhilesh's academic interests lie at the intersection of financial markets, entrepreneurship, and strategic management. He is especially passionate about leveraging data-driven insights to support innovation and drive sustainable business growth. His professional focus is informed by a strong fascination with the structure and behaviour of global financial markets, and he continuously builds on his expertise through the mastery of industry-recognised tools and ongoing study of market trends.

**Surjit Singha** is an academician with a broad spectrum of interests, including UN Sustainable Development Goals, Organizational Climate, Workforce Diversity, Organizational Culture, HRM, Marketing, Finance, IB, Global Business, Business,

AI, K12 & Higher Education, Gender and Cultural Studies. Currently a faculty member at Kristu Jayanti College, Dr. Surjit also serves as an Editor, reviewer, and author for prominent global publications and journals, including being on the Editorial review board of Information Resources Management Journal and contributor to various publications. With over 16 years of experience in Administration, Teaching, and Research, Dr. Surjit is dedicated to imparting knowledge and guiding students in their research pursuits. As a research mentor, Dr. Surjit has nurtured young minds and fostered academic growth. Dr. Surjit has an impressive track record of over 150+ publications (SCOPUS Indexed 100+), including articles, book chapters, and textbooks, holds two US Copyrights, one patent granted, and has successfully completed and published two fully funded minor research projects from Kristu Jayanti (Deemed to be University).

**Christo van der Westhuizen**, is Professor of Learning Technologies at the University of Johannesburg. With over 20 years in teacher education, his research focuses on ICT integration in blended learning to foster self-directed learning. He formerly led blended learning research at North-West University and serves on the editorial board of the Journal of Geography in Higher Education.

# Index

## V

www.ingramcontent.com/pod-product-compliance
Lightning Source LLC
LaVergne TN
LVHW062325300926
849161LV00007B/1570